A HISTORY OF PRE-BUDDHISTIC INDIAN PHILOSOPHY

A HISTORY OF PRE-BUDDHISTIC INDIAN PHILOSOPHY

BY

BENIMADHAB BARUA,

M.A. (CAL.), D.LIT. (LOND.)

GYAN

Published by

GYAN

Gyan Publishing House
5, Ansari Road
Daryaganj, New Delhi-110002
Phone: 011-47034999, 9811692060
E-mail: books@gyanbooks.com

Distribution Network
gyanbooks.com
India, USA, Canada, UK, Australia

ISBN: 978-93-6280-382-5 (PB)
First Published, 1921

2nd Impression 2024

Printed at: Gyan Press, Delhi.

A HISTORY OF PRE-BUDDHISTIC INDIAN PHILOSOPHY
Author: BENIMADHAB BARUA

A HISTORY OF
PRE-BUDDHISTIC INDIAN PHILOSOPHY

A HISTORY OF PRE-BUDDHISTIC INDIAN PHILOSOPHY

BY

BENIMADHAB BARUA, M.A. (CAL.), D.LIT. (LOND.)

POST-GRADUATE TEACHER IN THE DEPARTMENTS OF PALI AND ANCIENT INDIAN HISTORY AND CULTURE, CALCUTTA UNIVERSITY

PUBLISHED BY THE

UNIVERSITY OF CALCUTTA

1921

PREFACE

The present work is substantially my thesis "Indian Philosophy—its origin and growth from the Vedas to the Buddha," submitted in 1917 to the University of London and approved in the same year for the D. Lit. degree. I can no longer regard it as the same Doctorate thesis, since it has been revised, altered and enlarged, though slightly, in the light of subsequent research. Consequently the title of the original thesis has been done away with and replaced by the present title "A History of Pre-Buddhistic Indian Philosophy." The Supplementary Discussions in Chapter XII, the Post-Script in Chapter XXI and the whole of the concluding chapter are later additions. None the less, the original thesis remains almost intact in this work in that the changes made therein are immaterial, the general arrangement of its chapters and sections as well as its main conclusions having suffered no violent alteration.

It would no doubt have been of some advantage to me, a novice that I am, to get the thesis printed and published in its approved form with the stamp of the University of London upon it. I could not really have made up my mind to publish the thesis in its present form, with certain additions and alterations specified above, but for the precious suggestions from Professor T. W. Rhys Davids and the kind encouragement of the Hon'ble Justice Sir Asutosh Mookerjee, the President of the Council of Post-Graduate Teaching in Arts and the present Vice-Chancellor of the Calcutta University. I have nevertheless the satisfaction of seeing the work now published with the stamp of my former *Alma Mater*, the University of

Calcutta, and it has been to me not a little matter of pride that I found myself on my return from England in the midst of a band of arduous and talented researchers in the vast field of ancient Indian literature, history and culture, brought together from different parts of the world to advance the cause of learning under the guidance of so eminent a leader, scholar and educationist as Sir Asutosh. Nothing indeed could give me greater satisfaction than the relief I had felt on being back in the midst of my community which has not regarded me as an outcast, as well as my University which has not failed to afford me facilities for work; for, however rebellious in spirit one may be in matters of one's social and religious views, and however insignificant may be one's attainments abroad, nothing can be more painful and disappointing, I think, to a man than to find himself a stranger at home. What this strangeness of situation means to an Indian returning home from foreign sojourn and to an Indian student of ancient Indian literature, history and culture returning to the institutions of his country can better be imagined than told. Just fancy what chagrin a sensible man is apt to feel when after long absence he returns home only to find that his parents, brothers, sisters and others whom he regards as very dear and near to him, are all reluctant, because of the fear of society, to receive him back freely in their midst, or how depressing is the atmosphere to a student who finds, in spite of his earnestness, that in the educational institutions of his country the subjects generally neglected and undervalued are precisely those which are productive and really matter most. Happily the times are being changed.

While I leave the book to be judged for what it is worth, I must say that it is not a dissertation on the history of Buddhism or of Buddhist philosophy, the subject being reserved for a separate work. The investigation in it has been closed at a point where the philosophical thoughts and scientific speculations of ancient India reached a stage of development, advanced enough to provide for a necessary antecedent condition of the rise of a powerful movement of thought, wholly Indian in origin and character, seeking to evolve a system of religious philosophy with the theory of causal genesis as its mainstay or fundamental and central idea. But the genetic connection of this work with Buddhism is twofold: (1) that it embodies the results of an investigation which was at first undertaken, at the instance of the late Rev. Gunalankara Mahathera of Chittagong, to ascertain the immediate historical background of Buddhist thought; and (2) that the original data for the conception of a chronology of early Indian philosophy were derived from the Buddhist canon. It was mainly by the light of the evidence of the Tripiṭaka that I came to perceive three great synthetic divisions in the development of earlier thought. It was again a close comparative study of the first volume of the Dīgha Nikāya, published by the Pali Text Society, and the six Upaniṣads, edited and translated by Pandit Sitanath Tattvabhusan, that first suggested to me the prospect of a very fruitful study of Buddhism, keeping it in constant relation to the earlier and contemporary Indian thoughts in the midst of which it arose and without reference to which its true historical significance and value could not be properly comprehended, even if there were a hundred Buddhist commentators and exegetists like Buddhaghosa to write powerful expositions thereon. Further, I chanced upon a number of parallel passages in the Buddhist Piṭakas, the Jaina Aṅgas and the Mahābhārata, having bearing upon many daring philosophical ideas now found embodied in the older Upaniṣads, the Āraṇyakas and a few selected later hymns of the Ṛig and Atharvavedasaṁhitā. The evidences of these authorities have been found invaluable as throwing abundant light upon a very obscure but highly important period of thought evolution that had immediately preceded the rise of Jainism,

Buddhism and other later systems of Indian thought. An independent study of the Upanișads and the canonical works of the Jains and the Buddhists made it increasingly clear to me that the so-called traditional interpretation of the ancient Sanskrit, Pāli and Prakrit texts had much in it which was an after-thought on the part of the learned scholiasts who, as it seemed to me, were guided more by an etymological conjecture than by a true spirit of research which one must always understand as a quest of truth for its own sake. That there are immense possibilities of modern historical researches in the field of ancient Indian literature, history and culture can be accepted as a truism. When these researches will advance far enough, one is sure to find that the idea that has hitherto been formed of ancient Indian life and civilisation on the basis of traditional interpretation is in many regards misleading. I can say that this work is to a large extent the result of an attempt to interpret the texts in their own light and inter-connection as well as to trace up the development of early Indian philosophy on divergent lines, out of a common background and substratum, and that in defiance of the persistent endeavours of the Indian commentators to prove that in the Vedic hymns and the Upanișads there are to be found only the unsystematised ideas of Vedānta. But to minimise the importance of their works in all respects would be to push off the ladder whereby one climbs up; for the indirect value of their writings as a mine of historical information and suggestiveness is immense. The present work, when judged as a whole and contrasted with the previous works on the subject, will, I think, appear in many respects new of its kind. But here again to overlook the importance of the spade work done by the pioneers will be to show oneself wanting in gratitude for the invaluable services they have jointly and severally rendered. It is so easy for an unthinking youth to run into a mood of irreverence and to think that he is wiser than all his predecessors. My experience is that whenever a man begins to think he has discovered a new truth, he will be surprised some day to find that he was in some way or other anticipated by those who had gone before him. It is also my firm belief that no attempt is made in vain, and no work is useless if we know how to make proper use of it.

In a sense this book is the first definite expression of a dominant will to do some useful work in the world, regardless of the consideration of personal circumstances and equipment, no doubt under the belief, turning with every new success into stronger and stronger confidence, that present circumstances may be unfavourable and equipment nil, yet the very desire to do something and constant acting up to it render at last what was once thought impossible, possible. That is to say, it is the first visible fruition of a series of attempts on the part of a student to fulfil in all earnestness the expectations entertained of him by his teachers and many benefactors, Indian and English, who have in manifold ways helped his will to follow its natural bent.

Looking into the genesis of the work, that is, back into my own life, I find that I am just one of the many students of modern Bengal whom Sir Asutosh gave, by timely concessions and patronage, the opportunity of working out the innermost scholarly ambition of their lives. I am doubly indebted to Sir Asutosh for the arrangements he so generously made for the publication of the work by the Calcutta University and the opportunity he gave me for continuing my research work in Calcutta. I am one of those persons who, though born in poor circumstances, have been able to struggle in the race of life with the kind help and encouragement of their kinsmen and countrymen. Almost from the beginning of my school career the Government have liberally helped me by the grant of free-studentship and special scholarships in prosecuting my studies in India and in England. I need hardly say that but for such generous help from Government the desire that impelled me to move in this direction would have been baffled. The foremost among those whose sympathy was of great service to me in securing Government help, particularly in obtaining a special State scholarship in 1914 for the scientific study of Pali in Europe is the Hon'ble Mr. H. Sharp, Secretary to the Education Department of the Government of India. In connection with this State scholarship my gratitude is also due to H. E. Sir Harcourt Butler, then Education Member of the Governor General's Council and Sir E. Denison Ross, Keeper of Imperial Records, Calcutta, now Director of the School of Oriental Studies in London, who made out a special case for the Buddhist community of Bengal on the representation of its interests by the Chittagong and Bengal Buddhist Associations. Among my Indian teachers, the late Mahamahopadhyaya Dr. Satis Chandra Vidyabhusana, Principal of the Sanskrit College, Calcutta, had always fostered my literary aspirations and tried in every possible way to make my path smooth. His unexpected death has left a gap in the ranks of Oriental scholarship that will yet take a long time to be filled up in Bengal. I owe a very deep debt of gratitude to Professor T. W. Arnold, then Secretary, in the India Office, for Indian students, for it was mainly through his kind guidance and keen personal interest that I was able to complete my course of studies in England leading to the D. Lit. degree. I am also grateful to him for procuring for me permission of the authorities of the London County Council to use its library and see the working of the primary and secondary schools under its control. Here I must also mention the names of Mr. N. C. Sen, then Local Adviser to Indian Students in London, Mr. R. E. Field, Warden at 21, Cromwell Road and Miss E. J. Beck, Honorary Secretary to the National Indian Association, who by their sympathy and encouragement helped me a great deal in peacefully carrying on my research work. I would pay but a scanty tribute to Dr. Mabel H. Bode, then Lecturer in Pali, University College, London, were I merely to say that she ably guided me in my work; for she really helped me in a hundred other ways, particularly by placing me into close touch with many erudite scholars. I am ever so much indebted to Professor T. W. Rhys Davids and Mrs. Rhys Davids, neither of whom failed to guide me in my researches by their precious suggestions and constructive criticism. The fourteen discourses of Professor Rhys Davids on the scientific method of investigation, delivered at the instance of the India Office for my guidance, helped me considerably in imbibing the modern western spirit of research. But it is Dr. Dawes Hicks, Senior Professor of Philosophy, University College, London, who had initiated me in the present historical method of the study of philosophy. I must acknowledge that his lectures on Greek philosophy and modern European thought from Descartes to Kant were found much helpful to me. A deep debt of gratitude is due also to Professor L. T. Barnett, Keeper of Oriental Manuscripts in the British Museum, for he was the first to rouse in me an interest in the study of Jaina literature, and he helped me also considerably by calling my attention to a few important Tamil works bearing upon my subject. I do not find words to express my obligation to Dr. F. W. Thomas in whom and in whose wife I found much hospitality, the door of whose cottage was open always to the Indologists hailing from all parts of the world. Dr. Thomas never failed to show me kindness in allowing me, in the midst of his arduous duties as Librarian of the India Office Library, to read to him the successive chapters of my thesis as they were written out. I derived much benefit from discussion of several disputed points of interpretation and history, with him and with Dr. Barnett. Professor L. T. Hobhouse has placed me under a deep obligation by revising the thesis from the European point of view, particularly in regard to the interpretation of Greek Philosophy, before it was handed over to the press. The points in which he has differed have been mentioned in the foot-notes. The kind words of encouragement from Mr. H. M. Percival, late Professor, Presidency College, Calcutta, my friend Dr. Pramatha Nath Banerjea, Minto Professor of Economics, Calcutta University, then in England, the late lamented Sir Henry Cotton, Dr. Carveth Read and Sir Thomas Gregory Foster, Provost, University College, London, served as a great stimulant to my research work especially at its inception. Vivid in my mind is the memory of the goodness of Mr. and Mrs. Grubb, under whose roof and beneficent care I revised my work and profitably spent the last year of my sojourn in England in seeing something of the present social, religious and political life of the country. Sir Michael E. Sadler, late President of the Calcutta University Commission, has done me much honour by his courtesy in going through portions of the thesis and offering me some fruitful suggestions. In this connexion I have also to express my deep sense of gratitude to Mr. P. J. Hartog, Vice-Chancellor of the Dacca University, who as the then Academic Registrar of London University, had done all he could to see me established in Calcutta. Mr. W. R. Gourlay, Private Secretary to H. E. the Governor of Bengal and Rai Dr. Chunilal Bose Bahadur, Sheriff of Calcutta, are two of those kind-hearted gentlemen who have hitherto taken a keen interest in me and my research works at the Calcutta University. I must also put on record my deep sense of gratitude to H. E. Lord Ronaldshay, Governor of Bengal, who has very generously shown genuine sympathy with my researches in the field of early Indian Philosophy, particularly in that of Buddhism. His Excellency enjoys the reputation of a great champion of the cause of Indian Philosophy in that he has always tried to impress the importance of the subject on the minds of the framers of the University education scheme, and expressed it as a profound anomaly that the subject has not been given any place in Indian colleges.

My gratitude is also due to Mr. W. C. Wordsworth, Officiating Director of Public Instruction, Bengal, for the encouragement I received from him and his kind enquiries concerning the work I had done in England. He himself is interested in the study of Indian philosophy as he expressed to me in course of a conversation, and he too regretted the absence of any provision for the proper study of this subject in this country. Some important additions to the original thesis, made in this work, were kindly suggested to me by Kabibhaskar Sreejut Sasanka Mohan Sen, "Gopaldas Chowdhury" Lecturer in Bengali, Calcutta University, in whom I have found a great Bengali poet and a thoroughbred student of Hindu literature and philosophy. My sincere thanks are also due to my friend and colleague Professor Sailendranath Mitra, and to Rai Saheb Dineschandra Sen, the historian of Bengali literature, Mr. Johan Van Manen, Librarian of the Imperial Library, Calcutta, and my friend Babu Prabhat Chandra Chakrabartty, Lecturer in Sanskrit, Calcutta University, for kindly aiding me by reading occasionally through the proofs of the book and offering me some valuable suggestions. I am thankful to my pupil, friend and colleague Babu Prabodh Chandra Bagchi, Lecturer in Ancient Indian History and Culture, for the kind help he has rendered me by preparing the Indexes. Lastly, I must offer my sincere thanks to Mr. A. C. Ghatak, Superintendent of the Calcutta University Press, and his assistants for the keen personal interest they have taken in seeing the book through the press.

BALLYGUNGE,

The 27th July, 1921.

B. M. BARUA.

BIBLIOGRAPHY

(1) Standard Works

Adamson—The Development of Greek Philosophy.

Banerjea, Dr. P. N.—Public Administration in Ancient India.

Barth—Religions of India.

Barua, B. M.—Ājīvikas (Calcutta University publication.)

Blavatsky, Madame—The Secret Doctrine, I.

Deussen, Dr. Paul—Allgemeine Geschichte der Philosophie.
Outlines of Indian Philosophy.
The Philosophy of the Upanishads (Eng. transl.)

Erdmann—History of Philosophy, Vols. I, II (Eng. transl.)

Frazer—Indian Thought—Past and Present.

Hillebrandt—Vedische Mythologie.

Hopkins—Religions of India.

Hume—An Enquiry Concerning Human Understanding.

Kant—Critique of Pure Reason (transl. by Max Müller).

Max Müller—A History of Ancient Sanskrit Literature.
Six Systems of Indian Philosophy.

Macdonald—The Brahmanas of the Vedas.

Muir—Original Sanskrit Texts.

Oldenberg—Buddha (transl. by Hoey).

Rhys Davids, Mrs. C. A. F.—
Buddhist Psychology (Quest Series).
Buddhism.
Manual of Buddhist Psychological Ethics.
Points of Controversy (a joint work with Mr. Shwe Zan Aung).

Rhys Davids, T. W.—

Buddhist India.

Dialogues of the Buddha, Vols. I, II.

Rockhill—Life of the Buddha.

Scherman, Lucian—Philosophische Hymnen aus der Ṛig- und Atharvaveda-Saṁhitā.

Schrader—Uber den Stand der Indischen Philosophie zur Zeit Mahāvīras und Buddhas—Strassburg, 1902.

Stevenson, Mrs. Sinclair—Heart of Jainism.

Wallis—Cosmology of the Rigveda.

Windelband—A History of Philosophy (Eng. transl.).

Zeller—Stoics, Epicureans and Sceptics (Eng. transl.).

(2) Sanskrit Texts and Translations.

Saṁhitā—

Ṛig-Veda (with Sāyaṇa's Commentary) Ed. Max Müller—translations by Wilson and Griffith.

Atharva Veda (with Sāyaṇa's commentary)—translations by Griffith and by Whitney and Lanman.

Caraka (Calcutta Ed.).

Brāhmaṇa—

Aitareya (with Sāyaṇa's commentary)—translation (Bengali) by Ramendrasundar Trivedi (Sāhitya Parishat publication).

Śatapatha.

Taittirīya (Bibl. Ind.).

Āraṇyaka—

Aitareya (with Sāyaṇa's commentary). Bibl. Ind. —translation in S. B. E.

Taittirīya (Bibl. Ind.).

Upaniṣad—

Bṛihad-Āraṇyaka (with Śaṅkara's commentary)—translation in S. B. E.

Chāndogya (with Śaṅkara's commentary)—translation in S. B. E.

Kauṣītakī (with Śaṅkara's commentary)—translation in S. B. E. and by Cowell.

Śvetāśvatara (with Śaṅkara's commentary).

Taittirīya (with Śaṅkara's commentary)—translation in S. B. E.

Maitri (Bibl. Ind.).

The minor Upaniṣads, viz.—

Īśa, Kaṭha, Kena, Muṇḍaka, Paiṅgala, Subāla, Āruṇika, Yājñavalkya, Śarabha, Śārīraka—(Nirṇaya-Sāgar Press Ed.); English translation of Īśa, Kaṭha, Kena, Muṇḍaka in S. B. E.

Mahābhārata (with Nīlakaṇṭha's commentary), Bangabasi and Nirṇaya Sāgar Press Editions.

Bhagavad Gītā.

Rāmāyaṇa—Nirṇaya Sāgara Press Edition.

Yoga-Vāsiṣṭha Rāmāyaṇa and its English translation.

Smṛiti—

Manu (Ed. Jolly)—translated by Bühler in S. B. E.

Yājñavalkya.

Saṁkha.

Likhita.

Viṣṇu Purāṇa (Bangabasi Ed.)—transl. by Wilson.

Bṛihaspatisūtra—Ed. Dr. Thomas.

Vedāntasāra (Ed. Cowell).

Vedāntasūtras—Translated by Thibaut in S. B. E.

Dharmasūtras—

Āpastamba.

Gautama.

Baudhāyana—translations in S. B. E.

Śāṇḍilya Sūtras—Ed. Cowell.

Arthaśāstra of Kauṭilya—translation by Shamashastry.

Vātsyāyana—Kāmasūtra.

Sarvadarśana Saṅgraha (Cal. Ed.)—transl. by Cowell and Gough.

Vaiśeṣika Sūtras—transl. by Gough.

Śūkra-nīti—transl. in the Sacred Books of the Hindus.

(3) Buddhist Texts and Translations.

Pāli texts and commentaries consulted are publications of the Pāli Text Society except otherwise mentioned.

Divyāvadāna (Ed. Cowell and Neil).

Buddhacarita—Ed. and transl. by Cowell.

Mādhyamika-Vṛitti (Bibl. Buddhica).

Milinda-Pañho (Ed. Trenckner)—transl. by T. W. Rhys Davids in S. B. E.

Jātaka (Ed. Fausböll)—transl. by Cowell, Rouse, etc.

Āryaśūra's Jātakamālā (Ed. Cowell).

(4) Jaina Texts and Translations.

Aupapātikasūtra—Ed. Leumann.

Ayāraṅgasutta (P. T. S. Ed.)—with Śīlāṅka's commentary (Dhanapati Ed.)—translation by Jacobi in S. B. E.

Kalpasūtra—with commentary—translation by Jacobi in S.B.E.

Rāyapaseṇi (Ed. Dhanapati).

Samavāyāṅga (Ed. Dhanapati).

Sthānāṅga—(Ed. Dhanapati).

Sūtrakṛitāṅga—with Śīlāṅka's commentary (Ed. Dhanapati)—translation by Jacobi in S. B. E.

Uttarādhyayana (Ed. Dhanapati)—translation by Jacobi in S.B.E.

Uvāsaga Dasāo—(Bibl. Ind.)—translation by Hoernle.

(5) Tamil Text and Translation.

Śivajñānabodha and Siddhiyar—Translated by Nallasami.

ERRATA & CORRIGENDA

Page.		*Incorrect.*	*Correct.*
18	*l.* 21	ṛitā	ṛita
19	*f.n.* 1	canno	cannot
40	*l.* 13	ruh	truth
40	*l.* 14	isaianppearance	is an appearance
44	*l.* 2	o	to
61	*l.* 10	Put	But
63	*l.* 21	gods	goods
88	*l.* 28	Śāndilya	Śāṇḍilya
96	*l.* 30	pañea	pañca
109	*l.* 14	consonanee	consonance
116	*l.* 29	praṇaṁ	prāṇaṁ
118	*l.* 16	t	It
119	*l.* 11	ratardana	Pratardana
122	*l.* 27	Naciketā	Naciketas
194	*l.* 9	pratardana	Pratardana
214	*f.n.* 1	starling	starting
222	*l.* 24	pratardana	Pratardana
290	*l.* 9	Bibidhaprabandha	Nānāprabandha
297	*f.n.* 1 ; *l.* 1, 3	Monogram	Monograph
355	*l.* 1	dêtre	d'être

CONTENTS

PART I

VEDIC PHILOSOPHY

PART II

POST-VEDIC PHILOSOPHY

CHAPTER V

CHAPTER VI

CHAPTER VII

CHAPTER VIII

CHAPTER IX

CHAPTER X

CHAPTER XI

CHAPTER XII

PART III

PHILOSOPHY BEFORE MAHĀVĪRA AND BUDDHA

PART I

Vedic Philosophy

Introductory

Is there a system of Vedic philosophy?

Rightly or wrongly, it has long been doubted if we can speak of a *system* of Vedic philosophy. In order to avoid modern associations of the words "system" and "philosophy," the Vedic scholars have resorted to such expressions as "Vedic mythology," "Vedic cosmogony," and so forth. However, Dr. Lucian Scherman published in 1887 a German translation of a number of hymns belonging to the two collections called the Ṛig-Veda and the Atharva-Veda, under the title "Philosophische Hymnen aus der Ṛig-und Atharva-Veda Sanhita." Some seven years later was published the "Allgemeine Geschichte der Philosophie" by Dr. Paul Deussen. In this latter work, Dr. Deussen freely employs the expression "Erste Periode der indischen Philosophie," by which he means, of course, Vedic philosophy. Here the reader might be referred to an excellent treatise, "The cosmology of the Ṛig-Veda" by Mr. Wallis. The works of such writers as Kaegi, Frazer and others deserve special notice.

The aim of the work.

The aim of the writer of these pages differs from that of Scherman and Deussen. The principal object with which both the scholars seem to have started is to estimate the standard of philosophical speculations, embodied in a few hymns of the Vedas, belonging mostly to the tenth or last book of the Ṛik. Our aim is, on the other hand, not only to estimate such a standard, but also to bring out the individual element in each of these hymns. That is to say, we principally seek to show that each mode or system of speculation is a creation of individuality.

The authors of the Vedic hymns, specially of the philosophical ones, are not all known.

No one knows yet, and there is little chance of knowing ever, who the real authors of all these hymns were. Tradition attributes them to a number of names, such as Aghamarṣaṇa, Prajāpati Parameṣṭhin, Brahmaṇaspati, etc., most of which are in fact names of the deities to whom the hymns were addressed. It does not, however, make much difference whether the names, as given in these pages, be taken as fictitious or real, so long as we know that there is behind the expressions of each of these hymns an individual.

Philosophy as a doubting process of the human mind is eternal. As a structure of thought it has its beginning.

If we go by the dictum, that to doubt is to philosophise, it will not be easy to say exactly when the Indo-Aryan sages were not philosophers, for their inspired utterances, which still survive in the form of hymns and psalms, contain many and various inquisitive questions as to *whence*, *whither*, *when*, and *how*. Philosophy, viewed as a mere doubting process of the human mind, knows indeed no beginning of its own. If by philosophy is understood a structure of thought, which we consider permanently established where we find consciousness of the ultimate categories and also terms to express these, then we may suppose philosophy to have had its beginnings somewhere with individual thinkers, and with those individual thinkers in whose words we trace this consciousness.

A peaceful time following upon the struggle for existence is favourable to philosophical reflections, which start at first from a mythical basis.

Philosophy is the fruitful result of reflections on the riddle of existence. These reflections become possible, as Prof. Erdmann holds, only when "the heroic struggle to acquire the conditions of existence has been followed by its enjoyment." The reflective movement as a whole starts from the mythical stage, and it is only after many serious efforts on the part of the earlier thinkers that it succeeds afterwards in gaining an independent position.

This holds true of Greek thinking, and no less of early Indian philosophy. It is generally agreed among the historians of Greek philosophy that the lines of development which proceed from such a mythical basis may be distinguished as the cosmological and the psychological.

Difference between mythology and philosophy.

As to the difference between mythology and philosophy, the following observations of Prof. Adamson are here worth quoting. "The problem of cosmological speculation differs from the aim of mythology in this: that while the latter represented the connexions between its assumed ground and existing realities after the crude fashion of temporal sequence, the more philosophical view raised the question,—what is the permanent element in real existence and of what are actual things composed? The change of question implied a restriction upon the free play of imagination, which constitutes the difference between philosophy and mythology."[1]

The attitude of later thinkers towards the Vedas.

The attitude of later thinkers towards the Vedas was far from being one of warm appreciation. In a well-known passage of the Bhagavad Gītā (II. 42) the Vedic hymns are compared to lovely flowers, lovely only in appearance. In the Tevijja Sutta (Dīgha-nikāya, I. No. 13) Buddha distinguishes between the later Brāhmaṇa teachers and the earlier Vedic sages. Among these sages, again, he regards just ten as the ancient, and as the real authors and reciters of the mantras.[2] But they are all spoken of as those whose duty it was only to invoke several deities, such as Indra, Soma, Varuṇa, Iśāna, Prajāpati, Brahmā, 'Mahiddhi' (=Tvaṣṭar?) and Yama.

[1] The Development of Greek Philosophy, p. 8.

[2] The ten sages mentioned by Buddha are—Aṣṭaka, Vāmaka, Vāmadeva, Viśvāmitra, Yamadagni, Aṅgiras, Bharadvāja, Vasiṣṭha, Kāśyapa and Bhṛigu. This list differs to some extent from that given in the "Laws of Manu" (I-35). The latter gives—Marīci, Atri, Aṅgiras, Pulastya, Pulaha, Kratu, Vasiṣṭha, Pracetas, Bhṛigu and Nārada. Elsewhere only the first seven are mentioned.

The Brāhmaṇa schools mentioned in the Tevijja Sutta.

Regarding the Brāhmaṇa teachers, such as the Aitareyas,[1] the Taittirīyas, the Chāndogyas, the 'Chandavas' and the Bahvṛicas,[2] Buddha holds in agreement with the Brahmin youth Vasiṣṭha, a disciple of Puṣkarasādi,[3] that they taught various paths leading to a state of union with Brahman (God). An interesting account of this transition of thought from the earlier Vedic sages to the later Brāhmaṇa teachers is also given in the Dīgha-nikāya, Mahāgovinda Suttanta.

Buddha's estimate of cosmological speculation.

In the Pātika Sutta,[4] however, Buddha said to Bhaggava, "There are, O descendant of Bhṛigu, some śramans and Brāhmans to whom the teachers who ascribe creation to the hand of Îśvara,—to Brahmā (God) appear as the foremost of thinkers (agraṇya)." "But I, too, know, Bhārgava, this mode of cosmological speculation. I know this, and also know other things far beyond; and having known this, I do not tarnish my knowledge."

It is very remarkable that the speculations which Buddha alluded to and described in this connexion, correspond to those set forth in some of the later hymns of the Ṛig-veda and restated, explained and elaborated in the Atharva-veda, the Brāhmaṇas, and in other such texts.

The problems for cosmological speculation.

Furthermore, Buddha thought that these earlier speculations were concerned chiefly with the pre-ens or first beginnings (Pubbanta) and the post-ens or the other end (aparanta), that is to say, with the

[1] Pāli 'Addhariyā'—Sanskrit 'Adhvaryus.' Prof. Walleser identifies the Addhariyas with the Aitareyas. In the Aitareya Āraṇyaka (III. 2-3-12) the Bahvṛicas, the Adhvaryus and the Chāndogyas are alluded to apparently as three separate schools. If so, the suggestion of Prof. Rhys Davids would seem more acceptable. See Dialogues of the Buddha, Vol. II. p. 303.

[2] Ibid Dialogues, p. 303. Another reading of 'Bavharijā' is 'Brahmacariyā.'

[3] Sutta-nipāta, *Vāseṭṭha-Sutta.*

[4] Dīgha-nikāya, III. 28: "Santi Bhaggava eke samaṇa-Brāhmaṇā Issara-kuttaṁ Brahma-kuttaṁ ācariyakaṁ aggaññaṁ paññapenti." "Aggaññaṁ cāhaṁ Bhaggava pajānāmi tato ca uttaritaraṁ pajānāmi, tañca pajānanaṁ na parāmasāmi"; cp. ibid, I. 16-17.

problems as to the beginning and the end of the world as a whole.[1] In other words, the main problems of the Vedic speculation were: How does the world originate? In what manner are individual things created? By what have these their unity and existence? Who creates, and who ordains? From what does the world spring up and to what again does it return? These earlier speculations are to be called, in this sense, Purāṇa, Lokāyata, or the like.

The immediate background of Indian Philosophy is to be found in the cosmogonic hymns of the ancient and early Vedic sages. The first philosophic reflections received impetus from the daily experience of things, changing into one another, and appearing and reappearing at their appointed seasons. Such constant mutations of things of experience must have very early roused wonder in a people, so lively and such keen observers and so much at home with nature as the Indo-Aryans.

The cosmogonic hymns of the Rig-veda constitute the immediate background for Indian Philosophy.

Not confined to any particular orders of Brāhmans or warriors,—of householders, ascetics, or hermits, there arose a body of men who came to be known in the later literature as Brahmarṣis. To Vedic Indians they were known by the name of Poets (Kavis),[2] and Poets were the divine philosophers of ancient India. According as the Poets were the philosophers, philosophy itself was called Hymn (Uktha),[3] and hymn-chanting (udgītha)[4] denoted the act of philosophising. Indeed, there was no other name for philosophy in India than Hymn (Uktha or Udgītha) up to a certain late date, that is to say, until it was replaced by other epithets more suitable.

Philosophy and the Philosophers.

[1] Dīgha-nikāya, I, 12, 30; Dhammasaṅgaṇi, 1319, 1320.
[2] Rigvedá, I. 164, 6; X. 129, 4.
[3] Ibid, X. 82, 7, cp. Aitareya Āraṇyaka, II. 1, 2, 1.
[4] Chāndogya Upaniṣad, I, 8. 1, etc.

Definition of "Hymn" or philosophy.

"Prajāpati Parameṣṭhin" seems to speak of philosophy as search carried on by the Poets within their heart for discovering in the light of their thought the relation of existing things to the non-existent, *i.e.*, primordial matter.[1] Dirghatamas suggested altogether a different conception. For him philosophy was just 'ignorance for the sake of knowledge,' and knowledge consisted but in ascertaining the nature of the one, single, original cause to which the plurality of all known causes might be reduced.[2] Philosophy with "Viśvakarman" is "sampraśnaṁ,"[3] "information," "doubt," "true doubt," that is to say, doubt, as distinguished from that of a sceptic,—enlightenment, as distinguished from the ignorance of an agnostic.

When could philosophical question arise?

And if philosophy consists in rightly doubting, and if the immediate background for it was formed by the cosmogonic poetry which is interspersed throughout the Vedic hymns, conceivably it was only when, as Prof. Windelband would maintain, in course of time individual views were freely developed that the question at last arose as to "the unity and abiding original ground of changing things." The question, as formulated by a Vedic philosopher, was: what is the tree or wood (vṛikṣaḥ vanaṁ) out of which the visible universe was fashioned?[4]

How was the question answered?

Partly because of the legend of the flood in the time of Manu, which lived so deep in the mind of the Indo-Aryans, and partly because of the ordinary experiences concerning the existence, changeability, circulation, distribution, and mighty force of water in the world, the answer that naturally suggested itself was—Water. Water is the elementary matter or abiding original ground of things.

[1] Ṛig-veda, x. 129, 4: Śato baṁdhūn asati.
[2] Ibid, I. 164, 6-7: Acikitvāñ cikituṣaḥ.
[3] Ibid, x. 82, 3.
[4] Ṛig-veda, x. 81, 4.

From this the further question emerged as to what came into being immediately after water, and before all created things.

A further question, and answers.

As to the answer to this particular question, the Vedic thinkers differed from one another. Aghamarṣaṇa's reply was—the Year (Saṁvatsara, the time-principle, the natural seasons); "Prajāpati Parameṣṭhin" said, Cosmic Desire (Kāma, Eros); "Hiraṇyagarbha" said, the Golden Germ; and "Nārāyaṇa's" word was the Individualised Sun (Puruṣa).

A still further question.

A still further question had to be faced, and that was, from what did water itself spring? To this Aghamarṣaṇa's answer was, from Night or Chaos (Tamas); "Prajāpati Parameṣṭhin" said, "I know it or perhaps I know it not;" "Brahmaṇaspati's" answer was—from Nothing; "Anila's"—from Air; and so forth.

The historical significance and value of Vedic speculations.

The cosmological speculations of the Vedas are of the greatest historical importance as exhibiting Indian philosophy in the making. Infinitely great was their influence upon later thinking, whether Brahmanic, Jaina or Buddhistic; Vedic philosophy supplied abundantly rich food for later thought, so much so, indeed, that subsequent Indian philosophy might be viewed as a mere systematic carrying out of the general plan of a structure, tacitly implied or imperfectly conceived.

CHAPTER I

AGHAMARṢAṆA

Aghamarṣaṇa, the first philosopher of India.

We know nothing of the life-history of Aghamarṣaṇa, regarded here as the first philosopher of India, beyond the fact that he, like Viśvāmitra and other great sages, is said to have been a famous founder of family or school. He may be credited with having formulated the views which came to be known in later ages as 'the doctrine of time' (Kāla-vāda).

Comparison of Aghamarṣaṇa's hymn with that of "Prajāpati Parameṣṭhin."

The hymn X. 190 of the Ṛig-veda is ascribed to Aghamarṣaṇa. It is recommended in all the Brahmin Law-books [1] as one of the purificatory texts. Aghamarṣaṇa's hymn was, in no case, later than the hymn X. 129, which is ascribed to "Prajāpati Parameṣṭhin," and devoted to the same subject of creation. Rather judging from the more crude fashion in which it presents its author's doctrine, it ought to be placed a little earlier than the latter. The common feature of both the hymns is that their authors derive their idea of creation of the visible world from the action of Warmth,—Creative Fervour (Tapas), in the primitive substance called Water. But elements of difference in the two hymns are noticeable. The great peculiarity of the former is that in it the author, the poet Aghamarṣaṇa, allots, in one sense at all events, the principal part of creation to that which he calls the Year (Saṁvatsara), while in the latter the same part is attributed, in the same sense, to what its author calls Cosmic Desire (Kāma).

[1] Gautama, XIX-12, XXIV-10-12, Baudhāyana, III-5, IV-2-5, IV-Iv-7, Vasiṣṭha, XXVI-8 Manu, XI-260-261. Yājñavalkya, III-359.

His doctrine.

Aghamarṣaṇa laid down a theory of creation, involving what is known in history as the doctrine of time. But his is an exceedingly short thesis from which nothing, by way of a clear statement, can be elicited. Nor do we know either what led him to speak of the Year as being the lord, great creator, preserver and destroyer of all things, until we come to look through some of the older cosmogonic hymns which we understand to have constituted the immediate background for Indian philosophy, as well as through some of the latter Brāhmaṇas.

Conception of time or seasons in the cosmogonic hymns.

First, in those earlier Vedic hymns we see that Season or Seasons (Ṛitu, Ṛitus) are personified, and that things are said to have been done and also to have been revived, or readjusted at their due seasons. The Indo-Aryans used to perform sacrifices, and to drink soma-juice at seasons.[1] In two of them[2] their authors recognise that Dawn (Uṣā) and Varuṇa are 'the ever new,' and 'born again and again.' Regarding Dawn we further learn that 'like a dancing girl' she is adorned, and 'adorned always with the same colour.' 'As a cow gives milk, as a cow comes forth from its stall, so opens she her breast, so comes she out of darkness.' Again, "as a player conceals the dice, so keeps she concealed the days of a man; daughter of Heaven, she wakes and drives away her sister (Night)."[3] In the hymn VII. 6-1 the sun (Sūrya) is considered to be the 'lord of all that lives and dies.' We can even easily trace a Platonic view in many hymns, where Indra is represented as Tvaṣṭar,—the Artificer who repeatedly creates through his magic the world of generation.

[1] Rig-vēda, I. 15, II. 37, etc.

[2] Ibid, I. 113; I-4, X. 85-17.

[3] Religions of India, p. 76. 2. Taittirīya Brāhmaṇa, I. 6-2.

Exposition in the Brāhmaṇas.

Secondly, in a passage of the Taittirīya Brāhmaṇa we are told that the godly Aryans—both priests and peasants, were employed thrice in the year, that is to say, during the three seasons —winter, summer and the rains.

In the same passage Prajāpati is conceived as the year because it was by the Year that he generated living beings. Similarly, in a passage of the Śatapatha Brāhmaṇa (X. 4.2.2) the Year is said to have been Prajāpati, the creator of all things, whether animate or inanimate,—and of both men and the gods. As a sort of explanation, it is added that in the beginning the universe was water, and nothing but water. Water desired to produce individual things. It was stimulated into energy, and in consequence, a Golden Germ (solar body) came into existence. This floated about in space for the period of a year. In the course of a year the Sun (Puruṣa) was born from the Golden Germ. This Sun was Prajāpati. A woman, or a cow, or a mare brings forth within a year. A human child endeavours to speak in a year. For these reasons the year is to be regarded as Prajāpati, the lord of beings.[1]

Aghamarṣaṇa's doctrine continued.

Now Aghamarṣaṇa's views are not so childish as their exposition in the Śatapatha Brāhmaṇa. His hymn reflects a mind which had the clear perception of things. His thesis is too short for the purpose of elaborate exposition. But he plainly tells us that warmth (Tapas) is the first creative principle from which eternal law and truth were born. From these was produced the Night (Tamas). The Night produced water, and from water originated the Year (Saṁvatsara) or the time-principle. The Year formed 'in due order' the sun and the moon, the heaven and the earth, the firmament and light, and ordained the days and nights. The year is the lord of life and of death.

[1] Śatapatha Brāhmaṇa, X. 1.6.1, ff.

Two points are worthy of note : (1) Aghamarṣaṇa's naturalistic conception of the universe, and (2) his emphasis on the eternal existence of law and order in the universe. According to Aghamarṣaṇa's view, then, chance has no place in the creative evolution of nature.

So far the doctrine of time is extremely crude, and the term used, whether in Aghamarṣaṇa's hymn or in its exposition in the Brāhmaṇas, is Year.

The doctrine of time in the Atharva-veda.

In the hymns of the Atharva-veda[1] the Year (Saṁvatsara) was replaced by a more general and comprehensive term Time (Kāla). But the doctrine of time, as set forth in these hymns of the Atharva-veda, does not show originality of conception, except as regards a vague notion of infinity of time, or rather, of eternity of the time-principle. It is a curious mixture of the thoughts of several earlier hymns, addressed to the Sun, Death, Indra, Brahmā, Prajāpati, and what not ! Further, as Dr. Deussen points out, the Ātharvaṇa conception of time is naive fatalism.[2] Here is a summary of the doctrine of time as collected from the Atharva-veda :—Rohita—the radiant Sun, came into existence as Time. In the beginning the Sun was the lord of beings.[3] Time is no other than the Sun which is thousand-eyed, undecaying, a horse with seven reins or solar rays, the primal deity in the sense that the sun is the source of life, light and heat. Time has seven rolling wheels, meaning perhaps the seven divisions of 'the year, solstice, season, month, fortnight, day, night, hour.' The seven wheels of Time have seven naves.[4] Time

[1] Atharva-veda, XIII. 2; XIX. 53, 54.

[2] All. Gesch. der Philosophie, pp. 209, ff.

[3] Atharva-veda, XIII. 2: "Rohitaḥ Kālo abhavad, Rohitôgre Prajāpatiḥ."

[4] Dr. F. W. Thomas understands by 'seven naves' the seven planets.[1] Dr. Ehni, in his Der Mythus des Yama, pp. 116-117, suggests that "the seven wheels are the seven worlds which constitute the universe ; the seven naves are the seven seasons which are produced by the annual course of the sun brought about by time ; and the axle represents the world of immortality which remains firm and unmoved through all changes of time and season."

is the creator who creates the worlds of life, and Time again is the Death who destroys them all. Time was formerly the father of the Sun, the lord of beings, and subsequently became the son of those of which Time was the father. Time is Brahmā, the highest, the lord of all. Time is the eternal substance out of which all things are formed, and in which everything lives, moves and has its being. Time is indeed God supreme.

"Prajāpati Parameṣṭhin"

"Prajāpati Parameṣṭhin" or the Thales of India.

For various reasons, after Aghamarṣaṇa we turn to "Prajāpati Parameṣṭhin" whose naturalistic views and sceptical attitude are clearly set forth in the hymn X. 129 of the Ṛig-veda.[1] Speaking in the most general terms, he may be called the Thales of India.

His conception of original matter.

It appears from the above-mentioned hymn that the thinkers of "Parameṣṭhin's" time were divided on these two opposite theories,[1] that Being came out of non-Being, and[2] that Being came only out of Being. In his speculation on nature, "Parameṣṭhin" seems to have taken the middle course by rejecting both the theories; for him the original matter comes neither under the definition of Being nor under that of non-Being.[2]

The original matter is called Water: the point about which he was sceptical.

"Parameṣṭhin," like Thales, offered Water (Salila) as the fundamental principle of explanation. From Water all things are formed; Water is the original substance of all that exists. He refused accordingly to push his enquiry beyond water, and it was towards this particular question that his attitude was invariably sceptical.

[1] Śankara calls it the Nâsadiya-sūkta according to its theme. The subject of the hymn is Brahman. By this hymn Śankara seeks to establish that Prāṇa or spirit is uncreated. See his commentary on Vedânta-sūtra, II. 4-8.

[2] Ṛig-veda, X. 129, 1: "Nâsad âsîn no sadâsît tadânîṁ."

His fundamental thesis was :—there was then neither non-existence nor existence. Then the existent was not ; by this he denied of course the existence of all concrete things in the beginning.[1] In his own words, there was then no realm of air, no sky beyond it.[2] There was then neither death nor immortality, no visible sign wherewith to distinguish between days and nights,[3] that is to say, between light and darkness.

His fundamental proposition and its import.

If the existent was not in the beginning, is it, then, that the existent sprang from the non-existent ? No, even not that—was his reply. The reason is that the primitive element falls neither under the conception of the existent nor under that of the non-existent. And if he were asked, what was that primitive substance which is to be called neither Being nor non-Being, his answer would have been Water. There was then water, the unfathomable depth of water (gahanam gambhīram), and nothing but water. "Water was that one thing, breathless, breathed by its own nature."[4] There was darkness (tamas), and concealed at first in this darkness was Water in its indiscriminated or unmanifested form (apraketam). Water was all that existed (sarvamā idam).

The condition of cosmic matter.

Water, we may suppose, changed itself into the variety of things, and changed those things back into itself. "Parameṣṭhin" did not draw any distinction between matter and motive power. He identified Being with existence, *i.e.*, change. Water transformed itself into particular things by some inherent principle to which he gave the name Kāma, Cosmic

How the concrete existence proceeded from the universal substance.

[1] According to Sāyaṇa, tadānīm = pralaya-daśāyām avasthitam (while in the state of envelopment) ; no sat = naiva sat ātmavat sattvena nirvācyam āsīt (*i.e.*, no individual thing) ; in other words, no sad iti pāramārthika sattvasya niṣedhaḥ.

[2] "Lokā rajāṁsi ucyaṁta iti Yāskaḥ," says Sāyaṇa.

[3] "Nāsīd rajo no vyomā na tarhi na rātryā ahṇa āsīt praketaḥ."

[4] "Ānīdavātaṁ svadhayā tad ekaṁ, tasmād-dhānyan na paraḥ kiṁcan nāsa."

Desire. This 'will-to-be' or motive force was not distinct from the material substratum itself; it was regarded by him as the primal germ of Mind or Soul (manaso retaḥ). For "Parameṣṭhin" Kāma was not the will of God, as Sāyaṇa understands, although undeniably he thought the inherent reason for change was identical with that which is the greatest and most divine in nature, and with Mind or Soul. Moreover, the meaning of the term, Mind or Soul, is far wider with "Parameṣṭhin" than with us, rather cosmical, and it is no other than the principle of change in general.

His theory of progression.

We shall now endeavour to show "Parameṣṭhin's" notion of gradual development. The cause by which the series of transformations is produced in water is called Warmth (Tapas). This original principle of change is superseded, in process of time, by a higher principle, such as Kāma or 'the will-to-be' (Sāyaṇa's sisṛikṣā—the desire-to-create), which is one, and that by a still higher principle, such as Manas or Mind,—Intelligence or consciousness. Whilst everything was void[1] and shapeless, by the power of Warmth was born that unit[2] called Kāma. Kāma was the motive force of the changing universe,—the first germ of Mind (manaso retaḥ), and this Mind was no other than the Sun "whose eye controls this world in highest heaven."[3] The gods—heavenly beings or godly men—were produced later than this world, and people naturally attribute the creation to the sun, the first-born, self-conscious, individual being in the visible universe.[4]

[1] "Tucchyenâmvapihitaṁ." It is difficult to say if by this "Parameṣṭhin" meant to convey exactly the idea of void space, especially in view of the fact that he distinctly states there was then 'no sky beyond the mass of water' (no vyomā paro yat). In Sāyaṇa's interpretation tucchyena = sad asadvilakṣaṇena bhāvarūpajñānena.

[2] According to Sāyaṇa, ekaṁ—ekībhūtaṁ kāraṇam.

[3] "Ṛig-veda, X. 129. 7: Yo asyâdhyakṣa parame vyoman."

[4] Ibid, Iyaṁ visṛiṣṭir yata ābabhūva.

It will be noted that the philosophical position assumed by "Parameṣṭhin" was that of a naturalist, and that his conception of nature was entirely dynamic. Accordingly, for him the principle of movement or development is inherent in matter itself, and involved in the vast processes of nature. In other words, the world evolves from the immanent energy of nature (svadhayā); the movement as a whole is self-determined. It must also be recognised that the cosmic process in general is far earlier than the formation of the present sun from whom we derive life and light. He questioned, therefore, very candidly if the sun was the maker of the whole universe. It will be noted here that "Parameṣṭhin's" conception of water and its inherent principle of movement can in no way be identified with the full-fledged Sāṁkhya doctrine of Prakṛiti and Puruṣa. But one might perhaps say with better justification that the former exhibits the latter in the making.

His dynamistic theory of nature.

Aghamarṣaṇa, who is here considered to be a predecessor of "Parameṣṭhin," formulated, as we saw, a proposition, but offered no explanation. His proposition was: "From Fervour kindled to its height eternal law and truth were born."[1] As "Parameṣṭhin" seems to have understood it, the action of energy immanent in matter or nature is at its highest at the initial stage of the creative process, as also perhaps on the eve of destruction of the world-system. So he said: when, in course of time, the line of the firmament was extended across water, dividing the heaven from the earth, what was above it, and what below? There were to be seen below the firmament, *i.e.*, on the earth, generating factors (retodhā) or mighty forces (mahiman) at work, and free action or self-determined movement (svadhā). The heaven above the firmament was the scene of the action

"Parameṣṭhin's" explanation of his predecessor's thesis.

[1] Griffith's Ṛig-veda, X. 190.1.

of dynamic energy (prayati). Thus, indeed, is to be apprehended the connexion of the existent with the non-existent, *i.e.*, the primitive matter (sato baṁdhun asati).

His scepticism.

It is important also to note that "Parameṣṭhin" started his inquiry with water, and did not extend it beyond water. Whenever the question of looking beyond water did press itself upon him, he broke forth quite naturally and sincerely in scepticism. The world-process is far earlier than the thinkers among men, nay, earlier even than the sun, the seer who can view all that happens in this world from the highest heaven. Therefore, who indeed knows, and who can truly say, from what other element than water this universe came into existence? Even in the case of the sun, the first individual being we may conceive of, and who is generally believed to be God, it is as yet doubtful whether he formed it all, or did not form it,—whether he knows it all, or does not know it (veda yadi vā na veda). In a later interpretation of "Parameṣṭhin's" cosmical speculation in the Śatapatha Brāhmaṇa[1] we notice that water is altogether forgotten, and Mind is substituted for it.

A later exposition.

There was then neither non-existence nor existence, because Mind was at the time neither the existent nor yet the non-existent. The Mind being developed, wished to manifest itself. It sought after itself, toiled hard and swooned. It found 36,000 of its own fires, *i.e.*, suns, made up of mind, established by mind. Mind produces voice, voice produces breath, breath produces eye, eye produces ear, ear produces work, and work produces sacrificial fire. There may be some definite philosophical conception behind this exposition, but the language is too fantastic to make out of it any such meaning.

[1] X. 5.3.1 foll.

"BRAHMAṆASPATI"

"Parameṣṭhin" treated water or matter as the ultimate reality, and disavowed all possibilities of knowledge of the ultra-material substratum, if there be any. He refused to extend his metaphysical enquiry beyond matter, and when the question of getting beyond matter suggested itself to his mind, he indulged, as all open-minded naturalists usually do, in arguments which ended inevitably in scepticism. Moreover, in the expressions about his doctrine there is implied, as we have seen, a two-fold antithesis, the first of which has reference to the hypothesis that in the beginning Being came out of non-Being.[1] From this it would follow that the date of "Brahmaṇaspati" as a thinker was earlier than that of "Parameṣṭhin." But we do not know whether it was precisely the doctrine of "Brahmaṇaspati" that "Parameṣṭhin" was acquainted with. The utmost we can say is that some such theory was current in his time.

The historical relation of "Brahmaṇaspati to "Parameṣṭhin."

Whether of an earlier or of a later thinker, "Brahmaṇaspati's" doctrine must be regarded as representing a much more advanced stage of abstraction, on the ground that he, like Anaximander, conceived the cosmic matter far beyond experience.

"Brahmaṇaspati" and Anaximander.

"Bṛihaspati" is the name by which "Brahmaṇaspati" is traditionally known. He is said to have embodied his views about the origin of the world in the hymn X. 72 of the Ṛig-veda. It presupposes several earlier hymns. The hymn must be considered as one of the most unintelligible, and it would be vain to attempt to bring out anything very definite from it. So much is quite certain, however, that the main

His hymn.

1 Ṛig-veda, X. 72. 2: "Asataḥ sad ajāyata."

object of "Brahmaṇaspati" was to proclaim 'with tuneful skill' the order of generation of the gods. And it was in this connexion that he set himself to inquire into the nature of the world-ground, and its condition prior to the generation of heavenly beings and all elemental forces. "Brahmaṇaspati," so far as the philosophical side of his hymn goes, postulated the genesis of Being from non-Being. He nowhere tells us expressly what he meant by the terms Being and non-Being, though tacitly it is implied that the separation which he contemplated between these two was not exactly the strict logical distinction that is now possible for us to draw between what we term thing and nothing, existence and non-existence. As we now define the term non-Being implies nothing, absolutely nothing. With "Brahmaṇaspati," on the other hand, the non-existent (asat, non-ens) was the very world-ground,—the permanent foundation of all that is existent (sat, ens) and of all that is possible and yet non-existent (asat).[1] For "Brahmaṇaspati," we may take it, non-Being was and is the very genetrix of law or principle of order (ṛitā, dharma)[2] in the universe.

His fundamental problem.

His postulate of non-Being: its signification.

The existent originally sprang from the non-existent[3]—this is the fundamental proposition which "Brahmaṇaspati" laid down. By the term, non-existence, he denoted apparently the Infinite,—Aditi, corresponding almost to Anaximander's ἄπειρον.[4] Like ἄπειρον, Aditi is an ambiguous term of which we have not a precise explanation from "Brahmaṇaspati." Dakṣa, the cosmic force,

His principal thesis.

[1] Sāyaṇa also points out that Asat does not mean non-existent as a cause (asat kāraṇatva). It is, on the contrary, the adhiṣṭhāna, the generating cause of the gods. *cf.* Ṛig-veda, X. 5-7. Asacca sacca............janmannaditer upasthe.

[2] Ṛig-veda, I. 1.8, I. 2.8, I. 84.4, etc. For dharma, ibid, VIII. 85.13.

[3] Ibid, X. 72. 2.

[4] Deussen's All, Gesch. der Philosophie, pp. 145-146.

is born of Aditi, and yet Aditi is said to be generated, in her turn, from Dakṣa.[1]

The term, Aditi, is explained by Sāyaṇa as Earth; by Prof. Muir, as Nature; by Prof. Roth, as freedom or security; and by Prof. Benfey as sinlessness (anāgas).[2] The better interpretation would seem to be that of Prof. Max Müller. He says, "Aditi, an ancient god or goddess, is in reality the earliest name invented to express the Infinite; not the Infinite as the result of a long process of abstract reasoning, but the visible Infinite, the endless expanse beyond the earth, beyond the clouds, beyond the sky."[3]

The interpretation of the term Aditi.

The point in which we fully agree with Prof. Max Müller is that Aditi, in one sense, is nothing but the visible Infinite, the endless expanse beyond the earth, beyond the clouds, beyond the sky. This spatial Infinite is mighty, sinless, immortal, unchangeable, pure and free.[4] The earlier antithesis of Aditi is Nirriti, whom Sāyaṇa calls wicked goddess (pāpadevatā)[5]; and the later antithesis is Diti whom Sāyaṇa identifies with Niṣṭigrī.[6]

Criticism of Max Müller's interpretation.

Nirriti is decay, decrepitude and old age; Aditi growth, development and youth. Nirriti is death, Aditi immortal life; Nirriti is bondage, Aditi freedom; Nirriti is the mother of darkness, disorder, drunkenness, drought, ill-luck, sin, corruption, and so forth; Aditi the mother of light, eternal law, temperance, shower, good luck, virtue, continence and the like.

Aditi and Nirriti.

[1] Ṛig-veda, X, 72.3: "Aditer Dakṣōjāyata, Dakṣād u Aditiḥ pari." Yâska canno make out how this is possible. "They may have had the same origin; or according to the nature of the gods, they may have been born from each other,—hence derived their substance from one another." Muir's Original Sanskrit Texts, IV. 13.

[2] Griffith's 'Ṛig-veda,' I. 24.1.

[3] Max Müller's translation of the Ṛig-veda, I. 230.

[4] Ṛig-veda, I. 24.1; I. 24.15; etc.

[5] Ibid, I. 24.9; I. 29.6; V. 41.17; VI, 74.2; etc.

[6] Ibid, V. 62.8; "Aditiṁ Ditiṁ ca; X. 101.12.

Aditi as the endless expanse beyond the sky seems to have been described by "Brahmaṇaspati" as the daughter of Dakṣa—the potent energy, the Cosmic Force, the genetrix of the immortal gods.[1] But Aditi denotes also the Earth, meaning the endless expanse of the horizon. Aditi as the endless expanse of the horizon is said to have sprung from Uttānapada, a term of which the meaning is uncertain. From this Aditi were born the regions or quarters of the horizon.[2]

Aditi the visible Infinite.

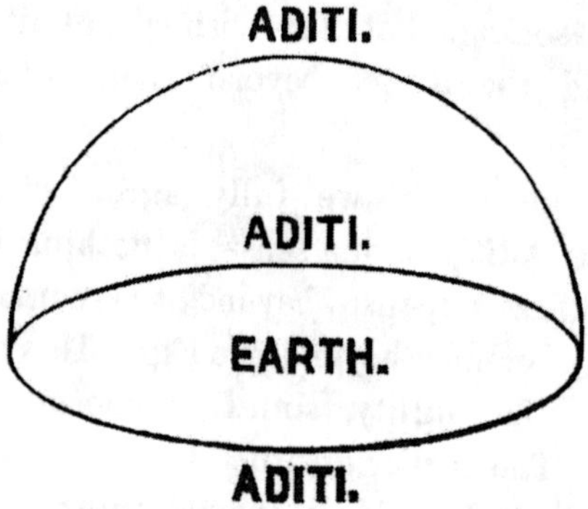

That which is generated from the infinite is infinite in nature, and that which is infinite in nature, is immortal in life. The regions are accordingly infinite and immortal, and so too are the seven sun-gods (Ādityas). The sun, from whom we derive light and heat is known as Sūrya or Mārtaṇḍa. He was recognised by "Brahmaṇaspati" as the last born among the sons of the Infinite, and as the first-born among the finite things of experience. The visible sun being finite in nature, is different in appearance from his elder brothers,—Mitra, Varuṇa, etc., who are all infinite, and considered therefore to be the darlings of their mother Aditi—the Infinite.[3]

The contrast of Infinity with finite things.

[1] Ṛig-veda, X. 74.5.

[2] Ibid, X. 72.4.

[3] Ṛig-veda, X. 72.8

The gods[1] who were born after Aditi, daughter of Dakṣa, as sharers of immortal life, brought forth the visible sun who was lying hidden in the sea. As "Brahmaṇaspati" put it picturesquely, they "kicked up in dancing"[2] the particles, which formed all existing things. Originally, they were "in yonder deep close-clasping one another," and it was therefore only by a process of separation that they attained their respective existences.

The process of generation.

The sun-gods, although represented as brothers, denote in a sense the ancestry of the visible sun. They were born, as we are told in the Taittirīya Brāhmaṇa,[3] at different times from the body of the Infinite, by the grace of the mighty gods of old.[4] From Dakṣa—the Cosmic Force—was born Aditi—the endless expanse beyond the sky. After her were born the Sādhyas or Elemental Powers, Potentialities. With the help of Elemental Powers Aditi brought forth the eight sun-gods at different times. Similarly, from Uttānapada ("Productive Power") sprang Aditi—the endless expanse of the horizon, and from that the regions. This is the order, this the mode, in which the gods were generated.

The order of generation of the gods.

We agree with Prof. Max Müller that the conception of Aditi as the daughter of Dakṣa or Uttānapada was not the result of a long process of abstract reasoning. But it cannot be denied that in "Brahmaṇaspati's" conception of Aditi as the mother of Dakṣa we reach a pure abstraction,—"a last remembrance of the religious home in which scientific reflection arose."[5]

Aditi—an abstract conception.

[1] Probably the Sādhyas whose dwelling place is the sky according to Yāska. Ṛig-veda, I. 164.50.

[2] Wallis: Cosmology of the Ṛig-veda, p. 43; Ṛig-veda, X. 72.6.

[3] I. 1.9.1 foll.

[4] The Sādhyas—Fire, Air, etc.

[5] Deussen says: "Die erste und alteste Philosophie eines liegt in seiner Religion." The first and oldest philosophy of a people lies in their religion. All. Gesch. der Philosophie, p. 77.

Aditi and Diti: Non-Being and Being.

Aditi as the daughter of Dakṣa was conceived as existence, while Aditi as the mother of Dakṣa was conceived as non-existence. For "Brahmaṇaspati" Aditi as the endless expanse beyond the sky did approximate to the conception of Aditi as non-existence.[1] Indeed, the former notion seems rather to have been represented by Diti, representing the bounded space beyond the heaven and the bounded horizon on the earth.[2]

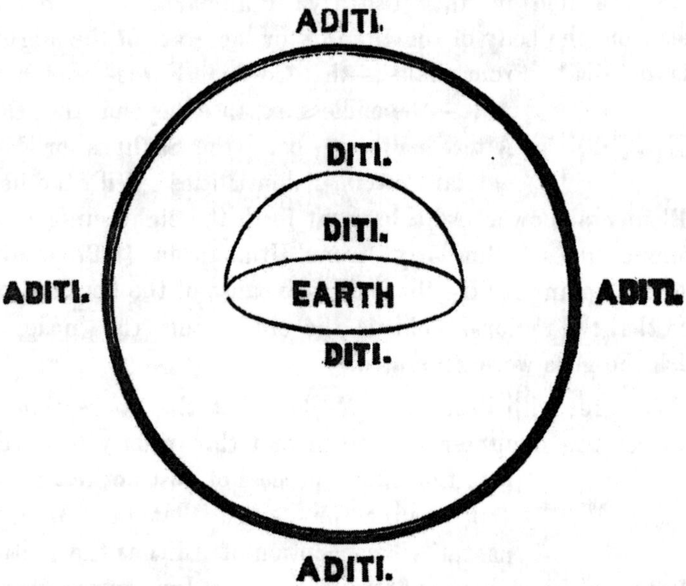

Thus "Brahmaṇaspati"[3] postulated Aditi or Infinity as the primitive matter which is non-existent in the world of

[1] Ṛig-veda, X. 72.9.

[2] Ibid, V. 62.9. By Aditi Sāyaṇa understands the earth as an indivisible whole, and by Diti the individual beings and things. According to Prof. Muir, the two words—Aditi and Diti, together denote "the entire aggregate of visible nature." Original Sanskrit Texts, V, pp. 42-43. Here we have followed Griffith's interpretation.

experience. This primitive matter was called by him the Infinite, for, were it finite, it would have exhausted itself in the ceaseless activity of production. But he had seen that the predicate, non-existent (asat), is essential to the conception of the Infinite. In calling Infinity the non-existent, he had probably meant only to insist that there is nothing in the universe of experience which corresponds to it, the fact being that it can be only approximately expressed by Diti or the so-called visible Infinite.

Why is Aditi called the non-existent?

Infinity is, according to "Brahmaṇaspati," the permanent world-ground from which we must derive all changes or existences, actual and possible (sacca asacca).[1] Thus he transferred the cosmic substance beyond experience, and in so doing he sought naturally to satisfy the demand made by the conception of the Immortal, Unchangeable, Pure and Free. Though no object of experience corresponds to it, he insisted that for explaining experience it is indispensable to assume such a conception behind experience. This seems to have been the meaning implied in the postulate of "Brahmaṇaspati," that in the beginning Being came out of non-Being.

The utility of the conception of Aditi.

A passage of the Taittirīya Brāhmaṇa[2] furnishes a later exposition of "Brahmaṇaspati's" doctrine, now intermingled with that of "Parameṣṭhin." The interest of this exposition is that it throws some light on the mode in which the sun-gods were conceived as generated from the Infinite. Stripped of Brāhmaṇic fancy, the exposition is as follows :—

The Brāhmaṇic exposition of "Brahmaṇaspati's" doctrine.

The universe was at first non-existent. There was neither the heaven nor the earth, nor the mid-air. Being non-existent,

[1] Ṛig-veda.

[2] I. 11.2.9.1. foll.

it desired to be, and thus the cosmic process set in. Consequently, smoke was produced. Smoke was followed by fire, fire by light, light by flame, flame by rays or radiance, that by blaze, which became gradually condensed like a cloud or vapoury mass. The cloud poured down rain which appeared as water, fluid. From water were formed the earth, the mid-air, and the sky. Mind (Manas) was, in like manner, generated from the non-existent. Mind created Prajāpati, and he the world of beings. On Mind rests all that is. Mind is therefore called Brahmā, the Divine.

"Anila"

"Anila's" doctrine: its defect.

The doctrine of "Anila," like that of "Parameṣṭhin," was kept within the bounds of experience. For "Anila" the principle of things (ṛitāvā) was Air (vāyu, αηρ).[1] This principle, like that of Anaximenes, possesses the inherent capacity for movement. Air was conceived accordingly by "Anila" as the monarch or ruling force of the universe (bhuvanasya rājā). He called Air the friend of water,—the first born, endowed with the generating principle.[2] Air travels, we are told by "Anila," without rest or sleep, on the paths of the firmament. Air is the soul or vital spirit of the gods, in air lies the origin of the Universe, Air wanders ever as it listeth.[3] Air has no visible form (na rūpam), but it has a voice of thunder. Its voice is heard, and by that its existence is made known to us. "Anila" attempted no solution of the main problem as to the source from which Air itself came into being.[4]

Once more we meet with the doctrine of "Anila" in a Vedic hymn, namely, the hymn XI. 6 of the Atharva-veda, and this time in a rather more developed and mystical form.

[1] Ṛig-veda, X. 168.

[2] "Apām sakhā prathamajā ṛitāvā." Ṛig-veda, X. 168.3.

[3] "Ātmā devānām bhuvanasya garbho yathavaśam carati deva eṣaḥ." Ṛig-veda, X 168.4.

[4] "Khasvijjātaḥ kuta ābabhūva." Ṛig-veda, X. 168.3.

In this hymn the term Vital Breath (Prāṇa) is substituted for Air (vāyu).

Anila's doctrine as expounded in the Atharva-veda.

We are told that the vital breath is the controlling power of all that we perceive, the vital breath is the lord of all, on the vital breath everything rests.[1] It is in obedience to the thundering voice of the vital breath that the plants are fecundated, that they conceive and multiply. When the season arrives, the vital breath causes the rejoicing of whatever is upon the earth. It is when the vital breath waters the earth with rain that the plants and all kinds of herbs spring forth. The vital breath, clothes the creatures, as a father his dear son. The vital breath, indeed, is the lord of all,—of all that is animate or inanimate.[2]

The vital breath is known, in respect of the universe, as Air (vāta) or wind (Mātariśvan, Air in motion), while as to man, it denotes in-breathing (prāṇa), the opposite of which is called down-breathing (apāna). Without doubt, air is the substance that a man breathes in (inhales) and also breathes out (exhales) while in the womb, and it is when the vital breath quickens the embryo that it is delivered forth. While a man sleeps, the function of breathing is carried on ceaselessly. It is therefore said that a man sleeps while the breath keeps guard over his vitality without sleep or rest. All that is (bhūta) and all that will be, truly, are supported upon the vital breath. But the vital breath is also death; it is fever (takman). The gods worship it,[3] for it shall place the truth-speaker (satya-vādina) in the highest world. It is the guiding power (virāṭ deṣṭrī), it is the sun and moon, and the lord of beings (Prajāpati).

[1] "Prāṇāya namo yasya sarvaṁ idam vaśe, yo bhūta sarvasyeśvaro yasmin sarvaṁ pratiṣṭhitam." Atharva-veda, XI. 6. 1.

[2] *Ibid*, XI. 6. 10: Prāṇoha sarvasyeśvaro yacca prāṇati yacca na.

[3] The gods regard Prāṇa as bhūti or being, while the demons regard it as abhūti or non-being. Aitareya Āraṇyaka II. 1. 8. 6-7.

CHAPTER II.

DIRGHATAMAS AND "NĀRĀYAṆA."

The central point of interest for Vedic speculation.

The strongest movement of Vedic thought is, as we have seen, in the direction of deriving philosophic abstraction from the world as experienced. A strikingly familiar example of this is afforded by the conceptions of the sun. From the very earliest times the sun was recognised "as at once the germ and the creator of the universe."[1] While these prehistoric notions were tending steadily towards a definite end, Dīrghatamas gave out his speculations about the visible universe and the position of the sun in the whole system.[2]

His conception of the sun.

Dīrghatamas[3] seems to have maintained[4] that all living beings rest and depend ultimately on the sun. He compared the sun to a chariot, fitted with one wheel, which revolves with its axle heavy-laden, but not heated, and with its nave unbroken from time immemorial.[5] The wheel has twelve spokes, representing the twelve months. A year with twelve months consists of seven-hundred and twenty days and nights together,[6] and the additional days and nights go to form the intercalary month. The year is divided into a certain number of seasons.

[1] Wallis: The Cosmology of the Ṛig-veda, p. 80.

[2] Dr. Deussen observes that the theme of both these hymns—X. 129, and I. 164—is the same. The unity in the plurality of the phenomena of the universe (Walterscheinungen),—except so far as the method goes, the latter is more analytic, and the former more synthetic than the other. All. Gesch. der Philos., p. 105.

[3] Dīrghatamas is alluded to in the hymns of the Ṛig-veda (I. 160. 6; IV. 4. 13; VIII. 9. 10), as a famous sage. He was the son of Ucathya, and his mother's name was Mamatā. He died probably at the age of seventy (Ṛig-veda, I. 160. 6). He lost his eye-sight at an early age, and remained blind during the remaining years of his life. A pretty long legendary account of his life is to be found in the Mahābhārata. We do not know exactly the cause of his blindness. So far as it may be premised from the hymn I. 160, he was a warrior—a charioteer who was cast by his enemies, bound hand and foot, in a river. But mysteriously his life was saved.

[4] Ṛig-veda, I. 164. 12. [5] *Ibid*, I. 164. 2. 13. [6] *Ibid*, I. 164. 48.

Dīrghatamas speculated about the nature and the cause of the motion of the sun. The sun, held up and propelled by its inherent force (svadhā),[1] goes backward and comes forward,[2] and clad in accumulative and diffusive splendour, travels without stoppage within the worlds.[3] Like a herdsman, the sun never stumbles as it moves on its fixed and familiar path across the sky. The sun and the moon move ceaselessly in opposite directions.[4]

The cause of the motion of the sun.

His account of the relation and the phases of the sun and the moon shows some acuteness. The sun is boneless, the moon bony, and the boneless supports the bony.[5] The moon is called bony, perhaps, because the bonelike spots are visible on its orb, and the sun boneless obviously for the reason that no such spots on its disc are visible to the naked eye. The sun is said to be born an immortal, the moon a mortal, and the relation between the immortal and the mortal is that of two brothers.[6] The sun is said to be immortal, because it does not apparently wax and wane, and the moon is said to be mortal, because its phases do change very often. Men can always mark the one, and are unable sometimes to mark the other.

The contrast between the phases of the sun and the moon.

Far more important is what Dīrghatamas said of the component substance of the sun. The sun is composed, we are told, of a grey coloured substance (palita), and so too are lightning and fire. Indeed, the sun, lightning and fire must, so far as their component substance goes, be looked upon as three brothers.

The component element of the sun; its relation to fire and lightning.

[1] Rig-veda, I. 164. 30.

[2] *Ibid*, I. 164. 31.

[3] *Ibid*, I. 164. 31.

[4] *Ibid*, I. 164. 38.

[5] *Ibid*, I. 164. 4. f. Hillebrandt's Vedische Mythologie, I, p. 338.

[6] Rig-veda, I. 164. 30. "Amartyo martyena sayoniḥ."

Of them, the sun is the first brother, lightning the second, and fire the third.[1] Fire is that brother whose back is sprinkled with ghee (ghritapriṣṭha); lightning is that brother who lies enveloped in his mother's bosom (cloud)[2]; and the sun is that brother whose body is effulgent, who possesses the seven rays, and who rested during his infancy "in the dank rows of cloud."[3]

The primitive substance, whatever it may be, is one.

The grey-coloured substance of which the sun, lightning and fire are composed is "the lovely germ of plants,—the germ of waters."[4] It is to the one and the same substance or principle that the savants give many a name.[5] They call it Agni, Yama, Mātariśvan. They call it sometimes Indra, Mitra, Varuṇa, Agni, Garutman.

The sun's part in the life-process of the world.

The sun delights men with rain in season. The tempest clouds (parjanyā) infuse life into the earth in the form of rain, and various kinds of fire reanimate the heaven. The clouds are formed by water, rising up in uniform manner and falling in the course of time again.[6] The clouds form the waterfloods, and low like a buffalo. From the clouds water descends in streams, and from this water the world of life derives its being or sustenance. Indeed, water is the imperishable substance wherefrom cloud and rain are formed.[7]

The five roots of things.

The heaven (Dyaus) is our father, this great earth our mother, and the mother shares the generating principles with the father. Obviously, the generating principles are, according to Dīrghatamas, these three—water, fire, and air. But it is also implied that the

[1] *Ibid*, I. 164. 1, lightning—aśnaḥ.

[2] *Ibid*, I. 164. 32.

[3] *Ibid*, I. 164. 9.

[4] *Ibid*, I. 164. 52. "bṛihaṁtaṁ apāṁ garbhaṁ darśatam oṣadhīnāṁ."

[5] *Ibid*, I. 164. 46. "Ekaṁ sad viprā bahudhā vadaṁti."

[6] *Ibid*, I. 164. 41.

[7] *Ibid*, I. 164. 42. imperishable = akṣara, "tataḥ kṣaratyākṣaraṁ, tad viśvam upajīvati."

roots of things are these five in all, earth, water, fire, air and heaven, and that all these are reducible to one and the same primitive substance.

His ignorance or agnosticism.

The farthest limit of the earth can be represented geometrically by the circumference of the altar, and the centre of our world by the sacrifice laid on the altar. It is conceivable that Brahman is the word (Vāk), the resting place of which is the highest heaven.[1] We can also conceive that the multiform principles of things are traceable in one and the same cosmic matter. And yet we have to confess "what thing I truly am I know not clearly: mysterious, fettered in my mind I wander."[2] If it can be reasonably supposed that we are from the same primitive substance of which the sun, lightning, and fire are composed, or briefly, if the sun be "the germ and the creator of the universe," even then we must be prepared to answer the question which Dirghatamas brought into the foreground, with a view to dispel his own doubt.[3] His question to all the great and wise thinkers was—What is that one original abiding element which, manifested in the form of the unborn sun, has established and upholds this world-system?

"Hence the trend of thought," as Dr. Henry Stephen would have put it, "is towards the idea of single absolute and self-subsistent principle which is infinite in the sense of being inexhaustible power; and towards the view that all finite things and products of the self-evolution of correlated

[1] Ṛig-veda, I. 164. 35. "Iyaṁ vedi paro antaḥ prithivyā, ayaṁ yajño bhuvanasya nābhiḥ—Brahmāyaṁ Vācaḥ paramaṁ vyoma."

The altar is the image of the earth or world. The signification of this dictum is twofold. In the language of art, it means that the altar is symbolical of the idea of the universe. Geometrically, it is the representation of the configuration of the earth.

[2] Ṛig-veda, I. 164, "na vijānāmi yadi vedam asmi niṇyaḥ saṁnaddho manasā carāmi."

[3] *Ibid*, I. 164. 6. "acikitvāñ cikituṣaś cidatra Kavin pricchāmi vidmane na vidvān."

factors of one universal system and plan, and that the world therefore is a unity."[1]

It is all very interesting to observe by way of retrospect that the attitude of Dirghatamas towards the deepest problem of philosophy savours of agnosticism. But he persistently tends to derive the many from the one single, ordaining, sustaining, co-ordinating self-existent principle of which all known forces, laws, and movements are various manifestations. The nature of ultimate reality is however unknown, and probably unknowable. The world of experience is conceived as a systematic unity, the whole of nature being a sort of Divine machine evolving and working itself to an end by some fixed and uniform laws of motion, interaction, and so forth.

All physical phenomena, states and processes can be accounted for by the principles of mechanics and physics, while the final question of their origin and interaction remains ever insoluble. There is nevertheless to be felt behind all these the presence of an unseen hand at work, the play of a deep mystery that ever eludes man's grasp. Although the mysterious is always the mysterious, Dīrghatamas advanced far enough to suggest that it is the unborn, unchanging cause of the ever-fleeting show of created things, and that whatever its real nature, it seems to partake more of the material and less of the spiritual. The world as a whole is guided on towards a path of progress by two principles—active and passive, compared to two birds roosting on the same world-tree. One of them eats fruits, while the other does not eat, but silently reflects only.[2] It is thus that the whole of nature is moving along the road to an end. These principles are however emanations from the same unborn, energising force. These are inseparable comrades.

[1] The Problems of Metaphysics, 5th edition, p. 311.

[2] Ṛig-veda, I. 164. 20. Yāska, Nirukta, XIV. 30.

(2) "*Nārāyaṇa*."—The theoretic desire to determine the nature of the first cause of the world was very keen among the Vedic thinkers, and conceivably it grew keener when Dīrghatamas formulated it into a definite problem. Dīrghatamas himself could quite realise that in order fully to apprehend the nature of the first cause of the world, it is not enough to accept the postulate of oneness of the cosmic matter as a mere truism. Assuming that the present sun is the source of life and light, the enquiring mind wants yet to have a clear and definite knowledge of that one original, undivided, universal being from which the sun derived its life, or of which the sun is the present representative.

Dīrghatamas's anticipation of "Nārāyaṇa's" views.

The view of "Nārāyaṇa" is embodied in the hymn X. 90 of the Ṛig-veda.[1] This hymn has two sides—the philosophical and the social.

As regards its philosophical side, this hymn exhibits clearly the mode in which "Nārāyaṇa" attempted for the first time to form the conceptions of God, soul and their relation.

"Nārāyaṇa's" philosophy.

"Nārāyaṇa" conceived the visible sun, whose diameter is ten fingers,[2] as the soul (Puruṣa) of the universe, and that soul as the principle of all that is and of all that is to be.[3] The sun as the soul of the universe was described by him as "The lord of immortality.[4]"

The sun is the soul of the universe; its diameter.

Far greater than Puruṣa the visible sun was Puruṣa the original sun.[5] This latter Puruṣa was posited by "Nārāyaṇa" as the one—the first cause of the universe, nay, the universe itself.

The original sun or solar body: it is God.

[1] See also Atharva-veda, XIX. 6.

[2] Ṛig-veda, X. 90. 1: "daśāṅgulaṁ."

[3] *Ibid*, X. 90. 2: "Puruṣa evēdaṁ sarvaṁ yad bhūtaṁ yac ca bhavyaṁ."

[4] *Ibid*, X. 90. 2: "amṛitatvasyēśāno."

[5] *Ibid*, X, 90. 3.

The visible sun and the original solar body were called alike Puruṣa, because both were regarded by "Nārāyaṇa" as identical in all respects save in size. According to "Nārāyaṇa," the sun from which we now derive light and heat must be viewed only as the present relic or representative of the original solar body.

The identity of God and Soul.

"Nārāyaṇa" also conceived the original solar body as split up, somehow or other, in two. Three-fourths of it went up, and the one-fourth remained here.[1] From the three-fourths which went up was produced Virāj,[2] the luminous body of which the sun, the moon, the planets and the myriads of stars are so many offshoots. And from the one-fourth which remained here below was formed, through the process of cooling, this earth with all animate and inanimate things. Thus in "Nārāyaṇa's" conception Puruṣa (God) is the first cause of the universe. It is from Puruṣa that the sun, the moon, the earth, water, fire, air, the mid-air, the sky, the regions, the seasons, the creatures of the air, all animals, all classes of men, and all human institutions had originated.

The process in which this universe was gradually formed from the primitive solar mass.

But since it is implied that cause and effect are identical in essence, Puruṣa must also be viewed as the universe or totality of things. As every particular thing is from Puruṣa, so the sum-total of all particular things is Puruṣa. True, that Puruṣa and the visible universe are identical in substance, which is a constant quantity. And yet this universe cannot be called Puruṣa, inasmuch as it is so transformed that it no more resembles the original solar body. If there be anything in the visible universe which has claim to the name of Puruṣa, it is the sun. The sun must then be considered to be the soul of the universe. This soul is in the universe; yet it is not the

God, World, and Soul.

[1] Ṛig-veda, X. 90. 3; X. 90. 4.
[2] Ibid, X. 90. 5.

universe, but something totally different in its nature. Indeed, the sun is but the eye of the universe. It is thus made increasingly clear that the famous Puruṣa Sūkta of the Ṛigveda is far from presenting us with a Sāṁkhya doctrine of Puruṣa and Prakṛiti, Soul and Matter. A mere analogy of two words cannot be held as a definite proof of the identity of two doctrines.[1]

"Nārāyaṇa's" social theory is an accidental secondary feature of his doctrine. As a philosopher, his object was to establish that everything in this universe is from Puruṣa. He found the four classes of men—Brāhmaṇas, Rājanyas, Vaiśyas, and Śūdras—already existing in his time within the pale of the Indo-Aryan community. He does not seem to have taken the least trouble to enquire whether the distinction of four classes was based originally upon a mere division of labour or otherwise. Taking these classes as he found them, he asserted that the Brāhmaṇa was the mouth, the Rājanya was made of the arms, the Vaiśya was the thighs, and the Śūdra was produced from the feet of Puruṣa,[2] and this was all that he said by way of illustration of his main doctrine. But it is clearly implied in his expressions that his views were absolutely in favour of the existing caste-system or class-distinctions. The ground on which he defended the theory of caste was that such a system obtains in the organisation of the universe, and why not, then, in human society? If there may be class-distinctions among the gods, then why not among men? Hence the Puruṣa-Sūkta may be rightly considered as the first theoretic basis of the Cāturvarṇya system of the Brāhmaṇs.[3]

"Nārāyaṇa's" theoretic defence of the system of class-distinctions in society.

[1] The view criticised above is to be found in the Maudgalôpaniṣad which is a commentary on the Puruṣa-Sūkta.

[2] Ṛig-Veda, X. 99. 12. "Brāhmaṇôsya mukham āsid bāhu Rājanya kṛita, urū tad asya yad Vaiśyaḥ padbhyām Śūdro ajāyata" Cf. Manu-Saṁhitā, 1. 31.

[3] Cf. Puruṣavidha-Brāhmaṇa in the Bṛihad Āraṇyaka Upaniṣad.

CHAPTER III.

"Hiranyagarbha" and "Viśvakarman."

It has been observed by Dr. Windelband that the inclination of philosophers to view "Deity" as the highest conception is a phenomenon which constantly recurs in history.[1] There arises an unavoidable necessity for uniting religion and philosophy in fruitful and indissoluble marriage. The chief aim of philosophy, as modern usage understands it, is to explain the world, and the religious consciousness leads man to rise above all that is multiform, finite, mutable, earthly and brutal in him to that which is one, infinite, immutable, celestial and divine. And it is thus that a need arises to build up a philosophical theory on a theistic basis.

Necessity for the conception of God.

"Brahmaṇaspati's" Aditi, as well as Anaximander's Infinity, was undoubtedly "the first philosophic conception of God, the first attempt, and one which remains still entirely within the physical, to strip the idea of God of all mythical form."[2] Almost in the same stage were "Nārāyaṇa's" conceptions of Puruṣa—God and Soul. The conceptions of "Hiraṇyagarbha" and "Viśvakarman" show, as it seems, a considerable advance in the direction of the idea of God.

The development of the idea of God.

But it also appears that the conceptions of "Hiraṇyagarbha" and "Viśvakarman" themselves differ fundamentally from each other in that the one is dominated by what may be called the religious motive, while on the part of the other we perceive a motive which is philosophical.

Distinction between "Hiraṇyagarbha" and "Viśvakarman".

1. A History of Philosophy, p. 34. In reference to Brahmaṇaspati's view, Madame Blavatsky pointedly says, "The whole range of physical phenomena proceeds from the primary of Aether—Ākāsh—as dual-natured Ākāsha proceeds from the undifferentiated chaos—so called, the latter being the primary aspect of Mūlaprakṛiti, the Root-matter and the first abstract idea one can form of Parabrahman." The Secret Doctrine I. p. 585.

The main question with "Hiraṇyagarbha" was, what God should we adore with oblation other than God (Prajāpati)?[1] Evidently it contained for him both an answer and a contention, namely, that there is no other god but God whom we should thus adore. "Viśvakarman", on the other hand, urged this thoughtful enquiry, what is the tree or wood out of which the universe was fashioned?[2] Thereby he did not intend, to be sure, to add anything further to his knowledge, but just to open the eyes of those who were in doubt to see for themselves that the world-tree was God. It will be remembered, however, that the religious element, too, is not entirely absent from "Viśvakarman's" idea of God, in the same way that "Hiraṇyagarbha's" doctrine is not devoid of the philosophical element.

The special feature of his doctrine.

I. As to "Hiraṇyagarbha's" doctrine[3] there is nothing very surprising about it. It stands mid-way between the doctrine of "Parameṣṭhin" on the one hand, and that of "Nārāyaṇa," on the other. As Mr. Wallis points out, Hiraṇyagarbha viewed the un, called metaphorically the golden germ, as the great power of the universe, from which all other powers and existences, divine and earthly, are derived, a conception which is the nearest approach to the later......conception of Brahmā, the Creator of the world."

The sun was thus conceived by "Hiraṇyagarbha" as the one (ekaḥ),—the sole ruler of all that breathes, and of all that sleeps (does not breathe). The sun is the lord of all beings (bhūta), the lord (īśa) of the bipeds and the quadrupeds. He is "the giver of vital spirit, of power and vigour."[4]

1 Ṛig-veda, X. 121. 1. "Kasmai devāya haviṣā vidhema?" We have followed above Ludwig's interpretation.

2 Ṛig-veda, X. 81. 4.

3 Ṛig-veda, X. 121.

4 Ṛig-veda, X. 121.2. (Griffith's translation) : "ātmadā baladā."

His is death, and his shadow again is life immortal.[1] These snowy mountains, and what men call seas and rivers are his possession ; the regions (pradiśa) his arms. It is he who fixed and holds up the heaven and the earth.

His conception of God.

Here by the term, Sun, "Hiraṇyagarbha" did not exactly mean the sun as we commonly understand it, but what he called the Golden Germ. This germ is Fire,[2] for Fire constitutes, according to him, the solar essence,—the generating principle of the universe. But this Fire itself was contained at first in water.

The solar essence is Fire.

Thus, like "Parameṣṭhin", "Hiraṇyagarbha" thought water to be the primitive substance of all that is. But he realised at the same time that to explain the world it is not enough to say that water is the first principle in itself, for conceivably there is a higher principle behind it. It is Prajāpati, and Prajāpati is the God of gods, and none beside him.[3] Prajāpati brought forth water,[4] and it is he who provided the generating principle and the ordaining power of things. All this leads back to the question, what other god should we adore with oblation than God ?[5]

"Hiraṇyagarbha" and "Parameṣṭhin".

II. Now we turn to "Viśvakarman", whose contribution to the Vedic thought was the abstract or metaphysical conception of God.

It is a noteworthy fact that "Viśvakarman" offered his view not so much in the form of a tenet as in that of a case against others. The chief object of his attack was, of course, "Parameṣṭhin", who refused in the traditional manner of a sceptic

His case against the sceptics.

[1] Ṛig-veda : X.121.2 . "yasya chāyâmṛitam yasya mṛityuḥ."

[2] *Ibid*, X.121.7

[3] *Ibid*, X.121.8.

[4] *Ibid*, X.121.9.

[5] *Ibid*, X.121.1.

to carry his research beyond water. From the point of view of "Viśvakarman" it is a quite inadequate and unsatisfactory explanation to posit water as the primitive substance of all that is, and then to derive from it this world as a whole by giving it an inherent power of movement. If water be the primitive substance which is endowed with the inherent principle of change, we have yet to account for that from which water derived its being, and derived the motive power, the generating principle, the elemental forces, the laws, and all the rest.[1]

God is the universal substance, the first cause of things.

Here "Viśvakarman" said, that is God. God is the first and the last. He is earlier than the visible universe; he had existed before all the cosmic forces came into being.[2] He is the sole God who created and ordained this universe.[3] He is yet again the tree or wood from which this universe was fashioned.[4]

God: his attributes.

God is one, and only one (eka eva). He is the unborn one (aja) in whom all the existing things abide.[5] He is that one who is mighty in mind and supreme in power.[6] He is the maker, the disposer, the most lofty presence.[7] As father he generated us, and as disposer he knows the fate of all that is.[8] It is from him that water derived its being, and received the motive power or generating principle.[9] He alone gave names to the gods, and it is he whom we all "seek for information,"—for explanation of the world.[10] The hymn-chanters or philosophers who doubt his

[1] Ṛig-veda, X.82.5: "Kaṁ svid garbhaṁ prathamaṁ dadhra āpo yatra devā samapaśyaṁta viśve."

Ibid, X.82.5: "paro divā para enā pṛithivyā."

Ibid, X.81.3.

Ibid, X.81.4.

Ibid, X.8.26.

Ibid, X.82.2.

Ibid, X.82.5: "dhātā vidhātā paramota saṁdṛik."

Ibid, X.82.3: "yo naḥ pitā janitā yo vidhātā dhāmāni veda bhuvanāni viśvā."

Ibid, X.82.6.

bid, X.82.3: "yo devānāṁ nāmadhā eka eva taṁ saṁpraśnaṁ bhuvanā yaṁtyānyā.

existence wander, *benighted as they are by the mist of ignorance* and speak with faltering voice.[1]

Thus in accordance with "Viśvakarman's" view, God is omnipresent, omnipotent, omniscient (paramota saṁdṛik) and one. But we cannot see him, because he is invisible, and we cannot find him because another thing—this delusive universe ?—has appeared before our eyes.[2] To know him or to apprehend his nature, therefore, we, as thoughtful men, must only inquire within our heart, *i.e.*, deeply think.[3]

How to know God ?

We must know him, for without knowing him, we cannot arrive at a satisfactory, all-comprehensive explanation of the world; and we must apprehend his true nature; for without apprehending it, we cannot establish that immutable ground of the unity of things upon which to fall back constantly.

Why should we know God ?

We must know God as the first principle of things,—the first cause in relation to which this universe must be conceived as the effect; and we must apprehend his true nature as identical in pith or essence with that of the universe.

"Viśvakarman's" doctrine is of immense historical importance. In it we see all the basic ideas of Vedānta in the making. Moreover, we perceive the two distinct conceptions or different points of view. One is logical, and the other ontological.

The historical importance of "Viśvakarman's" doctrine.

In the first place, God conceived as the first cause of the universe is logically distinguishable from the conception of the universe; and in the second place, God, viewed as identical in substance with the universe, is the universe.

The two points of view: logical and ontological.

[1] Ṛig-vada, X.82.7: "nihāreṇa prāvṛitā jalpyā......Ukthapāsaś caraṁti." nihāreṇa prāvṛitā="enwrapt in misty cloud"—(Griffith).

[2] *Ibid*, X.82.7: "na taṁ vidātha ya imā jajānānyad yuṣmākaṁ aṁtaraṁ babhūva."

[3] *Ibid*, X.81.4.

PART II.

Post-Vedic Philosophy.

Introductory.

(The name Post-Vedic period may require a word of explanation. It is possible that its upper limit can be fixed as far back as the last seer of the Ṛig-veda or even a little earlier. In any case, here we shall restrict the use of the name to the period covered by the history of the Aitareya, the Taittirīya, and a few other important Brāhmaṇa schools,[1] who were counted by Buddha as being among the oldest. The period thus chosen might be brought, for our present purposes, within smaller compass from Mahidāsa Aitareya to Yājñavalkya.

The historical features of the period.

The Post-Vedic period as a whole may be best distinguished from the Vedic by the fact that the intellectual centre is no longer the Brahmarṣideśa, but what is generally known as Madhya-deśa, the Mid-land. It is situated between the Himālayas on the north, and the Vindhya mountains on the south. It lies to the east of Prayāga (Allahabad) and to the west of Vinaśana ("Manu-smṛiti," II. 21), Kuru, Pañchāla, Matsya, Śūrasena, are four among the well-known republics, and Kāśī, Videha, and Kośala are three among the most powerful monarchies of the time. During this period—Benares the oldest of the three monarchies—is said to have changed its name many times (Jātaka, No. 460).

The contrast between the Vedas and the Brāhmaṇas.

The transition from the Vedic to the Brāhmaṇic period must have taken place gradually. Yet in leaving the one for the other, the historian turns his back upon the freshness of poetry only to face the dullness of prose. In the language of Dr. Hopkins, "With the Brāhmaṇas not only

[1] Dīgha Nikāya, I, p. 237.

is the tone changed from that of the Ṛig-veda, the whole moral atmosphere is now surcharged with hocuspocus, mysticism, religiosity, instead of the cheerful, real religion which, however formal, is the soul of the Ṛik. In the Brāhmaṇas there is no freshness, no poetry. There is in some regards a more scrupulous outward morality, but for the rest there is only cynicism, bigotry, and dullness. It is true that each of these traits may be found in certain parts of the Ṛig-veda; but it is not true that they represent there the spirit of the age, as they do in the Brāhmanic period."[1]

The judgment of of Brāhmanic religion by Hopkins.

But this careful observer adds: "Such is not altogether the case. It is the truth, yet it is not the whole r uh, that in these Brāhmaṇas religion isaianppearance, not a reality."[2]

Dr. Hopkins seeks to establish the link between the animistic worship of the Ṛig-veda and the stringent ritual of the Brāhmaṇas in the person of the priest, as his position is set forth in the liturgical hymns of the Yajurveda. This seems plausible, yet not very important to us. To us, in fact, the Sāman and the Yajur, however voluminous they may be in size, are but two large collections of excerpts from the older Ṛik. The important text for us is the divine Ṛik, and also to some extent, the Atharva.

The Sāma and the Yajurveda are of the least importance from the point of view of philosophy.

The transition period defined.

It is conceivable that there is a long interval separating the last sage of the Ṛig-veda from the thinker whom we may rightly take as the first philosopher of the Post-Vedic period. Probably, as may be easily deduced from the long string of names appended to some of the Brāhmaṇas, at this intermediate period a great many persons were born who kept alive the philosophic traditions of the past, and represented

[1] Religions of India, pp. 176-177.

[2] Religions of India, p. 180.

the highest wisdom of the time. From our point of view, this intermediate period is the one into which we can peep through the portals of the Brāhmaṇa sections of the Brāhmaṇa texts, as distinguished from the Āraṇyakas and Upaniṣads. It seems that the thinkers of the time kept things going, just in the same way that musicians play on various tunes to indicate that the performance is not over yet, only the scene is changing.

The historical value of this intermediate period consists chiefly in its being the period of transition from the Vedic to the Post-Vedic. At this period, philosophy, no less than Prajāpati,[1] was thinking herself "emptied" or exhausted in the activity of production. But the creative impulse led her to ponder over the minds of men, just as Prajāpati was brooding over the cosmic matter. Whilst thus Prajāpati and philosophy were toiling hard, and fainting in the struggle for existence, theology was not in any way less active on her own side.

Its intrinsic value in the history of philosophy

While Prajāpati was fusing the races of men, theology was spinning out the rituals in detail, while philosophy was busy, we saw, with intermingling Vedic thoughts; consequently the intermixture of blood among men, the painfully minute elaboration of rituals, and the intermingling of the doctrines of the earlier thinkers—these are among the most noticeable features of the transition period in question.

The peculiarities of the transition period.

So far as philosophy is concerned, it is just in this process of intermingling of the earlier thoughts that we can trace in India the origin of a something equivalent to that Sophistic maxim, that man is the measure of all things. Prajāpati generated man from his soul, therefore 'Man is all the

The Sophistic maxim; how did it originate?

[1] Śatapatha Brāhmaṇa, III. 9. 1. 1; Taittirīya Brāhmaṇa, II. 2. 4. etc.

animals,[1] *i.e.*, man is the prototype of living beings—such is, however, the precise Indian maxim and its argument. And we must note here that as soon as this maxim came to clear recognition, the course of philosophy was changed.

The transition from cosmological to psychological speculations is natural and inevitable.

Beyond a doubt, this transition from the geocentrism of Vedic speculations to the anthropocentrism of the Post-Vedic took place gradually, as well as harmoniously. The chief interest of the earlier thinkers was centred upon the physical world as a whole, and the later thinkers were chiefly concerned with the organic world and man. The order is perfectly natural.

The Post-Vedic thought is implied or anticipated in the Vedic. How?

Further, in spite of the fact that there are in the scheme of the earlier thought but 'very feeble indications of a zeal for knowledge applied to the organic world and man,' we have seen that in the speculation of Dīrghatamas was foreshadowed the whole character of Post-Vedic philosophy; his doctrine disclosed to us in an eminent degree as to what would be the exact lines on which the development of Vedic philosophy must proceed in future.

It was Dīrghatamas who considered the sacrificial altar as the navel or centre of our world, and set himself to inquire, What am I? And so it was Dīrghatamas whose somewhat paradoxical doctrine of Indra and Soma[2] (sun and moon, or heat and light) as the active principle and the passive spectator of the visible universe contained the later conceptions of the relation between life and soul. Besides Dīrghatamas, there is another Vedic sage whose name must be mentioned in this connection. She is "Sūryā". "Sūryā" conceived the son as the reproduction of the father,

[1] Śatapatha Brāhmaṇa, II. 1. 4. 11 ff. Professor L. T. Hobhouse points out that "this does not seem to have any real analogy with the principle of Protagorus."

[2] Ṛig-veda, I. 164. 19.32.

since a man is born in the womb of his wife in the form of a seed.[1] Inspite of the fact that this came to be regarded later as a popular view,[2] it will be remembered that "Sūryā's" was the first attempt to formulate a scientific theory about the origin and continuity of human life. We have further to admit here that "Sūryā's" speculations gave rise to the theory of heredity as expounded in the Post-Vedic literature.[3]

The conditions under which the question "Who am I"? permanently arose.

All this is true, and yet the fact remains that the primary concern of the Vedic thinkers was the world, not man. Therefore the question "Who am I?" could permanently arise only in the wake of the consciousness, that 'man is all the animals.'

Post-Vedic thought is just the repetition of the Vedic, in so far as the types of problems are concerned.

Once more, this one question "Who am I?" brought in its train many other questions, and here it is interesting to remark that almost all the fundamental questions raised by the Vedic thinkers with regard to the world were repeated in the Post-Vedic thought with regard to man. In this respect Post-Vedic philosophy may be looked upon as simply the repetition of the Vedic, although this repetition does not mean imitation, but continuation and development, in the truest sense of the terms.

The fundamental problem of the period, according to Buddha.

In the opinion of Buddha the period which closely followed upon that of the Vedic worship was religious-philosophical in character, the main problem of this period being "How can I hold communion or unite with Brahman?"[4]

The judgment thus summarized by Buddha may not be wholly true in the letter, yet it must be said to be true in the

[1] Rigveda, X. 85. 40; "ātmā vai jāyate putra." Kauṣītaki Upaniṣad, II. 1. 1. Aitareya Āraṇyaka, II. 5. 1. 2. ff.

[2] Vedānta-sāra, (ed. Jacob), p. 32.

[3] Kauṣītaki Upaniṣad, II. 15. Bṛihad Āraṇyaka Upaniṣad, I. 5. 1. 1.

[4] Brahmāṇam Sahabyatā, (Sanskrit, svabhavyatā ?)
Tevijja-sutta, see Dial. B. II. pp. 305 ff; Mahā-Govinda-suttanta, D. N. II., p. 240 ff.

spirit, considering that the highest religious aspiration of man to approach and unite with what he looks up to as the supreme, the mighty, the divine, the infinite, the immortal, the sinless, the merciful, the beautiful, the one, the all, was never absent, from the Vedic or Indo-Aryan minds.[1] This truly religious aspiration of man to unite with what is divine in nature found its earliest expression in one of the hymns of Śunaḥśepa. He aspired to know who among the immortal gods had the power to restore him to Aditi—the visible Infinite, that he might realise the nature of his father and mother (heaven and earth), and the reply that came to him was—Fire (Agni alone is powerful to do so).[2] In the case of "Brahmaṇaspati's" hymn, too, we could not but see the eagerness of the finite (*i.e.*, the bounded space beyond the heaven and the bounded horizon on the earth) to approach Aditi—the real Infinite. And yet again it was only in the views of Dīrghatamas that we had the first definite indication of the unity of man in essence with the rest of the universe,—with the whole. We know, however, that in the conception of Dīrghatamas this world-essence is no other than what he called the solar essence, that is to say, identical with the fire-essence. Thus all these are inter-connected, and their connection came about in natural, historical order.

Justification of Buddha's opinion.

Now in conformity with our theory, that in India as in Greece, the first philosophic reflections arose out of religion, we may hold with Buddha that the main question with the early Post-Vedic thinkers appertained to Yoga—the inner culture of faith and intellect. It seems probable even then, that from the question "How can I unite with him?" emerged these two apparently distinct problems for philosoyhy—(1) Who is he with whom I shall

Further demonstration of the main problem of Post-Vedic Philosophy.

[1] Ṛig-Veda, X. 88. 15; I. 125. 5; X. 107. 2.

[2] Ibid, I. 24. 1-2.

unite? and (2) Who am I who shall unite with him? Of these the former has already been answered by the Vedic thinkers, and now the latter must be answered by their successors. In reality, however, both of these problems are there for the Post-Vedic thinkers, and they are to them not exactly two distinct problems, but two aspects of one and the same problem. To them he is logically distinguishable from me as the object from the subject. But from the Yoga point of view, if I know him, I know myself, and if I know myself I know him. Thus the two questions—"Who is he?" and "Who am I?" are capable of being answered briefly by "I am he (so' haṁ)." In other words, according to the Yoga postulate, the two questions are reducible to this one - Who is he? or, Who am I?

The interest of the problem.

To the question—Who am I? the answers are given in an ascending series. The interest of these answers lies partly in the roughly outlined stages of transition, first, from the physical world to the organic; secondly, from the organic world to embryonic man; thirdly from embryonic to physiological man; fourthly, from physiological to psychological man; fifthly, from psychological to metaphysical man; and lastly, from metaphysical to religious-ethical man.

The solution of the problem.

Accordingly, the reply to the question—Who am I? may be stated in the following order :—

(a) I am an individual being, as all the animals of the earth and all the creatures of the air are. All organic beings and all inorganic things, said "Nārāyaṇa," are formed from Puruṣa—the sun or solar substance.

(b) I am annamaya—embryonic man, a man in the process of formation, that is to say, a seed or sperm, composed of food or five elements,[1] produced from the essence of food digested by the father, communicated to the mother and established in the womb.

[1] According to Buddha's enumeration, the elements are four in number.

(*c*) I am prāṇamaya—physiological man, a man born of the parents, brought forth by the mother, a living body, that is to say, a body imbued with life, composed of food or elements, nourished by food,[1] reduced at death to an anatomical man, a corpse dissolved hereafter into the elements or returned to the physical world.

(*d*) I am manomaya—psychological man, a conscious individual, who can perceive through the senses, who dreams, imagines, thinks, feels, wills, and who perceives duality and plurality among things, perceptual and conceptual.

(*e*) I am vijñānamaya[2]—metaphysical man, a thought-free, but conscious man who is beginning to sleep and sleeping a sound sleep, a man who is endowed with nothing but the inherent conscious sentient principle or soul—a thinker who realises the unity of cause in the variety of appearance.

(*f*) Lastly, I am ānandamaya—spiritual or religious-ethical man, who is enjoying the bliss of sound sleep, uncrossed by dreams, untouched by cares,—a blessed soul, united with the divine.[3]

According to the earliest, demoniac, or materialistic mode, I am the body; according to the later, corporeal or realisitic mode, I am the mind; and according to the last, incorporeal or idealistic mode, I am the soul.[4]

The dialectical aspect of Post-Vedic philosophy.

So far regarding the contemplative side of the Post-Vedic literature. But in dealing effectively with the subject of Indian philosophy, we must also take into consideration another side of it, which is of as much intellectual importance as the contemplative. Logic and dialectic (tarka, mīmāṁsā), formed the two wings of discussion, carried

[1] Pāli,—kabaliṅkāra-āhāra-bhakkho.

[2] Pāli,—saññāmaya.

[3] Taittirīya Upaniṣad, II. 1-5; Dīgha-nikāya, I. p. 34.

[4] Chāndogya Upaniṣad, VIII, 7. 1. ff (S.B.E.); Poṭṭhapāda sutta, D.N. I, p. 195; etc., Deussen's All. Gesch der Philosophie, pp. 89-90.

on by the Wanderers generally, and discussion involved, as a rule, a sort of "wrangling" in the learned circle. As Buddha described it humorously, the learned recluses and Brāhmans meet together, discuss problems, and wrangle in this manner :—[1]

"You don't understand this doctrine and discipline, I do. How should you know about this doctrine and discipline?

You have fallen into wrong views. It is I who am in the right.

I am speaking to the point, you are not.

You are putting last what ought to come first, and first what ought to come last.[2]

What you've excogitated so long, that's all quite upset.

Your challenge has been taken up.[3] You are proved to be wrong.[4]

Set to work to clear your views.[5] Disentangle yourself if you can."

The four laws of thought.

The problem in theological circles was concerned with the divine revelation of Word, or the Vedas, and duties enjoined therein. In other circles the subject was either philosophical or scientific. Whatever that might be, the happy result of this mode of discussion or "wrangling" among the learned Wanderers was that in the time of Buddha the four laws of thought were recognised as a matter of course. These are in their application to propositions :—

(If A is B), A is B.

A cannot be both B and not-B.

A is either B or not-B.

A is neither B nor not-B.

[1] Dīgha-nikāya, I. p. 8; Majjhima-nikāya, II. 3; see Dial. B. II, pp. 14-15.

[2] "Putting the cart before the horse."

[3] Āropito te vādo. The alternative rendering suggested by Rhys Davids is—"Issue has been joined against you."

[4] Niggahitôsi. Note the term nigraha.

[5] Cara vāda-pamokkhāya.

These are implied in such interrogative propositions as are met with throughout the Buddhist canonical texts.

Is there another world? Is A B? (The reply being, No).

Is it, then, that there is not another world? Is A not-B? (The reply being still, No.)

Is it, then, that there both is and is not another world? Is A both B and not-B? (The reply being as before.)

Is it, then, that there neither is nor is not another world? Is A neither B nor not-B?[1]

In reality this reference ought to have been discussed in the introduction to Part III. For all ancient documents at our disposal bear evidence to the fact that the recognition of four laws or principles was rather the outcome of a further penetrating analysis on the part of thinkers other and somewhat later than Post-Vedic. It was not possible until Sophistic activities in the country were in full swing. So far as Post-Vedic philosophers are concerned, they seem only to have vaguely and occasionally referred to these three laws, *viz.*, laws of Identity, Contradiction, and Double Negation. Yājñavalkya's "No-No Doctrine" affords no doubt the best example of Double Negation. Those who think merely of the forms of questions may not accept our interpretation in its principle or in its detail. Råther they might go so far as to assert that Indian minds were so illogical from the beginning that they could, and as a matter of fact did, with impunity set all the fundamental laws of thought at nought. But the critic, in order to avoid being one sided, must carefully examine the forms of interrogation, the modes of rejoinder, and above all, their motives. The example given, is of a controversy in the form in which it was carried on in the sixth century B.C., if not earlier. It is evident that the motive of the interrogator is to seek a dialectical advantage over the interlocutor who, as a professed sceptic, seeks to evade the position where he might commit himself to a flagrant logical absurdity.

[1] Dialogues of the Buddha, Vol. II, pp. 39-40

[Let us produce here at random the specimen of a controversy which dates as late as the third century B.C., for examination. "Th.—Does the past exist? A.—It exists on this wise, it does not exist on that wise. Th.—Does the past, as you describe it, both exist and not exist? You deny, then affirm—for you must affirm. And if this same past both exists and does not exist, then is also existence non-existence and conversely, then is the state of being a state of non-being and conversely, then are "is" and "is not" convertible terms, identical, one in meaning, the same, same in content and in origin? And this of course you do not admit." (Points of Controversy, P. T. S., pp. 108-9). The Syādvāda or Antinomian doctrine of the Jainas and of the Sarvāstivādins and their followers might be calculated to be a defiance of the established laws of thought. But this is not really the case, the doctrine being of a hypothetical character only. To affirm that A may be B in one sense, from one standpoint, and not B in another sense, from another standpoint, is not to deny the Law of contradiction, which teaches that A cannot be both B and not-B at the same time, and in the same sense. We might here refer the reader to a significant pronouncement of Buddha on the subject of the Law of Identity in its application to categorical propositions: "that which has passed away, ceased to be, completely changed, is to be designated, termed, judged as "something that was," and neither as "something that is" nor as "something that will be"; and so on (Saṁyutta, III, pp. 71-3).]

Later texts can furnish numerous passages giving us an insight into the exact use to which the fourth Law was put, that of Double Negation. It is implied that this is applicable to two extreme cases: either (1) to the conception of something which is really nothing, that is, non-existent as a fact in the world of experience, but possible as a product of fancy, *viz.*, "a barren woman's son," "the horns of a hare," "flowers in the sky;" or (2) to the conception of that which is the real of all that is relatively real, *viz.*, Brahman, Ātman, Nirvāṇa, that is, the Absolute. The significance of the Nêti Nêti doctrine of Yājñavalkya is that Brahman is definable only by negation of all the predicates assignable to the finite things of experience.[1]

[1] *Cf.* Brahma-Sūtra, III.. 2·22: Prakṛitaitāvattvaṁ hi pratiṣedhati tato bravīti ca bhūyaḥ.

The theological side of the older Brāhmaṇic activity. Its effect on the course of philosophy.

Now we sum up the result of the older Brāhmaṇic activity on the theological side. The overwhelming energy applied to the systematization of Vedic rituals was not without its salutary effect upon the course of philosophy itself. The oldest Vedic wisdom knew no division at all, nor the older Brāhmaṇic. But the arrangement and re-arrangement of current hymns and customary rites under various artificial heads, revealed in course of the Post-Vedic period the way in which the concrete sciences and practical philosophy might be separated from theology proper, and from theoretic philosophy.

CHAPTER IV

MAHIDĀSA AITAREYA

Mahidāsa: a short account of his life.

We begin the Post-Vedic philosophy with Mahidāsa Aitareya, to whom tradition rightly points as the founder of the Aitareya school. It appears from a reference made to him in the Chāndogya Upaniṣad[1] that he lived to the age of one hundred and sixteen years. The first twenty-four years of his life were spent as student, the next forty-four years as householder and the remaining forty-eight years as hermit or forest-dweller. The same Upaniṣad lays stress on the fact that the singular regularity which Mahidāsa observed throughout enabled him to attain such a long life, free from illness and from weaknesses.

He was in all probability a Brāhman. His parentage.

We do not know whether Mahidāsa was a Brāhman or a warrior by birth. The historical evidence seems to be to the effect that he was born in a Brāhman family. From a relatively late account of his life[2] it appears that he was the son of a sage who had many wives, among whom Mahidāsa's mother, Itarā, was one. In it we are told that the sage preferred the sons of his other wives to Mahidāsa, and did not scruple to insult him openly once by passing him over when he took all his children in his lap. Mahidāsa was, however, by far the most blessed in other respects. He was endowed with a natural aptitude for learning, and had the beneficent care of his mother. By dint of his genius he rose to eminence, while his half-brothers sank into oblivion for all their father's doting partiality.

[1] III. 16. 6.

[2] Sāyaṇa's introduction to the Aitareya Brāhmaṇa. *Vide* The Brāhmaṇas of the Vedas, p. 13. See for other legends the Upanishads (S.B.E.), Vol. I, pp. XCIV-XCV.

His works: their interconnexion. The historical interest of the third division of the Aitareya-Āraṇyaka.

The system of Mahidāsa was evidently named after his mother Itarā. It may be inferred from Sāyaṇa's account that while a house-holder he composed the Aitareya Brāhmaṇa, consisting of forty sections, and while a dweller in the forest he embodied his philosophical views in the Āraṇyaka of the same name. But the Aitareya Āraṇyaka as we now have it, does not seem to have been actually composed by Mahidāsa: it may no doubt be ascribed to his school. Further, this Āraṇyaka consists of three divisions, the second and third of which are comprised under the general title of the Bahvṛica, the Mahaitareya, or simply, the Aitareya Upaniṣad.[1] It also should be mentioned that the inter-connexion of the first and second divisions is far closer than that of the third with either. This being the case, it is particularly from these two divisions that a knowledge of his doctrine must be derived. These two stand moreover to each other in such a relation as to show how a certain doctrine passed from an immature to a mature stage. But the third division, too, is not without some special historical interest in that it contains views[2] other than those of Mahidāsa.

A few preliminary remarks concerning his main problem, services to science and philosophy, defects and difficulties. He is the incipient Aristotle of India.

The main problem with which Mahidāsa heroically grappled was but the problem of the origin of life and the development of consciousness. Again, an instructive feature of his system is that instead of a fantastic presentation,[3] we obtain with it a real fruitful synthesis of Vedic speculations. For a due appreciation of his system of speculation it will be worth while to take into consideration the supreme effort which Mahidāsa had to make in order to get over the difficulties as to language and method at a time when Indian philosophy was just passing out of its

[1] Upanishads, S.B.E., Vol. I, p. 200.

[2] Such as those of the Māndūkeyas, Sākalya, the elder Sākalya, Tārukṣya, Kauṇṭharavya, Pañcaślacanda, Bādhva, the Kāvaṣeyas, etc.

infancy, in the close environment of mythology and popular theology. But, in spite of the fact that his initial defects are in scientific nomenclature and methodical treatment of problems, when we fully consider his fundamental conceptions, and carefully compare them with those of Aristotle, we cannot help coming to the conclusion that, generally speaking, Mahidāsa is the incipient Aristotle of India. If such be the case, we have further to note that, in India, Mahidāsa, who compares favourably in a great number of points with Aristotle, preceded Gārgyāyaṇa, whose doctrine of immortality and theory of ideas lead us to think of Plato.

The division of his philosophy.

Now, as to Mahidāsa's philosophical investigation, we propose to summarise it under these four heads—metaphysics, physics, psychology and ethics.

I. *Metaphysics.*—As a preliminary to our estimate of the value of Mahidāsa's metaphysics, we must repeat the general statement that we nowhere meet with a systematic grouping or clear-cut division of his doctrine, taken as a whole. Hence it must be understood that the method of arrangement adopted in these pages is chiefly our own, whereas the conceptions are those of Mahidāsa.

A general explanation of the theoretic side of Mahidāsa's metaphysics or science of first principles might be offered as follows.

'Experience' in Mahidāsa.

(1) To begin with, Mahidāsa desired to point out that the task of philosophy is to explain experience, and by experience he understood evidently the physical universe, the organic world, a particular thing, a living substance, the heaven, the earth, the firmament, the sun, the moon, water, earth, fire, air, a metal, a plant, an animal, a man, a seed, a sperm.

The limits of knowledge.

If it be the principal task of philosophy to explain experience, then all philosophical investigations ought to be kept entirely within the bounds of experience. The axiom which Mahidāsa laid down for himself in this connexion may be rendered thus : I know the universe and myself as far as I know the gods, and I know the gods as far as I know the universe and myself.[1]

The five elements or material attributes.

In his phraseology, however, the mythological term "gods" is convertible into the theological term "hymns" (uktha), and that, in its turn, into the philosophical term "elements" (bhūtāni). Thus, if we say with Mahidāsa, "I am the five-fold hymn," this generally means that I am built up of these five—water and earth, fire and air, and space.[2] In other words, our ordinary, intuitive, unphilosophic, or objective knowledge of a particular thing of experience, taken as a whole, is divisible into the five subjective elements or material qualities enumerated also by him in the order of earth, air, space, water and fire (jyotis).[3]

Two methods of investigation: conventional and philosophic.

It follows that, in accordance with Mahidāsa's methodology there are these two methods of philosophical investigation--objective and subjective, called later conventional (sāṁvṛitika, vyavahārika), and philosophic (pāramārthika) respectively. That which we regard, therefore, from the subjective point of view as the five qualities are, when looked at from the objective point of view, but five elements or great beings (mahābhūtāni).

How to explain experience? The five material qualities defined.

Taking man as the most typical of particular things, the question now reaches the point, how are we to explain experience? Mahidāsa's reply to this is—By means of these five principles called water and earth, fire and air, and space, besides Life

[1] Aitareya Āraṇyaka, II. 1.7. 3-7; II. 1.8.2.
[2] *Ibid*, II. 1.2. 1-16; II. 3.1. 1-2; II. 3.4.2.
[3] *Ibid*, II. 3.1.1.

or the living principle (Prāṇa). Of these, water and earth are conceived as "food" or substance, for all food, Mahidāsa thought, consists of these two; fire and air are conceived as "the feeder" or something which is related to the living principle, for by means of them a man eats all food; and space is conceived as "the bowl," for all that exists is contained in it.[1]

His fundamental thesis: it is materialistic. The propositions and axioms.

From the five-fold hymn,[2] called otherwise the embodiment of Prāṇa, the living soul, springs, and to it returns all that is—such is apparently the fundamental thesis of Mahidāsa. But he insisted often that for working it out in detail the following propositions and axioms are essential.

Man is a microcosmos, and so is every living substance.

In the first place, man is to be conceived as the miniature universe, so that what is in the one, is in the other. His axiom is—"whatever there is belonging to the son, belongs to the father; whatever there is belonging to the father, belongs to the son."[3] If so, our concepts of the universe are translatable at last into those of man,[4] and *vice versâ*; and what is true, in this respect, of man, also holds of every living substance or particular thing, down to its very root, seed, germ, or atom.[5] Mahidāsa's assumption is that a finite thing of experience, taken as a whole, is not only a part of the sum-total of things, but in a sense, that is, in essence, the whole itself. In this case, the position of Mahidāsa may be defined by such an axiom as—I as a living monad am the universe.

But from this it does not necessarily follow that, according to Mahidāsa, the universal completely explains the particular;

[1] Aitareya Āraṇyaka, II. 3.1.2.

[2] Aitareya Āraṇyaka, II. 3.1.1. In his language: "He who knows himself as the five-fold hymn is clever."

[3] *Ibid*, II. 1.8.1., S.B.E., Vol. I., p. 212.

[4] *Cf.* Sākalya's views, Aitareya Āraṇyaka, III. 1.2. 6-7.

[5] *Cf.* Erdmann's History of Philosophy, Vol. I., p. 151.

it may be of course that the universal explains only that in the particular which is not different from the universal. And it would again be a mistake to suppose that Mahidāsa contemplated any hard and fast line of distinction between the two. For that would be incompatible with his conception of nature or cosmos as an interconnected whole. We might affirm, without doing violence to his position, that there is no difference in kind either between the physical universe and the organic world, or between the organic world and man. The fundamental difference, if any, which would be admitted by Mahidāsa, is what may be described as the difference in intensity or degree of growth, that is all. Admitted this, a so-called non-living thing is definable as an undeveloped man, in the same way that a man may be defined as a developed thing. It will be remarked that in Mahidāsa's language, the word development (āvistaraḥ āvirbhāvaḥ) is used rather in a limited sense ; it means no more than the manifestation (prakaṭatvam) in the particular of that which is hidden in the universal. Thus Mahidāsa's theory of development or specialisation exactly corresponds to Aristotle's conception of a transmission of the potential into actuality.

No difference of kind, but of degree, between these three—the physical universe, the organic world, and man.

Now the second proposition which forms the key to the whole philosophy of Mahidāsa is this. The things of experience are explicable only in the terms of "root" (cause) and "shoot" (effect).[1] These two called root and shoot are logically and for all practical purposes, distinguishable from each other, but identical in substance or essence.

Cause and effect are identical in essence.

(2) We have endeavoured so far to bring out that the philosophical investigation of Mahidāsa is concerned with the problems as to the visible universe, the organic world,

[1] Mūla and tūla. Aitareya Āraṇyaka, II. 1. 8. 1.

and man. Of these, the visible universe is a living form, man is a living thing, and the connecting link between the two is what is termed the organic world.

His general theory of knowledge.

According to Mahidāsa's general theory of knowledge, if we know the one, we know all the three. As a naturalist he perceived the difference subsisting between the things of experience, whereas, as a philosopher, he realised only the immutable ground of unity in the midst of all changes.[1]

Here by the visible universe Mahidāsa understood the physical world as a whole, and under the organic world he included the vegetable kingdom, the animal kingdom, and man. The distinction he thus implied between these two—the physical world and the organic—is no more than that which we now rather sharply draw between so-called "dead matter" and living matter. All these shining gods—the sun, lightning, the moon, the planets and the stars, and all these five great beings (mahābhūtāni)—the earth, air, the sky, water and fire—belong to the physical world; the herbs and trees, to the vegetable kingdom; the reptiles, birds, horses, cows, elephants, etc., to the animal kingdom; and a man naturally belongs to the animal kingdom, and is generally classed among the animals.[2]

The definition of, and distinction between, the physical universe and the organic world.

By the word difference he implied, first, the difference in form, habit and strength, and secondly, the difference as to the gradual development of self, that is, of life in the world as a whole, particularly of a thinking soul in man.

Difference is two-fold: in type of existence, and in degree of growth.

With regard to the first kind of difference, he insisted that there are beings developed from this or that kind of seeds,

[1] Aitareya Āraṇyaka, II. 3. 8. 2.

[2] Aitareya Āraṇyaka, II. 6. 1. 5; I. 5. 1. 9.

such as those born from eggs (oviparous), born from the womb (viviparous), born from sweat (moisture-sprung), and propagated from germs (plants); that there are beings movable and immovable.[1] Among the birds, the parrot is the one that is the most gluttonous, and the hawk that swoops on other birds is the strongest of all. Among the higher animals again, the two-footed man surpasses all the quadrupeds in strength. Therefore, the quadrupeds, such as cattle, horses and elephants obey man's commands.[2]

The four classes of beings.

Regarding the second kind of difference, too, Mahidāsa maintained that the soul or intelligent principle develops gradually in the world as a whole. In herbs and trees, for example, sap (life) only is seen, but thought (citta) in the widest sense is in the higher forms of life. Among the latter again, some show both vitality and intelligence, while others are devoid of intelligence. Among animals, man alone has the capacity for acquiring higher wisdom, yet in him, too, the soul develops gradually. A man differs from a lower animal in these respects:

The theory of the gradual development of soul.

"He says what he has known. He knows what is to happen to-morrow, he knows heaven and hell. By means of the mortal he desires the immortal—thus he is endowed."[3] With other animals, on the contrary, hunger and thirst (instincts and impulses) only are a kind of understanding; they possess voice, but no speech; mind, but no prudence."[4]

[1] Ibid, II. 6. 1. 5.

[2] Ibid, I. 5. 1. 9.

[3] Aitareya Āraṇyaka, S.B.E., Vol. I, p. 222.

[4] *Ibid*, II 3. 2. 1—5; *cf.* "The Questions of King Milinda," S.B.E., Vol. XXXV, pp. 50-51. According to Nāgasena, rudimentary reason (manasikāra) is one thing, and reasoned knowledge (paññā) is another. Sheep and goats, oxen and buffaloes, camels and asses possess rudimentary reason but reasoned knowledge they have not.

(3) Nature.

The two-fold conception of nature: as a system of numerous gradations of existence.

It has already been noticed that as a naturalist Mahidāsa, like Aristotle, conceived nature to be "a system of fixed types of existence," and recognised the difference which subsists between these types. Accordingly the heavenly bodies, the five elements, plants, creatures, animals, and men are all regarded as living things: they are taken to form a gradually ascending scale of concrete existents. The heavenly bodies are not included in the realm of constant change. Rather in his conception of nature as a gradation of fixed types of existence, Mahidāsa assigned to the heavenly bodies a place which does not strictly come within the general scheme of existence; each one of them is therefore taken to represent a separate type in itself. The same applies to each one of the five elements.

As an inter-connected whole.

On the other hand, as a philosopher Mahidāsa conceived nature as an inter-connected whole, and realised the immutable ground of unity in the midst of all changes.

Heaven, earth, and firmament.

He conceived the physical universe as a living form, which consists of the heaven, the earth, and the firmament.[1] In his language, the heaven denotes that from the gift (heat) of which arises all that exists; the object of its praise is the sun (āditya). The sun is regarded not only as the luminary of the heaven or the germ of the gods (deva-retaḥ), but also as the central, unifying power, nay, the soul (puruṣa) of the universe. The earth is similarly defined as that from which springs all that is; the object of its praise is fire (agni).[2] Fire is identical in essence with the sun. In fact, like Dīrghatamas, Mahidāsa conceived the sun and fire as but two

[1] Aitareya Āraṇyaka, I. 2. 3. 6; *ibid*, II. 1. 2. 4.

[2] *Ibid*, II. 1. 2. 1-2.

forms of one and the same thing, that is to say, like "Hiraṇya-garbha," he maintained that these two, called the sun and fire, are developed from what is known as the golden germ or primal form of heat. In the same way, the firmament is defined as the space between heaven and earth; the object of its praise is air (vāyu).[1] The earth is pervaded and purified by air.

The extent and duration of the physical universe.

As to the former, we are told by Mahidāsa that the universe, in its present form (mūrti) is co-extensive with the earth and fire, heaven and the sun, the cardinal directions and moon, water and the ocean, and that as long as these do not decay, so long the universe does not decay.[2]

The inter-connexion of heaven and earth.

The relation between the two, called heaven and earth, is described thus. All that dies on earth is consumed by heaven, and all that returns from heaven is consumed by earth.[3] Thus a sort of give and take is the guiding principle of the operation of nature, viewed as an inter-connected whole. Moreover, the axiom laid down by Mahidāsa in this connexion is: "No one possesses that which he does not eat, or the things which do not eat him," that is to say, the feeder and food are in reality food. Thus food may be described as that which feeds and is fed.[4]

(4) God and Matter.

God is the ground of unity, and Matter is the ground of plurality.

Lastly comes the question of the assumed ground of unity. Mahidāsa seeks for unity in the conception of God, the divine, immortal being. But evidently the predicate of unity assignable to the Divine implies only the negation of the plurality which is the characterstic feature of the concrete realm of change. Further, if God be conceived as the ground

[1] Aitareya Āraṇyaka, II. 1.2.3; I. 2. 3. 6.

[2] *Ibid*, II. 1 7. 1-7.

Ibid, II. 1. 2. 15.

Ib II. 1. 2. 16.

of unity or singleness of cause, we may in accordance with Mahidāsa's view take Matter[1] to be the ground of all plurality. In order to arrive at a concrete estimate of Mahidāsa's conception of God, we must first of all take into account his conception of Matter.

A. Matter and Form.

The real is that which is capable of development or transition from the hidden to the manifested.

From the foregoing analysis, it follows that Mahidāsa's picture of nature displays throughout his notion of development as alone real in the concrete world of generation. Put otherwise, there is nothing real but that which is actualised. As we saw, Mahidāsa understood by development nothing but a transition from the hidden to the manifested, that is, to put it in Aristotle's phraseology from the potential to the actual. And when his idea of development is carefully analysed, it yields us Aristotle's broad proposition: "Each existent in the realm of change comes to be from something, by something, to something."[2]

Numerous gradations exist between the first matter and the final form: the more developed a thing is, the more individual it is.

Taking "seed" in Mahidāsa's language to denote the something in Aristotle's proposition, it might be added that, according to Mahidāsa's theory, a seed is developed from a seed by the process of change or natural transformation. This process of change presents itself in the form of a rope[3] or chain of development, consisting of numerous links of relation between food and the feeder, the material and the individual, the potential and the actual, the indeterminate and the determinate.

There is, then, this broad distinction between the seeds. A developed seed is more individual, more actual, more deter-

[1] Mahidāsa did not coin a new term for Matter, but employed the Vedic term Water in the sense of matter. *Vide* Aitareya Āraṇyaka, II. 1. 8. 1; II. 4. 3. 1.

[2] The Development of Greek Philosophy, p. 153.

[3] Aitareya Āraṇyaka, II. 1, 6. 1.

minate, and more an object of knowledge,[1] than that from which it is developed. But the higher form often presupposes the lower. Moreover, in order to attain the higher form, a seed is bound to lose all its individuality, though not necessarily its materiality. Hence the individual also presupposes the material. But in this case the reverse is true as well. For, according to Mahidāsa's axiom, no one possesses that which he does not eat, or the things which do not eat him. The meaning of this axiom is that the two notions—food and the feeder—are correlative. What we therefore call this moment food, may appear the next moment as the feeder. It admits of another interpretation. As Prof. Adamson puts it in the case of Aristotle, "In the complete gradation there is thus, as it were, a scale of ascent and descent, descending towards privation of all that is determinate, and ascending towards completed actuality."[2]

The reason for change lies always in an individual agent. The agent itself participates in the general process of change.

The vital concern for us, is the process of development. It is conceived thus: the seed[3] reduced to the state of food (or potentiality) develops to a seed elevated to the rank of a feeder (or actuality) and this development is effected through a living, active, individual agent,—say, the present feeder on the food. Thus Mahidāsa's conception of the gradation of natural development is quite in accordance with, and furnishes enough justification of, his conception of the graduated scale of the types of existence. A living, individual agent is with Mahidāsa but one of many knots in the rope or chain of development; in other words, one of the many names given by speech[4] or convention to those forms which matter assumes, or is capable of assuming.[5] An agent, so regarded, must be said to stand in

[1] *Ibid*, II.3. 6. 15.

[2] Development of Greek Philosophy, p. 156.

[3] Aitareya Āraṇyaka, II. 1. 3. 1.

[4] *Ibid* II. 1. 6. 1.

[5] *Ibid*, II. 1. 8. 1.

relation to two consecutive seeds as at once a destroyer and a creator. But it must not be forgotten that, in bringing about the change necessary for the development of a seed from a seed, the agent itself must enter into motion, or undergo a certain form of change.

Now, to follow out Mahidāsa's conception of development a little further, a chain or rope has two extremities, two ends,—the two ultimate knots either way, between which all other knots fall, and which, therefore, determine the length of the whole change. These two ultimate knots are represented by Prajāpati and Brahman in the case of the universe, and by Prāṇa and Prajñā in the case of man, as we shall see; and in the case of Aristotle, by *causa efficiens* and *causa finalis.* But it should be borne in mind that what we call metaphorically two knots are really two aspects of one and the same first and last knot, *i.e.*, of the Divine. Thus God as Prajāpati is the efficient cause, the first unmoved mover; but he is again just Brahman the final cause or end, the very perfection on which all turn their thoughts,[1] after which all things strive.

God is the first and the last cause.

"The seed of Prajāpati is the gods; the seed of the goods is rain; the seed of rain is herbs; the seed of herbs is food; the seed of food is living creatures; the seed of living creatures is the heart; the seed of the heart is the thinking mind; the seed of the thinking mind is the thoughtful speech; the seed of the thoughtful speech is the thoughtful action; and the thoughtful action done is this reality in man (puruṣa), the abode of Brahman."[2] The prevailing tone of thought is teleological.

Finally, we must inquire into Mahidāsa's conceptions of Matter and Form. If his conception of development be strictly adhered to, it must be conceived as a transition from

[1] Aitareya Āraṇyaka, I. 3. 4. 9.
[2] *Ibid*, II. 1. 3. 1.

something to something, from something yet hidden or potential to something manifested or actual. That is to say, there is no transition from nothingness into Being, but only from that which is not yet, the matter or potentiality. Indeed, matter is, according to Mahidāsa, that out of which a thing becomes, that from which form (mūrti) or purposive order is brought forth.[1] Thus matter is related to form as the root to the shoot[2], and form is related to matter as that which manifests it. The more formed matter is, the more manifested, and thus the more recognisable it becomes.

Difference between Matter and Form: Form is the manifestation of Matter, and Matter is that which is capable of manifestation.

Mahidāsa gave an illustration: "A whispered voice is just breath, but if spoken aloud, it is form (śarīra). If whispered, it is as if hidden, for what is formless is as if hidden, and breath is formless. But if spoken aloud, it is form, and therefore it is perceptible, for form is perceptible."[3]

By this Mahidāsa seems to have meant that speech in itself is a kind of form, the materialised breath by reason of which a purpose, such as that of expressing thought, is carried out. Breath is in this case the root of speech. In like manner, breath may be regarded as a form in relation to air. Going in this way backward from form to matter, shoot to root, or perfection to presupposition, we are sure to arrive at the first or pure matter, which being entirely devoid of form, is incognisable in itself. On the other hand, going forward from matter to form, root to shoot, presupposition to perfection, we shall reach the ultimate matter which becomes so united with form that it is no more capable of separate manifestation.

An illustration: its bearing on the distinction Mahidāsa drew between the first and the final matter: the former is incognisable, the latter is cognisable.

[1] Aitareya Āraṇyaka, II. 4.3.1.

[2] *Ibid*, II. 1.8.1.

[3] *Ibid*, II, 3.6.15.

In agreement with the Vedic thinkers, particularly "Paramesthin," Mahidāsa posited water[1] as the original matter, the first root of which this purposive order, the universe of concrete existence, is the shoot. But this does not mean that matter in itself is the concrete existent. True, that it is the root which has the capacity of becoming the shoot. However, Mahidāsa nowhere tells us in what relation this first matter stands to the first mover, except in a passage[2] where he seems to regard matter as a passive principle, that on which form is imposed, something which requires to be energised, in order that it may become manifested. Under this aspect, matter is also to be conceived as the substratum of change. It is evident from his view of the chain of development that Mahidāsa did not look upon change as a series of isolated events. The world of generation has a unity of its own, and this unity implies obviously the identity and continuity of a common substratum of change, *i.e.*, matter. Thus matter is the ground of all plurality of forms, just as speech is the ground of all multiplicity of names.

The relation between the first matter and the first mover.

B. God.

The point in which Mahidāsa effectively opposed "Paramesṭhin" is that the reason of transition from the hidden to the manifested is not in matter, the principle of passivity. Matter does not come within the definition of either being or non-being.[3] Hence the principle of motion is in something other than matter; in God, the satyam of satyam,[4] the most real of all things real. God as Prajāpati is the lord of beings, the father and friend of all living creatures. He who is both individual and universal "brooded over"[5] the first matter, and thus stirred it up into motion or energy. The Deity

[1] Aitareya Āraṇyaka, II. 1.6.1.
[2] *Ibid*, II. 4.3.1.
[3] See *ante*, Parameṣṭhin's views, Pt. I.
[4] Aitareya Āraṇyaka, II. 3.6.2; *ibid*, II. 1.8.7.
[5] *Ibid*, II. 4.3.1.3; *ibid*, 1.3.3.6.

is a name which is "the best and without a flaw."[1] The Divine essence is in its nature immaterial, immortal, eternal, imperishable. The Divine essence is one, and unity of God can best explain the singleness of character which the world of generation presents within itself in very varied degree.[2] God excludes all idea of passivity, and therefore, of plurality. The yes and no of language, do not apply to God, for the Divine nature is eternally free from all that is hard and cruel.[3] Brahman enjoys bliss eternally. In order, therefore, to contemplate the nature of the Divine one must transcend the yes and no of language and all that is hard and cruel. Nevertheless, God may be conceived under these two aspects. In one aspect, God is Prāṇa, spirit, or the living principle of the universe, the pure vital energy and activity. In the other aspect, God is Prajñā (*νους*) the pure intelligence, the eternally active self-conscious reason (prajñāna).[4] The whole realm of change is led by Brahman, the self-conscious reason (prajñā-netra).

Mahidāsa's theology.

(5) The Soul (Ātmā).

Like Aristotle, Mahidāsa seems to have conceived soul as the complement of a living body. Soul is that single element in our existence which comes directly from the Deity, or in and through which we can approach the Divine. The function of reason (Prajñāna) is in the soul. The faculty by which we see form, that by which we hear sound, that by which we perceive odours, that by which we utter speech, that by which we taste food, and all that which comes from the heart and the mind, namely, apperception, comprehension, understanding, cognition, intellect, insight, retention, judg-

The psychological aspect of Mahidāsa's metaphysics.

[1] Aitareya Āraṇyaka. I. 3.3.6.

[2] *Ibid*, II. 3.8.2. foll.

[3] *Ibid*, II. 3.8.4.

[4] *Ibid*, II. 6.1.5-6.

ment, reflection, receptivity, remembrance (or memory), conceiving, willing, breathing, loving, desiring,—bear in varying degrees the name of Reason (prajñānasya nāmadheyyāni).[1]

On the other hand, soul is in its essence just the vital principle (prāṇa) in virtue of which we can discharge our functions as living beings. Thus for Mahidāsa, as for Aristotle, the complete fact is this life, and the central fundamental function of a fully developed organism is breathing or respiration. For even during sleep, when all sensations and all mental activities cease, the process of life, *i.e.*, respiration, goes on still the same.

As there are infinite gradations of types of existence, so there is a graduated scale of functions of the soul. The lowest function discharged by the soul is nutritive; the first desire felt by the soul is that for food; and the first feeling experienced by the soul is hunger and thirst. The next higher function of the soul consists of sense-perception and such motor activities as action, locomotion, excretion and reproduction. The functions which stand still higher in the scale are grouped, as we saw under the mind and the heart, the latter including what we now call the functions of understanding and reason. Once more, as there is no difference of kind between the types of existence, so between the various functions of the soul.

(6) Speech (Vāk).

The logical aspect of Mahidāsa's metaphysics.

Like matter or mind, speech is conceived as being a continuous structure. It is compared to a rope with many knots, a chain with many links (vāk tanti nāmāni dāmāni).[2] The knots or links are the names or concepts, corresponding to existent forms. The rope or chain runs in a straight line. It has a

[1] Aitareya Āraṇyaka, II. 6.3.

[2] *Ibid*, II. 1.6. 1.

first and a final knot, representing the first and the final cause respectively. Thus Mahidāsa, like Aristotle, avoided the absurdity of an infinite regress in proof. The difference between the first or the final knot and any intermediate knot is that the latter admits of the yes and no of language (*i.e.*, the law of contradiction), while the former does not. Mahidāsa, in agreement with all post-Vedic thinkers, found perfect correlation between thought and speech. "As far as speech goes, so far goes Brahman"[1] was his maxim. Further, he identified concepts with concrete facts, knowledge with existence.

The bearings of the maxim, that every individual thing is a microcosmos, on the investigation of physics.

II. Physics.—Mahidāsa started his physical inquiries by advancing as a general axiom, that man is a microcosmos, just as, on the other hand, the visible world as a whole is but a universal man.[2] Both are, so far as their organic constitution goes, complete individuals, and so are all known and unknown living bodies which form a scale of intermediaries between them. This means that between the one and the other of these fixed types of concrete existents, there is no difference in kind, but merely in intensity. The whole of nature is a purposive order, 'a system of ends.' In this great and eternal order of the universe there is nothing which does not partake of the Divine nature, and no point at which we cannot perceive a continual striving after perfection.

[1] Aitareya Āraṇyaka, I. 3. 8. 9: "Yāvad brahmā viṣṭitaṁ tāvatī vāgiti; yatra ha kva ca brahmā tad vāg, Yatra vā vāk tad vā brahmēti."

[2] *Ibid*, II. 1. 2. 5-12; II. 4. 2. 4; etc. In a passage of the Bṛihad Āraṇyaka Upaniṣad (1. 1) the solar universe (*i.e.*, "Nārāyaṇa's" Puruṣa) is compared to an ever-running horse, a horse fit for sacrifice, that is to say, subject to recurrent cycles of change, to envelopment and development. The dawn is described as its head, the sun as the eye, the wind as the breath, and the year as the body (corporeal form). This is followed by a further description of the anatomy of the organised universal horse. The heaven is its back, the sky its abdomen, the earth its thorax, the quarters its extremities, the intermediate quarters its ribs, the seasons its organs of sense, ... the half-digested food is the sand, the rivers its intestines, and so on and so forth.

As Sākalya puts it in agreement with Mahidāsa, and with more definiteness in expression than the latter, every individual being is like an egg, that is to say, very similar to the oval-shaped, spherical universe. Like the visible universe, the trunk of an animal is divisible into three parts. The heaven corresponds to the skull, the mid-air to the thorax, and the earth to the abdomen. As there are three luminaries attached to the three-fold division of the universe, so there are three luminaries joined to the three parts of the trunk. The sun in the heaven resembles the eye in the skull; lightning in mid-air is the heart (vital breath) in the thorax; and fire on earth is the seed in the propagative organ.[1]

Sākalya's view of the resemblance between the physical constitution of the Universe and that of individual beings.

But Sākalya omits or overlooks a few points of scientific interest in Mahidāsa's cosmology. For in accordance with the latter's view, we are to recognise that the formed universe is surrounded by Ambas (waters),[2] termed elsewhere the ocean,[3] denoting the concentric circle of Varuṇa (Neptune), a notion reminding us at once of "Brahmaṇaspati's" Aditi, or Anaximander's ἄπειρον. By the circle of Varuṇa, then, Mahidāsa understood not certainly any void space (śūnyākāśa, the notion of which was altogether foreign to post-Vedic thinking), but that eternally unmoved region of pure, unmixed and fiery ether of immeasurable brilliance (amitaujas, to use Gārgyāyaṇa's expression) from which energy is constantly generated, and transmitted in the form of a flash of lightning or solar ray to the formed universe, first, to the outermost part of space called heaven, the region of lights (maricis), and then from that to lower regions. The energy or stimulus which is thus imparted from the circle of

Mahidāsa's cosmological doctrine.

[1] Aitareya Āraṇyaka, III. 1. 2. 6-8.

[2] *Ibid*, II. 4. 1. 4.

[3] *Ibid*, II. 1. 7. 7.

Varuṇa sets the heavenly bodies, air, and all the rest in motion. This circle of Varuṇa or Infinity is conceived by Mahidāsa apparently as something similar to Saturn's ring. It lies above the formed universe, and yet is supported upon and encloses the universe within itself. As Yājñavalkya seems to have thought, the Oceanic ring surrounding the Earth (Pṛithivī, *i.e.*, Extension, the border of the formed universe) on every side, is twice as large as the Earth. The space separating the one from the other hardly exceeds the edge of a razor or the wing of a mosquito.[1] However, the notion of severance of the two concentric circles must by no means be lost sight of, inasmuch as it has most important bearings on the ontological views of Mahidāsa and other post-Vedic thinkers. The mental picture thus drawn of the eternal separation and inter-connexion (amounting to an inter-dependence) of Infinity and Finiteness (Aditi and Diti, ananta and sānta) enabled them to conceive of a first unmoved mover. And all this is but to repeat the general view, that "Brahmaṇaspati's" Aditi, like Anaximander's απειρον, was the first philosophic conception of God, and one remaining yet entirely within the physical.

Now, enclosed entirely within the Ocean or Infinity is the outermost border of the formed universe called Heaven, studded with lights (maricis). The number of these luminaries (stars and all the rest), as given in the Śatapatha Brāhmaṇa, is 36,000. Mahidāsa gives no number. And Gārgyāyaṇa, following an unknown but earlier thinker,[2] conceives heaven as the council-hall skilfully built by Vibhu,[3] a term corresponding to Vedic Viśvakarman (universal architect), now degraded evidently from a highest Deity to a mere god (devaputra). Further, Gārgyāyaṇa speaks, in agreement with Mahidāsa, of two door-keepers—Indra, the wielder of thunder,

[1] Bṛihad Āraṇyaka Upaniṣad, III. 3. 2.

[2] Chāndogya Upaniṣad, VIII. 5. 3 "Prabhu-vimitam hiraṇmayam."

[3] Kauṣītaki Upaniṣad, I. 3: "Vibhu-nāmakam pramitam sabhāsthalam."

and Prajāpati, the sun[1]—that is to say, of two gates opening apparently on two ways, and serving as the channels of communication between infinity and the finite. Yājñavalkya omits Prajāpati.[2]

Heaven surrounds this mortal earth (mara) on every side. The earth supports mid-air or the atmosphere filled with vapours above it,—the mid-air which is the scene of lightning (electrical phenomena), and itself is supported upon and encircled by waters (*Ap*-world, hell) beneath it.[3] A thin plenum of ether[4] divides the heaven from the mid-air. Strictly, this is the circle of Varuṇa below which lies the dominion of Indra, and above the dominion of Prajāpati. The earth is placed like a ship[5] lying at anchor in the midst of waters. It has nevertheless a local motion of its own, compared by Mahidāsa to that of a swing (preṅkha[6]). The sun rises in the eastern ocean and sets in the western. Pandit Sāmaśrami Satyavrata Śarmā has collected a few interesting references from the Brāhmaṇas and other sources, pointing to a different conclusion, *viz.*, that in the view of the Aitareyas and other Brāhman philosophers 'the sun neither rises nor sets, but stands alone in the centre.'[7] But it is to be doubted if we are really justified in drawing such an inference as that days and nights are caused by rotation of the earth. The passage quoted is this: "He (the sun) never sets nor rises. When people think he sets, it means that he having reached the end of day, conceals himself."[8] The belief in either revolution or in rotation of the earth does not

[1] Aitareya Āraṇyaka, II. 6. 1. 5; Kauṣitaki Upaniṣad, I. 3.

[2] Bṛihad Āraṇyaka Upaniṣad, III. 3. 2.

[3] Aitareya Āraṇyaka, II. 4. 1. 4.

[4] Bṛihad Āraṇyaka Upaniṣad, III. 3. 2.

[5] Aitareya Āraṇyaka, I. 2. 4. 6.

[6] Preṅkha seems to denote also the whole physical universe, divided into three parts *ibid*, I. 2. 3. 4.

[7] Chāndogya Up., III. 11. 1. 3; "naivôdetā nâstametā, ekala eva madhye sthātā.

[8] Aitareya Brāhmaṇa, III. 4. 6: "Sa vā eṣa na kadācanāstam eti nôdeti. Taṁ yadastaṁ etīti manyante, ahna eva tadantam itvā athâtmānaṁ viparyasyate; rātrim eva avastāt

follow from Sāyaṇa's interpretation which rather takes the earth as stationary, and represents the sun as moving round the pole.[1] The view in the Chāndogya Upaniṣad, inherited by Uddālaka Āruṇi from the past, emphatically declares that *the sun "neither rises nor sets at any time.* If this is not true, ye gods, may I lose Brahman."[2] "*The sun does not* rise and does not set. For him there is day, once and for all."[3] The expression "stands alone in the centre" is most significant, no doubt, and should the same mean that the sun remains fixed at the centre, it would necessarily follow that days and nights are caused by no other factor than rotation of the earth in its axis. But Śaṅkara and Ānandagiri throw no light on this disputed question.

Buddha merely reminds us of Mahidāsa's cosmology, when he says, "This great earth is established on water, water on air, and air on space. A time comes when the mighty wind blows, causing the commotion in waters which cause at length the earth to quake."[4] Śvetāśvatara,[5] as we know, endeavoured to formulate a Pythagorean notion of the Brahma-cakra, having one felly with three tires (trivṛit), sixteen ends, and so forth. He derived evidently from Uddālaka the conception of three tires of the wheel in question, that is to say, of the threefold division of the formed universe into the region of the element of fire, that of water, and that of earth. In the later Sāṁkhya cosmology the term trivṛit

The development of the notion of Brahma-cakra.

kurute ahaḥ parastāt. Atha yadenaṁ prātar udetīti manyante, rātrereva tadantam itvā athātmānam viparyasyate ; ahoreva ahastāt kurute rātrim parastāt. Sa vā eṣa na kadācana nimlocati na ha vai kadācana nimlocati." *Cf.* Gopatha-Brāhmaṇa, II. 4. 10. See for other references Aitareyālocanam by Pandit Satyavrata, pp. 107-8.

[1] "Meroḥ pradakṣiṇaṁ kurvan ādityo yaddeśavāriṇāṁ prāṇināṁ dṛiṣṭipatham āgacchati taddeśa-vāsibhirayam udetīti vyavahṛiyate......" (Sāyaṇa).

[2], [3] Chandogya Up., III. 11. 1-3.

[4] Dīgha-nikāya, II. 107 ; Dial., B. II., p. 114.

[5] Śvetāśvatara Upaniṣad, I. 4.

was conveniently replaced by triguṇa—sattva (brightness), rajas (redness), and tamas (darkness). But for the origin of the notion of Brahma-cakra one must go, in the last resort, to the philosophy of Dīrghatamas. As we saw, it was Dīrghatamas who vaguely conceived that the roots of things are five in all.

The five elements.

Thus we come to the main question of Mahidāsa's physics, namely, the question as to the nature of what he calls five elements or material qualities (pañca mahābhūtāni). Although the subject of immediate perception is a whole being or concrete individual, he insists repeatedly that on that we cannot establish a scientific knowledge of real facts. What we can preceive with Mahidāsa in scientific apprehension of each particular thing of experience is that it is a five-fold hymn (ātmôktham pañcavidham),[1] *i.e.*, composed of these five elements—earth and water, fire and air, and ether or space.[2] He who recognises the truth of this axiom is wise.[3] The antithesis of earth and water, just as the antithesis of fire and air, implies no more than a difference of aspects. This being the case, earth and water together may be contrasted with fire and air, as food with the feeder, or matter with energy. In fact, then, earth and water denote Mahidāsa's two aspects or conditions of matter or material substratum—solidity and fluidity. Similarly fire and air are to be conceived as denoting two aspects of energy—heat (static) and motion (dynamic). In addition to these four elements Mahidāsa mentions ether (ākāśa) or space in which things are contained, or by which things can be separated from one another in external perception.

[1] Aitareya Āraṇyaka, II. 3. 3. 3.

[2] *Ibid*, II. 3. 1. 1: "sa samprativit," "pṛithivī vāyur ākāśa āpaiyotimsi."

[3] *Ibid*, II. 3. 1. 2.

The only perplexing point in Mahidāsa's physics is whether he conceived the vital spirit (prāṇa) as a principle separate from the five elements or not. In one place he definitely states that so far as a living body is concerned, the vital principle has no *separate existence from the five elements*,[1] *while in another* place he considers Prāṇa as a principle in itself, a principle which is not altogether dependent on the body or material conditions.[2] However, the ambiguity thus involved in his physical conceptions is important to bear in mind, as it led at a later period to the opposition between Kakuda Kātyāyana's doctrine of soul being distinct from the body (añño-jīva-aññaṁ-sarīra-vāda) and Ajita Keśa-Kambalin's doctrine of soul being identical with the body (taṁ-jīva-taṁ-sarīra-vāda).

An ambiguity and its historical importance.

Biology.—The chief point to notice in Mahidāsa's biological speculations is his view of the gradual development of intelligence (citta) in the living world (prāṇa-bhṛitsu).[3] But to put it in this way would be to define rather too narrowly the broad proposition he himself laid down. His proposition is—"Know the gradual development of individual things" (ātmānām āvistāram veda[4]). We say "too narrowly" because, as he clearly points out, the development is not merely psychical, but also physical. And yet there is no statement from which it might be concluded that, according to his view, sense itself is developed into reason, or a plant becomes a man by gradual evolution. As to the first point, he considers that sense-perception and reasoning, considered as mental functions, are not different in kind but only in intensity. Indeed, according to him, the mental functions ranging from bare sensation (as we may say) to comprehension bear the name of Reason (prajñānasya

[1] Aitareya Āraṇyaka, II. 3.1.1.

[2] *Ibid*, II. 1. 8. 12-13: "The immortal dwells with the mortal."

[3] *Ibid*, II. 3.2.2. According to Sāyaṇa, citta=cidrūpa.

[4] By āvistāram Sāyaṇa understands "atiśayena prakaṭam."

nāmadheyyāni).[1] As regards the second point, he seems to have thought that the types of existence are almost as eternal as the world itself. It is needless here to repeat his classifications of living beings. But it is, at all events, interesting to note that he includes earth, water, fire, air and heaven among living things. Maskarin Gośāla and Mahāvīra, as we shall see later, grouped earth, water, *fire and air together with plants* under beings with one sense, the fundamental sense of touch.

Mahidāsa mentions plants as forming a type distinct from those of five elements. As Sāyaṇa rightly interprets his view, in earth, stone and such other unconscious objects mere existence can be conceived to prevail. They do not come under the strict definition of living beings.[2] They are, in other words, organic things as distinguished from organic beings. Plants and herbs in general can be distinguished from organic things by sap (rasa)[3] or moisture (ārdratvam) which the former possess. But like organic things the plants, too, are immovable (sthāvara).[4] Those that are higher in the scale can move from place to place at their will. They are called, therefore, movable (jaṅgama). Physically and mentally men are the best of created things.[5] But the difference is a mere question of degree.

Embryology.—In forming an idea of Mahidāsa's achievements in embryology, we must keep constantly in mind his classification of living beings. Proceeding from the theory of gradation in types of existence, Mahidāsa had to assume a similar gradation in the modes of generation. In this point Mahidāsa and Aristotle agree. With both, the highest

[1] Aitareya Āraṇyaka, VI. 1.3.

[2] "Āvirbhavôpadhayas tatra acetaneṣu mṛit-pāṣāṇādisu sattvamātram āvirbhavati na ātmano jīvarupatvaṁ."

[3] Aitareya Āraṇyaka, II. 3.2.3.

[4] *Ibid*, II. 6.1.5.

[5] *Ibid*, II. 4.2.2.

in the scale are those beings which are generated by means of separate sexes.

From the observation of the phenomena of nature, especially the phenomena of animal life, Mahidāsa was led to recognise it as a universal law (and perhaps Aristotle had to do the same), that a third something is always the *sequence of two opposed facts.* The expression *"opposed" is not very happily chosen,* considering that no opposition amounting to the notion of a difference of kind exists for Mahidāsa in the world as a whole. Prof. Erdmann observes in connexion with Aristotle's doctrine that in the act of generation, "the altogether more imperfect female supplies the matter in the menses and the male the form in the seed, which contains an ether-like breath. And as in the act of generation, so in its product also, the corporeal element is to be derived from the maternal, and the psychical from the paternal element."[1] The same holds true of Mahidāsa's view of generation, or propagation of species. The difference thus involved between the two elements called the paternal and the maternal is not of kind, but of degree.

Reproduction is the process by which seed and blood become united.

Thus Mahidāsa was led to think that the mother's blood is a form of fire (agni), and the father's seed is a form of the sun (āditya). But fire and the sun are not different in kind, their common essence being heat. Hence to say that life originates from the union of sexes would really mean, according to Mahidāsa, that the vital spirit is called forth into existence by the mutual reaction of two forms of heat or caloric energy.[2] Indeed, in agreement with all earlier thinkers, Mahidāsa maintained that the *tertium quid* of the origin of animal life is the combination of two elements

Between seed and blood there is no difference of kind: both are species of the same genus heat.

[1] History of Philosophy, Vol. I, p. 162.

[2] Aitareya Āraṇyaka, II. 3.7.3.

—maternal and paternal. The two elements become united, and develop into a fœtus in the woman.[1]

Thus in the act of generation, the father and the mother have almost equal shares. As Mahidāsa also put it paradoxically, "This self gives her self to that self, and *that* self gives his self to this self. Thus two selves thrive together." *It is not* easy now to make out the precise meaning of this paradox. But it seems to have prepared the way for a later view, that the paternal element gives rise to fat, bone and marrow, while from the maternal element are formed skin, blood, and flesh.[2]

Mahidāsa's paradoxical axiom: its bearing on a later scientific view of generation.

We have no right to read this later view back into Mahidāsa's axiom, especially as it seems utterly irreconcilable with his view expressed elsewhere, which is :—Led by hunger and thirst, the father eats food. From food digested in the stomach is formed ultimately the seed (or *manas*, the psyche, as Uddālaka calls it). He bears the seed as a self in his self (body). When he commits it to the mother, he causes it to be born. This is called the first birth of a man.

Thereafter the seed becomes the self of the mother, as though one of her limbs. It does not therefore do any harm to her. She bears and nourishes the germ, or fœtus, her husband's self (not hers) within her, and brings forth the child in due course of time. This is said to be the second birth of a man.[3] Historically this view is that of the Vedic thinker

[1] Aitareya Āraṇyaka, I. 4.2.11.

[2] In the legal philosophy of 'Manu' (X.70-72) we are referred to these two opposed views of generation—(1) That the seed (the psychical element derived from the father) is more important than the 'field' (the matter in the menses), and (2) that both—the seed and the field—are of equal importance. Being consistent with his rather unhappily chosen metaphor of seed and field, the unknown expositor of Manu's system favoured the former view, although the analogy enabled him to insist so far at least, that as, on the one hand, a seed cannot grow apart from the fertility of the soil, so, on the other hand, a fertile ground without a seed sown in it is virtually barren.

[3] Aitareya Āraṇyaka, II. 5.1.2-7.

"Sūryā," who mentions four stages through which the fœtus passes.[1]

Anatomy.—Mahidāsa's knowledge of anatomy is far from exhaustive, as compared with that of modern writers. But the bare outlines which he leaves behind him of his study of the human frame would seem more than enough to have marked an epoch in the history of Indian anatomical science.

Mahidāsa speaks of a human body as built up of the trunk and the extremities. The principal part of the body is of course the trunk, which is divided by him broadly into three portions—the skull, the thorax, and the abdomen.[2] He insists more than once that the trunk is indispensably necessary for our organic existence, because a man is seen to live even when he is deprived of hands, legs, eyes, ears, speech, consciousness, or sound mind, but life without the trunk as a whole is inconceivable.[3] The trunk is therefore called the Self (ātmā), the physical aspect of real being.

The threefold division of the trunk which is essential to our existence.

Of the three parts of the trunk, the abdomen seems to have been distinguished from the skull as the mortal or lower centre from the immortal or higher centre.[4] The abdomen is represented sometimes by a numerical figure, "The Twenty-one" (Ekavimśa)[5] for the reason that there are twenty-one separate parts in it. Three organs of sense (prāṇāḥ) are said to be joined with the abdomen.[6] These are apparently the legs or organ of locomotion, the organ of excretion, and the organ of reproduction. The abdomen contains the intestines which are of irregular shape, some are large, some small; some are long,

Abdomen.

[1] Ṛig-veda, X. 83.40.

[2] Aitareya Āraṇyaka, I. 5.1.2-7.

[3] *Ibid*, II. 14. 9-16.

[4] *Ibid*, II. 1.4. 2-6.

[5] *Ibid*, I. 5.1.2-3.

[6] *Ibid*, I. 5.1.7.

some short.[1] From one point of view, that is, as the support or source of nutriment, the abdomen is considered to be the chief of the three parts,[2] while from another point of view, that is to say, from the point of view of the development of intelligence, the skull is regarded as the chief of all.

Thorax.

The thorax stands mid-way between the two. There are two organs of sense, contained in, or joined with the thorax, to wit, the heart or the central organ, and the hands or the organ of action. The special function of the heart is called breathing.

Skull.

In the skull or head is located, as we said, the immortal or higher centre of organism. It is the abode or centre of activity of the higher self, consisting of sight, hearing, mind, speech, and breath.[4] The exact position of this brain-centre is just below the opening of the suture of the skull.[5] The two centres called the mortal and the immortal are physically connected by a main branch of the artery, as well as perhaps by the nerve fibres, while their physiological connection is maintained through the central uniting function of the heart. The organs of sense are in this way connected with the brain-centre and with the heart.[6] The skull is associated with seven organs of sense,[7] the two eyes, the two ears, the two nostrils and the tongue.

Extremities.

The extremities comprise two upper and two lower limbs. Each one of the two upper limbs consists of five fingers, of four joints each, two pits in the elbow and arm, the shoulder-blade, and so on. In like manner, the parts of each one of the two legs are to be

[1] Aitareya Āraṇyaka, I.5.1.4-5.

[2] *Ibid*, I. 5.1.3 ; *Cf.* I. 1.2.9 : The heart is the vital centre ; the stomach performs the nutritive functions.

[3] *Ibid*, I. 5.1.7.

[4] *Ibid*, II. 1.4.7.

[5] *Ibid*, II. 4.3.7-9. "Viditri."

[6] *Ibid*, I. 5.1.6.

[7] *Ibid*, I. 5.1.7.

enumerated. All these being added to the trunk make a total of one hundred and one. But when the parts of the extremities are not separately counted, the total is just twenty-five.[1] The two thighs consist of two large bones.[2] A man stands firm on two feet, and animals stand on four. Though a man is a biped (dvipada), he is generally placed among the quadrupeds (catuspadas).[3] Like men, the birds are called bipeds. The tail is the main support of a bird, just as the abdomen is that of a man. The left wing of a bird is larger than its right wing because it contains one feather in excess.[4] A woman is physically weaker than a man because of some organic defect.[5] Upon the whole, the human anatomy is the same as that of the beasts and birds.[6]

Physiology.—A living body is a body that is organised, and has the vital principle (prāṇa) for its potentiality. It must be sharply distinguished from a dead body because a body without life joined to it, so to speak, is but a decaying corpse (śarīra).[7] Whereas a living body is a self-working mechanism of nature, a system, nay, a body-politic (to put it figuratively) which is composed of several members skilfully joined together or united into a complete whole. The members, apart from their corporate life, are said to have a distinct place, function, or purpose of their own in the organism. Each member is perfect in its place,[8] while out of place, it is useless. Besides, each member has a function so peculiar to itself that no other member can take its place. The eye, for example,

The living body is a purposive order, and as such it is different from a dead body or corpse.

[1] Aitareya Āraṇyaka, I. 1.2.7; I. 1.4. 20-21; I. 2.2.20; etc.

[2] *Ibid.* I. 5.1.8.

[3] *Ibid*, I. 1.2.6; I. 5.1.9.

[4] *Ibid*, I. 4.2.5; I. 7.8.9.

[5] *Ibid*, I. 4.2.4.

[6] *Ibid*, I. 4.2.8; cp. II. 1.4.1: what people call the tips of the feet in man are but hoofs and claws in other animals.

[7] *Ibid*, II. 1.4.11; II. 1.8.13.

[8] *Ibid*, I. 5.1.7.

cannot hear, the ear cannot see, *the stomach cannot think*, the mind cannot digest.[1] Thus the *functions are distributed* among the members, as if, on a wise principle of *the division* of labour. Each member exercises its own function independently, in harmony and co-operation with other members, while the unity of the whole organism is maintained by the vital principle. The mouth, for instance, speaks, the nose smells, the eye sees, the ear hears, the skin feels, the mind thinks, the stomach digests, and the organ discharges virile matter.[2]

In order to participate in the general function called 'life,' the relation between the members should not only be that of a mere physical contact (to put it in a modern fashion), but also that of a physiological connexion. That is to say, each member of the organism must be animated by the same spirit, and stimulated into activity by the same motive. For, as a later thinker, Uddālaka, expounded it, no sooner does the animating principle leave a branch of a tree than it begins to wither;[3] or, as Aristotle steadfastly maintained, "a hand or arm when cut off ought not to have applied to it the same name which it bears when the same portion of matter is varitably an integral part of the living whole."[4] It is also worth while to bear in mind that according to Mahidāsa, all the members of an organism are not absolutely necessary for its existence.

The five systems into which organic functions are to be divided.

Mahidāsa seems to have thought that a living body is a system which is divisible into a number of component systems. The division of these systems varies according to the centre in reference to which we study the functions of animated bodies. Mahidāsa tells us that the Śarkarākṣyas ("The

[1] Aitareya Āraṇyaka, II. 4.3.2-3.
[2] *Ibid*, II. 4.3.6.
[3] Chāndogya Upaniṣad, VI. 11.2.
[4] The Development of Greek Philosophy, p. 164.

Sugarsighted") meditated on the stomach as Brahman, the Āruṇis on the heart, while he himself meditated on the head (*i.e.*, the brain).[1] But he makes it quite clear in many places that he considered the stomach to be the centre of nutritive *functions, the heart of vital*[2] *and the head that of psychical* functions. Thus we may designate them respectively as the nutritive centre, the vital centre, and the intellectual centre. From the gradual embryonic development of man, these three centres are regarded as successive in order of time.[3]

In the name of five-fold air (prāṇa), and with reference to the vital centre, Mahidāsa divides the physiological functions of the body into the following five systems.

(1) Prāṇa—The up-breathing or respiratory system.
(2) Apāna—The down-breathing or alimentary system.
(3) Samāna—The back-breathing or metabolism.
(4) Udāna—The out-breathing or special senses.
(5) Vyāna—The on-breathing or circulatory system.

The nervous system is not separately enumerated.

So far as the intellectual centre goes there is one system only, namely, the physio-psychological or nervous system, as represented by sight, hearing, mind, and speech. This latter system is included under the respiratory and alimentary systems on the ground that its existence depends on them.

Here we must not misconstrue Mahidāsa's doctrine. For what he really means is that all the systems are interdependent, just as the living body is an inter-connected whole—an order which is as much purposive as the universe itself. It will also be noted that in assigning the name air or breath (prāṇa) to the systems above mentioned, Mahidāsa seems to have two purposes in view: first, to bring home that the working of the systems depends ultimately on the vital breath; and, secondly, to point out that the functions of the body,

[1] Aitareya Āraṇyaka, II. 1.4., 5-6.
[2] *Ibid*, I. 1.2.9.
[3] *Ibid*, II. 1.4. 1-7.

such as eating, digestion, excretion, circulation, and the like, stand in need of the help of air, or atmospheric pressure, as we now say.

III. *Psychology.*—The details of Mahidāsa's psychology, have already been discussed under the preceding heads. Here we have to note just a few points which have not been clearly brought out. Mind is that faculty in an organised body which thinks.[1] All desires dwell in the mind, for it is with the mind that a man conceives all desires.[2] Mind is that faculty in us which thinks, wills, and feels.

All that is thought or conceived in the mind is expressed in speech. Thus in order of time, or at least logically, thought is always prior to speech.[3] In another place he distinctly states that thought and speech are interdependent (vāṅ me manasi pratiṣṭhita, mano me vāci pratiṣṭhitam).[4]

IV. *Ethics.*—In the background of Mahidāsa's ethics are his metaphysics and biological speculations. The former can be best understood when it is considered in constant relation to the latter. We have to recall in the first place that, according to his view, the whole of nature is a system of ends, and in the second place, that the self develops gradually in the living world (prāṇabhṛitsu). The ultimate aim of man's life, and of life as a whole is perfection, which consists of knowledge (prajñā), bliss (nandana), and immortality (amṛitatvam). The continual advance is one from Life (Prāṇa) to Reason (Prajñā [5]), from Prajāpati to Brahman, that is to say, from bondage to freedom of action.[6] The first and obvious sign of freedom is the power of free bodily movement, the power of which the stocks and stones, nay, the plants and herbs

[1] Aitareya Āraṇyaka, II. 4-3-6.
[2] *Ibid*, I. 3-2-2.
[3] *Ibid*, I. 3-2-5.
[4] *Ibid*, II. 7.
[5] *Ibid*, II. 6.1-6: prajñā or prajñāna. "Sarvantat prajñānetraṁ, prajñāne pratiṣṭhitaṁ prajñānetro lokaḥ prajñāpratiṣṭhā prajñānaṁ Brahma."
[6] *Ibid*, II. 1-3-1: "Karma tadidaṁ karmakṛitamayaṁ puruṣo, Brahmaṇo lokaḥ."

(the sthāvaras as discriminated from the jaṅgamas) are deprived. The second test of freedom is to be applied to the thighs (uru) or the power of generation by means of separate sexes, *i.e.*, by *mithuna.* The next higher test is by the stomach (udara), that is, the choice of food and power of assimilation, and so on, while the final test is applicable only to the head (Śīrṣaḥ), or to the powers of heart and mind" (hṛidayaṁ manas), by which a man is endowed with knowledge, says what he has known, sees what he has known, knows what is to happen to-morrow, knows heaven and hell, and desires the immortal by means of the mortal.

The highest in the scale of development is man who alone is endowed with the faculty of reason (prajñānena sampannatama). His highest aspiration is the attainment of the immortal by means of the mortal, and his principal means is prajñāna. In performance of duty lies humanity which is the Brahma-world. The highest duty of man is of course the contemplation of the Divine manifesting or realising itself through various forms and in varying degrees. In order to enjoy full freedom, a philosopher or a god must transcend in his thought all material conditions of existence, and rise above the sensuous. But what is the real significance of his phrase, to desire the immortal by means of the mortal (martyena amṛitaṁ īpsā) ?

All forms of life eat and drink. All lower animals propagate the species. Even the plants, when they are grown up, bear fruits.[1] This alone cannot be the whole duty of a human being who is endowed with the extraordinary faculty of reason by cultivating which he can acquire wisdom, build up his moral self, and perfect his conduct. This is however no reason why we should forego like some of the ascetics the legitimate pleasures of the sense, legitimate in so far as these are in harmony with the purpose of the whole of nature, that

[1] Aitareya Āraṇyaka, I. 2.4. 14.

is, in so far as these subserve the real end for which these are meant, and no other. Take, for instance, the question of the propriety of marriage on which the opinion of the time is divided. Marriage in popular usage of the term means the union of father and mother, whereas scientifically viewed, it is just the union of "seed" with "blood," that is, a mutual reaction of two forms of heat, energy in its solar (āditya) and its fire (agni) stage of manifestation.[1] The Aitareya views expressed in an older document, the Aitareya Brāhmaṇa (VII. 3. 1), are here worth considering. The extract is from the story of Hariścandra, the interest of which is that it fully exhibits how the Aitareyas, and with them all the Brāhman schools, came into sharp conflict with those for whom the road to the Brahma-world lay through ascetic practices: "What is filth, what is goat's skin, what are beards, what is penance (in comparison with the son [2]) ?" "The father always overcomes by a son darkness in large measure. The son is the self in whom the father himself is reproduced.[3] He is like a vessel carrying ample provision of food to the father......The Brāhman should desire a son, since he himself makes a blameless world. Food is the subsistence of life, protection is afforded by a garment,[4] beauty is gold, the animals are marriages, the comrade is wife, poverty is the daughter, and the son is a luminary shining in the highest heaven."

"To one without a son the world is (as if) non-existent" (nâputrasya lokôstîti). All the lower animals are conscious

[1] Aitareya Āraṇyaka, II. 3. 7. 3.

[2] "Kin nu malaṁ kim ajinaṁ kimu śmaśrūṇi kiṁ tapaḥ ?" Filth, goat's skin, beards, and penance—these four are the characteristic symbols of an ascetic. But Sāyaṇa takes them as the characteristic marks of the 'four estates,' "atha malājina śmaśrutapaḥ śabdaiḥ āśramacatuṣṭayaṁ vivakṣitam." *Cf.* Buddha's pronouncement against asceticism: "Kinte dummedha jaṭāhi, kinte ajina sāṭiyā | Abbhantaran te gahanaṁ bāhiraṁ parimajjasi | |".

[3] Śaśvat putreṇa pitaro atyāyan bahulaṁ tamaḥ, ātmā hi jajña ātmanaḥ sa irāvatī atitāriṇī......".

[4] Śaraṇaṁ hi vāsa. (Aitareya Brāhmaṇa, VII. 3. 1).

of this truth, and for this reason even a son amongst them rides upon the mother and sister in the excitement of sexual passions."

Elsewhere the Aitareyas declared :

"All human arts, *viz.*, elephant, brass-work, garment, works in gold, mule and chariot, are an imitation of Divine arts or works of nature. All skilful works that appear in this light are to be regarded as arts; self-building is one of the arts by which the devotee should so build up his self that it becomes *chandomaya*, self-building inclusive of the art of reproduction."

Marriage is a sacred human institution which must be respected by all mortal beings. It is good in so far as it subserves the Divine purpose, which is the preservation and betterment of the race. All that the Aitareyas wanted to say might be summed up in the expression: Live the life of nature. The art of self-building or the art of conduct is to be based upon the art of the Divine, that is, to be in complete accord with the general laws of nature. Nothing is bad in its right place, and everything is useless when out of its place. Everything gains in value and significance in so far as it discharges its proper function and in proportion it contributes to the general well-being of the whole system of which it is an integral, organic part. The eye, for instance is good, as long as it discharges the function of seeing for which it is intended, and remains an integral part of the organism. "The eye cannot hear, the ear cannot see, and so on." When out of place, it is absolutely useless. Thus Mahidāsa Aitareya and his school left many inferences relating to practical life to be drawn from their study of the human organism or of the constitution and working of the physical universe. The family or the society or the state should be so constituted that each will appear as an organism in which all the parts will be harmoniously related together.

Each member will be given a free scope for a proper discharge of his or her function, or for the proper use of his or her capacity.

As for practical life, Mahidāsa thought life is altogether imperfect and bitter without marriage and children.[1] A happy life is said to be that which is lived for a hundred years in health, strength, and brightness (indriye, vīryye, tejasi). The greatest virtue of man is truth (satya), the flower and fruit of speech. The tongue that utters what is not true dries up and perishes like an uprooted tree.[2] The term truth had a far wider connotation with him than with us. Truth means a perfect harmony in conduct between one's thought, speech and deed, as in philosophy between knowledge and reality.

[1] Aitareya Āraṇyaka, I 3. 4. 12-13.

[2] *Ibid*, II. 3. 6. 9-10.

CHAPTER V

Of the Thinkers before Uddālaka

We have seen in the last section that there are few problems, so familiar to us in philosophy and natural science, which Mahidāsa did not touch upon. We may now conclude on a careful examination of the mode in which he endeavoured to find the solution of those problems, that it was he who prepared the way for almost all the thinkers who succeeded him in India, just as, on the other hand, it was he who made a profitable and scientific use of the earlier types of Vedic thinking. Mahidāsa must be recognised, therefore, as the father of Indian philosophy.

Mahidāsa is the father of Indian philosophy.

Of the thinkers who preceded Uddālaka and came immediately after Mahidāsa, the two most distinghished in history are Gārgyâyaṇa and Pratardana. There were undoubtedly a great many other thinkers. It will be presently shown that they did not apparently succeed in evolving any new system of philosophy. However, they were engaged in their own humble way in shaping the destiny of Indian thinking.

Mahidāsa's successors: The characteristic features of their speculations.

The constant topic of discussion among the thinkers of Mahidāsa's time was whether the vital or the intelligent is the first principle of change. One party, headed by Suravīra Māṇḍukeya, the Elder Sākalya, Raikva, and others maintained that the vital principle—Life (Prāṇa)—is the highest principle in man, and in the world of generation at large, while the other party, headed by Bādhva, Śāndilya, and

The vitalists versus the psychologists.

others, contended that the highest principle is the intelligent principle—Brahman. And Mahidāsa, as we have seen, tried to reconcile the two views by teaching that the soul is the manifestation of life, and indeed in essence, just life. But whenever there arose occasion for him to pronounce judgment upon the relative importance of the two principles, he was inclined in favour of the vital.[1]

The view of thinkers who preceded Uddālaka can be summarised as follows :—

I. Suravīra-Sākalya.

Sūravīra Māṇḍūkeya and Sthavira Sākalya.

First of all, it was stoutly maintained by Suravīra Māṇḍūkeya that the vital breath is the beam.[2] The argument came from the Elder Sākalya, who held the same view on the ground that the eye, the ear, the mind, the speech, the breath, in short, the whole self or whole tabernacle of individual existence rests ultimately on the vital principle.[3]

Māṇḍukeya-Kauṇṭharavya.

Hrasva Māṇḍūkeya and Kauṇṭharavya.

This brings us to consider other thinkers—Hrasva Māṇḍūkeya and Kauṇṭharavya. In their views are embodied the germs of the later physiological theory, that seed is formed from marrow as marrow from bone. In Hrasva Māṇḍūkeya's enumeration the parts of our body are altogether 720,[4] while according to Kauṇṭharavya, these are 1,080 in all.[5] However that may be, the Elder Sākalya and Kauṇṭharavya fully agreed in viewing the higher self in man as consisting of sight, hearing, æsthetic faculty,[6] mind, and speech.

Raikva.

Of this class of thinkers, Raikva must be said to be the chief of all. From a brief account of his life given in the

[1] Aitareya Āraṇyaka, II. 1. 4. 9-15. [2] *Ibid*, III, 1. 4. 1.
[3] *Ibid*, III. 2. 1. 1. [4] *Ibid*, III. 2. 1. 4. [5] *Ibid*, III. 2. 2. 7.
[6] *Ibid*, III. 2. 1. 5; III. 2. 2. 8. Their category for æsthetic faculty is chhandas or harmony.

12

Chāndogya Upaniṣad we learn that he lived under the patronage of King Mahāvṛiṣas.[1] The part of the country where he lived became famous under the name of Raikva-parṇa villages. Raikva was a far-famed teacher in his time.[2]

Raikva's doctrine.

As regards his philosophical views, they bear a close relation to the doctrine of "Anila." For Raikva, as for "Anila," the fundamental fact is Air (Vāyu). But there is again this difference between them. "Anila" held that the principle is one: Raikva, that the principles are two—Air as energy with relation to the universe, and the Vital Breath with regard to man. But Air and the Vital Breath are with Raikva identical in substance. When fire is extinguished, he said, it goes into air; when the sun goes down, it goes into air; when the moon goes down, it goes into air; and when water dries up, it goes into air. Similarly, when a man sleeps, speech, sight, hearing, mind—all these active faculties go (to be absorbed) into the vital breath.[3]

II. Bādhva.

Bādhva's pantheistic doctrine.

Opposed to the view, that the vital principle is the first principle of things, was the view, that that principle is the conscious principle. Among the earlier supporters of this latter view, the name of Bādhva ought to be mentioned first.

According to Bādhva, the animating principle of the body is the corporeal or animal soul, the essence of which is the incorporeal or nöetic soul, comprising sight, hearing, æsthetic faculty, mind, and speech.[4] Bādhva goes the length of maintaining that the incorporeal, conscious principle in us is what the solar essence is to the universe. Thus he takes the solar essence to signify the soul of the universe, namely, that soul which is in this earth, in heaven, air, ether, water, herbs, trees, moon, stars, in fact, in whatsoever that exists.

[1] Chāndogya Upaniṣad, IV. 2. 5.

[2] *Ibid*, IV. 1. 4. [3] *Ibid*, IV. 2. 5. [4] *Ibid*, III. 2. 3. 1-13.

This soul must be viewed under all conditions as Brahman, the conscious, teleological principle of the universe.

SĀṆḌILYA.

Far more important, as far more advanced in abstraction, are Śāṇḍilya's speculations about God and Soul. We learn on the authority of Pravāhaṇa Jaivali that the nick-name of Śāṇḍilya was Udara-Śāṇḍilya.[1] He was a disciple of Atidhanvan Śaunaka, who taught him that like ether (ākāśa), Brahman is greater than the great, and without limit. It should be borne in mind that this statement of Jaivali is in perfect agreement with the doctrine of Śāṇḍilya which is frequently quoted in the Vedānta texts[2] as Śāṇḍilya-Vidyā.[3] A later book of aphorisms on the doctrine of Faith or Devotion (Bhakti) is ascribed to Śāṇḍilya.[4] Whether the tradition that Śāṇḍilya is the originator of Bhaktivāda is true is reserved for discussion elsewhere.

His doctrine of faith.

As a fitting introduction to his main theory, Śāṇḍilya disposed of the question why a knowledge of the absolute being is necessary. His motive was religious philosophical. It is indispensable that we should form a definite and clear idea of the nature of the absolute being, inasmuch as without such an idea it is impossible for us to be free from doubt, to elevate our moral being or attain eternal life. In his own words, a man is a creature of will (kratumaya). As he wills or believes here, so will he be hereafter. He should therefore have this will and belief:—That God (Brahman), in the first place, is all that is. In God the universe has its origin, consummation and existence. He whose teleological aspect is intelligence,[5] he whose mechanical aspect is life,[6] whose form is light,[7] whose will is true, whose nature is infinite and all-pervading like space, he from

[1] Chāndogya Upaniṣad, I. 9. 2-3. [2] Vedānta-sūtra, III. 3. 31.

[3] *Cf.* "Iha Śāṇḍilyaḥ Śāṇḍilyaḥ." Chāndogya Upaniṣad, III. 14. 4.

[4] Śāṇḍilya Sūtras, translated by E. B. Cowell, Calcutta, 1878.

[5] Manomayaḥ. [6] Prāṇa-śarīraḥ. [7] Bhārūpaḥ.

whom all works, all desires, all odours, all tastes proceed, he who embraces within his infinite nature all existences, who does not speak and has no partiality,[1] such a Divine, absolute being is indeed God.

Soul is the Divine element in man.

Secondly, that in relation to man the absolute being is the soul within our heart, smaller than a grain of rice, smaller than a grain of barley, smaller than a mustard seed, and greater than the earth, greater than the sky, greater than all these worlds.

Realisation of the Divine nature is the supreme end of man's life.

And thirdly, that we shall obtain him from whom all works, all desires, all odours and all tastes proceed, and who is the soul within our heart, the smallest of the small, the greatest of all that is great.[2]

III. Satyakāma Jābāla.

Jābāla and Uddālaka.

Among the immediate successors of Mahidāsa, Philalethes Jābāla deserves to be considered before all. The Bṛihad Āraṇyaka Upaniṣad provides us with a list of six teachers, headed by Uddālaka Āruṇi. The list is spurious; in it Jābāla is represented as the last of the six, and also as the disciple of a Jānaki Āyasthuna.[3] As we learn from an older document in the Chāndogya Upaniṣad,[4] Jābāla's teacher was Gautama Hāridrumata, and not Jānaki Āyasthuna. Even in another list of teachers given in the Bṛihad Āraṇyaka Upaniṣad,[5] Jābāla is mentioned as an earlier thinker. This view is warranted by the close inter-connexion which exists between the doctrine of Jābāla and the philosophy of Mahidāsa.

[1] Anādaraḥ.

[2] Chāndogya Upaniṣad, III. 15. 1-4.

[3] Bṛihad Āraṇyaka Upaniṣad, VI. 3. 7-11; *cf. Ibid*, IV. 1. 6, where Janaka alludes to Jābāla's conception of Mind (manas) as Brahman.

[4] Chāndogya Upaniṣad, IV. 4. 3. foll.

[5] Bṛihad Āraṇyaka Upaniṣad, IV. 6. 2: "Uddālakâyana from Jābālâyana."

The fundamental assumption in which Jābāla stands nearest to Mahidāsa is that the vital principle is the highest principle in man. Even their expressions are the same. Jābāla's doctrine exhibits a crude notion of the immortality of soul, and the trinity of God. Such a notion was but an historic derivation from Mahidāsa's philosophy.

Jābāla's eschatalogical view of the progress of soul from light to light.

Jābāla thought there is in the corporeal form an incorporeal person (Puruṣa)—the soul or the immortal, fearless Brahman. When a man dies, this soul in him, made up of light (Jyotismat) as it is, goes to light, thence to day, from day to the bright half of the moon, from that to the six months when the sun goes to the north, thence to the year, from the year to the sun, from the sun to the moon, and from the moon to the lightning. There is a super-human soul (puruṣa=person) that receives the human soul, and escorts it to Brahman, the Supreme Being. In short, soul conceived as a luminous form, passes from light to light, from the light lesser, to the light greater, till it is merged or absorbed in Brahman, who is the eternal source of all life and light. This is the path of the gods, the path that leads to Brahman.

IV. Jaivali.

Jaivali and his contemporaries.

Śilaka of Śālāvatī, Dālbhya of the school of Cikita, Pravāhaṇa Jaivali, King of Pañcāla, are described in the Chāndogya Upaniṣad as three contemporaries.[1] The same Upaniṣad refers to a discussion held between them touching the origin of the world. Śilaka found the solution of this great problem in water; Dālbhya in heaven; and Jaivali in space or ether (ākāśa). Moreover, in support of his theory, that from infinite space proceed and to it return all existing things,

[1] Chāndogya Upaniṣad, I. 8. 1.

Jaivali quoted an ancient view, from which it follows that he was born later than Udara Śāṇḍilya.[1] Not only that. As a thinker, Jaivali came even after Philalethes Jābāla. Our main authority for Jaivali's views is an interesting dialogue put into the mouth of Jaivali and Uddālaka Āruṇi.[2]

The points noteworthy in connection with Jaivali's speculations are three in number. These are,—(1) the doctrine of the immortality of soul; (2) the first philosophic recognition of the popular belief in rebirth and retribution,—in heaven and hell; and (3) the virtual denial of soul and its immortality in lower animals. But, on the whole, his speculations presuppose Jābāla's doctrine of immortality and remind us of the views of such Vedic seers as "Damana" and "Mūrdhanvan."[3]

The remarkable features of Jaivali's philosophy.

Thus according to Jaivali's view, when a man dies, his friends carry him, *i.e.*, the dead body, to the funeral place, where it is consigned to fire, from which it came originally into being.

Jaivali's eschatological view of the soul.

Now if that man be one of those wise, godly and saintly philosophers who had deep insight into the reality of things, and who as forest-dwellers cultivated faith and practised the inner culture of intellect, his soul as a luminous form passes from light to light, from the light lesser to the light greater, exactly in the same way as described by Jābāla, until it reaches Brahman, the Divine Being. This is the path of the gods, the path that leads to Brahman. In other words, this is the process onward, carrying the soul up to immortality, as distinguished from metempsychosis.

The rational or transcendental soul.

[1] Chāndogya, 9, 1, 3.

[2] *Ibid*, V. 3. 1 ff. *Cf.* Bṛihad Āraṇyaka, VI. 2.

[3] Ṛig-veda, X. 16; 1. 5; X. 88.

Secondly, if that man be one of those worldly men who performed sacrifices, and works of public utility and practised penances, his soul goes to smoke, thence to night, from night to the dark half of the moon, from that to the six months when the sun goes to the south. His soul does not reach the year, but goes straight off to the world of the fathers, from that to the ethereal region, and from that to the moon. Having dwelt there till the reward of his good works is consumed, his soul returns to the region of ether, from that to air (atmosphere). Having become air, it becomes smoke; having become smoke, it becomes mist; having become mist, it becomes cloud; having become cloud, it comes down as rain. Then it is born as rice and corn, herbs and trees, sesamum and beans. These are eaten by men as food; from food is formed the seed; from seed, the germ; from that it is at last born as a man, and so on. Here again is this distinction. If that man's conduct was good, he will attain the birth of a Brāhman, of a warrior, or of a trader; and if otherwise, he may be born as a dog, or a hog, or a Caṇḍāla. This is the path of average worldly men, the ascent and descent, as it were, which brings the soul back to a new round of mundane existence.

The mundane soul.

Thirdly, should that man be one of those who were in the habit of, or in any way associated with, stealing gold, drinking spirits, violating the teacher's bed, or killing a Brāhman, the soul is doomed to hell. So far as to men.

The infernal soul.

Fourthly, with regard to lower creatures, deprived as they are of the higher self or soul, the door of immortality is closed to them. It may be said of them that they continually "live and die," and nothing more.

The animal soul.

The ethical bearing of Jaivali's doctrine.

In this quaint fancy of Jaivali's there is nothing more to comment upon than the ethical bearing or moral consequence of his doctrine of immortality. There is implied in his doctrine something of a Socratic maxim, such as knowledge is virtue. But Jaivali would insist that knowledge is not the only virtue, *it being just one of many. That is to say,* knowledge or inner enlightenment, taken by itself, is not enough. The argument practically comes to this. Knowledge cannot be regarded as virtue in itself, unless it be coupled with the higher moral condition of soul, and consistent throughout with man's spiritual outlook on life. Jaivali tends to maintain in the same breath that such an ideal life as this is not within the reach of those who are not wholly detached from the world. The best that a worldly man can possibly do is to observe the rules of outward morality, and to be pious patriotic, and spiritually minded. Jaivali by his doctrine of immortality and general eschatological theory tried to answer the question why the world of generation is never full. Further, these afforded a metaphysical basis for his rules against the "five fires of immoral conduct (pañcâgni)." "Hence let a man take care to himself.[1] A man who steals gold, who drinks spirits, who dishonours his Guru's bed, who kills a Brāhman, these four fall, and as a fifth he who associates with them. But he who thus knows the five fires is not defiled by sin even though he associates with them. He who knows this is pure, clean, and obtains the world of the blessed." Herein one can trace the origin of Pārsvanātha's doctrine of four-fold restraint (cāujjāma saṁvara), Mahāvira's five great vows (pañea mahāvvayas) and of Buddha's five moral precepts (pañca-sīlas).

[1] Chāndogya Up. V. 10. 8-10. Max Müller's translation: 'Let a man take care to himself' is not a literal translation of Jugupsati.' The commentators suggest "fear" (vibhatsota) or "hate" (ghṛiṇī bhavet). "Fear, therefore (such a wretched state of existence)," would seem rather nearer the mark.

CHAPTER VI.

V. GĀRGYĀYAṆA.[1]

Jaivali's speculations on the fate of soul after death occur again, with certain variations, yet on the whole with the same purpose, in the Kauṣītaki Upaniṣad, in a dialogue between Gārgyāyaṇa and Uddālaka.

Jaivali and Gārgyāyaṇa.

There is involved in Jaivali's speculations, we saw, the distinction so sharply drawn between the two main roads by which souls proceed on their destined course. The roads are described in the Chāndogya Upaniṣad as the Deva-yāna and the Pitṛi-yāna ; they are sometimes called the right and the left, or the southern and the northern. Prof. Max Müller observes that "The northern or left road, called also the path of the Devas, passes on from light and day to the bright half of the moon: the southern or right road, called also the path of the fathers, passes on from smoke and night to the dark half of the moon. Both roads therefore meet in the moon, but diverge afterwards. While the northern road passes by the six months when the sun moves towards the north, through the sun, (moon) and the lightning to the world of Brahman, the southern passes by the six months when the sun moves towards the south, to the world of the fathers, the ether, and the moon."[2] "The great difference, however, between the two roads is that while those who travel on the former do not return again to a new life on earth, but reach in the end a true knowledge of the unconditioned Brahman,

[1] The full name of Gārgyāyaṇa is Citra Gārgyāyaṇa. The name is spelt also as Gārgyāyaṇi and Gāngyāyaṇi. Prof. Weber in his Indische Studien (I. 395, II. 395) adopts both the forms. Prof. Cowell prefers Gāṅgyāyaṇi to Gārgyāyaṇi. Here we have followed the authority of the Bṛihad Āraṇyaka Upaniṣad (IV. 6. 2): "Gārgyāyaṇa from Uddālakāyana." In the Kauṣītaki Upaniṣad (I. 1-2) Gārgyāyaṇa is mentioned as a contemporary and teacher of Uddālaka. Like Jaivali, Gārgyāyâṇa was of a warrior family. Nothing more is known of his life.

[2] S. B. E., Vol. I, p. 272.

those who pass on to the world of the fathers and the moon return to earth to be born again and again."

According to Jaivali and Gārgyāyaṇa, there are these two paths open to men after death—that of immortality, and that of mortality or metempsychosis. The godly men who travel on the former reach finally the Ideal world, the world of Brahman, while the average men who pass by the latter are reborn on this earth, according to their deed and thought, as a worm, an insect, a fish, a bird, a lion, a bear, a serpent a tiger, a man, or as something of the kind.[1]

Gārgyāyaṇa's question as to soul, and answers.

Though there is in regard to the problem of future existence so close a resemblance as between Jaivali and Gārgyāyaṇa, the main task which the latter set himself to fulfil was rather to answer the more serious question, *viz.*, who am I?[2]

To this question Gārgyāyaṇa's answer was:[3] "I am a living body, consisting of fifteen parts, brought forth originally from the moon who orders the seasons, and is the home of my ancestors. That is to say, I am he who is connected by blood and traditions with the long line of ancestors through the father's seed. The seed itself was called forth into existence in the father's body by the elemental forces. The father was then a living energetic man, when he was united with the mother, and the seed was through a natural process transferred from him to her. In this manner I was born in a family of men so that I might acquire the knowledge of Brahman, the Divine being."

The identity of Soul and the Divine essence.

"What Brahman is, that am I."[4] This is apparently the simple metaphysical answer offered to the question by Gārgyāyaṇa. But in finding an answer for one question, he had to face these two separate questions—Who is he? and Who am I?

[1] Kauṣītaki Upaniṣad, I. 2.
[2] *Ibid*, I. 6.
[3] *Ibid*, I. 2.
[4] *Ibid*, I.6.

First, as to "Who am I"? said Gārgyāyaṇa, "I am a season (ṛitu, animus, caloric energy), a child of the seasons, brought forth from the womb of endless space, and generated from light or luminous Brahman.[1] In short, I am *tyam*, meaning he who is from Brahman."

The generic character of soul.

Who is Brahman? He is light, the luminous, golden germ,[2] the primal form of heat, which is the origin of the year (seasons, time-principle), the past, the present, the all.[3] In short, Brahman is *sat*, *i.e.*, Being or existent.[4] "I am from Brahman, Brahman is Being, I am, therefore, Being."

Brahman.

What is Being or existent? It is that which is different from the gods—such as Fire, Air, Varuṇa, Indra, Prajāpati[5]—and from prāṇas—living beings.[6] In relation to Being Gārgyāyaṇa insisted on the conception of the gods and animated bodies as *tyam*, meaning that which is from Being. Here is implied again the logical syllogism: the gods and prāṇas are from Brahman, Brahman is Being, the gods and prāṇas are, therefore, Being. It follows that Brahman is not only *sat*, but both *sat* and *tyam*—Being and all that is derived therefrom. In truth, then, Brahman is all that is (sarvamidaṁ).[7]

The Divine being is both *sat* and *tyam*—Universal and individual.

We imagine Gārgyāyaṇa proceeded on these assumptions to conceive two sets of two Brahma-worlds. In the first set are the world of Brahman the universal spirit and that of Brahman the individual spirit; in the second set are the world of Brahman the unconditioned and that of Brahman the conditioned.

Two Brahma-worlds.

1 Kauṣītaki Upaniṣad, I 1. 6.
2,4 *Ibid*, I. 6.
6 *Ibid*, I. 6.
3 *Ibid*, I. 3.
5 *Ibid*, I. 3.
7 *Ibid*, I. 7.

His view of the world of generation. It is incompatible with his Doctrine of Immortality.

Following the line of thought of "Parameṣṭhin," and to a certain extent, that of Mahidāsa, Gārgyāyaṇa understood by the world of universal spirit, Water,[1] and by that of individual spirit, what we may call intelligible corporeality. There is no difference of kind between the universal spirit and the individual. For the former is conceived to be a primal form of heat, the latter a form of ṛitu; both are in essence heat. Thus it is implied in this wholly mechanical conception of the universe that primal heat is the unchanging principle of all change. By the power of primal heat, water—the eternal imperishable substance—is developed from "the potential stage of existence" (mānasa) to that of "completed actuality" (cākṣuṣa). Before water can become evolved into multitude of developed forms, it has to pass through various stages, and in this connexion Gārgyāyaṇa felt like Mahidāsa the necessity of introducing the gods—Fire, Air, Varuṇa, Indra, Prajāpati—as the intermediaries. We understand with Gārgyāyaṇa that the cosmic matter water in itself is eternal, imperishable and that the cosmic energy heat in itself is unchanging, indestructible. In other words, the world of generation is actually existent, and eternally present. And yet we do not see clearly enough how Gārgyāyaṇa can eliminate the notion of mutability from that of immortality.

Criticism of the last point.

Here the position of Gārgyāyaṇa may be approached from two points of view, *viz.*, that of the changing individual, and that of the changing universe. As long as the caloric energy which informs a particular intelligible corporeality can maintain itself as such in the continual change from the coming-to-be into the ceasing-to-be so long there is metempsychosis for the individual; and as soon as that energy is completely absorbed into the universal

[1] Kauṣītaki Upaniṣad, I. 3.

spirit—the primal form of heat—the individual attains immortality.

We may make this admission with Gārgyāyaṇa that, from the one point of view, the immortality of the variable particular is but its total absorption into the relatively invariable universal. Our difficulty is, the immortal life being thus attained, how to conceive it preserved from the smuggling, deceitful hands of mutation or change? For it is in the very nature of the universal spirit to render itself actual and effectual in the individual. Such being the case, the difference that can be conceived to subsist between the two notions of metempsychosis and immortality is nothing but this. In the case of metempsychosis the change takes place from the particular to the particular, while in the case of immortality the change is from the individual to the universal. Moreover, in the former case some sort of continuous personal identity is conceivable, while in the latter case, it is not. Thus the fact remains that the universal is not immune from mutation.

Being and change.

In the second set of two Brahman worlds are included the world of Brahman the unconditioned, and that of Brahman the conditioned. By the former Gārgyāyaṇa meant, we may take it, "the non-temporal, unchanging realm of absolute existence," and by the latter, "the temporal, changing cycle of merely relative being." Strictly, however, the latter comprises the first set of two Brahma-worlds which we might perhaps describe here, for convenience' sake, as the heavenly world and the world of man.

In the Kauṣītaki Upaniṣad[1] we have from Gārgyāyaṇa a semi-mythical, semi-philosophical description of the heavenly world, as contrasted with the world of man. It will not be an exaggeration to say that this particular conception of

[1] Kauṣītaki, I. 3-5.

Gārgyāyaṇa deserves the name of "a philosophical romance," couched for the most part in allegorical terms. It is difficult to read into these terms which he employs the exact meaning they conveyed to him. Perhaps much more or perhaps much less was meant by these terms than we can make out now with our limited knowledge. We are forced to realise the difficulty of judging Gārgyāyaṇa, born as we are too late, or it may be, too soon, to be able to place ourselves wholly at his point of view.

What little seems obvious to us is that in assigning to the heavenly world these two predicates—undecaying and unconquerable—(vijara, aparājita), Gārgyāyaṇa kept in his mind something of a sharp antagonism between the world of concrete existents (prāṇāḥ) on one hand, and that of the gods (devas) on the other. The former is in its nature mutable, while relatively to it the latter is of an immutable nature. Reducing, then, all our concepts pertaining to the world of generation to these two opposite correlatives—the mutable and the immutable, we might perhaps hold with Gārgyāyaṇa that there is a third, so to speak, which is different from either and yet embraces them both. This is what was called the world of absolute existence which in itself is neither this nor that—Brahman the unconditioned, who is neither good nor evil, neither death nor immortality, in fact, to use a familiar expression of Mahidāsa, who is beyond the yes and no of language,[1] beyond all contradictions, beyond all correlatives, beyond all descriptions. This is the perfect model of which the soul must be a perfect copy. It is this Brahman the unconditioned towards whom soul, the knower of Brahman, should advance by being trained to the highest excellence, by shaking off, as Gārgyāyaṇa puts it, the good and the evil, by looking at all pairs of correlative opposites—day and night, joy and sorrow, etc., with perfect indifference.[2]

[1] Aitareya Āraṇyaka, II. 3. 8. 4.

[2] Kauṣītaki Upaniṣad, I. 4.

Now in taking the world of generation as a whole, and on contrasting it, if any contrast is possible, with the Ideal world, we find ourselves again in the midst of the same opposites from which Gārgyāyaṇa always recoiled. The one is characterised throughout by change and multiplicity, the other is not. It is reasonable to allow that to render the world of generation intelligible we require a ground beyond it, namely, that which has just the opposite attributes. But the question arises, how to connect the one with the other? If we separate them widely, how can we solve the problem? Is it possible, following Gārgyāyaṇa, to postulate first the realm of change, then, by a second process of thought, to take the world of absolute existence as starting point and from it deduce the world of change? Is this deductive construction of absolute existence justifiable? In what way can the world of Brahman the unconditioned and the world of Brahman the conditioned be brought into the closest possible connexion?

His failure.

It has to be acknowledged that the gulf between the world of absolute existence and the world of generation is too wide to bridge over so easily. Being fully aware of the difficulty in connecting the one with the other except in Idea, Gārgyāyaṇa interposed—and we learn from our authority that Plato did the same—the soul and space as intermediaries. It is then doubtful in Gārgyāyaṇa, as in Plato, if the world of generation is necessarily implicated in the realm of absolute being. Here the position of Gārgyāyaṇa is so exactly similar to the position of Plato that nothing perhaps would be better than that we should quote Prof. Adamson with regard to the latter. "His nearest approach thereto is in the correlation he quite empirically makes between Reason (νοῦς=prajñā)[1] the one function of which is the contemplation of the Ideas,[2] ....and soul. Reason, he *tells* us, is in soul; he almost

[1], [2] Kauṣītaki Upaniṣad, I. 5; I, 7.

lays down the general proposition that reason is actualised only in soul. The indestructibility of soul doubtless enables it thus to serve as that concrete in which the eternal reason is made actual."[1]

The knower of Brahman should advance towards Brahman. This proposition enables us to see further resemblance between Gārgyāyaṇa and Plato. For, in the first place, both of them contemplated some finest distinction between the eternal Reason and Soul. So, in the second place, both, as we know, generalised soul and conceived it to be the principle of all change. In order to clear up our position, we quote once again Prof. Adamson. "But now and again, one must say, on empirical grounds, it is assumed that in the process by which the principle of change unfolds itself it follows the direction prescribed in and by contemplation of the Ideas. But the soul shares also the nature of the mutable; and in this finally Plato has to find a solution for that deviation from the perfect model which cannot but be allowed in the world of generation; so much so, indeed, that, as we saw,......... he is ready even to distinguish between the good and the bad soul. Finally, the soul as principle of change, as working out a copy of absolute existence, has to operate under conditions that are so far foreign to its own nature."[2]

First Ideal Theory in India --

Development of the Doctrine of Immortality.

On taking leave of Gārgyāyaṇa's doctrine of immortality, we should call attention to the fact that it is not in the history of post-Vedic thought altogether new. The root conceptions of which it was a development in the fullest sense are to be found in the thoughts of his predecessors. As a matter of fact, Mahidāsa and Jaivali were the principal sources from which Gārgyāyaṇa drew largely the materials for his thought.

[1] The Development of Greek Philosophy, p. 131.

[2] *Ibid*, p. 132.

Yet it must be conceded, in justice to Gārgyāyaṇa, that he made the doctrine of Immortality entirely his own by giving a definite form to it. It was chiefly at the hands of Gārgyāyaṇa that the doctrine of Immortality came to occupy so prominent a place in Indian philosophy. Even those who are fascinated by the Buddhist conception of Buddha Amitābha and of Sukhāvatī, the Buddhist Land of Bliss or Paradise cannot but note with profit Gārgyāyaṇa's conception of Brahman as Amitaujas (of infinite radiance) and his eternal abode.

Gārgyāyaṇa is the incipient Plato of India.

One may rightly question whether we are justified in attaching any very great importance to Gārgyāyaṇa's doctrine of Immortality for its own sake. Far from that. In truth, the importance of his doctrine of Immortality lies in the intimate relation in which it stands to his theory of Ideas. In Gārgyāyaṇa, these two—the doctrine of Immortality and the theory of Ideas—are so closely connected that it is impossible to separate them. The doctrine of Immortality is historically the basis of the theory of ideas, whereas logically the former is but a deduction from the latter. If originality be denied to Gārgyāyaṇa on the side of his doctrine of Immortality, it does not materially affect his position as an original thinker, the incipient Plato of India, on the side of his theory of Ideas. Gārgyāyaṇa's was, so far as evidence goes, the first ideal theory in India. It must be carefully noted that in his phraseology the word Idea (mānasa) does not convey the Platonic sense of the eternal relation of things but just the existence of a thing as an idea in the divine mind before its actualisation.

The theory of Ideas.

Turning at last to Gārgyāyaṇa's theory of Ideas, we have to confess, at the outset, that it is not within our power to bring out from his scanty expressions anything beyond a few fundamental points which are as follows :

Antagonism between Mahidāsa and Gārgyāyaṇa.

In the first place, the general problem with which his Ideal theory is concerned seems to have been the life of soul and its relation to reason (prajñā). It is moreover the point in which Gārgyāyaṇa was chiefly indebted to Mahidāsa, and yet came into direct conflict with him. But it is in the light of this conflict between the two thinkers that we can best read where the real defect of each is.

From the metaphysical position which he assumed, Mahidāsa was driven to the conception of soul as a part of actuality, *i.e.*, change or process. According to him, what is given in the life of soul within the world of generation is not so much an object known as the mode of cognition. Thus he was led to view every mental fact in the light of an act of cognition. Further, in accordance with his view, we should try to understand not what we know, but how we know. In fact Mahidāsa maintains that soul as a principle of all change lends its name to the active exercise of the function of reason (prajñāna) which is directly connected with the mode of cognition, and only indirectly connected through it with the object cognised. In this respect, he drew no distinction of kind between abstract reasoning and sense-perception.

Just the reverse was the conclusion reached by Gārgyāyaṇa. For according to him our concern should be not so much how we know as what we do know or ought to know. According to him, the essence of the life of soul is eternal Idea (mānasa) in contemplation and actualisation of which is the true function of reason (prajñā). Soul has three names, which are expressive of the three aspects under which the absolute being is conceived by a finite mind. The masculine name is obtainable, *i.e.*, can be represented, by vital breath or life (prāṇena), the feminine name by speech or language (vācā), and the neuter name by mind or thought (manasā). Under the masculine aspect, Gārgyāyaṇa held in common with Mahidāsa that soul is in essence but life itself. But it is the neuter or neither-masculine-nor-feminine name which brings us nearest to the realm of pure idea, through idea human to idea divine. In the scale of ideas, the lowest are the joy, delight and offspring, obtainable, *i.e.*, can be actualised, by way of reproduction, and the highest is the idea of absolute existence by way of philosophic contemplation. Locomotion, action, sight, sound, odour, taste, touch, thought—all these are in various measures but divine ideas translated into the terms of actuality; all these therefore belong to the realm of divine ideas, to soul the divine in man. For Gārgyāyaṇa the really existent are ideas, although not in the Platonic sense of relations but things, and the function of reason has meaning—is existent, only through its realisation of the various shades of ideas; the mode of cognition exists only for the sake of ideas. According to him, as eternal reason in man is directly connected with the object known or idea realised, and connected only indirectly through it with the mode of cognition. Lastly there lies in the background of Gārgyāyaṇa's theory of Ideas the identification of knowledge with real existence.

Ethics.—Gārgyāyaṇa's ethical doctrine is generally on the same level with that of Jaivali save where he strikes a loftier note by his lofty metaphysic. As conceived by him, the highest duty of man, or the only duty of the divine philosopher, is to copy the perfect model of absolute being known by the contemplation of eternal idea. For this he must be above all distinctions which obtain in the world and society, and must abandon all works and sacrifices which have nothing but material gains or heavenly joys in view. Gārgyāyaṇa unlike Mahidāsa found no coördinating link between the transcendental order and practical life save in the generic character of soul, the contemplator of absolute being. However, as for practical life, he maintains that the best thing is to act according to the Divine purpose as manifested in the phenomena of nature. For nothing is good which conflicts with that purpose. Thus it is implied that a knowledge of the constitution of the visible world,[1] no less than the study of the physiology of man,[2] will at once reveal the art of building cities, governing kingdoms, and regulating life and society. Art is no art unless it actualises what is in the Divine mind, or in other words, the Divine purpose is realised in and through it. Accordingly, all objective knowledge must be deduced from the idea of the universal being.

This idealistic conception of art implied in Gārgyāyaṇa's expression "mānasī pratirūpā cākṣusī," "the visible or actual is but a reflection of the mental," is different from and yet follows closely on the line of Aitareya philosophy which regards all human arts, including the art of generation, as an imitation in some way of the works of nature, the Divine arts. "The Divine arts," the Aitareyas proclaim, "are praised as arts indeed. All human arts, *viz.*, brass-work,[3] garment, works in gold,[2] and such toys as elephant, mule and chariot, appear to be but a reproduction of nature.[4] All skilful works that appear in this light are to be known as arts, self-building is comprised in those arts by which the Yajamāna should so build up his self that it becomes chandomaya,[5] endowed with harmony, *i.e.*, in tune with the whole of nature, or vedamaya, endowed with intelligence as Sāyaṇa interprets the same. The generation of offspring is such an art.[6]"

[1] Kauṣtiaki Upaniṣad, I. 3.

[2] *Cf.* Bṛihad Āraṇyaka Upaniṣad, IV. 3. 38; IV. 4. 22. Note the conception of state as an organism of seven limbs in Kautiliya Artha-Śāstra, VI. 1. See for other references Banerjea's "Public Administration in Ancient India," p. 63.

[3] Sāyaṇa takes Kaṁsa in the sense of darpaṇaḥ, mirror.

[4] Hiraṇyāni=Suvarṇābharaṇāni (Sāyaṇa).

[5] All Brāhman schools took the same view of art, *e.g.*, "Yadvai pratirūpam tacchilpam," *i.e.*, "whatever is a facsimile is art" (Śatapatha Br., III. 2. 1. 5); "divaḥ silpam avatatam," *i.e.*, "art has descended from heaven" (Taittirīya Br., II. 7. 15). See other references collected by Pandit Satyabrata Sāmaśrami in his Aitareyālocanam, p. 117, Aitareya Brāhmaṇa, IV.

[6] Aitareya Brāhmaṇa, V.I. 5. 1; "Śilpāni Śaṁsanti devaśilpāni eteṣāṁ vai Śilpāṇām anukṛitī ha Śilpaṁ adhigamyate hastī kaṁso vāso hiraṇyam aśvatarī rathaḥ Śilpāni. Śilpaṁ hāsmin adhigamyate ya evaṁ veda yadeva Śilpāni. Ātmasaṁskṛitirvāva Śilpāni chandomayam vā etair yajamāna ātmānaṁ saṁskurute......" The above rendering is rather free and condensed.

Thus the Aitareya conception affords on the whole a mechanical, not to say a materialistic, explanation of art as teaching that art is but an imitation of nature, or conformation of human action to the established order of things. If so where is the free play of imagination in art except in finding out the hidden reason manifesting itself through works human and divine? It is therefore in Gārgyāyaṇa's view that we obtain the first reference to an attempt at defining art in terms of mind which is a divine element,—a faculty which imposes its own form upon nature. Nevertheless, the historian can trace the background of this Kṣatriya Idealism in art in the Brāhman teleological view of nature as a purposive order of things, to conform to which is to act according to a set purpose in consonanee with the whole. Gārgyāyaṇa's conception of art itself is not as yet stript of its cosmical implication as it presumes the existence of a divine order actualising itself through the mysterious manifestations of nature. This defect of his theory was to some extent made good by the Buddha who came to regard art as a product of human imagination, a representation of ideas conceived in the mind of the artist. The difference in so far as Gārgyāyaṇa's view is concerned is that Buddha precluded all idea of a Divine Being external to man. Thus in speaking of a famous picture of his time, Buddha pronounced that the *caraṇa*-citra was really conceived by the mind.[1] The Buddhist Commentator Buddhaghosa explains Buddha's theory as follows: "In the world there is no finer artmanship than that which is displayed in a piece of painting, and of paintings the one called *Caraṇa* is admitted to be the very best. In drawing this class of pictures the thought arises in the mind of the painters: "Such and such kinds of figure are to be drawn in this picture." By this thought the drawing of outline, colouring, polishing, and

[1] "Caraṇaṁ cittaṁ citteu eva cintitaṁ." Saṁyutta, Khandha-Saṁyutta, 5. 8., quoted in the Atthasālinī, p. 64.

such other detail works of drawing follow, in consequence whereof a wonderful figure appears on the caraṇa-citra.[1] "Let that go above this figure, let this go below that"—the finishing touch is given afterwards to the picture according to thought. Similarly whatever products of art there are in the world, all are wrought by the mind.[2]" The Buddha introduced this psychological view of art by way of analogy of his explanation of the diversity of the forms of life and of their experiences. Hence there can be no doubt that Buddha's was a later development on psychological lines of Gārgyāyaṇa's ideal theory.

---

[1] According to Buddhaghosa, caraṇa-vicaraṇa, *i. e.*, "rambling" or "wandering." He adds by way of explanation: "Saṁkhā brāhmaṇā pāsaṇḍikā honti, paṭakoṭṭhakaṁ katvā tattha nānappakārā sugati-duggati-vasena sampatti-vipattiyo lekhāpetvā idaṁ kammaṁ katvā idaṁ patilabhati, idaṁ katvā idanti dassentā taṁ cittaṁ gahetvā vicaranti." (Sāratthappakāsini, Ceylonese Ed., p. 469.)

[2] "Citten'eva cintitanti cittakārena cintitvā katattā, cittena cintitaṁ nāma." (*Ibid*, p. 469).

CHAPTER VII

VI. Pratardana.

Passing over Kauṣītaki, Painga, and others who declared themselves to be among the upholders of the theory of life as the first principle of things (niḥśreyas, neplus-ultra),[1] we come to Pratardana, son of Divodāsa, King of Kāśi.

Pratardana and his predecessors.

In post-Vedic philosophy many thinkers worked out Mahidāsa's line of thought but none perhaps achieved so grand a result as Gārgyāyaṇa and Pratardana did. Both were warriors, royal princes, and so, too, was Jaivali, King of Pañcāla. Gārgyāyaṇa's achievement was metaphysical, and Pratardana's was psychological, broadly speaking. But Pratardana owed his philosophical knowledge to both Mahidāsa and Gārgyāyaṇa, so much so indeed, that we may regard him as a richer combination of the two. And though his achievement was psychological, his main task was really one of metaphysics.

The doctrine of Inner Offering.

The Kauṣītaki Upaniṣad[2] speaks of Pratardana as the famous institutor of a new system of self-control (saṁyamana), generally known by the name of Inner Offering (āntaram agnihotram). It is said that he introduced this new system as an improvement on the prevailing mode of Vedic sacrificial offering. We think the fact is historically true, since the reference given comes in purely by accident, though at the same time, we have reason to deny the exclusive right of Pratardana to this honour. For we learn on an earlier authority, such as that of the Aitareya Āraṇyaka, that the Kāvaṣeyas (one of the earlier schools) were the first to raise a voice against the

[1] Kauṣītaki Upaniṣad, II. 14.

[2] II. 5.

existing system of Vedic sacrifice, and to think of a better system. So they asked, saying, "Why should we repeat (the Veda), and why should we sacrifice? We offer as a sacrifice breath in speech, or speech in breath. What is the beginning (of one), that is the end (of the other)."[1]

The Kauṣītaki Upaniṣad itself bears evidence to the fact that the doctrine of Inner Sacrifice was not invented by Pratardana.[2]

His own teaching was:—

(1) That whatever other forms of offering there are, they have an end, for they consist of work, which, in common with all works, has happiness for its end, but the system of Inner Offering does not aim at any such material or sensuous end.

(2) That breath and speech are the two inexhaustible and immortal oblations that a man may offer always, whether he is awake or asleep.

(3) And that it is by offering breath in speech, and speech in breath, that a man can withdraw himself from the senses and the sensuous, and exercise perfect control over his passions and emotions.

Here the third argument is of great importance. In working it out Pratardana arrived at a psychological truth quite unforeseen. When a man speaks, he cannot breathe, and when he breathes, he cannot speak. For, as he discovered, when a man speaks, he offers all the while his breath in his speech, just as when he breathes, he offers all the while his speech in his breath. It is evident from a dialogue in the Kauṣītaki Upaniṣad (which is our sole authority for Pratardana's doctrine) that this truth was generalised by him and applied to every act of cognition. Thus he came

The bearing of the third argument upon Pratardana's psychology.

[1] Aitareya Āraṇyaka, III. 2.6.8. S. B. E., Vol. I, pp. 265-266.

[2] "The ancients, knowing this better form of offering, did not offer the ordinary sacrifice." This is Max Müller's rendering of Kauṣītaki passage (II. p).

to lay down almost as a general proposition : when we see we cannot hear ; when we hear, we cannot think, at the same time, at he same moment.

I. Psychology.

Pratardana's psychological doctrine is not, in principle and detail, new, and yet it is new in the sense that it cast the two older doctrines of Mahidāsa and Gārgyāyaṇa into a new mould and crystallised form of its own. He combined the two antecedent views in his system, not in a mechanical mixture but in a chemical union. There must be no mistake about that. Even while admitting that he shared with Mahidāsa and Gārgyāyaṇa all their fundamental metaphysical ideas, and brought them to bear on his psychology, we have sufficient reason to hold that, in this respect, his indebtedness goes only to testify to his greatness. For the very fact of his acquaintance with the earlier views explains clearly enough how he could make an advance upon them.

Indebtedness constitutes his greatness.

A great intellect ought not to be judged, at all events, by his indebtedness. That is to say, in judging the merit of a philosopher, we should never forget two things : the circumstance, however little an incident it may be in its own nature, that stimulates him to reflection, and the conception that lies nearest to his heart, that by which he achieves a real contribution to philosophy as a whole.

To judge of Pratardana's originality we must return to his conception of what he called, in contradistinction to the ordinary vedic sacrifice, the system of Inner Offering. For this led, it might be *per accidens*, to his important psychological conception of the central sense or uniting function of Prāṇa (vitality and sensibility in the soul), and of the unity of the conscious principle (prajñātman). But we have two further reasons for calling Pratardana's psychological doctrine new.

Pratardana's claims to originality.

In the first place, Pratardana defined the province of psychology within narrower limits by restricting its investigation to the human mind, and this enabled him certainly to prepare the way for Yājñavalkya, Buddha, and other later psychologists. Besides, this gave him an advantage over Mahidāsa (whose psychology is of far wider scope) that he could thereby be more precise in his language, and more rigorous in his treatment of problems than the latter. However, what he did was but to fulfil the brilliant work of his two predecessors Mahidāsa and Gārgyāyaṇa.

In the second place, we call his psychological doctrine new, because it is with the help of this doctrine that Pratardana was able to insist, for the first time in India, in regard to the theory of knowledge, that cognition in the widest sense is impossible, except, as it were, by way of a subject-object-relation, involved in the common process of consciousness.[1]

A. The uniting function of Prāṇa—the physiological aspect of Pratardana's psychology.

In expounding his doctrine of Inner Offering as a sacrifice of breath in speech, and of speech in breath, Pratardana eventually made a psychological discovery, which is: so long as a man breathes, he cannot speak, just as, conversely, so long as he speaks, he cannot breathe.[2] Carrying the investigation over to every act of sense-perception or cognition in general, Pratardana arrived always at the same result.[3] Being in this way convinced that no one can at the same time see a form with the eye, hear a sound with the ear, and think a thought with the mind, but that he can apprehend sight, sound, odour, taste, touch, thought, one by one, each as a unit Pratardana, like Aristotle,[4] set himself to inquire, how is it so?

[1] Kauṣītaki Upaniṣad, III. 8.

[2] *Ibid*, II. 5.

[3] *Ibid*, III. 2.

[4] The Development of Greek Philosophy, pp. 204-213. According to Prof. L. T. Hobhouse, 'Aristotle with his *Κοινη αισθησις* rather implies the opposite view."

First, we must consider his enumeration of the senses called prāṇas. There are the eleven senses correlated with the sensibles as the subject with the object: (1) vital breath and breathing,[1] (2) speech and word, (3) nose and odour, (4) eye and sight, (5) ear and sound, (6) tongue and taste, (7) hands and action, (8) body and pleasure-and-pain (*i.e.* sensation of touch, muscular sensations, hunger and thirst, etc.), (9) propagative organ and delight-joy-and-offspring, (10) feet and locomotion, and (11) mind and thoughts-and-desires.[2]

The senses and objects.

Historically this enumeration of the senses belongs to Gārgyāyaṇa.[3] There is nevertheless a little difference between the two enumerations. Gārgyāyaṇa regarded what he called the vital breath (prāṇa), speech (vāk) and mind (manas) as three names expressive of the three aspects (masculine, feminine, and neuter) of the faculty or functional activity of the soul. Pratardana, on the contrary, discriminated the vital breath from the remaining ten senses. Moreover, Gārgyāyaṇa assigned as functions thinking and willing to Reason (prajñā), while Pratardana assigned them to Mind (manas).

There is something perplexing in both the enumerations. With regard to the subject, there is apparently a confusion between the organ of sense on the one hand, and the sense-faculty or active exercise of it on the other. And as to the object, there is involved a general confusion between the object of sense on the one hand, and the awareness and discrimination[4] of the active exercise of a faculty on the other.

The defect of terminology.

But in the case of Pratardana, too, there is a clear way of escape from this confusion, and that is to

[1] Kauṣītaki Upaniṣad, III. 2.

[2] *Ibid*, III. 5. See for Śaṅkara's views about the enumeration of the senses Thibaut's "Vedānta-sūtras," S. B. E., Vol. XXXVIII, II. 4. 5-10.

[3] *Ibid*, I. 7.

[4] Prajñāpana, vijijñāsā.

restrict, as he was ready to do,[1] the meaning of the term subject to a special faculty and its active exercise, and the meaning of the term object to the content of perception and of thought.

Pratardana's enumeration of the senses and the objects of sense is defective. But the defect lies merely in the detail. Essentially, there is no reason why we should not appreciate his discovery of the uniting function of Prāṇa, the central sense. He conceives that there are the special senses (such as the eye, the ear, etc.,) each of which is 'bound up' (sahâpyeti, goes together), or correlated with the specific sensibles (sight, sound, etc.,) as the subject with the object. Conversely, there are the specific objects defining the faculties of the special senses. Every process of sense is an act in some measure complete in itself, according as every sense apprehends its own object, and apprehends it as a unit, even with regard to the time, the moment at which the sense-operation takes place.[2] Hence it must be said that every act of sense-perception is in its own nature a mode of cognition. Pratardana presses nevertheless the inquiry: are not the special senses with their plurality of functions and multiplicity of modes in some way expressions of a common central sense?

If the special senses are expressions of a common central sense, then further questions are bound to emerge, what is it? and what is the nature of that relation in which the function of each special sense stands to the common central activity? And if, on the other hand, they are not expressions of a common central sense such as Prāṇa, then how is it that life pulsating, all the special senses are enlivened, *i.e.*, stimulated into action (praṇaṁ prāṇantaṁ sarve prāṇā anuprāṇanti)? Similarly if they are not animated and unified by a common principle, then how is it that the special senses can not exercise

[1] Kauṣītaki Upaniṣad, III. 8.

[2]. As Śaṅkara says, "ekasmin kāle sūkṣma sucyagrena śatapatravedhanavad aspaṣṭa vibhinna kālāni vyākhyeyāni."

their functions all at the same time, at the same moment, but that they can do so only one at a time, each as a unit (ekaikam)? What does this striking fact of our mental life point to? All this consideration forced upon Pratardana this conclusion: Each special sense, in the exercise of its function becomes in some way united with the rest.[1]

Conclusion as to the unity of mental life.

Even mind, the functions of which are thinking and willing, is not an exception to this rule. The uniting function thus involved in the process of sense, nay, in all forms of mental process, is assignable to nothing but Prāṇa—vitality and sensibility in the soul. For, proceeding from an empirical foundation, we cannot but admit, first, that the complete fact of our existence is Life (Prāṇa),[2] and secondly, that the fundamental function of a living body is breathing or respiration. In regard to the former truth Pratardana, following Mahidāsa and others, argued that the organ or faculty of speech, sight, hearing, thinking, action, or locomotion is not essential to or absolutely necessary for organic existence. For we see there are dumb men who cannot speak, blind who cannot see, deaf who cannot hear, infants who cannot think, and so on, whereas the notion of a living body without life is impossible.[3] And as to the latter truth, that respiration is the fundamental function of life, he calls upon us to consider these two facts of common experience:

(1) The presence of the function of breathing during dreamless sleep, that is to say, during the periodical cessation of all sensations, nay, all forms of mental activity.

[1]. Kauṣītaki Upaniṣad, III. 7; "ekabhuyāni vai prāṇa bhutvaikaikam etāni sarvāni prajñāpayatīti." By ekaikam (one by one) Śaṅkara understands that when any one of special senses "svavyapāram kurvat sarve prāṇa nikhilāni indriyāni.........eka-helayā vyapāram kurvanti." Cowell follows in his translation the interpretation of Śaṅkara. But Max Müller seems to have taken a diametrically opposite view, when he translates the passage thus: "The prāṇas become one, for (otherwise) no one could at the same time make known a name by speech, see a form with the eye, hear a sound with the ear, think a thought with the mind, etc., etc."

[2]. Kauṣītaki Upaniṣad, III. 2; III. 8.

[3]. *Ibid*, III. 3; S.B.E., Vol., I. pp. 294-95.

(2) The final cessation of all sensations and all active functions of the mind previous to death, and the presence of the process of respiration till the last moment.[1]

Pratardana was thus inclined to maintain that what we call breathing is but an active manifestation of what vital breath is potentially, just as vital breath, in its turn, is the potentiality of an organic body. This remark holds good of every special sense, for the operations of the senses are no more than manifold expresions of one and the same activity that characterises Life itself. And what we call the vital principle is just again the animating drinciple. All the organs of sense are but so many animated parts of the animated body taken as a whole. This is evidently the reason that led Pratardana to give the general name prāṇa to all the senses.

Life, soul and the senses.

.t is made clear that the metaphysical foundation of Pratardana's psychology lies in the earlier views of Mahidāsa. The complete fact of our existence is Life. In other words, Life is the potentiality of a living body. It is besides the one fact which is conceivable as outlasting the dissolution of body, and without which a living being is inconceivable. Life is therefore the first principle of things, and that which is the first cause is again the final cause or end and *vice versa* (yo vai prāṇaḥ sā prajñā, yā vā prajñā sa prāṇaḥ).

Life as the first cause is not many, but one. So conceived, the self or soul presents within the realm of change its two-fold aspect. In one aspect, it is the vital principle—the principle in virtue of which we can discharge all functions as living beings; and in the other aspect, it is Reason inherent in the soul—Reason, in virtue of which we can discharge all functions as rational beings. Under the former aspect, Life represents the central sense, by the uniting function of which we can account for the common feature exhibited by manifold activities of the animated organism. It is natural, then, to assume that Pra-

[1]. Kauṣītakī, III. 3.

tardana considered the heart to be the central organ of sense; the faculty of the central sense is the vital breath, and the active exercise of this faculty goes by the name of breathing. Each special sense can exercise its function, can realise its object, only in co-operation with the central sense described here as life or vitality. The view which Pratardana thus took of life is the teleological.

B. The unity of Prajñātman—the cognitive aspect of Pratardana's psychology.

Sentience or consciousness in general was viewed by Pratardana as but one of the two aspects of the self which here represents the concrete subject in reference to which we form all judgments concerning the physical and psychical activities; its other aspect is vitality. Pratardana is right to observe that the mere active exercise of a faculty does not complete the work of the sense. For beside it, or in it, there is involved another function, which may be described as the passive impression of the object of sense on the conscious sentient soul. The function thus described may be simply the awareness of the process of thought or the knowledge of the content of thought, or the discrimination of the objects of sense-perception. How can we account for this function but by the unity of the conscious sentient soul? For, were there no such unity, then why should a man sometimes say, "My mind being absent, attending elsewhere, I did not apprehend that vision with the vision, that sound with the hearing, and so forth?"[1]

Theory of attention.

This common sensibility, as distinguished from the specific sensibility of the special senses, belongs ultimately to the conscious self.[1] The conscious self must be in its own nature all-embracing so as to comprehend all differences within

The relation of objects to Prajñā.

[1] Kauṣītaki Upaniṣad, III. 7. "anyatra me mano'bhūd ityāha nāham etān nāma prajñāsiṣam."

its unity. It represents the same element of consciousness or reason (prajñā) in special forms of expression. The so-called objects are directly related to this common element of consciousness—to Prajñā, the innate discriminating reason in the soul. Pratardana perhaps thought, in agreement with Gārgyāyaṇa, that it is the inherent desire of the eternal Reason to express itself that calls forth the thinking faculty of the soul into an active exercise. It may be said that the impression of a specific object on the sentient soul is accountable at last for the active exercise of the function of a special sense.

It is noteworthy that Pratardana's ground for the discrimination of the sensibles from one another is teleological. For he repeatedly insisted that we should not attempt to investigate so much the knowledge of what speech is, as of who speaks, —not so much the knowledge of what odour is, as of who smells, and so on.[2]

The teleological view of the conscious subject which Pratardana thus adopted was not free from ambiguity but lent itself naturally to the interpretation that the mode in which the senses receive impressions from the objective world is passive. The theory of the passive receptivity of impressions is discarded by Nāgasena.[3] It is doubtful whether the theory is reconcilable with Pratardana's central conception. Perhaps the following remarks of Prof. Adamson on Aristotle's view will throw some light on Pratardana's position. "Sense-perception, for example, taken as a whole, is the actualisation of what the organ of vision is potentially, and in strictness the

[1] *Cf.* Buddha's theory of mind as a *sensus communis* or a coördinating factor in sense: "these five senses...have different fields, different ranges; they do not share each other's field and range. Of them thus mutually independent, *mano* is their resort, and *mano* pertakes of, enjoys, the field and range of them all." Mrs. Rhys Davids, "Buddhist Psychology," pp. 68-69.

[2] Kauṣītaki Upaniṣad, III. 8.

[3] "The Questions of King Milinda," I. pp. 86, 133. The gist of Nāgasena's contention against the theory of soul (Vedagū) as the knower is that "there is no agent in sensation independent of the specific functioning of each sense," See Mrs Rhys Davids, "Buddhist Psychology," p. 164.

concrete subject about which predicates relating to vision may be made is here neither the eye taken in abstraction nor the activity of seeing taken in abstraction, but the seeing eye."[1]

2. *Theory of Knowledge.*

One of the principal ends to which Pratardana directed his speculative efforts was to explain away the opposition implied between the views of his two predecessors Mahidāsa and Gārgyāyaṇa. To Mahidāsa that which is fundamental or integral to the life of soul, taken as a part of actuality, is the subject or act of knowing, and accordingly the object or content of knowledge comes into existence only for the sake of the subject. To Gārgyāyaṇa, on the contrary, that which is fundamental to the soul, conceived as the self-conscious subject, is the object, and accordingly the subject exists only for the sake of the object. Pratardana found that both of them were right, and that both of them were wrong. For, as he thought, there can be no subjects apart from or independent of objects, as there can be no objects apart from or independent of subjects. For on either side alone knowledge is impossible,[2] a theory of cognition that was latterly developed by Buddha and his disciples to its fullest possibilities.

The object is generally said to be placed outside or external to the subject (parastāt prativihita). But the distinction is only in our own mind. They are really not separable the one from the other, representing as they do two aspects of one and the same act of perception or cognition. Taking the object to mean the content of perception, and the subject to

The subject and the object are not separable from or independent of each other.

[1] The Development of Greek Philosophy, pp. 202-203.

[2] Kauṣītaki Upaniṣad, III. 8 : " yaddhi bhūtamātrā na syur na prajñāmātrāḥ syur yad va prajñāmātrā na syur na bhūtamātrāḥ syur na hyanyatarato rūpam kiñcana sidhyan no... " *Cf.* Buddha's theory of knowledge : " Because of sight [lit. eye] and visible matter (rūpa) arises visual consciousness, etc." Mrs. Rhys Davids's "Buddhist Psychology," p. 68 *foll.*

mean the act of perceiving, it may be said that the content is a mental fact not separate from the perception itself. In other words, it is in the actual exercise of the function of the conscious subject that we can realise both perception and what is perceived. Pratardana gave the following as an illustration of his point. "As in a car the circumference of a wheel is placed on the spokes, and the spokes on the nave, thus are the objects (circumference) placed on the subjects (spokes), and the subjects on the Prāṇa."[1]

3. *Ethics.*

There is seemingly a marked contrast in tone between Pratardana's psychological doctrine and its ethical conclusions. Prāṇa the substratum of consciousness or cognitive soul (prajñatman) is the sustainer of the world, the supreme monarch, the sovran Lord of all, and alike the individual ego 'bodiless, changeless and deathless,' and so substantially untouched by moral consequences of action which passes in the world by the name of good or evil.[2] By no deed of a person is "his life harmed, not by the murder of his mother, not by the murder of his father, not by theft, not by the killing of a Brāhman. If he is going to commit a sin, the bloom does not depart from his face."[3] Prāṇa as a universal principle is the creator of circumstances that lead a person to do good or evil.[4]

This theory of Pratardana which runs apparently counter to Jaivali's doctrine of five Fires was subsequently developed and followed in its letter and spirit by Naciketā, Pūraṇa Kassapa, Pakudha Kaccāyana and the author of the Bhagavad Gītā. And the same was subsequently criticised by Mahāvīra, Buddha and Śvetāśvatara as Yadṛcchāvāda or Chance-theory of action.

[1] Kauṣitaki Upaniṣad, III. 8.
[2] *Ibid*, III. 9.
[3] *Ibid*, III. 1.
[4] *Ibid*, III. 9.

Some of Buddha's expressions in two Dhammapada verses "mātaraṁ pitaraṁ hantvā, etc."[1] reminds one of Pratardana's actual words "na mātṛivadhena na pitṛivadhena, etc." The very language of the Dhammapada verses indicates that Buddha was remembering some such theory as that of Pratardana while contrasting with it his own theory, metaphorically inculcating the moral excellence of an Arahat through the killing of his desires and other sundry causes of moral bondage.

CHAPTER VIII.

UDDĀLAKA.

With Uddālaka Āruṇi Indian wisdom seems to have taken a turn which may, for want of a better expression, be called systematic. Both in his tendency towards biological speculations and in his conceptions of Matter and Spirit Uddālaka shows a close resemblance to Anaxagoras. Like Pythagoras again, he seems to have conceived a tripartite (trivṛit) universe, or contemplated a three-fold division of the formed universe into the region of the element of fire, that of water or air, and that of food or earth.

Uddālaka, Anaxagoras and Pythagoras.

Uddālaka was born in a Brāhman family. He was son of Aruṇa and father of Śvetaketu, a famous Vedic scholar of his time. In fact the whole family of the Āruṇis is distinguished in history for Vedic learning.[1] In the Chāndogya Upaniṣad[2] Uddālaka is described as a younger contemporary of Jaivali. In another passage of the same Upaniṣad[3] we have mention of Aupamanyava[4] of the old school (Prācīna-śālā), Paulușī Indradyumna, Śārkarākṣya,[5] Buḍila-Āśvataraśvi,[6] and Aśvapati Kekaya as being among the contemporaries of

His life and works.

[1] Oldenberg pointedly says: "When the time shall have come for the inquiries, which will have to be made to create order out of the chaotic mass of names of teachers and other celebrities of the Brāhmaṇa period, it may turn out that the most important centre for the formation and diffusion of the Brāhmaṇa doctrine will have to be looked for in Āruṇi and in the circles which surround him. The most divergent lines of tradition meet in the person of Uddālaka Āruṇi."—"Buddha," translated by W. Hoey, 1882, p. 396.

[2] Chandogya Upaniṣad, V. 3-10; cp. Bṛihad Āraṇyaka Upaniṣad, VI. 2. 1-16.

[3] *Ibid*, V. 11. 1-4.

[4] In the Jaina Rājavārttika, VIII. 1, Aupamanyava is classed among the Vinaya-Vādins (Moralists).

[5] Āruṇis and Śarkarākṣyas are mentioned in the Aitareya Āraṇyaka, II. 1.4.5.

[6] In the Bṛihad Āraṇyaka Upaniṣad, V. 14-8, Aśvataraśvi is referred to as a contemporary of King Janaka, that is, of Yājñavalkya.

Uddālaka. The Kauṣītaki Upaniṣad[1] alludes to him as a contemporary of Gārgyāyaṇa, while the Bṛihad Āraṇyaka Upaniṣad refers to him in several places as a contemporary of Yājñavalkya.[2] It also appears from two separate lists of teachers in the latter Upaniṣad that Yājñavalkya was one of the successors and pupils of Uddālaka or of his son Śvetaketu. Among the Buddhist records, the Uddālaka Jātaka[3] has a very special interest for the historian, as it adds some new information regarding the life of Uddālaka.

The Uddālaka Jātaka associates the origin of the name Uddālaka (Sk. Auddālaka=Śvetaketu),[4] with the Uddāla tree under which he was conceived, and would have us believe, among other things, that Auddālaka or Śvētaketu was the fruit of an illegal union of his mother with a wise, learned Brāhman who was the prime-minister to the then King Brahmadatta of Benares. The account is not only false, but categorically malicious There is nevertheless a truth behind it, namely, that the Buddhist historian evidently confounded Auddālaka with Philalethes Jābāla.[5]

Evidence of Uddālaka-Jātaka.

It is recorded in the Uddālaka Jātaka that Auddālaka was educated at Takkasilā in Gandhāra. In the Chāndogya Upaniṣad[6] Uddālaka himself clearly points to Gandhāra as a famous seat of learning, and his is perhaps the earliest mention of Gandhāra as a seat of learning in Sanskrit literature.

We further learn from the above Jātaka that Auddālaka, giving up ascetic life, entered the service of the King

[1] Kauṣītaki Upaniṣad, I. 1.

[2] Bṛihad Āraṇyaka Upaniṣad, VI. 5.3; VI. 3.7.

[3] No. 487. Translated by Mr. Rouse, and also in Fick, Sociale Gliederung zu Buddhist zeit, p. 13 ff.

[4] Pali Uddālaka is equivalent to Sanskrit Auddālaka, *i.e.*, the son of Uddālaka. *Vide* Setaketu Jātaka (No. 377) in which Setaketu is represented as the son of a Udicca-Brāhman, Brāhman of Northern India, *i.e.*, of Uttara Pañcala, *cf.* Fausböll's Jātaka, I, p. 401.

[5] Chāndogya Upaniṣad, IV. 4. 1-5.

[6] *Ibid*, VI. 14. 1-2.

of Benares as a sub-minister under his father. As we also learn from the Upaniṣad under reference, he was generally addressed by his family-name Gautama. From this a question is apt to arise if Uddālaka's son Śvetaketu was the author of the legal treatise, entitled the Gautama Dharma-sūtra in the sense that the existing Dharma-Śāstra of this name was a later compilation mainly based upon an older manual by Auddālaka or Śvetaketu. It seems very likely that he was so. Without dogmatising, however, on so difficult a question as this, we shall urge here a few points in support of our hypothesis.

Auddālaka or Śvetaketu was probably the author of the Gautama-Dharma-sūtra in its older form.

(1) The following quotation from Mr. Rouse's translation of the Uddālaka-Jātaka shows how Auddālaka's social and ethical views might be influenced by his father's philosophy, embodied in the Chāndogya Upaniṣad (VI. 1.). The quotation is from a conversation between Auddālaka and his father the primeminister of Benares. The former inquires.

"What makes the Brahmin? how can he be perfect? tell me this. What is a righteous man? and how wins he Nirvāṇa's bliss?"

The latter replies,

> "He has no field, no goods, no wish, no kin,
> Careless of life, no lusts, no evil ways;
> Even such a Brahmin peace of soul shall win,
> So as one true to duty men him praise."

The former again asks,

> "Khattiya, Brahmin, Vessa, Sudda and Caṇḍāla, Pukkusa,
> All these can be compassionate, can win Nirvāṇa's bliss:
> Who among all the saints is there who worse or better is?"

The other replies,

> "None among all the saints is there who worse or better is."

Auddālaka retorts,

"You are a Brahmin, then, for nought : vain is your rank I wis."

Now in his further reply, the prime minister strikes the key-note of Uddālaka's philosophy :

"With canvas dyed in many a tint pavilions may be made :
The roof, a many-coloured dome : one colour is the shade.[1]
Even so, when men are purified, so is it here on earth :
The good perceive that they are saints, and never ask their birth."

(2) The Bṛihad Āraṇyaka Upaniṣad [2] refers to a doctrine, called the doctrine of Mortar (Mantha). Uddālaka is said to have been its original author. The interest of the Mortar-doctrine is two-fold, first, that it illustrates Uddālaka's conception of original matter as the finest mixture of things—of all that is qualitatively distinct. It has also an interesting ritualistic aspect and touches on the general topics of the Gṛihya and Dharma-sūtras. Uddālaka's one invariable cry in regard to his Mortar-doctrine is marriage, and the same cry we hear, more or less, throughout the Gautama Dharma-Śastra. In the Jaina Rāja-vārttika, the Mānthanikas are classed among the Kriyā-vādins. The Aśvalāyana Gṛihya Sutra seems to have cited this Mantha-doctrine in the Bṛihad Āraṇyaka as a canonical basis of its rules regarding the practical application of the principles of eugenics. It is not improbable that Erotic science (Kāma-sūtra) developed on the lines of Uddālaka's Mantha-doctrine. The Vātsyāyana Kāma-sūtra singles out Śvetaketu as the first human originator of the Indian Erotic science. It is also likely that the Upaniṣad passages, no less than the Uddālaka Jātaka, confounded Uddālaka with his son Auddālaka, *i.e.*, Śvetaketu, and mixed up their doctrines. The Mahābhārata tradition that Śvetaketu was the first institutor of marriage seems to point indirectly

[1] Fausböll's Jātaka, IV, p. 304 : Nānārattehi vatthehi vimānaṁ bhavati chāditaṁ, Na tesaṁ chāyā vatthānaṁ, so rāgo anupajjatha.

[2] Bṛihad Āraṇyaka Upaniṣad, III, 7, 1.

[3] *Ibid*, VI. 3, 1.

to the same conclusion, *viz.*, that Śvetaketu was the originator of Erotic science.

(3) Among the existing Dharma Sūtras and Śāstras Gautama's is the least philosophical, and this fact can be explained on the hypothesis that the author of an older Dharmasūtra, probably bearing the same title, was no other than Śvetaketu who, although a talented Vedic scholar and honoured in the Apastamba Dharmasūtra as a *śrutarṣi*, is said to have been puzzled whenever a question touching the genesis of life or the nature of soul was put to him. The Vṛiddha-Gautama-saṁhitā expressly mentions a legal manual prepared by Uddālaka (Uddālaka-kritā-dharmā, Ch. I), and it is not impossible that the Saṁhitā supplies us just with another instance where the father has been confounded with the son.

Other views of Uddālaka referred to in the Milinda,

In addition to the Mortar-doctrine another view is ascribed to Uddālaka in the Chāndogya Upaniṣad.[1] Uddālaka said to Aśvapati Kekaya, "The earth (pṛithivī) is the self, the essential part of the solar system (vaiśvānara-ātmā)." The king could not agree with Uddālaka, that he considered the earth to be the feet or resting-place (pratiṣṭhā) of the solar universe, the world of life, the soul of the solar universe being the sun. Uddālaka elsewhere designates earth as food (anna)[2] on which the world of life depends for sustenance. Some such view as this was in the mind of King Milinda, when he refers to the view, that the earth sustains the world,[3] and wrongly attributes the same to Pūraṇa Kassapa.

and in he Sūtrakṛitāṅga.

In the Jaina Sūtrakṛitāṅga [4] Sudharman, the chief disciple of Mahāvīra, calls attention of Jambusvāmin to a current philosophical view, which may be aptly described as a type of materialistic pantheism. The view seems to have a direct reference

[1] Chāndogya Upaniṣad, V. II, 1, ff.

[2] *Ibid*, VI. 2, 4, *cf.* Thibaut's "Vedānta-sūtras," S. B. E., Vol. XXXVIII, II, 3.12.

[3] "Paṭhavi...lokam pāleti." *Vide* The Questions of King Milinda, S. B. E., XXXI, p. 9.

[4] Sutrakṛitāṅga, I. 1.1. 7-9.

to the philosophy of Yājñavalkya,[1] and only an indirect reference to the philosophy of Uddālaka. "Some foolish philosophers say that there are these five elements—earth, water, fire, air and ether. These are the five original principles of things. From them emerges one (imperishable, intelligible essence.[2]) On the disintegration of the five elements, the materiality of the embodied soul vanishes. But just as the earth, though it is but one mass,[3] presents manifold forms, so the intelligent principle appears under various forms."[4]

Uddālaka's thirst after knowledge, and simplicity of character.

All the existing records, whether Brāhmanical or not in origin speak of Uddālaka as a life-long student: one who was old in years, but never too old to learn. This would seem to be true, because the verdict is so unanimous. He was an earnest seeker of truth, and an intense lover of wisdom. He sought after truth without stopping for a moment to consider from whom he might learn it. His conduct, in this respect, was in harmony with his philosophy. By his personal example he tried to establish a commonwealth of thought and culture, which admitted of no distinction of age or colour. The boy Śvetaketu goes to learn, but his father stops him, saying, "Wait, we shall both go." The charm of Uddālaka's character is no doubt his native simplicity, the simplicity with which we are all born, and which never left Uddālaka. All his words which now survive are impregnated with this one element of his personality. It surprised Jaivali, King of Pañcāla, to see Uddālaka, though a teacher of high renown, coming as a pupil, with his son Śvetaketu. Gārgyāyaṇa, too, well remarked, when he said, "You are worthy of Brahman, the Divine knowledge, O

[1] Bṛihad Āraṇyaka Upaniṣad, IV. 4.4; IV. 5.13.

[2] Śīlāṅka explains "ega" as "ekaḥ kaścid cidrūpaḥ bhūtavyatirikta ātmā."

[3] "Ahatesiṁ vināsenaṁ vināso ho-i dehino."

[4] "Jahā ya pudhair thubhe ege nānāhi disa-i, evaṁ bho kasiṇe lo-e viṇṇu nānāhi dīsa-ī."

Gautama." Even the malicious Uddālaka Jātaka cannot help noting, "so eager he was for knowledge, and did menial service for them, begging them to teach him their own wisdom." It is not impossible that the Sophistic movement, characteristic of Indian philosophy before Mahāvīra and Buddha, had originated with Uddālaka Āruṇi. The method of his quest of knowledge is a singular and most striking fact, and when a history of Indian Wanderers is written, his name must be singled out as almost a starting point. At any rate we cannot resist here the temptation of quoting the views of Dr. Rhys Davids: "The early history of the Wanderers has yet to be written. We hear of a similar custom as already followed in one isolated case by a sacrificing priest. Uddālaka Āruṇi, of the Gotama family, of whom so many other legends have been preserved, is said to have wandered about the country offering a gold coin, as a lure for the timid, to any one who, in a disputation on spiritual matter, could prove him wrong. When defeated he becomes the pupil of his conqueror (Buddhist India, p. 249).

Cākrāyaṇa and Jābāla.

It also may be noted that among Uddālaka's predecessors, Uṣasti Cākrāyaṇa and Philalethes Jābāla set two other noble examples. Of them, Uṣasti was ready to eat any kind of food, and from the hands of any one, in so far as it was a question of bare necessity with him.[1] The personal example set by Jābāla was moral courage to confess his obscure origin.

His Philosophy.

Uddālaka and Mahidāsa compared.

By whatever name—Pantheism or otherwise—Uddālaka's philosophy be called, we ought to bear in mind that its entire metaphysical foundation is laid on an empirical basis. For, like his predecessor Mahidāsa, he was unwilling to enlarge the scope of his philosophical investigations beyond experience.[2]

[1] Chāndogya Upaniṣad, I. 10, 1-6.

[2] "Na nūdya kaścanāśrutam amatam avijñātam udāhariṣyati." Chāndogya Upaniṣad, VI. 4. 5.

He shows, moreover, a resemblance to Mahidāsa by stedfastly maintaining that there can be no transition into Being but from Being. How could it be, he asked, that something should come out of nothing?[1] Thus in the fullest agreement with Mahidāsa and Gārgyāyaṇa, Uddālaka thought the reason of a transition from the root to the shoot is in the Deity (Devatā).[2] The Deity is an actually existing being, and such a being is one, one only, without a second.[3]

The task of Uddālaka was to transcend dualism.

Even then, Uddālaka had, in one respect, a far harder task before him, and that within the realm of the physical. For Mahidāsa, as we saw, did not succeed in getting beyond dualism, the dualism involved in his conceptions of the first matter and the first mover. The following verdict of Prof. Erdmann on Aristotle applies equally to Mahidāsa. "In common with the whole of antiquity, Aristotle also fails to transcend dualism, because he excludes matter from the Deity, to which it therefore remains opposed, even though reduced to a mere potentiality."[4] In taking God and Matter to denote two distinct principles, Mahidāsa had doubtless this advantage on his side, that he could thereby easily account for the two constant phenomena of nature, called life and death. The task Uddālaka set himself was to transcend the dualism in which Mahidāsa was entangled. But in accomplishing this task, he had to admit that every shoot presupposes a root. The point on which he differed from his predecessor was that Water cannot be posited as the first root, because Water is itself but a shoot to which Fire (tejas) is the root. In the same way, Fire, too, must be viewed as a shoot, though it is indeed the first shoot in relation to the

[1] "Kathaṁ asataḥ sajjāyeteti? Sat tveva somyedam agra āsīd ekam evādvitīyam." Chāndogya Upaniṣad, VI. 2. 2.

[2] *Ibid*, VI. 3. 1.

[3] *Cf* Śaṅkara's interpretation, in Thibaut's 'Vedānta-sūtras,' S. B. E., Vol. XXXVIII, II. 3. 5 foll.

[4] History of Philosophy, I. 87. 9.

first root, that is, the Deity.[1] Thus when we come to the Deity, all grounds of distinction between Mind and Matter disappear. For these two— Mind and Matter—are no more than two aspects of one and the same Deity, the manifestations of the same single Being.

1. Physics.

The metaphysical unity of Deity is the ground of explanation for the duality between matter and spirit.

Uddālaka's Deity (Devatā), which occurs here and there in Mahidāsa's phraseology,[2] is a most baffling term. But nothing is more certain than that it is on the whole a physical conception. We may suppose that in the realm of change the term applies to Matter or the material, as distinguished from Prāṇa, the Universal Spirit which is a living principle in a concrete existence (jīvātmā). This admitted, it would follow that the metaphysical unity is with Uddālaka but a mere presupposition or ground of explanation for the duality which obtains in the empirical world between what we call Matter and Spirit. Accordingly, in dealing with his physics we shall understand by the metaphysical Deity the original Matter which is pure and unmixed, one and indivisible, universal and unmanifested,—the Deity or whatever it is which lies wholly outside the material, and from which motion is generated and imparted to the material universe. Or, at best, we might interpret the term Deity as meaning that highly concentrated or attenuated form of matter which admits of no distinction whatever from mind, spirit or energy,—a condition in which matter is transformed into energy, acts as the vivifying principle, and therefore not distinguishable from motion itself. For the present we must leave aside any further consideration of the metaphysical Deity of Uddālaka, and shall concentrate our attention on his conceptions of Matter and Spirit.

[1] Chāndogya Upaniṣad, VI. 8. 4-6.; *Cf.* Buddhist India, p. 257, Uddālaka's influence on pantheistic thought.

[2] Aitareya Āraṇyaka, II. 4. 2. 1-2.

A. Matter.

Uddālaka had no other expression for Matter than Deity (Devatā). The three preponderating elements which Matter presents to experience are Fire (tejas), Water (āpa), and Earth (anna).[1] All these are called deities (devatās) because all are, according to Uddālaka, inhibited, inspirited, animated and motivated, in various measures, by one and the same Spirit,[2] that is, the Deity or living principle (prāṇa),—because, in other words, the will-to-be-many (bahu-bhavitum-icchā)[3] is inherent in each of them, in all things. In the case of the physical world, the subtilest or finest condition of Fire is ether (ākāśa—aditi, αειρον), the material foundation of sound; of Water the subtilest condition is air, the material foundation of motion in general; and of Earth, the subtilest condition is food or fertility (anna), the material foundation of life at large. In regard to an organism, the subtilest condition or particle (aṇiṣtha dhātu) of Fire (oily substance swallowed) is ether, the material basis of voice or speech (vāk); the intermediate condition (madhyama dhātu) is marrow (majjā); and the grossest condition (sthaviṣṭho dhātu) is bone (asthi). Of Water (liquid substance drunk), the subtilest condition is air or vitality (prāṇa), the material basis of all bodily functions; the intermediate condition is blood (lohita); and the grossest condition is urine (mūtra). Similarly, of Earth (solid food eaten), the subtilest condition is virility, the material basis of germ, psyche or mind (manas); the intermediate condition is flesh (māṁsa), and the grossest condition is fæces (purīṣa).[4]

Three preponderating elements: Fire, Water, and Earth.

Here three points deserve special notice. (1) That in Uddālaka's theory, as in that of Anaxagoras, the ultimate fact is

[1] Chāndogya Upaniṣad, VI. 2. 3-4. *Cf.* Śankara's opinion, Thibaut's 'Vedāntasūtras,' S. B. E., Vol. XXXVIII, II. 3. 12.

[2] *Ibid*, VI. 3.2.

[3] Implied in "aikṣata bahu syām," *ibid*, VI. 2. 3-4.

[4] *Ibid*, VI. 5. 1-4; VI. 6. 1-5.

that things are all qualitatively distinct from one another—(dhātus).[1] (2) That the parts into which each qualitatively distinct thing is divisible are not only three, but infinite. (3) That in adopting a doctrine of Being similar to the Eleatic, Uddālaka could not reasonably maintain that things become or qualitatively distinct kinds of matter are transformed into one another. As Prof. Adamson explains the position of Anaxagoras, "If then an empirical fact, such as the assimilation of nutriment, appears to show us the conversion (say) of corn into flesh and bone, we must interpret this as meaning that the corn contains in itself, in such minute quantities as to be imperceptible, just that into which it is transformed. It veritably consists of particles of flesh, and blood, and marrow, and bone."[2] It is very curious, indeed, to discover that the resemblance between the two thinkers of two distant countries should be so close, or that their expressions should be almost identical. But Uddālaka gave another illustration. Take, for instance, the case of curds. When curds are churned, the minutest portion rises upwards, and becomes butter.[3] From this it does not follow that curds are transformed into butter, but that the seed of butter is already contained in curds, and so as to everything else. In other words, things are contained in one another.

Things being qualitatively distinct, cannot transform into one another.

It is clear that Uddālaka conceived the Deity or Matter as a continuous, indivisible whole, in which are mixed up all things which are infinitely divisible, and qualitatively distinct.[4] His conception of the All must, under all conditions be elicited from what is generally known as the Mortar-doctrine. According to Jaimini's interpretation, "Various things

Matter is a complete mixture of various kinds of seeds.

[1] "Attano sabhāvam dhāretīti dhātu," says Buddhaghosa

[2] The Development of Greek Philosophy, p. 50.

[3] Chāndogya Upaniṣad, VI. 6. 1: "dadhnaḥ somya mathyamānasya yo aṇima sa ūrddhaḥ samudīṣati tat sarpirbhavati."

[4] *Cf.* Śaṅkara' discussions in Thibaut's Vedānta Sūtra, S. B. E., Vol. XXXVIII, II.3.7.

are put into it, pounded and mixed—such is the meaning of the term mortar (mantha)." [1] As Uddālaka himself puts it, "Just as in a mortar various kinds of cultivated seeds—rice, barley, sesamum, and so forth—are pounded and mixed, and moistened, first with curds, honey and ghee, and finally with clarified butter (ājya), so as to make a smooth paste," so is Matter.[2] Matter consists of innumerable seeds of things (bījāni), or minds (manas, monads?), so mixed together that there is no void space. The image is appropriate. By curds, honey and ghee he signifies three preponderating elements, or secondary deities, as he also calls them—namely, Fire, Water, and Earth. And by clarified butter he signifies the Deity or pure, unmixed Matter or Spirit.

Two objections to Uddālaka's theory of Matter, and how he met them.

In establishing his conception of the nature of Matter as a complete whole, without having in it any absolute parts, as well as his notion of the immutable relations of things among themselves, Uddālaka had to give satisfactory answers for these two questions, First, if there be no void space in the material, how can we conceive motion? Uddālaka's simple answer is, it is a motion within, a churning motion, corresponding to what Anaxagoras describes as the whirling or vortex motion. And secondly, if the things be so mixed together and contained in one another, how to account for the development or manifestation of names and forms (nāmarūpam), *i. e.*, of individual things? Things emerge out of things by the aid of the churning motion within the material, by the gradual spontaneous unfolding of nature.

B. Spirit.

Besides the ambiguous terms Being and Deity (Sat, Devatā), Uddālaka uses other expressions to denote universal Spirit in various degrees of manifestation. These are vital

[1] "drāvyadravye prakṣipta mathitaḥ saktavaḥ." (quoted by Max Müller, S. B. E., XV, p. 210).

[2] Bṛihad Āraṇyaka, VI. 3. 4 ; VI. 3.13.

spirit (prāṇa), living principle (jīvātmā), and mind or psyche or monad (manas). It is remarkable that the so-called Mortar doctrine[1] of Uddālaka was interpreted by Śaṅkara as the vision of life (prāṇa-darśana). Like some of his predecessors, notably Mahidāsa and Jaivali,[2] Uddālaka observed in the general scheme of existence the working together of two principles,—combination and separation, so to speak, of two elements—the feminine and the masculine, the material and the spiritual or psychical. From this we may further presume that his speculations, no less than those of Anaxagoras, were influenced by his observation of nature, especially the phenomena of animal life, and represent thus a landmark in the history of Sāṅkhya ideas of Puruṣa and Prakṛiti.

Śaṅkara's interpretation of the doctrine of Mortar. Two principles of things.

By the term living principle (jīvātmā) Uddālaka understood the atom of atoms, so to speak, or that pure, unmixed and indivisible matter which acts as the animating principle (aṇima) of things which are mixed together and divisible into an infinite number of parts. For him it is in every respect identical with universal spirit, except that it is individual or connected in some mysterious way with concrete things. The living principle is, in other words, for Uddālaka, as for Mahidāsa, the potentiality of living bodies,—the real seed of things. It is, for example, that potentiality or vitality in an infinitesimally small seed from which a huge banyan tree springs into existence.[3] Thus we are to understand that a living body is an animated whole, and that it is one and the same spirit which animates all its parts. When this spirit[4] leaves any branch of a tree, that withers,

The living principle.

[1] The earlier form of the doctrine is to be found in the Chāndogya Upaniṣad, V. 2 4. Its rudiments are also to be traced in the Kauṣītaki Upaniṣad, II. 3.

[2] Chāndogya Upaniṣad, V. 4-9.

[3] *Ibid*, VI. 12. 1-2.

[4] It is in Śaṅkara's phraseology "Mukhya prāṇa," see his comments on the Vedānta-sūtra, II. 4. 17.

i.e., ceases to be an integral part of the living whole. When it leaves another branch, that too withers. And when, in this way, it leaves finally the whole tree, the whole tree withers and perishes. But the living principle never dies. According to Uddālaka, there are chiefly beings of three origins[1], while Mahidāsa spoke of four. These are described as the oviparous, the viviparous, and those which are propagated from germs (*i.e.*, plants). All these are in various degrees animated by the living principle, that is to say, there are the manifestations of the same universal Spirit. The living principle being of an imperishable nature, whether a lion, or a wolf, or a boar, or a worm, all are born again and again.[2] Prāṇa (spirit) is what is really existent in the universe. The functions of the mind die out with the body. He tells us explicitly that mind is joined to life, and that sleep results from the absorption of the mind into Praṇa. Mind is linked to Prāṇa which is its abode (āyatana) or resting place (upaśraya), *i.e.*, substratum. While a person sleeps, his mind subsides in its bond the Prāṇa like a string-bound bird obtaining no other shelter resorts at last to the chain itself.[3]

The main question remains yet to be answered. What was the original condition of Matter, and how were concrete things gradually formed from it? Uddālaka's reply to this is exactly similar to that of Anaxagoras. Matter was at first a chaotic mass, like the juices of various trees indiscriminately blended together in honey.[4] In order to develop names-and-forms, to discriminate things from one another, or to set them in order, the universal Spirit came not in its universal form, but as the living principle, and entered into Fire, Water, and Earth. After separating their component

Uddālaka, Kātyāyana, and Kaṇāda.

[1] Chāndogya Upaniṣad, VI. 3. 1: "bhūtānām trīṇi eva bījāni." Note that three is for Uddālaka a number of sacredotal character.

[2] *Ibid*, VI. 10. 2.

[3] *Ibid*, VI. 8. 1.

[4] *Ibid*, Upaniṣad, VI. 9.1-2.

18

but qualitatively distinct parts (dhātus), it made numerous new combinations of them.[1] By propounding the theory of combination and separation of particles, Uddālaka anticipated the atomic theory of Kaṇāda, as by maintaining that all things are qualitatively distinct, he prepared the way for Kakudha Kātyāyana (Pakudha Kaccāyana).

2. Theory of knowledge.

In accordance with his physical doctrine, Uddālaka propounded an empirical theory of knowledge. Henceforth let no one speak, he asserts, of anything but that which is heard, perceived or cognised.[2] He seems repeatedly to point out:—The only right method of scientific investigation into the nature of reality is that of inference by way of induction. He defines the method of induction as that procedure of reasoning which enables the knowing subject to infer the nature of the All from the observation of the nature of any one of particular objects. Hence the process of inference by way of induction lies from the particular to the universal, from the contingent to that which is necessary (to put it in a little more modern fashion), from species to the genus, or from appearances to reality. In his own words, "As by one clod of clay all that is made of clay is known, or as by one nugget of gold all that is made of gold is known, or as by one pair of nail-scissors all that is made of iron is known, the difference being only a name, arising from speech, but the truth being that all is either clay or gold or iron,"[3] so is the method of inference by way of induction. And the truths that Uddālaka thus sought to establish are these two:—

Uddālaka's empirical theory of knowledge. His method of inquiry is inductive. The truths.

(i) That there is nothing unmixed in nature but the Spirit Prāṇa, (jīvātmā), or that the material is the one continuous

[1] Chāndogya Upaniṣad, VI. 3. 2-3.

[2] *Ibid*, VI. 4.5.

[3] *Ibid*, VI. 1.4-6. In this translation of Prof. Max Müller "difference" does not seem to be a very happy rendering of "Vikāro." Nor does Śaṅkara's interpretation "na

whole in which qualitatively distinct particles of matter are mixed together; and (2) That there really exists in nature that Spirit or living principle which animates all kinds of matter in varying degrees, and yet in itself is immaterial and imperishable—both immanent and transcendent by its nature.

With regard to the first truth that there is nothing unmixed in nature but the Spirit, Uddālaka holds that we, following the common usage of naming things, assign such names to the various objects of experience as the sun, the moon, the lightning, and the like. All these names, established by convention and current in the daily use of men, indicate or denote, at most, the notions or judgments that the knowing mind forms of external objects perceived according to this or that preponderating element which this or that particular object presents actually to our sense-experience. But there is sufficient reason for questioning the validity and cogency of all these ordinary popular notions. For there is nothing in nature, according to Uddālaka's theory, alike the theory of Anaxagoras, which is unmixed. All things are mixed, but not the elements (dhātus). The things are mixed, and yet the particles of which they are composed are qualitatively distinct from one another. Once more, the things themselves are so mixed together that there can be conceived no absolute parts to exist in nature, in the life of the All. That is to say, the material, inspite of the qualitative distinctness of the particles of matter and inspite of the difference of degrees perceivable between the

vikāro nāma vastvasti paramārthato" commend itself to us as absolutely a true one. We think that Uddālaka meant by Vikāra transformation, transfiguration of Matter or the material, in short, phenomenal changes. We perceive in him no conscious attempt at explaining away all objective changes by saying like a Buddha or a Śaṅkara that "It is a mere name arising from current language, and nothing more." He did not certainly deny the reality of change, change in respect of form, not of matter, otherwise what is the force of "nāmarūpe vyākarot" (Chāndogya, VI. 3.3), vyākarot, a verbal form of Vikāro. We take accordingly the passage to mean that it bears a name, a linguistic expression, corresponding to a palpable formal change in matter.

types of existence, is a continuous indivisible whole. Such is the sum and substance, as we saw, of what is known as the Mortar-doctrine. This doctrine of Uddālaka anticipates in history the Sāṅkhya theory of Prakṛiti or Primordial Matter with all its potentialities, and the antecedent of the Buddhist psychological doctrine according to which Mind is a mixture of numerous states and distinct processes of the mind,—a mixture so fine and complete that it renders impossible the effort to distinguish any one of these states and processes absolutely from any other, as well as fron the whole—illustrated in the Milinda [1] and other later Buddhist works by similar examples.

Uddālaka's Mortar-doctrine is the anticipation of the Sāṅkhya theory of Prakṛiti and the Buddhist psychological theory of mind.

If the ultimate fact of nature be, according to Uddālaka's theory, that there is nothing unmixed in it. Then the question arises, how is it possible for the thinking subject to cognise that fact? Can sense-perception give us the knowledge of nothing being unmixed? To this Uddālaka's answer is that the senses do not give us the knowledge of nothing being unmixed. The knowledge is in a sense subjective, being possible in thought. But Uddālaka neither trusts the testimony of the senses nor quite distrusts it. This is a most important point to remember in Uddālaka's theory of knowledge. According to his own showing the senses furnish us with sufficient indications from which the knowing mind can easily infer the nature and relations of things in themselves. In this connection Uddālaka raises a question for the first time which constitutes one of the fundamental problems of knowledge. As preceding the Analytical or Critical philosophy (to render perhaps loosely the term vibhajja-vāda) of Buddha, the question is of great

Uddālaka neither trusts nor yet distrusts the evidence of the senses.

[1] "The Questions of King Milinda," p. 97; op. the simile of the royal cook mixing the ingredients of a sauce. The doctrine was originated by Mahā Koṭṭhita. See Majjhima-nikāya, I. 292-293; "Ime dhammā saṁsaṭṭhā no visaṃsaṭṭhā, na labbhā .....nānā-karaṇaṁ paññāpetuṁ."

importance historically. What can we perceive of objects through the senses? And to this his answer is nothing but sensations, no more than impressions. We can become aware, for example, of the sensation of colour through vision. Leaving aside other senses, Uddālaka only dealt with the organ of sight. The impression of Fire on the organ of vision produces or is followed by the sensation of red; the impression of Water produces the sensation of white, and the impression of Earth is followed by the sensation of black. Whenever therefore there is an occasion of the sensation of red, we must infer, that it is due to the impression of Fire on the organ of vision; whenever there is an occasion of the sensation of white, that it is due to the impression of Water; whenever there is an occasion of the sensation of black, that it is due to the impression of Earth; and whenever there is an occasion of the sensation of a combination of red, white and black, that it is due to the impression of a corresponding combination of Fire, Water and Earth in the external object. The impression produced by each external object on the organ of vision is followed by the sensation of a combination of all these fundamental colours. Therefore everything is mixed; Sun, Moon, etc., are all similar in substance to other things of experience, to this mundane mixture—the earth.

The second truth relates to the existence of Spirit or living principle. The living principle is that which actually exists in nature and is identical in almost every respect with the universal Spirit. It animates in varying degrees all kinds of matter and yet in itself is immaterial and imperishable; but the proof of its existence is beyond sense-cognition. It is possible only in reasoning, but only in that kind of reasoning which is based upon actual sense-perception or observation of facts. In support of his theory he examines an atomically small seed of the banyan tree. Break it, though you perceive nothing there and yet you know that this tiny seed as a whole is pervaded by a subtle spirit, the real potentiality of the seed. It is that potentiality of the seed without which the seed is no seed, the potentiality by virtue of which the seed can grow into a huge banyan tree.[1] It is needless to repeat here other illustrations which he gives.[2]

Another important point to notice in connexion with Uddālaka's theory of knowledge is that the power of human cognition is limited and does not extend beyond the domain of mind and ceases on the complete absorption or recess of mind in Prāṇa. This is illustrated by the gradual cessation of mental process and consciousness of the dying man.[3]

CHAPTER IX.

VARUṆA.

Varuṇa, father of Bhṛgu Vāruṇi,[1] may rightly be regarded as the best exponent of the Taittirīya system. He resembles Diogenes Apollonius in his marked eclectic tendency. He sought to combine the principle[2] of his immediate predecessor with that of an earlier thinker. In his case the immediate predecessor was Uddālaka, and the earlier thinker Mahidāsa. Varuṇa offers us four conceptions which we may call four developmental gradations. Of these, the first is physiological, being the gradation of a natural development from chaos to man; the second is psychological, being the gradation of functions of the soul from nutrition to philosophic contemplation. These two gradations form the subject-matter of the third chapter of the Taittirīya Upaniṣad, entitled Bhṛigu-vallī. The third gradation is spiritual, being the gradation of degrees of happiness from the mere satisfaction of appetite to a participation in the eternal bliss of the Divine. This forms the subject-matter of the second chapter of the Taittirīya Upaniṣad, fittingly described as Brahmānanda-vallī. The fourth gradation is educational, being a serial enumeration or systematic statement of various duties of a person of good breeding, particularly of a Brahmacārin who has been trained up in the Taittirīya school. This important subject is treated of in the first chapter of the Taittirīya Upaniṣad, known as Śikṣāvallī or Śikṣopaniṣad. We shall take up these four points and four gradations, one by one.

Four points in Varuṇa's philosophy. His contributions.

I. Physiological Aspect of the Taittiriya System.— The first point connects Varuṇa with Uddālaka. The

[1] Taittirīya Upaniṣad, III. 1; III. 6.

[2] The Development of Greek Philosophy, p. 54.

latter, like Anaxagoras, based his conception of the material as a continuous whole on this principle: out of nothing comes nothing.[1]

Varuṇa and Uddālaka.

At the same time Varuṇa, whom we take to be the best exponent and representative of the Taittirīya system, unreasonably tends to differ from Uddālaka in attempting to accommodate to the Eleatic principle[2] a non-Eleatic thesis; out of nothing comes something.[3] However, the difference involved here between the two thinkers is a verbal rather than a material one. The reason perhaps is that Varuṇa does not apparently attach the same meaning to the word *nothing* in each case. In the former case he seems to understand by *nothing* the opposite of something, meaning Existence, Being, Reality, Brahman, Uddālaka's Deity; and in the latter case, the opposite of something, meaning Order, System, Cosmos. Accordingly, we must interpret the Eleatic principle as meaning to Varuṇa: the multiplicity of concrete existence comes only out of Brahman; and the non-Eleatic thesis as meaning: the Cosmos comes out of the chaos—Aditi or Infinity.

In the second place, Varuṇa unites with Uddālaka against Mahidāsa by holding that Brahman in order to create out of himself a purposive order of the universe hitherto non-existent broods over himself (tapaṁ tapati),[4] and certainly not over Water, as Mahidāsa thought.

And in the third place, for Varuṇa, as for Uddālaka, nature is a system of spontaneity, a self-evolving autonomy, so to speak. Therefore, the principle of movement in general, the reason of development from one into many is inherent in Brahman, as well as in things themselves. In things

Causality is not antagonistic to the spontaneity of nature.

[1] Taittirīya Upaniṣad, II. 6.

[2] Prof. Hobhouse notes:—"I am doubtful about the use of the term Eleatic here. The Eleatic principle may be taken as that of unity *excluding* all multiplicity.

[3] Taittirīya Upaniṣad, II. 7.

[4] *Ibid*, II. 6.

themselves, because they are, according to Varuṇa and Uddālaka, inhibited, inspirited, animated, motivated in various degrees by one and the same eternally existent Being, *i.e.*, Brahman, the first cause of things. Further, in the view of both Varuṇa and Uddālaka, the theory of spontaneity does not exclude causality. Both of them seem rather to have thought that causality has its right place only in the spontaneity of nature. There is nevertheless this slight difference between them.

Difference between Uddālaka and Varuṇa.

(*a*) With Uddālaka three preponderating elements are Fire, Water and Earth. Of these, in order of time, Fire has its root in the Deity, Water has its root in Fire, and Earth has its root in Water. Besides, of Fire, the subtilest or finest condition is ether, the material basis of sound; of Water, the subtilest condition is air, the material basis of vital breath; and of Earth, the subtilest condition is food, the material basis of germ or psyche (manas).

(*b*) For Varuṇa, on the other hand, the elements are these five—Ether (ākāsa), Air, Fire, Water, and Earth. Of these, in order of time, Ether springs from Brahman; Air from Ether; Fire from Air; Water from Fire; Earth from Water; herbs from Earth; food from herbs; seed from food; and man from seed.[1] Such is the physiological scale, the teleological gradation of a natural development from Ether[2] or "Brahmaṇaspati's" *nothing* to man.

II. *Psychological Aspect.*—Varuṇa's agreement with Mahidāsa and Aristotle is beyond question. For, as we

[1] Taittirīya Upaniṣad, II. 1. Cp. Thibaut's 'Vedānta-Sūtras,' S. B. E., Vol. XXXVIII, II. 3, 8.

[2] *Ibid*, II. 7. The order of succession involved in the conception of the gradual unfolding or retraction of relatively unreal elements of experience into the self-subsisting, single reality is causal or logical Cp. the views of Bādrāyaṇa and Śaṅkara in the Vedānta Sūtras. *Ibid*, II. 3. 10 14.

know, Varuṇa's conception of Brahman is but a pure activity of thought, of thinking upon nothing but himself (tapaṁ tapana). It is thus indeed that Brahman enjoys bliss (ānanda) eternally. The nature of the Divine, as conceived by Varuṇa, is absolutely free,—fearless, invisible, incorporeal, undefined, unsupported by anything material.[1] Brahman is the first cause; he is one, the one from fear of whom the wind blows, and the sun rises. He is again just the final cause, the end, the best. The end consists in an eternal enjoyment of bliss by thinking upon nothing but his own nature. This end is beyond all principles. The best thing for the soul to do is to approach Brahman, to unite with the God, to participate in the eternal bliss of the Divine, by contemplating on its eternal nature. But the first requisite, Varuṇa insists at this point, for such a contemplation on the part of the soul is to be completely free from fear, and to transcend all kinds of distinction, obtaining in this world or in our mind.

Varuṇa and Mahidāsa.

Varuṇa's Theology.

With regard to the functions of the soul, too, Varuṇa's resemblance to Mahidāsa and Aristotle is indisputable. For in Varuṇa's opinion, the soul is but a form of the living body, a complement of the organism. The soul is therefore capable of development, that is to say, there is a gradation of functions of the soul. The lowest grade of activity of the soul, the activity which is fundamental to life, is nutritive (annamaya).[2] In this respect man is in the same predicament with the rest of material nature. Life depends on food, the soul depends on life, and what do we find in nature at large but "food resting on food" (annavān annādo)? So Varuṇa declares: Life is food, the body eats this food. The

Graduated functions of Soul.

[1] Taittirīya Upaniṣad, II. 7, S. B. E., Vol. XV, p. 59. "abhaya, adṛśya, anātmya, anirukta, anilayana."

[2] *Ibid.* III. 2.

body depends on life, life depends on the body. This is the food depending on food. Let a man therefore by all means acquire such food, and let him never refuse hospitality to a guest, although a stranger. "If he gives food amply, food is given to him amply. If he gives food fairly, food is given to him fairly. If he gives food meanly, food is given to him meanly."[1]

The next higher forms of activity of the soul are prāṇamaya[2]—'sense-perception and motor-activity.' Still higher in scale are manomaya[3]—psychical activities in general, those of which sense-perception is in some way the foundation. Higher than these are Vijñānamaya[4]—a group of activities called by the general name of understanding. And at the top of the scale is ānandamaya[5]—the philosophic contemplation of the eternally blissful nature of Brahman—the Divine.[6]

Happiness is the end of concrete activities of life, and Bliss the *summum bonum*.

III. *Mystical, Ethical or Æsthetic Aspect.*—Varuṇa's original contribution is the conception of happiness (ānanda) as the end of all kinds of activity in man and in the world of nature at large. As regards men, beginning with the enjoyment of food, ending in the enjoyment of contemplative joy, and including as the intermediate the delight in action, locomotion, wife, children, cattle, wealth, society, friendship, power, pomp, learning, fame, and the rest, all are in various measures but bliss divine.[7] Thus we see how the teleological instinct which prompted the ancient thinkers of India and Greece asserts itself with full force in Varuṇa's conception of bliss which admits of degrees but of no difference of kind. This supreme end, the enjoyment of bliss, is not confined to human nature. The whole of external nature has

Taittirīya Upaniṣad, III. 7-10. S. B. E., Vol. XV, p. 67.

Literally, consisting of activities of the senses.

Lit. consisting of activities of thought.

Lit. consisting of activities of understanding.

Lit. blissful.

Taittirīya Upaniṣad, II. 2.—III. 6.

Ibid, III. 10. 1-2.

her due share in this divine blessing ; delight in rain, power in lightning, light in the stars, generation, immortality and joy. *in the ether or Infinite*, all these are expressive in various measures of the same bliss divine.[1] This explains clearly the reason why Varuṇa, "in giving the various degrees of happiness,...gives us at the same time the various classes of human and divine beings." [2]

Suppose there is a noble-looking young man who is learned, healthy and wealthy. Varuṇa reckons this as one measure of human bliss. One hundred times this human bliss is said to be one measure of the bliss of human Gandharvas (musicians,) and likewise of a great seer who is free from sensual desires. One hundred times this bliss of human Gandharvas is said to be one measure of the bliss of celestial Gandharvas, and likewise of a great seer who is free from passions. The comparison being thus continued, extends up to Brahman and the greatest seer among men, conceived as the highest pinnacle of blissful nature. Varuṇa tells us that the blissful nature in man and the blissful nature in the sun, are both one.[3]

Gradations of bliss.

This adhidaivata-ādhyātmika—macro-micro-cosmical, cosmo-anthropological or physio-psychological parallelism between bliss divine and human, can be traced back in its germinal-form to the Vedic conceptions of the dual personality of the gods, and it is but a corollary of the *Sôhaṁ* or *Tattvamasi* doctrine of post-Vedic philosophy. The Taittirīya doctrine recurs with certain minor changes in the teaching of Yājña-valkya,[4] and seems to have afforded a basis for the Jaina and Buddhist cosmographies, introduced by way of analogy with the progressive course of a person aspiring to attain *Arahatship*.

[1] Taittirīya Upaniṣad, III. 10. 2-3.
[2] S. B. E., Vol. XV, p. 61, f. n. 2.
[3] Taittirīya Upaniṣad, II. 8. 1-5.
[4] Bṛihad Āraṇyaka, IV. 3.33.

IV. *Śikṣavalli—Educational, Religious or Moral Aspect.*—The first chapter of the Taittirīya Upaniṣad is a connected discourse on the various duties of a religious student who has been brought up in the Taittirīya tradition, and *a posteriori*, of a person who desires to be faithful to the religious instincts of his Aryan forefathers. The eclectic tendency which characterises the Taittirīya system as a whole is no less prominent in its practical aspect. The historical significance and value of this Śikṣôpaniṣad is that it seems to reveal for the first time a conscious attempt to conceive a structure upon which the entire Brāhmanic or orthodox system of the Smṛitis was subsequently super-imposed. It is a literary as well as a doctrinal synthesis of the Vedāṅgas, and on the other hand it appears to be the first synthesis of the Varṇāśrama ideal in its social and religious aspects.

This spirit of synthesis is enunciated by the Taittirīyas as a law of the universe which is manifest everywhere in nature striving to maintain a harmony or autonomy in things, keeping them in a working order. This law is observed by them in its five-fold jurisdictions (pañcasu adhikaraṇeṣu), *viz.*—

1. In the material world (adhilokam),
2. In the shining things (adhijyautiṣam),
3. In the world of knowledge (adhividyam),
4. In the world of generation (adhiprajam) and
5. In individual life (adhyātmam).

The relations of things are illustrated under these five heads. To quote their own examples:—

1. Earth denoting the anterior side of relation (pūrvarūpam), and Heaven the posterior (uttararūpam), Void or Firmament is the connecting link (sandhi), and Air the incoming, inhibiting, cohesive and mobile element (sandhāna).

2. Fire denoting the anterior, and Sun the posterior, Water is the connecting link and Lightning the in coming and in-dwelling element.

3. Teacher denoting the anterior and Pupil the posterior, Knowledge is the connecting link and Instruction the functional feature.

4. Mother denoting the anterior and Father the posterior, Offspring is the connecting link and Generation the process of creation.

5. Lower maxilla denoting the anterior and upper maxilla the posterior, Voice is the connecting link and Articulation the out-coming result.

These five-fold relations furnish a logical mould into which all Brāhmanical thoughts can be cast, *e.g* :—

(*a*) Relating to syllogism—there must be a *pūrvarūpa* or major premise, a *uttararūpa* or minor premise, a *sandhi* or middle term to connect the two, and a *sandhāna* or outcoming conclusion,

(*b*) Relating to varṇāśrama—there must be a *pūrvarūpa* or natural social order of *varṇas* with their distinct functions, a *uttararūpa* or natural development of individual in unison with the developmental stages of life (āśramas), a *sandhi* or man in natural development and a *sandhāna* or performance of duties in accordance with *varṇāśrama* ideal.

(*c*) Relating to *āśrama* ideal—there must be a *pūrvarūpa* on lower functions of life, *annamaya*, *prāṇamaya*, etc., a *uttararūpa* or higher functions such as *vijñānamaya* and *ānandamaya*, a *sandhi* or religious man in the making, and a *sandhāna* or perfection of human life.

The duties to be gone through by the Taittirīya man in the making are reserved for discussion in Part III in connexion with Muṇḍaka philosophy. Here it remains only to note that the Taittirīya teaching which serves as the foundation of entire Brahmanism, promulgated in the Sūtras and Smṛitis is logical, consistent and comprehensive. If there are any defects in it, those pertain to their defective observation of facts rather than to their mode of reasoning.

CHAPTER X.

Bālāki and Ajātaśatru.

Gārgya Bālāki was known as a thoughtful scholar who lived among the Uśīnaras, the Satvat Matsyas, the Kuru-Pancālas, and the Kāśi-Videhas. Bālāki was a Brāhman, Ajātaśatru a warrior. Bālāki was a contemporary of Yājñavalkya, Ajātaśatru that of Janaka, King of Videha. King Janaka was a patron of philosophy. King Ajātaśatru was a philosopher. It is said that a philosophical discussion was held between Bālāki and Ajātaśatru. The Kauṣītaki Upaniṣad [1] and the Bṛihad Āraṇyaka [2] furnish two accounts of the same. These are not without some important variations, as Prof. Max Müller notices, but on the whole to the same purpose. It is evident from both the records that the main object of the discussion was to determine the nature of soul and its abode in the universe and in man. Further, in the self-same discussion, Bālāki plays the part of a philosophical maniac, and Ajātaśatru that of a doctor, a physiologist, who cures him.

The contrast between a Brāhman thinker and a Warrior. The former seeks for soul in everything, while the latter limits its existence to living bodies.

Bālāki, for instance, meditates on the soul (puruṣa) in the sun, while Ajātaśatru regards the sun only as a great, powerful, shining object of nature, the source of life and light. Bālāki begins then to meditate on the soul in the moon, while Ajātaśatru regards the moon only as the source of animal seed. Bālāki comes next to meditate on the soul in lightning, while Ajātaśatru regards lightning only as a brilliant form of

[1] IV.1-20

[2] II. 1-20.

fire or heat (electrical phenomenon). Passing over the soul in ether, air, fire and water, Bālāki fastens his mind for a while on the soul in the mirror (ādarśa), while Ajātaśatru regards that only as a reflection (pratirūpa). After meditating on the soul in the echo, in the sound that follows a man, in the shadow, Bālāki concentrates his mind on the soul, embodied (śārīraḥ), on the self-conscious reason (prajñā), on the soul in the right eye, on that in the left eye, one after the other. But having failed to convince the King, Bālāki demands at last an answer from him. Ajātaśatru offers this answer to Bālāki: The complete fact of a living being is Prāṇa—Life. Prāṇa is to be conceived as the embodied soul (śārīraḥ). Prajñā, or Reason is in Life, just as a razor is fitted in a razor case, or as fire in the araṇi wood. There are arteries (nāḍī) of the heart called Hitā, small as a hair divided a thousand times. These arteries are filled with a thin fluid of various colours—white, black, yellow, red, and extend from the heart towards all parts of the body, even to the very hairs and nails. During sound sleep the living, conscious soul dwells in these arteries of the heart.

This is the answer of Ajātaśatru according to the Kauṣītaki version of the above Dialogue. The Bṛihad Āraṇyaka version is silent about fluid and colours, but adds that there are 72,000 arteries. During sleep the soul moves forth through these arteries and rests in the surrounding body. Its movement is analogous to that of a spider along its thread.

Lastly, there is a parallel passage in the Chāndogya Upaniṣad which is equally silent about the thin fluid, but adds that there are 101 arteries in all. One of these penetrates the crown of the head, thus connecting the mortal or lower centre with the immortal or higher centre. Besides, according to this passage, the arteries of the heart consist of a brown (piṅgala) substance, of a white, blue, red and yellow substance. The sun, too, consists of a substance of these five colours.

CHAPTER XI.

Yājñavalkya.

The pronouncement of Erasmus about Seneca applies very well to Yājñavalkya. Judged by the standard of post-Vedic period, Yājñavalkya is pre-Buddhistic and later, by that of pre-Buddhistic and later times, he is post-Vedic. It may truly be said, therefore, of Yājñavalkya that with him the thought of the post-Vedic period is closed, and that of subsequent ages is implied. Manifold interests—religious, speculative, moral, social—centre round his person.

His predecessors and successors.

On the one hand, Uddālaka's biological speculations,[1] Ajātaśatru's physiological researches,[2] Varuṇa's conception of bliss (ānanda) as the summum bonum of life,[3] Dadhyāc Ātharvaṇa's doctrine of honey (madhu-vidyā),[4] Pratardana's psychology[5] and transcendental ethics,[6] Śāṇḍilya's views on will and belief,[7] Jābāla's conception of Brahman as light,[8] Jaivali's distinction between the good and the bad soul,[9] Gārgyāyaṇa's doctrine of immortality,[10] Mahidāsa's conceptions of matter and form,[11]—all these make a fitting introduction to, and are harmoniously combined in Yājñavalkya's Doctrine of Double Negation, of "No No" (Nêti Nêti).[12]

[1] Brihad Āraṇyaka Upaniṣad, III. 9. 28.

[2] *Ibid*, IV. 3. 20; IV. 4 9.

[3] *Ibid*, III. 9. 28; IV. 3. 32-33.

[4] *Ibid*, II. 5. 1-19.

[5] *Ibid*, IV. 3, 23-30: Sight is inseparable from the seer; smelling from the smeller;...... knowing from the knower.

[6] *Ibid*, IV. 4. 22; Soul as the immortal, intelligible essence does neither wax by good works nor wane by evil.

[7] *Ibid*, IV. 4. 5.

[8] *Ibid*, IV. 4. 7.

[9] *Ibid*, IV. 4. 4. 8.

[10] *Ibid*, IV. 4. 25.

[11] *Ibid*, IV. 3. 32.

[12] *Ibid*, II. 3. 6; III. 9. 26; IV. 4. 22; IV. 6. 15.

And on the other hand, Yājñavalkya anticipates the Epicureanism of Ajita,[1] Buddha's conception of Śūnya, the Vedānta of Bādarāyaṇa, the Māyā doctrine of Śaṅkara, and the ethical and social problems of Mahāvīra and Buddha.

The fact need hardly be mentioned that with Yājñavalkya is immortalised the name of King Janaka Vaideha, the most renowned patron of philosophy.[2] It is moreover with Yājñavalkya that the names of two Indo-Aryan mothers—Gārgi Vācaknavi and Maitreyi—are so intimately associated. Of them, Maitreyi was one of the two wives of Yājñavalkya, his other wife being Kātyāyani. Kātyāyani did not so much care for her husband's speculative dream as Maitreyi. She was content and occupied with her household problems and domestic politics. In the estimation of the author of the Yājñavalkya-Upaniṣad, Gārgi's was a more philosophically trained mind than Maitreyi's. However, both Gārgi and Maitreyi prove that women of India were not altogether indifferent and inactive at the time, when the whole kingdom of Janaka, nay, the whole of northern India was resounding with the clash of philosophic battles. It is said that the eloquent Gārgi engaged Yājñavalkya twice[3] in such a contest. The two questions which she put to him seem to have been very skilfully "warped and woofed." On the other hand, the tender-hearted Maitreyi was bewildered at a covered attack of materialism on the part of her husband.

The Bṛihad Āraṇyaka Upaniṣad records a great many names of others who gave battle to Yājñavalkya. Among them, Sākalya is said to have asked Yājñavalkya this question: Where does the heart abide?[4] Yājñavalkya said: O

[1] Bṛihad Āraṇyaka, II. 4. 12; IV. 6. 15: "Idaṁ mahad adbhūtam anantam aparam vijñāna-ghana evaitebhyo bhūtebhyaḥ samutthāya tānyevānu vinaśyati; na pretya saṁjñā astīti."

[2] Kauṣītaki Upaniṣad, IV. 1; Bṛihad Āraṇyaka Upaniṣad, II. 1. 1; III. 1. 1; IV. 1. 1. ff.

[3] Bṛihad Āraṇyaka Upaniṣad, III. 6. 1; III. 8. 1-12; "Then Vācaknavi said; Venerable Brāhmaṇas, I shall ask him two questions. If he will answer them, none of you, I think, will defeat him in any argument concerning Brahman."

[4] *Ibid*, III. 9. 24

Ahallika! if the heart were anywhere but in us, then either dogs might eat it or birds might tear it. This is apparently a story, a story that reminds us of the Sumsumāra Jātaka, in which a big-bellied but poor-witted crocodile is censured by an intelligent monkey in these words: O fool! if my heart were suspended from the fig-tree, it would have been smashed to pieces as I go up and down the tree.

The sources of information.

In treating of Yājñavalkya's philosophy, it is fundamentally necessary to sift the sources of information. Our main authority is the Bṛihad Āranyaka Upaniṣad of which there are two somewhat different recensions now extant. There is besides a whole Upaniṣad entitled the Yājñavalkya-Saṁhitā, consisting of some twelve chapters. It is written entirely in verse, and from beginning to end is a Dialogue between Yājñavalkya and Gārgi. It is evidently a later composition, embodying the later development of Yājñavalkya's speculations. Another text, generally known as the Yājñavalkya-Smṛiti contains a number of semi-legal, semi-moral injunctions of Yājñavalkya. This text, as its title shows, belongs to the Smṛiti class, and ranks almost with the Institutes of Manu. Perhaps, in one respect, its place is higher than that of the Manu-Smṛiti, if we consider the wide influence which Mitakṣarā, the commentary on the Yājñavalkya-Smṛiti, exercises all over India, except Bengal, where the Dāyabhāga system appears in some respects to be a powerful rival. But the Smṛiti, as we now have it, seems to belong to a later period than that to which Yājñavalkya himself may be supposed to belong. Nevertheless, it does not seem impossible that some of the important injunctions which this Smṛiti embodies may have come originally from Yājñavalkya himself. For the Bṛihad Āraṇyaka Upaniṣad embodies what Yājñavalkya had taught before his retirement from the world. Supposing that the age for his retirement was between fifty and fifty-five, and that he was alive some years after it,[1] is it not reasonable to surmise that a great mind such as Yājñavalkya should leave a few legal and moral injunctions for the guidance of his posterity? The long-cherished tradition which ascribes the injunctions to Yājñavalkya may bring home, we believe, one great truth regarding his philosophy, namely, that it is dominated throughout by a kind of practical or ethical end. But there are points in which his philosophical predilection is stronger than his ethical tendency.

Now, as regards the Bṛihad Āraṇyaka Upaniṣad itself, we have much reason to question the reliability of its evidence here and there. The work is not a homogeneous whole. At the most it is a compilation. What concerns us is that it puts a world of views into the mouth of Yājñavalkya. But his own views are so deeply stamped with his personality that we can discriminate at once those which are personal to him from those which are not. We are inclined to consider the Dialogue between Yājñavalkya and Maitreyī as our best and safest authority to rely upon. This Dialogue occurs twice in the same Upaniṣad.

His Philosophy.

When we read and ponder over the famous Dialogue between Yājñavalkya and his wife Maitreyī, the first impression, and that which remains, is that Yājñavalkya's is the practical mind of Socrates proceeding to the abstract thinking of Plato, or it may well be that his is a Platonic mind learning to be Socratic. In formulating "a pure dogma of soul," he naturally seeks to combine all that is visionary with all that is vivid, and all that is subtle with all that is ennobling. In every direction we find that he endeavours to prepare for the mind the steps leading up from the lowest to the highest, from

[1] The Yājñavalkya Upaniṣad seems to contain certain views of Yājñavalkya which he formulated during his Āraṇyaka life.

the worst to the very best. And as we advance step by step, we feel as though it were a journey from darkness into light. But once we have reached the ethereal height of the eternal light, and look down, we find, to our great wonder, that now even the very darkness partakes of the nature of light, falsehood of truth, ignorance of knowledge, enmity of love, theft of honesty, sorrow of joy, pain of bliss, and death of immortality. Such is the charm of Yājñavalkya's doctrine of soul!

1. *Self-love* (*ātma-kāma*).

Now we proceed to consider the above-mentioned Dialogue between Yājñavalkya and Maitreyī. This Dialogue opens really with the problem of self-love.[1] Yājñavalkya seems to have maintained that self-love lies at the foundation, is the spring of all kinds of love. Love is therefore in its nature egoistic: it begins with the love of self,—(with the instinct of self-preservation,[2]) and reaches a termination in the love of Self, that is, of God (Brahman). Conjugal love, the love of children, wealth, cattle, class, society, gods, creatures, religion and scripture, patriotism, philanthropy,—all are in various degrees the same love of self,—the self-love in special forms.

Between the instinct of self-preservation and love of God there is no difference of kind but of degree.

Love is for Yājñavalkya the cheerful heart that finds everything cheerful in the world. As Yājñavalkya puts it, a wife is not dear (priya) that we may love the wife; but because we love the self, therefore a wife is dear; and so as to everything else. Even the love of God is not an exception to this rule. As for the love of God, however, there is this difference that, while in all other forms of love, the object is something other than the self, the love of God does not recognise anything but self for its object. The love of God is what may be called in modern phraseology love for love's sake, in as much as God dwells, according to

[1] Bṛihad Āraṇyaka Upaniṣad, II. 4. 5; IV. 5. 5.

[2] *Ibid*, IV. 1. 3; IV. 1. 5.

Yājñavalkya, in love (kāma-āyatana), nay, God is love (Kāma).[1]

Moreover, in all other forms of love, there being no complete gratification of desire, perfect bliss (paramānanda) is not attainable by them. Whereas, in the love of God, there being nothing more to wish for, the result is perfect bliss. The love of God is in its nature all-embracing, it comprehends within itself all other forms of love. Thus this altruism, the love of God, is just the expansion or consummation of self-love.

2. *Desire* (*Kāma*).

With Yājñavalkya this altruism, the love of God,—love for love's sake, is not different in kind from the self-love which is implanted in our nature. For every form of love is in itself a type of desire,—desire the gratification of which is happiness (and the non-fulfilment of which is sorrow).

Between sensual desires and the desire for a higher life there is no difference of kind.

For instance, when a man desires a woman, and a son resembling him is born of her, it is happiness.[2] In all other types of desire the consequence is either happiness or sorrow. Whereas, in the case of the desire for the self, there being no fear of disappointment, the result is always happiness. Therefore, giving up all kinds of sensual desire, we should desire only to love, to seek, to know the self. For to love the self means to love God, and to love God means to desire knowledge, bliss and immortality, because God is all this. Negatively, then, not to love the self means not to love God, and not to love God means to welcome ignorance, doubt, delusion, hunger and thirst, and sorrow and pain and decay and death.[3] We must seek the self. For to seek the self is to seek God, and

[1] Bṛihad Āraṇyaka Upaniṣad, III. 9. 11.

[2] *Ibid*, IV. 1. 6.

[3] *Ibid*, III. 5. 1

to seek God is to seek for knowledge and bliss and immortality. We must also know the self. For to know the self is to know God, and to know God is, on the one hand, to shake off doubt and ignorance, to rise above all desires for sons and wealth and worlds[1]; and, on the other hand, to know, to seek, to obtain, to enjoy all that is desirable. Once more, we must know the self. For in Yājñavalkya's opinion, he who knows it, does not attach himself to evil action; but being unperturbed, subdued, restrained, patient, and collected, he sees self in self, and all of self. Evil does not overcome him, he overcomes all evil. Evil does not burn him, he burns all evil. Sinless, stainless, doubtless, he becomes a Brāhman. This is (the attainment of) the Brahma-world.[2]

Now, knowledge and ignorance, bliss and sorrow, immortality and death, being contradictory of each other, in seeking the one, we must abandon the desire for the other. To seek knowledge or bliss or immortality is to seek God, to desire the self, that is, to be above all desires for sons and wealth and worlds. Thus when we desire the self, then we seek, reach the state of God, that is, the end of all desires, of all seeking (eṣaṇā).

God is the ultimate end of all desires. There may be an end of desires, but no end to the act of desiring.

Here the expression 'the end of all desires' is ambiguous. Obviously it means to Yājñavalkya that when we reach the end of all desires, then the mind no more desires sons or wealth or worlds. But it does not certainly mean to him that the mind ceases at any time from desiring or the act of seeking. The mind then desired other objects, and now it is desiring itself; that is all. Besides, in

[1] Worlds are enumerated generally as three—that of men, that of fathers, that of gods. The first can be gained by a son, the second by Karma or sacrifice (yajña), and the third by vidyā or knowledge. Bṛihad Āraṇyaka Upaniṣad, I. 5. 16. Yājñavalkya adds the Brahma-world to these three.

[2] *Ibid*, IV. 4. 23: na lipyate karmaṇā pāpakēnēti tasmād evam vicchāṇto dānta uparatas titikṣuḥ samāhito bhutātmānyēvātmānām sarvam ātmānam paśyati......vipāpo virajo vicikitso Brāhmaṇa bhavatyēṣa Brahma-lokaḥ.

this transition—if transition we may call it, from desiring other objects into desiring the self, there is elimination of this or that object, but not of the thought-activity called desiring or the act of seeking. He is therefore He, desiring is desiring, and it makes no difference to the thought-activity called desiring, whether we desire this or that,—sons or wealth or worlds or Brahman. In accordance with Yājñavalkya's view, then, the Deity is like Aristotle's *actus purus*, the pure activity of thought, the thinking upon thought, the desiring of the desirable, the knowing of the knowable, the enjoyment of the enjoyable, and so forth. This being the case, that which is given into our power, that which is in our free-will, is not to eliminate from the mind the thought-activity called desiring or the act of seeking, but only to eliminate one object by substituting for it another. And it is in this process of elimination and substitution, indeed, that the idea of gradual sublimation consists. So Yājñavalkya said to Kahola Kauṣītakeya: A desire for sons is desire (eṣaṇā; for wealth, a desire for wealth is desire for worlds. These two are desires indeed. A Brāhman, therefore, after he has completed his Vedic studies—after erudition (pāṇḍitya), wishes to indulge in folly[1] (*i.e.*, to be wise by marrying); after he has accomplished the duty of a father, and previously that of a student, he wishes to become a Muni—silent thinker; and after he has done with the duty of a Muni, and previously those of a father and a student he wishes to become a Brāhman, a philosopher who apprehends the nature of Brahman, the Divine. By whatever means, he becomes a Brāhman, he remains such indeed. Everything except this highest contemplation of the Divine nature is of evil.[2]

This reminds us at once of Mahidāsa's pithy sentence: Man is an ever-swelling sea (eṣa puruṣaḥ samudraḥ).[3]

[1] Bālyena tiṣṭhati. This expression is explained in the Subālopaniṣad as meaning "he lives with the child-like simplicity of outlook on life (bālasvabhāvo)."

[2] Bṛihad Āraṇyaka Upaniṣad, III. 5. 1.

[3] Aitareya Āraṇyaka, II. 3. 3.1.

Whatever he reaches, he desires to go beyond. When he reaches the heaven, the celestial region, he desires to go beyond. If he should reach the heavenly world, he would desire still to go beyond.[1] Mahidāsa's meaning is that this desiring of the immortal by the mortal constitutes the greatness of man and his ultimate aim.

3. *Good and Evil (Puṇya-Pāpa).*

In inquiring into Yājñavalkya's conceptions of good and evil, we must by no means lose sight of the distinction which he draws between a man of desire and a man of no desire, that is to say, between a bad and a good, a mortal and an immortal soul. A man of desire is he who desires sons or wealth or the worlds of men, fathers and gods, while a man of no desire is he who desires only the self, that is, only the world of Brahman. In the Brahma-world there is nothing material, nothing conditional, but whatever there is, is immaterial and absolute. None the less, there is between the Brahma-world and other worlds no difference of kind but of degree.

A man of desire and a man of no desire defined.

According to Yājñavalkya, whatever lands us in doubt, darkness, delusion, dualism and ignorance, and increases hunger, thirst, sorrow, pain, decay and death is evil; and that which makes us free from all these, and leads to knowledge, bliss and immortality is good. A man is like this or like that—noble or wicked, virtuous or sinful—according as he acts and behaves.[1]

Definition of good and evil.

It is therefore well said: A man is of desire. As is his desire, so is his will. As is his will, so is his action. And as he acts, so he attains.[2] In this connexion Yājñavalkya also quotes the

His doctrine of Karma.

[1] Bṛihad Āraṇyaka Upaniṣad; IV. 4. 5. Tad yad etad idam mayodemaya iti. Yathākārī yathācārī tathā bhavati; sādhukārī sādhu bhavati pāpakarī pāpo bhavati..........

[2] *Ibid*, IV. 4. 5: Atha khalvāhuḥ: kāmamaya evāyaṁ puruṣa iti. So yathākāmo bhavati tat ṛitur bhavati. Yat ṛitur bhavati tat karma kurute. Yat karma kurute tad abhisampadyate.

following maxim from some unknown source: A man attains with his action the object to which his mind is attached. And after having reached the end (reaped the fullest consequence), of what was done here, he returns again from that world to this world of action.[1]

The highest good is above both good and evil as commonly understood.

This applies to a man of desire, one who desires sons or wealth or the worlds of men, fathers and gods, that is to say, one who is involved in materiality and conditionality,—is in the midst of knowledge and ignorance, joy and sorrow, death and immortality. He is not fitted, as Gārgyāyana pointed out long before, for the Brahma-world, the realm of absolute knowledge, bliss and immortality. For it is only he who does not desire, who is free from desire (niṣkāma), who has obtained the desirable (āpta-kāma), or who desires only the self (ātma-kāma), being Brahman goes to Brahman.[2] Hence it follows that, according to Yājñavalkya, the highest good is something beyond both good and evil, both knowledge and ignorance, joy and sorrow, death and immortality.

Yājñavalkya and Varuṇa.

Yājñavalkya's conceptions of bliss are essentially the same as those of Varuṇa. The points of difference are these: Varuṇa's list of gods begins with Gandharvas, while Yājñavalkya's list with Fathers. For Varuṇa a Śrotriya among men should be free from desires (akāma-hata), while Yājñavalkya adds a new element: he must also be free from fault or sin (avṛijino).[3] Yājñavalkya gives a beautiful illustration of his conception of the final bliss, of the enjoyment of the enjoyable: "As a man, when embraced by a beloved wife, knows nothing that is without, nothing that is within."[4]

[1] Bṛihad Āraṇyaka Upaniṣad, IV. 4. 6. Tad eva saktaḥ saha Karmaṇā liṅgam mano yatra nisaktamasya: prāpyantam karmaṇos tasya yat kiñceha karotyāyaṁ, tasmāt lokāt punar etyāsmin loka ya karmaṇa iti.

[2] *Ibid*, IV. 4. 6.

[3] *Ibid*, IV. 3. 33. This new element shews that Yājñavalkya's conception is later than that of Varuṇa.

[4] *Ibid*, IV. 3·21.

4. *Knowledge* (*Vidyā*).

Yājñavalkya's conceptions of Vidyā and a-Vidyā, knowledge and ignorance are in a sense diametrically opposed. For knowledge is to him faith (śraddhā), while ignorance is doubt (vicikitsā); knowledge is light (jyotis), ignorance is darkness (tamas); knowledge is truth (satya), ignorance is falsehood (anṛita); knowledge is virtue, ignorance is sin; knowledge is bliss (ānanda), ignorance is sorrow (śoka); knowledge is immortality (aṁṛitatva), ignorance is death (mṛityu). To this we may add: knowledge is universal, ignorance is conditional; knowledge is necessary, ignorance is contingent.

Knowledge and ignorance contrasted.

In fact, knowledge implies in Yājñavalkya's language the knowledge of God, that is to say, the knowledge of knowledge, for God is all knowledge (jñāna, prajñā); and ignorance implies that which is not such knowledge, the opposite or want of the knowledge of God. God is what really is (satya), and not-God is what is not (anṛita). That which really is, is oneness (ekatā), the unity of God and soul. Therefore, the true knowledge consists in the full recognition of the truth "I am He" (sôham). What is really not? That which is really not is duality, the distinction between self and not-self, between good and evil, desire and not-desire, anger and not-anger, dear and not-dear, between knowledge and not-knowledge, truth and falsehood, right and wrong, justice and injustice, moral and immoral, between God and soul, world and men, a father and not-a-father, worlds and not-worlds, gods and not-gods, Vedas and not-Vedas, a thief and not-a-thief, a murderer and not-a-murderer, a Caṇḍāla and not-a-Caṇḍāla, a Paulkasa and not-a-Paulkasa, a recluse (śramaṇa) and not-a-recluse, a hermit (tāpasa) and not-a-hermit.[1]

Definition of the term knowledge.

[1] Bṛihad Āraṇyaka Upaniṣad, IV. 3. 22; etc.

This dualism, this logomachy, the verbal distinction of this from that, is recognised by, or rather is the creation of logic, and logic is with Yājnavalkya that wrangling about words which "is mere weariness of the tongue" (vāco viglāpanam).

Psychological theory of one-ness in regard to knowledge.

The ultimate knowledge is beyond the reach of mere logic. It is clearly implied in his expressions that the greatest logical doctrine is the principle of contradiction. But this principle which admits of no application to his conception of ultimate knowledge—the doctrine of "No No." He certainly means to say that knowledge is not possible except in and through reason. What he seems to have maintained, on the other hand, is that the ultimate psychological fact is the one-ness of mental processes. For, considered from the psychological point of view, even what we call doubting is in itself a process of the mind, a seeking after truth,—an act of thinking which is not different in kind from the pure cognition or thinking upon thought. The real fact is this eternal activity of thought,[1] and the truth is that all activities ranging from the bare sensation to the pure cognition are in various degrees the same activity of the Divine thinking in man, or as Yājñavalkya would have expressed it, the self-activity in special forms.

Viewed under this aspect, ignorance becomes transmuted into knowledge, doubt into faith, darkness into light, falsehood into truth, multiplicity into unity. Furthermore, viewed in this light of the knowledge of God, language, literature, scripture, history, fables, myths, cosmogony, Upaniṣads, Sūtras and expositions, all appear to be, in themselves, a kind of knowledge.[2] These are the various manifestations of knowledge, the subjects of study, the objects of knowledge, and all are breathed forth from, are revealed by, and are therefore the expressions of the self-same eternal activity of thought.[3]

[1] Brihad Āraṇyaka Upaniṣad, IV. 3. 14: "There is no intermission of the knowing of the knower."

[2] *Ibid*, IV. 1. 2.

[3] *Ibid*, IV. 5. 11.

Whether by the study of the Veda or by sacrifice, penance and fasting, the Brāhmans seek to know Brahman.[1] But we must not forget that with him the highest knowledge consists in the universal recognition of the truth of the dictum "I am He" (sôhaṁ).

(a) *God* (*Brahman*).

If knowledge be rightly conceived as the knowledge of God, we ought to inquire, who is God? To Yājñavalkya God is the Deity (devatā), the Unity (advaita), the Light, the Divine, the Knowledge, the Bliss, the Immortality. The Deity is the first root, the first cause, the principle of all motion, the reason for all change, the creator (viśvakṛit), the protector (bhūta-pāla) the undecaying one (akṣara), at whose command heaven and earth stand apart, at whose command the rivers flow, and by whose ordination men praise the charitable, the gods follow the sacrificer, and the fathers love the *darvi*-offering.[2] In the imperishable one there is nothing either rough or refined, short or long, red or white. The Divine is without shadow, without darkness, without air, ether, toughness (touch), taste, smell, eyes, ears, speech, mind, breath, and yet the Divine is the life of life, the eye of the eye, the ear of the ear, the mind of the mind.[3] The immortal is immeasurable, has no within or without.[4] God is undecaying time,[5] is eternity: He is one, one only without a second.

Theology.

Brahman is Being (sat), the most real of all things real. The Brahma-world is the realm of absolute existence. But Brahman is also tyad, that which emanates from Being. The nature of Brahman is eternally free,—free from all fear, doubt,

[1] Bṛihad Āraṇyaka Upaniṣad, III. 5. 1.
[2] *Ibid*, III. 8. 9.
[3] *Ibid*, IV. 4. 18.
[4] *Ibid*, III. 8. 8.
[5] *Ibid*, IV. 4. 16.

delusion, ignorance, hunger, thirst, sorrow, pain, decay and death. That is to say, Brahman is pure knowledge, pure bliss, pure immortality. Moreover, the Divine essence is one (eka). Therefore the diversity of things finds its best explanation in this unity of cause. If experience brings home that the principle of life (prāṇa, spirit) animates a living body, a tree, for instance, that principle itself requires an explanation, and the explanation is in God, and not in Matter, because apart from God Matter is altogether lifeless. The Divine is besides all-embracing in its nature, like an ocean, all finite things are contained within its infinity, all small things within its greatness. In the Deity there is nothing passive, no imperfection, and accordingly no idea of Matter attaches to him.

God is immanent (antaryāmin), for he is in all things, as all things are in him. God is transcendent, for he is above all duality, all plurality, all increase and decrease,[1] all that is material. Lastly, God is a pure activity of thought: "Unseen, but seeing; unheard, but hearing; unperceived, but perceiving; unknown, but knowing."[2]

God is unknowable by a finite mind. How to know God?

Like Locke's Substance, Yājñavalkya's conception of God is a bundle of negations. All predications therefore that one may reasonably make about God are negative, No No (nêti nêti),[3] neither this nor that. This view being logically worked out, comes to this. The infinite is beyond the comprehension of a finite mind. It is therefore only an infinite mind, a mind without any idea of the many or plurality,[4] that can indeed comprehend the infinite. There is only this one way of apprehending the eternal Being that can never be proved[5] or measured, namely, to know that it is pure, beyond ether or space, the unborn one,

[1] Bṛihad Āraṇyaka Upaniṣad, IV. 4. 23.

[2] *Ibid*, III. 7. 23; III. 8. 11. S. B. E., XV, pp. 136, 138.

[3] *Ibid*, IV. 4. 20.

[4] *Ibid*, IV. 4 19 manasaivânudraṣṭavyam nêha nânâsti kiñcana. Cp. Kaṭha Upaniṣad, IV. 10-11.

[5] Aprameyam, *ibid*, IV. 4. 20.

great and immutable.[1] This implies a negative way of knowing God, namely, not to indulge in many words, "for that is mere weariness of the tongue."[2]

But we must know God, because without a knowledge of him, we know really nothing. We must know God, because when we know God, nothing more remains to be known. We shall know God, because he is that perfect model of knowledge, bliss and immortality which the mind may copy, in order to complete our knowledge, to perfect our conduct, to confirm our faith, to stimulate our charitable feeling, to increase our joy, and to save us from death. In other words, we shall know God, because he is not only the first, but also the best (prathamôttama)—he is the end. The end is, as we saw, threefold,—knowledge, bliss and immortality. With Yājñavalkya, too, knowledge is first, for without knowledge life is of no use. If the good be such, it would further follow that we must know God, because no one desires to be in doubt, to be ignorant, unhappy, and mortal. But how shall we know him? First, as Mahidāsa and Aristotle did: God is the pure activity of thought; and secondly, as Uddālaka did: The Deity is one, one only, without a second. Above all, we must recognise with Yājñavalkya this dictum: "I am He" (Sôham).

Necessity of a knowledge of God

(*b*) *The Soul* (*ātmā*).

Like his conception of God, Yājñavalkya's conception of soul is a synthesis of the speculations of previous thinkers, and yet not without an original stamp of its own. In agreement with the earlier thinkers, and also to a certain extent, with his contemporary Ajātaśatru, Yājñavalkya radically distinguished, in one sense at all events, Prajñā, the intelligent principle, from

Life and Soul.

[1] Virajaḥ parā ākāśād aja ātmā mahān dhruvaḥ.

[2] Bṛihad Âraṇyaka, IV. 4. 21.

Prāṇa, spirit, breath, the principle of life. Life is called Śarīra, the embodied soul,—a term corresponding to jīvātmā, the living principle. Life or the embodied soul is compared by an earlier thinker to "a horse attached to a cart."[1] Life is joined to the body, just as a horse is yoked to a cart. This means that Life is in its nature something totally different and accordingly separable from the body. Life is the essential form of the soul. That is to say, apart from the conscious activities, the soul is just this principle of Life.

Ajātaśatru maintained, as we saw, that Prajñā is in life, just as a razor is fitted in a razor case, or as fire in the araṇi wood.[2] In the language of Yājñavalkya, Life is surmounted by, loaded with, Prajñā νοῦς.[3] And we may put it thus: the soul is something superadded to Life. With Yājñavalkya, the fundamental fact is this Life, the embodied soul, and the soul in the strict sense is a pure mass of consciousness (vijñāna-ghana),[4] the intelligible essence of a living body, and also, as we might express it, a pure activity of thought.

Together with Prāṇa and Prajñā, Yājñavalkya inherits from the past the conceptions of Puruṣa, the incorporeal reflex or shadowy double of the corporeal, the immortal essence of the mortal, the immaterial soul in the material body. The pupil of the eye may be taken as a visible pattern of this soul, the divine person.

As we observed in connexion with Bālāki and Ajātaśatru, some of the thinkers of the post-Vedic period did not succeed,

An animistic notion of soul.

in spite of their great wealth of philosophical abstractions, in getting rid of a partly animistic and partly poetic notion of the soul. But when we seriously inquire into the root of such a notion, we can discover that nothing but their defective

[1] Chāndogya Upaniṣad, VIII. 12. 3.
[2] Kauṣītaki Upaniṣad, IV. 20.
[3] Bṛihad Āraṇyaka Upaniṣad, IV. 4. 35.
[4] *Ibid*, IV. 5. 13.

physiológical knowledge is accountable for it. Just as there is a person, the seer, in the eye, so there is a person in every organ of sense, in every particle of marrow, in every living cell. Thus the soul is the seer, while the eye is the instrument of seeing; the soul is the speaker, the tongue is the instrument of speaking; the soul is the hearer, the ear is the instrument of hearing; the soul is the thinker, the mind is to it the Divine vision.[1] In other words, the soul is the life of life, the eye of the eye, the ear of the ear, the mind of the mind.[2]

The Divine person, whose breath is life, body is intelligence, form is light, and the eye is the mind, is conceived as the master of a house, the ruler of all.[3] This person is the same as that in the disc of the sun. It is sometimes compared to a tiny, lonely bird (hamsa), which, like Wordsworth's skylark, soars up, during sleep (suṣupti), into the ethereal region of eternal light, and descends, when the sleep is over, to its lower nest,[4] this material world, the perishable body. The ethereal region of eternal light is the heart (hṛidaya)[5] which is also conceived as the city of Brahman (Brahmapura).[6] In this city there are two lakes, Ara and Nya. There is a third lake called Airammadiya between these two. There is in the city of Brahman an aśvattha tree which showers down soma, and there is in this third lake a lotus which is the seat of Brahman. The city of Brahman is unconquerable (aparājita), and the hall of Brahman is built by Prabhu or Vibhu. This account of the city of Brahman occurs in the Chāndogya Upaniṣad,[7] and recurs with some variations in the

[1] Chāndogya Upaniṣad, VIII. 13. 4-5.

[2] Bṛihad Āraṇyaka Upaniṣad, IV. 4. 18.

[3] *Ibid*, IV. 4. 22.

[4] *Ibid*, IV. 3. 12.

[5] Chandogya Upaniṣad, VIII. 3. 3.

[6] *Cf.* Leibnitz's "City of God" as distinguished from St. Augustine's *civitas Dei*. The Monadology (R. Latta's translation), p. 267.

[7] Chāndogya Upaniṣad, VIII. 5. 3.

language of Gārgyāyaṇa.[1] Yājñavalkya himself alludes to a playground[2] (ārāma), and affirms: one may see the playground of soul, the Divine person, but never itself.[3] This means that soul is incorporeal or immaterial. Now to return to the simile of the bird.

The theory of sleep.

During sound sleep, when all sensations cease, and all fancies, foolish imaginings, and representative cognitions of the mind are over, Soul, the lonely bird, living in the cavity of the heart, rises above the material, gets beyond the sensuous, and moves about in serenity (samprasāda) in the ethereal region of eternal light, assuming its true form, singing its own music, viewing its own vision, hearing its own voice, smelling its own scent, enjoying its own bliss, thinking its own thought. Hitherto the soul is unconscious (asaṁjñi), in the sense that it is above all duality, *i. e.*, not conscious of anything material, conditional, perishable, painful, and delusive.

But immediately after the sleep is over, the soul awakes, becomes conscious (saṁjñāna), and then, as the master of the house, it commands all the members, the senses, to awake and arise. This latter function of the soul was described by Mahīdāsa as commanding (ājñāna).[4] The communication is the easiest possible. For the arteries, capillaries, veins, and also perhaps nerves extend from the heart towards all parts of the body, even to the very hairs and nails.[5] With the awakening of the cognitive consciousness (vijñāna), all previous cognitions, sense-perceptions, motor-activity and actions, and also the reminiscence or past impressions (pūrva-prajñā) overtake the soul. The soul then becomes, in the language of Mahīdāsa, prajñāna.[6]

[1] Kauṣītaki Upaniṣad, I. 3.
[2] Brihad Āraṇyaka Upaniṣad, IV. 3. 14.
[3] *Ibid*, IV. 3. 15-30.
[4] Aitareya Āraṇyaka, II. 6. 3.
[5] Brihad Āraṇyaka Upaniṣad, IV. 3. 20.
[6] *Ibid*, IV. 3. 9.

Waking, dream and sleep compared to birth, last moment and death.

Yājñavalkya broadly conceives three states of the soul, corresponding to three worlds. The three states are the waking state (jāgrat), that of dream (svapna), and that of sleep (suṣupti). The three worlds are enumerated as this world, the intermediate world, and the world beyond.[1] The connexion or continuity of these three states, and of these three worlds is sought in the life of the soul. Yājñavalkya accepts and explains this expression of an unknown but earlier thinker[2]: The soul is a bank and a boundary.[3] The soul is a bank and a boundary. Yājñavalkya's interpretation of this dictum is very simple. Just as a fish swims along two banks of a river, so does the soul move along the two states—sleeping and waking.[4] Or, as a falcon or any other bird, after it has roamed about in the air, becomes tired, and folding its wings, descends to its nest, so does the Soul hasten from the waking state to sleeping. Between these two states there is an intermediate state, the dreaming.[5]

In the waking state, the soul becomes united with all evils, senses, desires, and all the rest, in fact, works under conditions foreign to its nature.[6] When in the intermediate state, the soul finds itself in between the waking state and sleeping.[7] Indeed, the dreaming soul moves along these two states, 'as if thinking, as if moving.'[8] Going up and down in its dream, the soul imagines manifold shapes for itself, either rejoicing with women, or laughing with friends, or witnessing

Dreaming.

[1] Chāndogya Upaniṣad, VIII. 4. 1

[2] Setu = literally, bridge, embankment. Bank is the rendering of Max Müller. Maryādā.

[3] Saṁjñānam anvavakramati sa eṣa jñaḥ savijñāno bhavati (Mādhyandina reading). *Ibid*, 4.2.

[4] Bṛihad Āraṇyaka Upaniṣad, IV. 3. 18.

[5] *Ibid*, IV. 3. 19.

[6] *Ibid*, IV. 3. 8.

[7] *Ibid*, IV. 3. 9.

[8] *Ibid*, IV. 3. 7.

terrific sights.[1] The soul is then out from the chamber of the heart for sport, and passes along the arteries, capillaries, veins, and also perhaps nerves, connecting the heart with various organs of sense. Now while dreaming, the soul sees, as if, some one kills it, some one overpowers it, as if, an elephant chases it, as if it falls into a well.[2] All these are the mere fancies, the vain imaginings of the soul, due to ignorance (avidyā), or, as we now say, due to hallucination and illusion of the mind. Here Yājñavalkya shows a genuine psychological insight, when he admits that the soul fancies in dream only that fear which it sees in waking.[3] This is in accord with a current, earlier view to which Yājñavalkya refers elsewhere,[4] provided that we may suppose Yājñavalkya to have used the word "asleep" (supta) in that passage rather loosely, in the sense of one who is dreaming. Dr. Deussen translates the passage thus : "Therefore it is said : It (sleep) is to him a place of waking only, for what he sees waking, the same he sees in sleep. Thus this spirit serves there for his own light."[5]

Dr. Roer and Prof. Max Müller take, in agreement, with Śaṅkara and Dvivedagaṅga, altogether a different view. According to them, the passage implies a very serious contention on the part of Yājñavalkya : the sleeping state is not the same as that of waking, for the soul, when asleep, becomes self-illuminated.[6]

That the passage does or does not imply a contention on the part of Yājñavalkya depends on the sense in which he employs the word "asleep" (supta). If it is meant in the sense of one who is dreaming, there is no ground for dispute ;

[1] Bṛihad Ārayaka Upaniṣad, IV. 3. 12.

[2] *Ibid*, IV. 3. 20.

[3] *Ibid*, IV. 3. 20 ; yad eva jāgrad bhayaṃ paśyati tad atrâvidyayā manyatê.

[4] *Ibid*, IV. 3. 14 ; jāgarita deśa evâsyaiṣa iti yāni hyêva jāgrat paśyati tāni supta ityâtrayaṁ puruṣaḥ svayaṁjyotir bhavati."

[5] "Vedānta," p. 205.

See for Śankara's interpretation—S. B. E., XV, p. 165, f. n. 3.

and if in the sense of one who is sleeping, as distinguished from dreaming, *i.e.*, imagining only what is experienced in waking, then there is ground for dispute. It may well be, as Dr. Deussen seems to think, that Yājñavalkya cited this older view simply in support of his own opinion. In fact, the point which goes on the side of Deussen, and contrary to Max Müller's view, is that Yājñavalkya repeats the same view on his own account. The soul fancies in dream that fear which it experiences in waking. But there is again a point which goes against Dr. Deussen. For, evidently, Yājñavalkya is not ready to admit that the mere imagining of a fear which has been previously experienced in waking completes the function of dreaming. In dreaming, according to Yājña-valkya, the soul displays something more than such an imagination, something of a prophetic vision,[1] that is to say, something relating to, and determining the nature of its future career ; imagination is not only reproductive, but also productive. This vision comes to the soul with the dawn of the consciousness (prajñana).—I am this or that,—a god or a king. With the dawn of such a consciousness dreaming is over and sleeping begins. The soul is then fully aware of itself, reaches the highest world (parama loka),[2] assumes its true form (rūpam), becomes in the language of an earlier thinker the best soul (uttama puruṣa).[3]

Dreams may be prophetic.

The sleeping state (suṣupti) is the end of dreaming (svapnānta), and is a state between the end of dreaming and the state of waking (buddhānta).[4] In this sleeping state, the soul transcends all that is material, fanciful, terrifying and painful, and becomes whole (samasta), and serene (samprasanna);[5]

Sleeping.

[1] Bṛihad Āranyaka Upaniṣad, IV. 3. 20.

[2] Chāndogya Upaniṣad, VIII. 12. 3.

[3] Bṛihad Āraṇyaka Upaniṣad, IV. 3. 18.

[4] Chāndogya Upaniṣad, VIII. 11. 1.

[5] Ia. *cf.* Thibaut's "Vedāntasūtras," III. 2. 4; K. C. Bhattacharyya's "Studies in Vedāntism," chapter on "Approach through psychology ;" *cf.* Thera Nāgasena's theories

and self-illuminated. Embraced by its self-consciousness, as though by a beloved wife, the soul knows nothing that is within, nothing that is without. Thus transcending all duality, and reaching this unity with itself, the soul thinks upon its own thought, sees its own vision, hears its own voice, smells its own scent, tastes its own bliss.[1] Blissful indeed is this sleeping state, when the soul becomes immortal, of an immaterial nature as it is.

Death and after.

Now, just as a dreaming state precedes sleeping, in the same way a dreaming state prevails on the eve of death. Besides, just as during sleep all sensations cease, so at death. Hence, to all appearance, death is the same as the state of dreaming (and partly that of sleeping), and re-birth is the same as the state of waking. Thus to complete the analogy, this world is the state of waking, the intermediate world is the state of dreaming, and the next world is the state of sleeping.

A psychological theory of death and re-birth.

We do not know whether Yājñavalkya cared to study, like Bādhva,[2] the premonitory symptoms of death. He thought that at death the soul recollects all that it has known and done in this life, and according to its knowledge and action, a consciousness dawns upon the mind: I am a father, or a Gandharva, or a God, or a Prajāpati, or a Brahman. With this consciousness settled upon the mind, the soul departs, mounted on spirit (prāṇa), retaining in some mysterious way the reminiscences or impressions of the past (pūrvaprajñā).[3] Here Yājnavalkya's idea of soul is thoroughly Platonic.

of dreams in the Milinda-pañho, pp. 298-300 (Rhys Davids' translation, ii, pp. 159-61). See also Shwe Zan Aung's Introductory Essay in the Compendium of Philosophy, P. T. S., 1910, pp. 48-49.

[1] Bṛihad Āraṇyaka Upaniṣad, IV. 3. 18, ff.

[2] Aitareya Āraṇyaka, III. 2. 7-17.

[3] Bṛihad Āraṇyaka Upaniṣad, IV. 4. 2. The Mādhyandina recension reads: saṁjñānam anvavakramati sa eṣa jñah savijñāno bhavati. The Kāṇvas read: savijñāno bhavati, savijñānam evānvavakramati.

Śāṇḍilya left behind him this dictum: A man is a creature of will. As is his will in this world, so will he be hereafter.[1] A passage in the Chāndogya Upaniṣad[2] adds, with clear consciousness, a new element—desire (kāma). And now Yājnavalkya introduces a third element—action (karma), and completely works out the view thus: A man is of desire. As is his desire, so is his will. As is his will, so is his action. And as he acts, so he attains. To put it otherwise, a man attains with his action the object to which his mind is attached. And after having enjoyed the full benefit of his deeds, he returns again from that world to this world of action.

The effect of the law of action upon the soul.

Although the soul is never born in the sense of becoming, a bad soul is bound to embody itself, owing to the inflexible law of action (karma). Karma draws the soul back into a new corporeality. In the language of Yājñavalkya, "as a grass-leech[3] after having reached the end of a blade of grass, and after having made another approach (to another blade), draws itself together towards it, thus does this self, after having thrown off this body and dispelled all ignorance, and after making another approach (to another body), draws himself together towards it. And as a goldsmith, taking a piece of gold, turns it into another, newer and more beautiful shape, so does this self, after having thrown off this body and dispelled all ignorance, make unto himself another, newer and more beautiful shape, whether it be like the Fathers, or like the Gandharvas . . . or like Brahman, or like other beings."[4]

[1] Chāndogya Upaniṣad, III. 14. 1. kratumayaḥ puruṣo: yathā kratur asmin loke puruṣo bhavati tathetaḥ pretya bhavati.

[2] *Ibid*, VII. 2. 1-9.

[3] Prof. Max Müller translates *triṇa-jalāyukā* as caterpillar, which does not seem to be correct. Though the St. Petersburg Dictionary and Monier Williams in his latest edition, translate the term as caterpillar, this is not the geometer caterpillar so well known in Europe, the German *Spannraupe*, but a leech, moving in a somewhat similar way and familiar to visitors of the northern hills in the rainy season.

[4] Bṛihad Āraṇyaka Upaniṣad, iv. 4. 3-4.

It is conceivable that even a bad soul remains for a time totally unconscious or forgetful of this world of action. But with its awakening from a slumber of death (saṁjñāna), the soul becomes conscious of a tendency to rebirth (savijñānaḥ bhavati). And with it, the potentiality of action, and the reminiscences or impressions of the past overtake the soul. Thus it returns to this world. "And as policemen, magistrates, equerries, and governors wait for a king who is coming back, with food and drink," so do all the elements wait on the soul when it returns.[1]

The case of a good soul (uttama puruṣa) is however different. As it is above all desires for sons or wealth or worlds, and having no other desire but for itself, karma cannot touch it, the law of action can exert no influence upon it. Consequently, the soul being Brahman, goes to Brahman beyond ether. Thus the mortal becomes immortal indeed.[2]

Here we must point out that, for Yājñavalkya, as for Mahidāsa and Aristotle, the immortality of soul does not mean corporeality or individuality, but simply immateriality. The soul is, therefore, in a sense, mortal or immortal as the body in which it is. In truth, there is an expression of Yājñavalkya's which is utterly irreconcilable with his general theory of re-birth. The expression is: The soul, conceived as a pure mass of consciousness (vijñāna-ghana), rises out from the elements, and perishes on their dissolution. (It may be in the sense, as Prof. Max Müller suggests, that it "vanishes into them"—tānyêvānu-vinaśyati.) And after death there is no more consciousness.

In the opinion of two later critics, Śīlāṅka[3] and Mādhavācārya[4], Yājñavalkya laid in this expression the foundation of materialism. The expression occurs in the dialogue between Yājñavalkya and his wife Maitreyī, referred to above.

[1] Brihad Āraṇyaka Upaniṣad, IV. 3 38.

[2] *Ibid.* IV. 4. 7,

[3],[4] Sūtrakṛitāṅga (ed. Dhanapati), pp. 290; Sarvadarśanasangraha, p. 2.

This dialogue shows that even Maitreyī was utterly bewildered at such an utterance on the part of her husband. Yājñavalkya offered to her this explanation:[1] The soul is of an imperishable, indestructible nature. And yet the soul must be said to be unconscious after death, in the sense that it transcends then all duality, that is to say, rises above all material conditions, and is, therefore, unaffected by the fate of a living body. It is not unlikely that some such idea is referred to and criticised by Buddha in the Brahmajāla and several other Suttas under the types of eschatological views: "After death the untouched soul (arogi attā) is unconscious."[2] This corresponds exactly to Yājñavalkya's expression—pretya saṁjñā nāsti.

Karma and Materialism.

Nevertheless, the great philosopher himself seems to have felt more than once the difficulty of maintaining his theory of rebirth or doctrine of karma in the face of all overpowering physical laws. This point is well brought out in a dialogue in the Bṛihad Araṇyaka Upaniṣad.[3] A thinker named Ārtabhāga says to Yājñavalkya, "If the speech of a dead man passes into fire, breath into air,.........the blood and seed are deposited in water, where is then the soul?" Yājñavalkya thereupon says, "This question is not to be discussed in public." The point which they discussed, we are told, was the mysterious effect of Karma.

(c) *The Mind* (*Manas*).

As with some of the earlier thinkers, so with Yājñavalkya, the mind is the Divine thinking in the soul. If the soul can

[1] According to Prof. L. D. Barnett, Yājñavalkya's expression is that of a materialist, but the argument is that of an idealist. According to Śankara's interpretation, Yājñavalkya meant only the dissolution of the limiting adjuncts (the mind, intellect, etc.) of the soul, but not the dissolution of the soul itself. *Cf.* Vedānta-Sūtras, II. 3. 17.

[2] Uddham-āghātanika-asaññi-vāda.

[3] III. 2. 13.

act at all, it acts in and through the mind. It is only in the power of an infinite mind to apprehend the absolute. Indeed, we may say that, as regards the realm of change, the mind is the soul. The soul is an ever active mind. It, therefore, always thinks, wills or feels. But as there cannot be thinking without an object to think upon, the mind thinks, in the absence of any other object, upon itself. Strictly, the best soul is nothing but this thinking upon thought. Sense-perception and the higher functions of the mind are not different in kind; all are in various degrees the same thinking upon thought.

Mind is the Divine thinking in man.

Yājñavalkya accepts in his system Mahidāsa's three-fold division of the functions of mind into sense-perception and the functions of heart and mind. The senses and objects are conceived as the seizer (graha) and the seized. Yājñavalkya conceded to Uddālaka that by the organ of vision we can only perceive the sensation of colour. The testimony of the senses is in general untrustworthy. The true knowledge is in the heart. The following is the enumeration of subjects and objects: Skin and touch; tongue and taste; nose and smell; eye and sight; ear and sound; mind and concepts (saṅkalpa); heart and knowledge (vidyā); hands and action; organ and delight; anus and excretion; legs and locomotion.[1]

The senses and objects.

(d) *Matter* (*Rūpa*).

In agreement with his predecessor Uddālaka Āruṇi, Yājñavalkya allows no difference of kind between mind or spirit on the one hand, and matter on the other. For, according to his view, matter is in various degrees the manifestation of the same *Actus Purus*, the endless activity of thought. Matter consists

No difference of kind between Mind and Matter.

[1] Bṛihad Āraṇyaka Upaniṣad, IV. 5. 12.

of the elements (bhūtāni), of which the number is nowhere given. In one passage,[1] he speaks apparently of these four elements: earth, water, air, and (heated) ether (ākāśa). But fire, too, is referred to elsewhere. As Yājñavalkya seems to have thought, the extension of earth, the flow of water, the motion of air, the burning of fire, the flash of lightning, all these natural phenomena which are of daily occurrence are activities, the same in kind as the higher vital and psychical functions.

Like Uddālaka and other earlier thinkers, Yājñavalkya had to recognise the presence of two distinct elements, masculine and feminine,[2] in the phantasmagoria of nature. Of these, the masculine element is called spirit (prāṇa) or the psychical principle,—soul (ātmā), and the feminine element constitutes matter, the principle of passivity, the substratum of change. The existence of spirit is not dependent on material conditions. But in order to create individuality, the soul is bound to unite with matter. Matter supplies the soul with nutrition.[3] As matter supplies the soul with nutrition, so the soul transforms matter into various types of existence, in the same way that a goldsmith fashions a piece of gold into various shapes.[4]

The correlation between soul and matter.

In passage of the Brahmajāla Sutta,[5] Buddha gives an analysis of the current views of his time on the finiteness or infinity of the world. He reckons them as four in number, and catalogues them all under the name Antânantika-Vāda. Elsewhere [6] he enumerates them under Loka-cintā (Thoughts regarding the world of existence). In the Sthānāṅga (IV. 4), as Dr. Schrader points out, Mahāvīra calls them Mita-vāda.

[1] Bṛihad Āranyaka Upaniṣad, IV. 4. 5.

[2] *Ibid*, I. 4. 3.

[3] *Ibid*, IV. 3. 37 (S. B. E.)

[4] *Ibid*, IV. 4. 4.

[5] Dīgha-nikāya, I, pp. 22-24.

[6] *e.g.*, Aṅguttara-nikāya, Vol. II, p. 80.

The passage in the Brahmajāla-sutta presupposes a few passages in the Bṛihad Āraṇyaka Upaniṣad (III. 3; III. 6; III. 8), the dialogue between Bhujyu Lahyāyani and Yājñavalkya, and that between Yājñavalkya and Gārgi. The four views are stated by Buddha as follows:—

Infinity and finiteness.

(1) Finite is the world, so that a boundary may be conceived round it.[1]

(2) Infinite is the world, and limitless.

(3) The world is limited above and below, but infinite across.

(4) The world is neither finite nor infinite.[2]

Finite is the world, surrounded by a boundary. This reminds us at once of a Pythagorean view put into the mouth of Yājñavalkya in a dialogue of the Bṛihad Āraṇyaka Upaniṣad (III. 3.). Lāhyāyani, the interlocutor of the dialogue, asked Yājñavalkya: What are the ends or limits of the worlds (lokānām anta)? and where are gone the Pārīkṣitas? (an old royal family, who are believed to have disappeared from the face of the earth). Yājñavalkya said in reply: "Thirty-two journeys of the car of the sun is this world,"[3] that is to say, the boundary of this world is equal to thirty-two times the orbit of the sun. It is surrounded[4] on all sides by Pṛithivī (Extension, the boundary of the formed Universe?), twice as large. Pṛithivī is surrounded on all sides by the Ocean (samudra=varuṇa), twice as large. The space between the zone of Pṛithivī and that of the Ocean hardly exceeds the edge of a razor or the wing of a mosquito. This space is filled with air (vāyu). The Pārīkṣitas are gone there where people go who have performed a horse sacrifice, *i.e.*, to the region of Air.

[1] "antavā ayaṁ loko, parivaṭumo." Rhys Davids translates parivaṭumo by "so that a path can be traced round it.

[2] Dial., B. II, p. 360.

[3] Max Müller's translation of "dvātrimśat vai devarathanhyāṇvayaṁ lokaḥ."

[4] paryeti=literally, surrounds; cp. parivaṭumo, Dīgha-nikāya, I. 23.

This doctrine does not seem to be an integral part of Yājñavalkya's system. Besides, the passage in which the doctrine is set out is corrupt. But the doctrine has some historical connexion with Uddālaka, who, like Pythagoras, divided the formed universe into the three regions (Trivṛit) of Fire, Water, and Earth.[1]

(Infinite is the world, and without limit. This view is opposed to that which is discussed above.)

The world is limited above and below, but infinite across. This reminds us of the views of Gārgi Vācakñavi and Yājñavalkya, as set out in two dialogues of the Bṛihad Āraṇyaka Upaniṣad (III. 6; III. 8.). In the first of these dialogues, the clever Gārgi lays down a proposition which is fully worked out by Yājñavalkya: Everything on this earth 'is woven, like warp and woof' (ota-prota) in water. The view is briefly put thus in the second dialogue: In space or ether (ākāśa = aditi, απειρον) is 'woven, like warp and woof,' all that is 'above the heavens, beneath the earth, embracing heaven and earth, past, present, and future' (bhūta, bhava, bhaviṣya). And space or ether is woven in like manner in Brahman, the Imperishable One (Akṣara).

CHAPTER XII

Supplementary Discussions.

In closing the history of post-Vedic philosophy with Yājñavalkya it is necessary to draw the reader's attention to a few Upaniṣads dealing more synthetically as well as systematically certain aspects of post-Vedic philosophy, as also to a Chāndogya Dialogue which may be said to serve the purpose of a glossary to the philosophical views hitherto considered. These are highly important as indicating the possibility of an internal chronology of the Upaniṣad literature, taken as a whole. The Upaniṣads under reference are the Māṇḍūkya, the Subāla and the Paiṅgala, to leave out of account the Āruṇika and the Yājñavalkya which inculcate the duties and ideals of recluse life. The dialogue forms the seventh chapter of the Chāndogya Upaniṣad, and it appears to embrace in its terminology a compendium, so to say, of post-Vedic philosophy. Here we shall be content with mentioning only some salient features of these Upaniṣads and the Dialogue.

1. Māṇḍūkya.—The Upaniṣad of this name seems to belong to the same age as the Muṇḍaka, the Kaṭha, etc., and probably it embodies, like them, the views of a school of wanderers which went by that name. It remains to be seen whether the Māṇḍūkya was derived from a Paribbajaka teacher who is described in the Majjhima Nikāya[1] as Samaṇa Maṇḍikā-putta or Recluse who was the son of Maṇḍikā.

The most notable point in the teaching of this Upaniṣad, considered apart from the Gauḍapāda-Kārikā, is that instead of the three states of consciousness, recognised by Yājñavalkya

[1] Majjhima, II, 24. p.

and other previous thinkers, it speaks of four planes (catuspāda), *viz.* :—

(*i*) Jāgarita-sthāna or waking plane, corresponding to Yājñavalkya's waking state (jāgrat).

(*ii*) Svapna-sthāna or dreaming plane, corresponding to Yājñavalkya's dreaming state (svapna).

(*iii*) Suṣupta-sthāna or sleeping plane, corresponding to Yājñavalkya's end of dreaming state (svapnānta) which is not separately counted as a state by itself but considered as the sleeping state in its inception.

(*iv*) The fourth plane, designated in the later Upaniṣads as *Turiya*, which corresponds to *Suṣupti* proper in Yājñavalkya's phraseology.

Though the Māṇḍūkya has no claim to originality, the conception of four planes being distinctly implied in Yājñavalkya's definition of three states, its treatment of the subject is doubly significant in history, *first*, that it made clear and definite what was vague and indefinite in earlier thought, and *secondly*, that it shows an advancement in mystical perception of reality. No less remarkable is the fact that the Māṇḍūkya definition of four planes was a fruitful synthesis of Yājñavalkya's psychological doctrine of three states and Varuṇa's *pañcakoṣa* doctrine :

(*i*) Annamaya and Prāṇamaya souls coming under the Māṇḍūkya's waking plane.

(*ii*) Manomaya under the dreaming.

(*iii*) Vijñānamaya under the sleeping.

(*iv*) Ānandamaya under the fourth.

Buddha's representation of the Taittirīya doctrine in the Brahmajāla Sutta precisely follows the Māṇḍūkya line. Further, we need hardly mention that the Māṇḍūkya conception of four planes of consciousness is closely connected with the Buddhist discrimination of four planes, *kāmāvacara*, *rūpāvacara*, *arūpāvacara* and *lokuttara*. The Māṇḍūkya conception also may be said to have afforded a basis for the four-fold modes of meditation, analysed and amplified differently by the Jainas, the Buddhists and the Pātañjalas. Buddha's conception of four kinds of food, material, sensuous, intellectual and so forth, also can be traced back to the Māṇḍūkya doctrine.

2. Subāla.—This Upaniṣad, as its name implies, inculcates a religious ideal of child-like simplicity of outlook on life. *Bālyena tisthāsed bāla-svabhāvo asaṅgo niravadyo.*[1] Like the Māṇḍūkya, the Subāla, too, seems to embody the religious and philosophical views of a school of wanderers, and possibly those of the Māṇḍūkyas themselves, as may be surmised from a Majjhima Discourse[2] where the Buddha sharply criticises a similar view, ascribed to the wanderer Uggahamāna, son of Samaṇa-Maṇḍikā. Uggahamāna is said to have maintained that 'child is the very model of moral perfection (sampanna-kusala).' The Upaniṣad under reference seems to be later, in point of date, than the Chāndogya, the Bṛihad Āraṇyaka, the Muṇḍaka and the Kaṭha, and even it may be post-Buddhistic. It is throughout an imaginary dialogue between Raikva and Prajāpati. The chief interest of this work lies in its synthetic treatment of Vedic and post-Vedic philosophy, particularly of the teachings of the Puruṣa-Sūkta and Puruṣavidha-brāhmaṇa and the philosophical views of Uddālaka, Yājñavalkya, the Muṇḍakas and the Gotamakas identified in Part III with the Kaṭhas.

The Subāla upholds Yājñavalkya's theory of the revealed character of Vedic literature and connects the same historically with the teachings of the Puruṣa-Sūkta and Puruṣavidha Brāhmaṇa.[3] It is important to note that in the Subāla list of the Vedic texts and systems which are said to be breathed out or revealed by the Supreme Being, we have the mention of Nyāya, Mīmāṁsā and Dharmaśāstras, replacing

[1] Subāla, 13.

[2] Majjhima, II, pp. 24-25.

[3] Subāla, 1-2.

Sūtras in the list of Yājñavalkya. This goes not only to prove that the Subāla, as we now have it, is later than the Bṛihad Āraṇyaka containing the views of Yājñavalkya but also to indicate that the Nyāya, the Mīmāṁsā and the Dharmaśāstras as three separate systems of thought were but fruitful results of a gradual differentiation of the three aspects of one and same older system. The Subāla is just one of the many Upaniṣads which furnish the historian with sufficient evidence to justify the hypothesis that like the Vedānta, the Sāṁkhya-Yoga,[1] an expression applied probably to the Sāṁkhya, the Yoga, the Nyāya, the Vaiśeṣika and the Mīmāṁsā in their undifferentiated forms were developments out of the philosophy of the Upaniṣads.

Yājñavalkya's expression *bālyena tiṣṭhati*, which lent itself to different interpretations, is explained in the Subāla as 'living with the child-like simplicity of outlook and purity of life, an ideal which a European writer, unacquainted with the history of Indian thought, would be easily tempted to attribute to the Christians.

In interpreting the theory that something came out of nothing (*asato sat ajāyata*) we pointed out in connexion with "Prajāpati" and "Brahmaṇaspati" hymns, as well as in connexion with Taittirīya philosophy, that the term nothing (*a-sat*) does not denote nothing in the abstract but the cosmic substance or first cause of the universe which is non-existent in the sense that it cannot be defined except by the negation of all predications applying to concrete things of experience. The Subāla fully corroborates our interpretation of the theory in a significant passage[2] which throws abundant light on the Muṇḍaka view[3] of the *prima causa*. One must admit that Śaṅkara's interpretation of the Muṇḍaka view is similar to

[1] Subāla, 9.
[2] *Ibid*, 3.
[3] Muṇḍaka, I. 6.

that in the Subāla and it is not improbable that his interpretation was actually based upon the Subāla.

Among other notable points the Subāla will always be highly valued as indicating the process of the development of the conception of Nirvāṇa in its Buddhistic as well as in the Gītā sense out of and on the lines of Yājñavalkya's conception of the Suṣupti state of soul.

The Subāla has no claim to originality of conception, and its chief interest lies in its application of the fundamental truths of post-Vedic philosophy to life.

3. Paiṅgala.—It may turn out that the Upaniṣad of this name contains certain advanced philosophical views of Yājñavalkya, those which he formulated after his withdrawal from the world, *i.e.*, during his Araṇyaka life. This Upaniṣad, as we now have it, is composed of four separate dialogues between Yājñavalkya and Paiṅgala of which the fourth seems to be in style much later than the first three. The future student of the Upaniṣads has to decide whether the Paiṅgala borrowed from Śaṅkara's Vedānta commentaries or Śaṅkara borrowed from the Paiṅgala. The point which is of importance to us is that the Upaniṣad clearly bears out our views that Uddālaka's conception of matter and of tripartite universe afforded a basis for the Sāṅkhya conception of Prakṛiti, characterised by three qualities.

4. Chāndogya Dialogue.—This forms the seventh chapter of the Chāndogya Upaniṣad, and like the dialogue forming its eighth or last chapter, it differs by its imaginary character from other dialogues where we feel throughout personal touches of the interlocutors. The dialogue under reference supplies us with a general glossary of philosophical terms and embraces in its terminology the entire philosophy of post-Vedic period. The terms explained are logically connected and arranged in an ascending order of importance to human interests, though the logical sequence established between them does not seem to be a very happy one, when judged

from our modern standpoint. It is difficult for us to understand how *water* is more potent or important a factor than *food*, and *food* than *strength*, unless we study this terminological discussion in the light of Vedic and post-Vedic philosophy to which it applies. The terms explained are 23 in number, headed by *Nāma* and ending with *Bhūmā*: *Nāma*, *Vāk*, *Mana*, *Saṅkalpa*, *Citta*, *Dhyāna*, *Vijñāna*, *Bala*, *Anna*, *Āpa*, *Teja*, *Ākāśa*, *Smara*, *Āśā*, *Prāṇa*, *Satya*, *Vijijñāsā*, *Mati*, *Śraddhā*, *Niṣṭhā*, *Kriti*, *Sukha*, and *Bhūmā*. All these terms are explained in a pantheistic vein and in their practical and religious bearings. It will be going beyond our present purpose to enter into a detailed discussion of the terminology which is better suited for a separate treatise. It is enough to say that there are matters in this dialogue which throw light on the development of Logic, and ideas which were followed up and expanded in later popular literature.[1]

PART III.

PHILOSOPHY BEFORE MAHĀVĪRA AND BUDDHA.

(Circa 800-600 B.C.)

Introductory.

The title chosen for the third part had its origin in a well-known remark of Dr. Jacobi, who says:[1] "The records of the Buddhists and Jainas about the philosophical ideas current at the time of the Buddha and Mahāvīra, meagre though they be, are of the greatest importance to the historian of that epoch. For they show us the ground on which, and the materials with which a religious reformer had to build his system."

Origin of the title.

In commenting upon this remark of Dr. Jacobi, Dr. Rhys Davids adds these words: "The philosophical and religious speculations contained in them (the Buddhist and Jaina records) may not have the originality or intrinsic value, either of the Vedānta or of Buddhism. But they are nevertheless historically important because they give evidence of a stage less cultured, more animistic, that is to say, earlier. And incidentally they will undoubtedly be found, as the portions accessible already show, to contain a large number of important references to the ancient geography, the political divisions, the social and economic conditions of India at a period hitherto very imperfectly understood."[2]

Throughout the Buddhist texts, earlier as well as later, there are numerous references to, and a number of direct and side attacks upon a body of six famous founders of schools,

[1] Introduction, Jaina Sūtras, II, S. B. E., p. XXVII.

[2] Buddhist India, pp. 163-164. See also Schrader's *Uber den stand der Indischen Philosophie zur zeit Mahaviras und Buddhas*, Strassburg, 1902, for a useful classification of pre-Buddhistic philosophical notions.

all opposed to the Buddhists.[1] On the one hand, they are classed by the Buddhists as the six Heretics or Sophists (cha titthiyā). And on the other hand, they are distinguished from Uddaka Rāmaputta and Ālāra Kālāma, who are recognised as the two successive teachers of the young ascetic Siddhattha. In all probability, the designation Śramaṇa (recluse, *religieux*) which came into vogue at least as early as the time of Yājñavalkya was also applied to them—the titthiyas or Tīrthaṅkaras. Further, to all appearance, these teochers, whether Brāhmans or not by birth,[2] were in their general attitude as anti-Vedic and anti-Brāhmanic as perhaps the Buddha himself. Indeed, Buddha often thought that he had been all along fighting and reconciling these two great opponents—the Śramans on one side, and the Brāhmans on the other. But the same may very well be said, positively, of Mahāvīra, and negatively, of Sañjaya the Sceptic.

The six Sophists.

Now these six teachers are mentioned in the oldest Buddhist records (which are all in Pali) in this order: Pūraṇa Kassapa, Makkhali Gosāla, Ajita Kesa-Kambala, Pakudha-Kaccāyana, Sañjaya Belaṭṭhaputta, Nigaṇṭha Nāta-putta.[3] Of them, the last-mentioned is identified by Profs. Jacobi and Hoernle (giving strong reasons on their side) with Mahāvīra, the founder of Jainism, or better, of Kiriyā-vāda—the doctrine of free-will activity, Dynamism.

The title "Philosophy before Mahāvīra and Buddha" will show that we exclude, contrary to the Buddhist scheme, the name of Mahāvīra from the company of six Titthiyas.

Three orders of teachers:

Besides the teachers above mentioned there are others who represent a period of thought which is not precisely post-Vedic, but later than it, i.e., neo-Vedic. The oldest Jaina and Buddhist

[1] Sākya-puttiya-samaṇas.

[2] Sutta-nipāta, p. 79; "muṇḍāpi hi idha ekacce brāhmaṇā bhavanti."

[3] *E.g.*, Dīgha-nikāya, I. 48-49.

records, together with Pāṇini's Aphorisms and Patañjali's commentary give, indeed, evidence of a continued existence of the old order of things at a time when many new orders have sprung up.

Thus, for instance, in the Tevijja Sutta, Buddha says to Vāseṭṭha (Vasiṣṭha): "The Brāhmans of to-day chant over again or repeat (the mantra, sacred verses), intoning or reciting exactly as has been intoned or recited (by the Ṛiṣis of old)."[1]

Secondly, the Tevijja Sutta makes mention of the following Brāhman schools as representatives of the post-Vedic order: the Aitareyas, the Taittirīyas, the Chāndogyas, the 'Chandavas' and the Bahvṛicas.[2]

Lastly, the same Tevijja Sutta introduces us to "many very distinguished and wealthy" Brāhmans of the neo-Vedic order, such as Kaṅki (Caṅki), Tārukkha (Tārukṣya),[3] Pokkharasāti (Puṣkarasādi),[4] Jānussoṇi (Jānaśruti),[5] Todeyya (Taudeya),[6] and others.

With the close of the post-Vedic period, we enter upon a third period which is so far removed from the ancient Vedic that people have begun to doubt if there is any longer a Ṛiṣi (Brahmarṣi, divinely favoured seer) among them. Āpastamba in his Dharmasūtra[7] states that no sages are born among the men of later ages.[8] It is, then, merely by way of courtesy, or as a recognition of the worth of religion and Vedic learning that Āpastamba concedes to Śvetaketu[9] and others the title of a Ṛisi-like scholar (śrutarṣi).[10] Again, in a passage of

[1] Dial., B., II. 304. *Cf.* Pāṇini's list of Vedic Ṛiṣis, Aph. II. 4. 65.

[2] *Cf.* Pāṇini's list, Aphs. IV. 3. 102, 209.

[3] Aitareya Āraṇyaka, III. 6. 1-4, *etc.*

[4] Āpastamba, I. 10, 28, 1; I. 6, 19, 7.

[5] *Cf.* Jānaśruti Pautrāyana, Chāndogya Upaniṣad, IV, 2, 1.

[6] Dial, B., Vol. II, pp. 300-301; Majjhima-nikāya No. 48—Suttanipāta, III. 9. *Cf.* Pāṇini, IV. 3.94.

[7] I. 2. 5. 4-5.

[8] Bühler's Āpastamba, S. B. E., II, p. XXXVII.

[9] Son of Uddālaka Āruṇi, grandson of Aruṇa.

[10] Āpastamba, I. 2. 5. 6.

the Śatapatha Brāhmaṇa,[1] it is alleged that Śvetaketu was a contemporary of Yājñavalkya.

The last mentioned facts give some support to our assumption that Yājñavalkya is the great landmark between the post-Vedic period and the neo-Vedic and later ages. In the history of Indian literature the period with which we are dealing is unanimously called the Sūtra period. In the history of Indian religions the same may be designated as the period of Śramans and Brāhmans. And it is remarkable that Yājñavalkya, so far as we know, is the first among the post-Vedic thinkers to have called attention to Śramans. Besides the Śramans Yājñavalkya expressly refers to the Tāpasas (Hermits). In point of fact, we regard the period in question as that which shows the germs, the beginnings of all that we find later.

The most remarkable feature of Indian life at this period, which bears upon the progress of thought and the development of social life, is the existence of various orders of teachers, both Vedic and anti-Vedic. These orders represent differing groups or schools of thought. These groups may roughly be divided into either Śramans and Brāhmans or Hermits and Wanderers.

Hermits.

The following note of Professor Rhys Davids applies to the Hermits (Tāpasas) in general: "In the forests adjoining the settlements, the disciples of the various schools, living a hermit life, occupied themselves, according to the various tendencies of the schools to which they belonged, either in meditation or in sacrificial rites, or in practices of self-torture, or in repeating over to themselves, and in teaching to their pupils, the Suttas containing the tenets of their school. Much time was spent in gathering fruits and roots for their sustenance...........And there was difference of opinion, and of practice, as to the comparative importance attached to the learning of texts.

[1] History of Ancient Sanskrit Literature, p. 421.

But the hermitages where the learning, or the repeating, of texts was unknown were the exceptions."[1]

Wanderers.

As regards the wanderers (parivrājakas) we can add little to what Prof. Rhys Davids in his Buddhist India (pp. 141-160) has said concerning them. This important body or order of teachers was not known in India much before the rise of Buddhism. Apart from, and other than, the order of the Hermits, the institution of the wanderers was held in great respect throughout the country. Like the Greek Sophists, the Indian wanderers, too, differed in many respects, in attitude, opinion, intelligence, earnestness and purpose. As Professor Rhys Davids describes them, "They were teachers, or sophists, who spent eight or nine months of every year[2] wandering about precisely with the object of engaging in conversational discussions[3] on matters of ethics and philosophy, nature-lore and mysticism."

The system of education then prevalent in India demanded of every student, every learner, to travel, after he had finished his course under a certain teacher, or in a certain institution, in order to acquire experience, to better his conduct, to seek a more proficient teacher, to carry on learned discussions with others who were well-versed on the subject in which he was interested, in short, to further his own knowledge. There was no question raised as to rank, age, sex, or colour. He who was defeated or convinced in the discussion openly declared himself to be a disciple of the disputant who baffled him by his argument and superior wisdom.

It is a generally accepted opinion that a spirit of toleration is one of the fundamental features of the religious life of India. As the existence of an institution, such as that of the wanderers, proves, this spirit of toleration was not confined to

[1] Buddhist India, pp. 140-141. Also pp. 246-7.

[2] Bühler's Gautama III. 13: "He must not change his residence during the rainy season," *cf.* III. 21.

[3] Vitaṇḍā, Tarka, Nyāya, Mīmāṁsā.

religion or matters of belief, but permeated also every department of life and thought. Even we have instances where in the same family the members (as is now the case in Japan) were adherents of different schools and yet lived happily together.

Now to turn to Indian philosophy, the neo-Vedic period was so far removed from the ancient Vedic that thinkers had in course of time ceased to feel the fascination of, and cherish admiration for, Vedic learning and Vedic rites. Some of the rightminded philosophers, with their later successors, were all ranged against the Vedic theologians, the Brāhman priests. All of them agreed in viewing Vedic study in the light of not-knowledge or ignorance (avidyā),[1] in estimating the four Vedas and the Vedic Sciences as the lower knowledge,[2] in teaching that the Self (ātman) was not obtainable by the study of the Veda,[3] in holding that the three Vedas were subject to the three qualities (guṇas[4]), in questioning the divine origin of the Vedas[5] and all efficacy of the sacrifices, funeral oblations, or the gifts to the priesthood, enjoined in the Vedas,[6] and in stoutly maintaining that the observance of moral precepts and the contemplation, knowledge, and realisation of the nature of Brahman were far superior to the performance of Vedic sacrifices, and the acquisition of Vedic learning.[7]

Anti-Vedic movement.

1—2 Muṇḍakôpaniṣad, I. 1. 4-5 : "aparā vidyā."

3 *Ibid*, III. 2. 3 ; Kaṭhôpaniṣad, I. 2. 23.

4 Bhagavad-gitā, II. 4. 5 ; "Traiguṇya-viṣayā vedā nistraiguṇyo bhavārjuna." *Cf.* the Sāṁkhya-kārikā, 2.

5 "Na hyāptavādā nabhaso nipatanti." Viṣṇupurāṇa.

6 The views of Ajita Keśa-Kambalin, and of those of his school.

7 Here is the summary of the Buddha's views on sacrifices. The sacrifice performed with ghee, oil, butter, milk, honey, and sugar only is better than that at which living creatures are slaughtered. Better than this mode of sacrifice is charity, especially that which is extended to holy and upright men. Better still is the putting up of monasteries. But better than this is certainly the observance of moral precepts. And the best of all sacrifices is the four-fold meditation or philosophic contemplation. See Dial, B. II. 180-182. *Cf.* Bhagavadgitā, IV. 33 : "Śreyān dravyamayāt yajñāj jñāna-yajñaḥ parantapaḥ" ; Śaṅkara's Vivekacūḍāmaṇi, 2 ; The Jaina Uttarādhyayana Sūtra, XIV. 12.

25

The history of such a revolt against the Vedic modes of learning and sacrifice goes back to ancient times. It can be traced, at least, as far back as the celebrated hymn on Frogs,[1] which is hurled, according to Prof. Max Müller,[2] as a satire at the Vedic priest-hood, or better, at the system of hymn-chanting. But, as we saw, it was the school of thinkers called the Kāvaṣeyas who were the first to raise this question: "Why should we repeat the Veda or offer this kind of sacrifice ?[3] Their views were, later on, worked out by pratardana.[4] In the meantime, Mahidāsa asked himself this important question: 'People say—Hymn, Hymn (uktha, uktha)! But do they know what Hymn means ?'[5] A little earlier than Pratardana's view, that like all ordinary works, the sacrificial oblations have an end, some unknown thinker felt himself bound to express this view: "What people call sacrifice (yajña),[6] that is really holy life (brahmacarya)."[7]

The end of philosophy not yet realised

Although the neo-Vedic period is so far removed from the ancient Vedic, the task of philosophy is not, as yet, accomplished. This fact is nowhere so clearly brought out as in the famous episode of Indra and Prajāpati, contained in the Chāndogya Upaniṣad.[8] The gods deputed Indra to Prajāpati to gain a knowledge of the Self,—Brahman the source of immortality and fearlessness. Indra lived with Prajāpati as a pupil for thirty-two years. The first answer of Prajāpati was: The body is the self (ātmā),—the immortal, fearless Brahman. Indra was satisfied in his heart for the time being. But on further reflection, his faith was shaken, and he began to think, if the body be the self or

[1] Ṛigveda, VII. 163.
[2] History of Ancient Sanskrit literature, pp. 494 ff.
[3] Aitareya Āraṇyaka, III. 2.6.8.
[4] Kauṣitaki Upaniṣad, II 5.
[5] Aitareya Āraṇyaka, II. 1.2.1.
[6] Chāndogya Upaniṣad, III. 16.1: "Man is sacrifice."
[7] *Ibid*, VIII. 5.1.
[8] *Ibid*, VIII. 7.15.

the organism be the highest reality, where is then immortality? So he came again as a pupil to Prajāpati, and lived with him another thirty-two years.

The second answer of Prajāpati was—The dreaming, imagining mind is the Self,—the immortal, fearless Brahman. It satisfied Indra for the time being. But he began again to feel doubt. Though the dreaming, imagining mind is not entirely dependent on the body or affected by material conditions (like the senses), yet it is not altogether unconscious of pleasure and pain. If so, where is immortality or fearlessness (amṛitam abhayam)?

The third answer given by Prajāpati was—The soul, whole and serene in the state of dreamless sleep, is the Self,—the immortal, fearless Brahman. Indra remained content with it for a while. But further reflection led him to feel doubt. The soul in the state of dreamless sleep knows neither itself, nor other existent things (bhūtāni), It goes then into utter annihilation (vināśam evāpito bhavati).[1] If this be the case, there is no good in it. So he came again as a pupil to Prajāpati. This time Prajāpati plainly told Indra that his knowledge did not reach further. However, he asked Indra to stay another five years. Prajāpati did not mean to express any further opinion, but just to offer an explanation (anuvyākhyā) of that which he had said before.

This episode poetically illustrates the fact that the thought of the post-Vedic period was troubled by the consciousness of failure in its quest of immortality and fearlessness (amṛitam, abhayam). Only the material or physical, or the mental or psychical had been assumed as the ultimate ground of immortality. The neo-Vedic thinkers sought, therefore, to

[1] See for the analysis of this Upaniṣad passage by the Buddha, first, the Poṭṭhapāda Sutta in the Dīgha-nikāya, I, p. 195 (Dial. B II. 259-260), and then, the Brahmajāla Sutta, Dīgha-nikāya, I, p. 34 (Dial. B, II, pp. 46-49). See also D' Alwis's "Buddhist Nirvāna," p. 47; and Jacobi's Jaina Sūtras, II. 236, 339. Note carefully why Buddha catalogues the views under the name of Annihilationism (Ucchedaṁ, vināsaṁ).

establish it on the basis of pure metaphysics or logical abstraction.

Method of arrangement.

We must call attention here to the method adopted by Mahāvīra and Buddha in dealing with the philosophies of the period. In contradistinction to his own system called Kiriyaṁ or Kiriyāvāda, Mahāvīra, as his disciples tell us, broadly divided the philosophical views of his time into three groups—(1) Akiriyaṁ, (2) Aṇṇānaṁ, and (3) Vinayaṁ.[1] Buddha's division into (1) Sakkāya-diṭṭhi, (2) Vicikicchā, and (3) Silabbataṁ [2] is almost identical, as we shall see, with that of his predecessor. According to this grouping, we propose to consider the teachers of the philosophies in question under these three heads—(1) Metaphysicians, (2) Sceptics, and (3) Moralists.

I. The Metaphysicians.

(*Akriyāvādins.*)

By the term Akiriyaṁ or Akriyāvāda Mahāvīra understood a theory of life and existence, or any mode of speculation, which was in some way antagonistic to, or which did not fit well into, his own doctrine, rightly described as Kiriyaṁ or Kriyāvāda—the doctrine of free-will activity, Dynamism.[3] Kriyāvāda is otherwise called implicitly in the language of Mahāvīra,[4] and explicitly in the language of Buddha,[5] Kammavāda or the Doctrine of Action. Accordingly, the term Akiriyaṁ may be held as equivalent to Akammavāda or the Doctrine of

[1] Uttarādhyayana Sūtra, XVIII, 23; Sūtrakṛitāṅga, X. 12.4.f.; etc.

[2] Ratana-Sutta; Dhammasaṅgaṇi, 1002; etc.

[3], [4] "Acchitti Kiriya-vādi vayanti, nacchitti Akiriya-vādiyā The Kriyāvādins speak of existence, while the Akriyāvādins of non-existence." Quoting this verse from a canonical source, Śīlāṅka says: Kriyā Jivādi padārthôstîtyādikaṁ vaditum śīlaṁ yeṣām te Kriyāvādinaḥ. Etad viparyastā Akriyāvādinaḥ. Lokāyatikaḥ Śākyādayāś ca teṣām ātmaiva nāsti kutas tat kriyā tajjanito va karmabandha iti," Sūtrakṛitāṅga (ed. Dhanapati), p. 456.

[5] Aṅguttara-nikāya, I, p. 286.

non-Action. As Suddharman, the chief disciple of Mahāvīra, expounds his master's view,[1] the Akriyāvādins or pure Metaphysicians teach the annihilation of good actions by denying the potentiality of Karma in future existence. Referring obviously to the Muṇḍakas, the Gautamakas, the Kātyāyanas, and others, Suddharman adds: They declare that the sun does not rise there (in the Brahma-world), nor does it set. The moon does not wax, nor does it wane. No rivers flow there, nor do any winds blow.[2] The whole world is said to be barren, eternal and solid.[3] Just as a blind man, surrounded though he be with light, does not see objects because of his blindness,[4] so the Akriyāvādins having a perverted intellect (niruddhapaṇṇā), do not apprehend the laws of action, though they really exist.

In the Sthānāṅga (IV. 4), Mahāvīra alludes to eight classes of thinkers all under the same name of the Akriyāvādins, *viz.*, (1) Ekkāvādins or Monists, Theists, Monotheists; (2) Aṇikkavādins or Pluralists; (3) Mitavādins or Extensionists; (4) Nimmitavādins or Cosmogonists; (5) Sāyavādins or Sensualists; (6) Samucchedavādins or Annihilationists; (7) Ṇiyavādins or Eternalists; and (8) Ṇa-santi-paralokavādins or Materialists.[5]

In the Brahmajāla Sutta (Dīgha-nikāya, I. 12-39), Buddha adopts almost the same method of classification. Omitting the Eel-wrigglers or Sceptics (Amarā-vikkhepakas), Buddha mentions (1) Sassatavādins or Eternalists; (2) Ekaccasassatavādins or Semi-eternalists; (3) Antānantikas or Extensionists; (4) Adhicca-samuppannikas or Fortuitous Originists; (5) Uddham-āghatanikas or Eschatologists including Saññivādins, Asaññi-vādins, and Neva-saññi-nâsaññi-vādins;

[1] Sūtrakṛitāṅga, I. 12. 4: "Lavâva saṁkiyā anāgachi no kiriyaṁ āhaṁsu Akiriyavādi." Śīlāṅka wrongly interprets Lavâva saṁkiyâ as meaning the Lokâyatas and the Śākays (Buddhists), and others. The expression lavâva saṁ-kiyâ: laya eva satkriyâ.

[2] *Cf.* Muṇḍaka-Upaniṣad, II. 2. 10; Kaṭha, V. 15; Śvetâśvatara, VI. 14; Bhagavad Gītā, IX. 15. 6.

[3] Kaṭha Upaniṣad, I. 2. 13; Bhagavad Gītā, II. 19-20; etc.

[4] Muṇḍaka Upaniṣad, I. 2. 8; Kaṭha, II. 5.

[5] Schrader's Indischen Philosophie, pp. 54-57.

(6) Ucchedavādins or Annihilationists; (7) Diṭṭha-dhamma-nibbānavādins—the Sensualists or Positivistic Hedonists.[1]

Śīlāṅka in his Ācārāṅga-Ṭīkā (ed. Dhanapati, p. 14), gives the following six types of Akriyāvāda, each considered from two standpoints—subjective and objective (svataḥ, parataḥ). (1) Kāla-vāda; (2) Īśvara-vāda; (3) Ātma-vāda; (4) Niyati-vāda; (5) Svabhāva-vāda; and (6) Yadṛcchā-vāda. A similar classification can be traced in several older texts.[2] The historical value of this mode of classification is very slight. Instead of enlightening us, it serves in many places only to confuse us. The terms sometimes overlap one another in their denotation, and are hardly used with precision of meaning. The significance is not at all clear, unless they are studied in constant reference to those individual thinkers to whose views they actually apply.

---

[1] *Cf.* Kathāvatthu-commentary, p. 6.

[2] *E.g.*, Śvetāśvatara Upaniṣad (I. 2) gives Kāla-vāda, Svabhāva-vāda, Niyati-vāda, Yadṛcchā-vāda, Bhūta-vāda, Puruṣa-vāda, and Īśvara-vāda. Aśvaghoṣa in his Saundarānanda Kāvya (XVI. 17) adds to these Prakṛiti-vāda; *cf.* Buddhacarita, IX. The text of Suśruta (ed. Calcutta, p. 256) refers also to Pariṇāma-vāda. *Cf.* Bṛihat-Saṁhitā, I. 7. The Mahābodhi Jātaka (No. 528) gives them as Ahetu-vāda, Issara-kāraṇa-vāda, Pubbekata-vāda, Uccheda-vāda, besides Khatta-vijjā-vāda; *cf.* the same in Āryaśūra's Jātakamālā. See also Aṅguttara-nikāya, I, p. 173 f.; Sūtrakṛitāṅga I. 12. 11.

CHAPTER XIII.

The Doctrine of Time.

(*Kāla-vāda.*)

The Doctrine of Time, as set forth in the Atharva-veda, is restated in the Mahābhārata more than once, and with some important variations indicative of its later development. The doctrine, so far as it can be traced, here and there, in the words of some of the post-Vedic thinkers, such as Bādhva, Yājñavalkya, and others, may be said to have followed the lines of Aghamarṣaṇa's hymn in the Ṛig-veda.[1] Their expression, be it remembered, like that of Aghamarṣaṇa, is not exactly Time (Kāla) but rather the Year (Saṁvatsara).

It is of great historical importance to notice that the conception of *post-ens* (aparanta-kappanā) or speculation concerning the future (aparantānudiṭṭhi)[2] plays no important part in the earliest types of Indian thought.

No doubt, among the post-Vedic thinkers, many spoke of Prajāpati as the Year. But Bādhva was perhaps the first to maintain : The Great Person is the Year, which causes some beings to fall together, and causes others to grow up."[3] And Yājñavalkya only added that from Brahman the speechless Year revolved with the days.[4] We have speculations of several earlier thinkers, since Mahidāsa, about the future of man.

The earlier speculations were not much concerned with the future of the world.

As regards the future of the world-system as a whole, it is merely implied in the hymn of "Parameṣṭhin" that the generating principles, the elemental forces, the self-determined movement and the dynamic energy, from which

[1] Ṛig-veda, X. 190.

[2] Dīgha-nikāya, I. 30; Dhammasaṅgaṇi, 1320.

[3] Aitareya Āraṇyaka III. 2. 3. 7. (S. B. E, Vol. 1).

[4] Bṛihad Āraṇyaka Upaniṣad, IV. 4. 16 : "Yasmād arvāk saṁvatsaro......parivartate."

the cosmos originates, reduce it, now and again, to a state of chaos or shapeless water.[1] A vague notion of the recurrent cycles of change also prevails in the hymn of "Brahmaṇaspati," where we are told how the gods, raising the cosmic dust by dancing, and by a process of combination and separation, cause all existent things to spring from non-existence (Chaos), and how the visible Infinite with her first-born seven sons goes to meet the primeval age of the gods, that is to say, Chaos or the real Infinite (Aditi)[2] With regard to the duration of the Cosmos, Mahidāsa alone, among the post-Vedic thinkers, expressly said this: As long as the earth and fire, the firmament and air, the heaven and the sun, the quarters and the moon, or water and Varuṇa exist, so long the world does not decay.[3] But he says nothing whatever regarding the recurrent cycles of change. As regards the future of man, Jaivali was the first to teach that travelling on the Southern road, the bad souls of those worldly men who followed the path of their ancestors, reached after their death the moon as the highest point, and returned thence, by a kind of gradual natural transformation or ascent and descent, to this earth, in order to pass through new cycles of mundane existence; while, travelling on the Northern road, the good souls of those holy men who followed the path of the gods or divine philosophers, reached as far as the sun, or perhaps beyond the solar region, but returned no more to this dark spot which men call the earth.

From these passages, the conclusion is obvious. The conception of *post-ens*, or the speculation concerning the future of the world is far later than the Vedic period, but pre-Buddhistic and pre-Jaina. That is to say, the enveloping aspect of nature did not so much engage the attention of the earlier thinkers as her developing aspect.

[1] Ṛig-veda, X. 129. 5.

[2] *Ibid*, X. 72. 6-9.

[3] Aitareya Āraṇyaka, II. 1. 7.

If the Ātharvaṇa doctrine of time be closely examined, we hardly find any emphasis laid on the side of cessation, destruction, dissolution, disappearance, or absorption.[1] Almost all that is said in the hymns of the Atharvaveda regarding time relates to its eternal existence, and its creative and ordaining power. On the other hand, the Epic doctrine of time seems to lay the whole stress on the destructive phase of nature; in other words, the optimism of earlier thought is overshadowed by the pessimistic gloom of later speculations. Moreover, the Ātharvaṇa doctrine of time is cosmological in its main conception, while the Epic doctrine is anthropological, being concerned chiefly with the fate, or the joy and sorrow, weal and woe, of the individual. The point in which the two doctrines show a resemblance to each other is that both are garbed in naive, poetic or unsystematic expressions.

The Epic doctrine of Time contrasted with the Ātharvaṇa.

I. The Epic Doctrine of Time.

A systematic exposition of the Epic doctrine of time is attempted, with considerable success, by Dr. Schrader.[1] According to his exposition, time is conceived, in the Mahābhārata, under its various aspects.

(1) As Diṣṭa or the Determined comprising the natural, and that which is willed by the individual. The life-term of living beings is called the determined, *i.e.*, natural time.[2] When the time-factor is brought into play by the will or act of man it is said to be willed by the individual.[3]

(2) As Daiva or the Fateful. The state of time, which prevails due to the works of the gods, demons, or such natural causes as cold, heat, rain, hunger, thirst, and disease, goes by the name of Daiva. The Daiva may be distinguished from the Diṣṭa as the non-human or super-human from the human (pauruṣa), the pre-destined or unforeseen from the foreseen,

[1] Indischen Philosophie, pp. 21-27.

[2] Atharva-veda, X. 3. 16; XII. 3. 55: "Pūrā diṣṭāt pūrāyuṣaḥ; diṣṭaṁ nôtra jarase hi nesat."

[3] Mahābhārata, V. 77. 10: "yad anyad diṣṭa-bhāvasya puruṣasya svayaṁ-kṛitam."

or as the ante-natal from that which belongs to the present existence.[1]

(3) As Haṭha[2]—the Fortuitous or Accidental.

(4) As Bhavya[3]-Bhavitavya—the Inevitable or that which must happen in the future even in defiance of the series of natural causation.

(5) As Vihita[4] or that which is regulated (niyata) by men, for instance, the time to sit, the time to lie down, the time to walk, stay, eat and drink.

(6) As Bhāgadheya or that which acts as the cause of happiness and misery in the world. There are many passages of the Mahābhārata illusrating this aspect of the doctrine of time.

Bali's views of Time.

For instance, in the Śānti-parva Bali says to Śakra:[5] All beings, whether strong or weak, handsome or ugly, fortunate or wretched, are swept away by time. Time is too deep to be fathomed. It is like an ocean without any island in it. Endless is the ceaseless flow of time. Time ordains all things, and destroys all creatures. As it produces everything, so it takes away everything. Time works upon all things, and it is through time that all things reach a termination. Time protects, time shatters. Persons well-versed in the Vedas conceive time as Brahman. The months and fortnights are its body, which is invested with the days and nights as its garments. The seasons are its senses, and the year is its mouth. Time as Brahman has neither beginning

[1] "Pūrva.janma-kṛitaṁ karma tad daivam iti kathyate," Hitopadeśa, Prastāvanā, 32. daiva-pūrva-kṛita (pūrva-daihika), at Manu, VII. 166, XI. 47, and Yājñavalkya, I. 348.

[2] Haṭha—Kākatālīya, yādṛicchika, ākasmika, akāraṇa, ahetuka, adhicca-samuppanna. According to Nīlakaṇṭha, "acintitasyātarkitasya ca lābho haṭhaḥ."

[3] *Cf.* "avaśyam bhāvino," Kāma-Sūtra, II. 31.

[4] *Cf.* paripanita-kālaḥ, Kauṭilīya Arthaśāstra, VII. 5. III: "Tvam etāvantam kālam ceṣṭasva, ahaṁ etāvantam kālam ceṣṭisva iti" paripanitakalaḥ; *ibid*, VI. 1. 13. Yaśodhara in his commentary on the Kāmasūtra, II. 31, reads palāyati instead of plavati.

[5] *Śānti-parva, sections* 223-225.

nor end ; it is eternal. Brahman in the form of time is the refuge of all creatures. Who can go beyond time ? Time cannot be evaded by running or standing still. Some say that Brahman is fire ; some that it is Prajāpati ; some that it is the seasons or the month, or fortnight, days, hours, morning, noon, evening, twinkling, or moment. Thus people speak diversely of time which is one. Time is Brahman, the eternity.

Secondly, from an important passage in the Ādiparva we learn : Time is the root cause of all that are and are to be, and of pleasure and pain. Time creates, time destroys. Time is vigilant while all are asleep. Time is unconquerable.[1]

II. Criticism of the Epic doctrine of time.

The Buddhist Jātaka (No. 245) offers, a criticism of the Epic doctrine of time. In former ages, when king Brahmadatta reigned in Benares, there lived a Brāhman who was well-versed in the three Vedas and became a far-famed teacher. He had five hundred pupils under him. It happened that in course of time his pupils began to think, "We know as much as our teacher : there is no difference." The teacher knowing this, put to them a question—a paradox, in order to tame them, proud and stubborn as they had all become. The question was this—Time consumes all things, including even itself. Can you tell me who consumes time—the all-consumer ?[2]

Strange to say, there was not one amongst them who could answer it. It came to them as a riddle of the Sphinx. Seeing that none succeeded in solving the riddle, the

[1] "Kālaḥ pacati bhūtāni, Kālaḥ saṁharate Prajāḥ. Kālaḥ gupteṣu jāgarti, Kālôhi dūratikramaḥ." This verse is quoted in Śīlāṅka's Ācārāṅgaṭīkā (ed. Dhanapati, p. 14), *cf.* "Kālāt prasūtiṁ bhūtānāṁ," Gauḍapāda-Kārikā ; "Tataḥ Kāla-vaśād eva"; Mukti Upaniṣad, 1. 43 ; etc.

[2] "Kālo ghasati bhūtāni, sabbānêva sahattanā. Yo ca kālaghaso bhūto so bhūtapacaniṁ pacati."

teacher said in a bitter tone of irony : "Do not imagine that this question is in the three Vedas. You think that you know all that I know!"

Here the Brāhman is represented as a Vedic thinker, but he was rather a Bodhisattva or a pre-Buddhistic thinker on Buddhist lines who opposed the Vedic or Epic doctrine of time. According to the Vedic theory, time not only consumes everything, but also itself in the sense, as the commentator points out, that even the time-before-meal and the time-after-meal do not abide (na pāpuṇāti). According to the Bodhisattva's view, an Arahat is the consumer of time (kālaghaso), inasmuch as he is not bound to be reborn. Having completely rooted out the inherent tendencies to sensuality, eternalism, orthodoxy and ignorance, he is released for ever from metempsychosis.

A second, but far more philosophical criticism is offered by Śvetâśvatara.[1] Some wise men, deluded, speak of time as the first cause of everything. But time cannot be regarded as the first cause. For God is the first cause, while time, like nature, fate, chance, and soul, is but one of the proximate or secondary causes. It is God by whose power (Śakti) and might the Brahma-wheel is made to revolve. God covers this world. He is the knower, the time of time (kāla-kāla).[2] It is at the command of God that this world unfolds itself,—the world constituted of earth, water, fire, air, and ether. God is the beginning. It is God who produces the causes uniting the soul with the body. God is above the three kinds of time—past, present, and future; He is without parts. God is beyond all forms of time; He is the other, from whom this

[1] Śvetâśvatara Upaniṣad, I. 2-4; VI. 14-16.

[2] The time of time—the destroyer of time. Vijñānātman explains Kāla-kāla as "Kālasya niyantā, upahartā—the ordainer, regulator of time." Śaṅkarânanda explains the same as "Kālaḥ sarva-vināśa-kārī, tasyâpi vināśa-karaḥ"—time is the destroyer of all, even of that God is the destroyer." This is a common sentiment in the later literature, *e.g.*, The Mahānārayaṇa Upaniṣad says: "I am time, but of time I am not." (Ahameva kālo, nâhaṁ kālasya.)

world moves round. God makes all, God knows all; He is the self-caused, the knower (jña), the time of time.

Aśvaghoṣa criticises the view according to which time is the root-cause of weal and woe. He maintains that the pain of existence, the pain as a common accident experienced (pravṛittiduhkha), is due to our craving, and other such mental causes, but not to time. It is, in other words, on account of craving (tṛiṣṇā), and not on account of time, nature, or the like, that men, imbued with passionate and delusive qualities (sarajastamaskā), become subject to death, while those who are without these qualities are not reborn.[1]

The author of the Śāṁkhya-sūtra[2] maintains: Bondage does not befall man because of time. For time being all-pervading and eternal in its nature, is equally and also perhaps eternally associated with all. Or, as the commentator puts it, "The bondage of man is not caused by time; because if it were the cause, there could be no separation such as that of the liberated and unliberated, because time, which applies to everything, and is eternal is at all times associated with all men, and must, therefore, bring all into bondage, if any."[3]

"Everything is caused by time. Time alone determines men's prosperity and adversity, victory and defeat, and happiness and misery. By time Bali is made Indra. By time he is removed elsewhere.[4] And by time again he will be restored to his former position. All are due to time."[5] Vātsyâyana discards this view, and holds, on the contrary, that manly strength, self-help, or free-will activity is the principal means and cause of success in all matters.[6]

[1] Saundaranandā-kāvya, XVI, 17.

[2] I, 12: "kāla-yogato vyāpino nityasya sarva-sanibandhāt."

[3] Ballantyne's Sāṁkhya Aphorisms of Kapila, I. 12. *Cf.* Bübler's "Vishṇu" XX. 43: "Kāla (time) is no one's friend and no one's enemy."

[4] Vyavaropita—pātāle niyojita—Commentator.

[5] Kāma-sūtra, II. 27-29.

[6] *Ibid*, II. 30: "puruṣa-kāra (=prayatna) pūrvakatvāt sarva-pravṛittīnām upāyaḥ pratyayaḥ."

Cāṇakya's view seems, in this respect, reconciliatory rather than polemical. Of strength, place and time, strength is superior to the rest. Such is the view of some teachers. Some give predominance to place on the ground that on land a dog baffles a crocodile, while in water a crocodile defeats a dog. There are some teachers with whom time is predominant. Their reason is this. At day-time a crow kills an owl, while during night an owl kills a crow. But according to Cāṇakya's view, the three factors—strength, place and time, are auxiliary to one another.[1]

We have no criticism whatever of the doctrine of time from Mahāvīra and Buddha. But Kriyāvādins (Dynamists) as both of them were, it may be safely imagined that their views would have been identical in their general spirit with those attributed to Vātsyāyana and others. Their general attitude is clear, at any rate, from the manner in which they have attacked the hypothesis of any efficient cause, such as God, Fate, Chance, or the like.[2]

III. Defence of the Epic doctrine of time.

The Vedic or Epic doctrine of time, was not without its strong defenders among the philosophers, the chief of whom was Śākāyanya in the Maitri Upaniṣad.[3] As a later thinker, Śākāyanya deals with various questions as to the form, manifestation, division, existence, and infinity of time. But the main problem with which his speculations are concerned is whether time is the original cause of everything or not.

In the language of Śākāyanya, Time (Kāla), Death (Yama) and Life (Prāṇa) are, in a sense, identical. Like fire, air, sun, food (anna, earth), Brahmā, Rudra, and Viṣṇu, time is one of the chief manifestations of Brahman, the highest Deity.

[1] Kauṭilya-Arthaśāstra, IX. 1. 135-136 : "paraspara-sādhakā hi śakti-deśa-kālaḥ."

[2] Sūtra-Kṛitāṅga, I. 12; II. 2-79; I. 6-27; I. 10-17; Aṅguttaranikāya, III. 135; Mahābodhi Jātaka in Fausboll's Jātaka and in Aryaśūra's Jātaka-mālā.

[3] Maitri Upaniṣad, IV. 5-6.

He quotes several earlier views[1] in support of his own theory, but curiously enough some are quite contradictory. His quotations are these :—

(1) Food (anna) is the cause of all that is time of food, and the sun is the cause of time. The visible form of time is the year, consisting of twelve months, made up of twinklings (nimeṣas) and other measures.

(2) As many portions of time as there are, the sun moves through them. He who meditates on time as Brahman, from him time moves far away.

(3) As from time all beings flow, so from time they grow, and in time they rest. Time has form, and time is formless.[2]

(4) "Time ripens and dissolves all beings in the Great Self, but he who knows into what time itself is dissolved, he is the knower of the Veda."

Śākāyanya's personal views are given as follows. Time in itself is imperceptible by the senses. The progress of the sun, for instance, is the evidence of its existence. There are in fact two forms of Brahman, time (kāla) and non-time (akāla). That which had existed before the sun came into existence is non-time. Non-time is without parts, *i.e.*, indivisible. That which originates from the sun, and has parts (*i.e.*, is divisible) is Time. Of time that is divisible, the year is the form, from which all creatures are born. As they are generated from the year, so they return to rest in the year. Thus the year is Prajāpati, is time, food, the embodiment of Brahman, nay, Brahman himself, the self. This manifest time is the great ocean of beings. The sun, the source of all life (Savitṛi), dwells in it. The moon, stars, planets, the year, and the rest

Śākāyanya's views of Time.

[1] Maitri Upaniṣad, VI. 14-16.

[2] "Kālo mūrtir amūrtimān." Max Müller translates "time is visible (sun), and invisible (moments)."

are generated from it. These are, in their turn, the causes of all that is good or evil in this world. Therefore, Brahman is the Solar Self, the soul of the sun, and the sun must be conceived under the name of time.

In the second place, all that human imagination can depict of time is to be found in a passage of the Yoga-Vāsiṣṭha Rāmāyaṇa, the date of which is evidently far later than that of the Mahābhārata and the Maitri Upaniṣad. This passage is put into the mouth of Rāma, the mystic interlocutor of the dialogue, in order perhaps to keep the view quite distinct from the real system of the Yoga-Vāsiṣṭha-Rāmāyaṇa, as expounded by Vasiṣṭha. Of three long chapters (33-35) of the first book called Vairāgya-prakaraṇa, we shall be content with giving a brief summary:—

Rāṃa's views of time.

Time is known under three names as Daiva, Kāla and Kṛitānta.[1] Time is called the Universal Soul because it swallows the universe within itself. Time is all-pervading, but it has no perceptible form of its own, except that it is imperfectly known by the names of years, ages (yugas) and aeons (kalpas).[2] Time is divided, though in itself indivisible; consumed, though incombustible; perceived, though imperceptible in its nature. Time is the subtlest of all things. Time has no other character or function but that of action and motion.[3] It is by its action and motion that the existence of time is made known to us. Thus according to mystic Rāma, as according to Zeno and Chrysippus, time is to be defined as "the extension of the motion of the world,"[4]—a ceaseless motion of the universe, an endless succession of external events.

[1] Yoga-Vāsiṣṭha-Rāmāyaṇa, I. 25. 1, 5: "Daivam Kālaś ca kathyate.—Tṛitīyañ ca Kṛitānteti nāma."

[2] Yoga-Vāsiṣṭha I. 13. 7: "Yuga-vatsara-kalpâkhyaiḥ kiñcit prakaṭata gataḥ. Rupairalakṣyarūpātma sarvam ākramya tiṣṭhati."

[3] *Ibid*, I. 25, 2: "Kriyam-atradṛite yasya svaparispandarūpiṇaḥ. *Nânyad dlakṣyate* rūpam na karma na samāhitam."

[4] Zeller's "Stoics, Epicureans, and Sceptics," pp. 186-187.

The function of time consists in the act of creating and dissolving the world-system. Time stands the foremost of all deceitful players, the artificer who, sporting for the period of an aeon, loses his own existence in the eternity of Brahman, the spirit of spirits. But time after a short rest, as it were, reappears as at once the creator, the preserver, and the destroyer of the world,—as the remembrancer of the past. Action (karma), also described as Fate (niyati), is to time as a wife to a husband.

Time is the source of all hatred and greed,—the cause of misfortunes and vicissitudes. Hundreds of great kalpas may even pass away, yet there is nothing to move eternity to pity or to stop its course. At the close of an aeon (kalpānte), time dances about, like a skull-bearer (kāpālika), with a long chain of the bones of the dead. Time then assumes its terrifying form of fire (pralayâgni), to dissolve the world in empty space, or to reduce the cosmos to a chaos. Even Brahmā, Indra, and such other gods cease then to exist. Although thus the world is destroyed and renewed alternately and endlessly, the seeds of things are never destroyed. From these seeds arise in course of time the four types of existence (the oviparous, the viviparous, etc.). These types of concrete existence are to be regarded, contrary to the modern view of evolution, as eternally fixed.

IV. Infinity of Time: The constant cycle of existence.

Although a later authority, the Śūkranīti makes us understand that matters with which a Purāṇa deals broadly fall under two heads: cosmology and history.[1] The creation of heaven and earth and firmament, the upheaval of land from water, the distribution of mountains, plains and waters, the apparition of the sun, the moon, the stars and the planets, the formation of clouds, the circulation of water, the exchange

Two aspects of Purāṇa: Cosmological and historical.

[1] Śūkranīti, IV. 3. 104-105.

of heat and cold between land and sea and sky, the origin and propagation of species from the primordial (or, protoplasmic) matter, the evolution of social grades and all other human institutions, the elevation and degradation of the moral sense, etc., form the subject-matters of a Purāṇa.[1] In the language of Buddha, Purāṇa, Lokāyata, or cosmology consists of speculations 'about existence and non-existence' (bhava-kathā, vibhava-kathā).[2] A Purāṇa in its historical aspect is sharply discriminated from an Itihāsa or legend as we generally understand it. Strictly, Purāṇa is not history, but rather the philosophy of history.[3] It is not the aim of a Purāṇa or "Universal History" to produce any record of 'hard facts' associated with fixed dates, but to indicate philosophically, or perhaps scientifically, the successive stages of natural evolution,—to speculate, in other words, about the cycles or epochs of events, natural and historical, physical, psychical, social and individual, in their uniform and endless succession.

Literary significance of the term Purāṇa. The earlier specimens of Purāṇas.

The two aspects of a Purāṇa are so closely interconnected that it is impossible to separate them. In the history of Indian literature, after the Vedas are to be placed the Brāhmaṇas (including the Forest-books and Upaniṣads); after the Brāhmaṇas, the Itihāsa-Purāṇas; after these, the six Vedāṅgas with which the Sūtra-literature begins; and after the Vedāṅgas, the Aṅgas, the Piṭakas, the Nīti-śāstras, the Dharma-śāstras, the Epics, and all the rest. Among the Vedāṅgas, the Kalpa-sūtras and the Jyotiṣas have to deal with divisions of time. The same holds true of the Nīti-śāstras and the Dharma-śāstras. At first the name Purāṇa denoted cosmological speculations embodied in the Brāhmaṇas.

[1] Manu, I. 21-34.

[2] Dīgha-nikāya, I, pp. 8-9.

[3] *Ibid*, p. 178. Buddha's expression 'loka-akkhāyikā' corresponds almost to Huxley's 'history of the earth' or 'Universal history.'

Later on, a class of literature arose to which the use of the name Purāṇa came to be restricted. The earlier specimens of Purāṇas are to be found in the Vedic hymns, the Brāhmaṇas, the Aggañña sutta, the Manu-smṛiti, the Mahābhārata, and the like. There is a great deal of truth behind the tradition that the Purāṇas are Upa-vedas—'Those which stand close to the Vedas.' For in the Vedic speculations we find nothing but the bare outlines of the Purāṇas.

The science of Time.

Towards the close of the post-Vedic period, Nidhi appears in a list of science.[1] Nidhi or the so-called sciences of time is in reality nothing more than a systematised division of time. It is incorporated in the Kauṭilīya Artha-śāstra,[2] the Manu-Smṛiti, the Mahābhārata, the Bṛihat-saṁhitā, and several other later texts. A practical division of time into year, half-year, five or six seasons, months, fortnights, is indeed as old as the Vedas. In the earlier reckoning, however, the greatest limit of time does not seem to have extended beyond a year (saṁvatsara), and a hundred winters.[3] Evidently, then, the conception of four yugas (ages) : Satya (Kṛita), Tretā, Dvāpara, and Kali—is post-Vedic, and occurs for the first time in the Taittirīya Brāhmaṇa.[4] Still later, we have the conceptions of Manvantaras (intervals of Manus) and Kalpas or Mahākalpas (Epochs, Aeons, Cycles, or Millenniums). When the Greek ambassador Megasthenes visited India in the fourth century B.C., he found the yuga-measurement of time already in existence. The Kauṭilīya Artha-śāstra bears testimony to the same fact. But it can be proved on the evidence of the Jaina and Buddhist texts, that the conception of Kalpas and Mahākalpas, not to say of yugas, became prevalent in the country

[1] Chāndogya Upaniṣad, VII. 2. 1; VII. 7. 1.

[2] The divisions of time as given in the Kauṭilīya Artha-śāstra (II. 20. 38; IX. 1. 135-136) differ in certain respects from those in the Manu-Smṛiti (I. 63-64), the Mahābhārata (XII. 232. 12-31; XII. 233. 4-7), and the Institutes of Viṣṇu (XX. 1-20).

[3] Ṛig-veda, X. 190. 2; VII. 66. 11, 16; etc.

[4] See Rules of human sacrifice.

sometime before the rise of Jainism and Buddhism. The conception played some part not only in the teachings of Mahāvīra and Buddha, but also in those of Gosāla,[1] their common predecessor, the reputed leader of the Ājīvika school. Thus the date of the conception of Kalpas and Mahākalpas may be safely placed somewhere in the neo-Vedic and pre-Buddhistic-period. Further, it would seem that the conception of Manvantaras (Manu-intervals)[2] is historically later than that of Kalpas, just as the theory of Incarnations (Avatāras)[3] is posterior to the conception of Manvantaras.

In connexion with these ancient cosmological speculations we have to note three points of philosophical importance. (1) That they all imply a certain reference to infinity of time and eternity of the world of generation. (2) That they involve something of a Stoic notion of the infinite divisibility of time, —the notion which forms the basis of the atomic theory of time in the Jaina Dravya-saṁgraha (V. 22). (3) That in their purely cosmological aspect they seem to be either Platonic or Aristotelian in character. "Platonic"[4] because they have reference to the notion of a Player,[5] who, sporting as it were, or of an artificer (māyin), who by his artifice (sva-māyayā),[6] repeats the world again and again *ad infinitum*. And "Aristotelian" because they presuppose a fully real individual as the originator of all changes.

---

[1] Dial. B. 11, p. 72 : "8,400,000 periods" (Mahā-kappas). See my 'Ājīvikas,' I, p. 25.

[2] Manu, I. 79-80. There is no reference to Incarnations.

[3] Macdonald's 'Brāhmaṇas of the Vedas,' p. 90 f.

[4] Development of Greek Philosophy, pp. 115-116; 161-235.

[5] Manu-smṛiti, I. 80.

[6] Śvetāśvatara Upaniṣad, IV. 9-10.

CHAPTER XIV.

Āsuri.

Yājñavalkya's speculations led to the development of a theistic doctrine (Īśvara-vāda), which was strongly opposed by both Mahāvīra and Buddha. It was in fact an old Brāhmanic belief for which Yājñavalkya's philosophy afforded a fresh ground. An account of this theistic doctrine is given in the first chapter of the Bṛihad Āraṇyaka Upaniṣad, divided into six sections, each of which is called a Brāhmaṇa. The doctrine, as we now have it, is interwoven with cosmological speculations, and reminds us, in many points, of the Mosaic doctrine of Genesis. And the Upaniṣad-passage[1] in which the doctrine is inculcated is historically important as forming the basis of all later cosmologies, especially those which are embodied in the Brahma-jāla and Aggañña suttas, the Manu-Smṛiti[2] and the Mahābhārata.

It is a generally accepted opinion that the Manu-Smṛiti contains not one, but two distinct doctrines of creation. The accounts in the Brahma-jāla and the Aggañña suttas also differ. In point of fact the origin of this difference or discrepancy is in the Upaniṣad passage itself. The first three sections set forth a theory of creation which is different from

[1] Bṛihad Āraṇyaka Upaniṣad, I. 3. 27:

"Lead me from the unreal to the real!
Lead me from darkness to light!
Lead me from death to immortality!" (Max Müller).

"Asato mā sad gamaya!
Tamaso mā jyotir gamaya!
Mṛityor mā amṛitam gamaya!" See Deussen's Vedanta, p. 86.

This passage contains the famous prayer-formula (stotra) of the Brāhmo Samāj, founded by Raja Ram Mohan Roy (1830 A.D.).

[2] Muir's "Sanskrit Texts," IV. 26.

that embodied in the remaining three. The fourth section in particular is called the Puruṣa-vidha Brāhmaṇa by the Mādhyandinas. As its name implies, the fundamental problem with which the Brāhmaṇa is concerned is the generation of things from Puruṣa or the universal soul. The Brāhmaṇa in question is of the greatest importance for the historian of Indian juristic thought, and of the Sāṁkhya views. In it we discover the immediate background for Purāṇic Sāṁkhyam, an expression by which we must understand here only an attempt at a rational theory of the universe, inclusive of all human institutions,—such Sāṁkhya views as we find, for instance, in the Manu-Smṛiti and the Mahābhārata. It seems to us possible that we may find here one way to answer the question whether the Sāṁkhya system is prior to the advent of Buddha or not.

Two theories of creation.

We learn from the concluding verse of the Sāṁkhya-Kārikā which is the first systematic exposition of the Sāṁkhya dualism, that Kapila, Āsuri, Pañcaśikha and Īśvara-Kṛiṣṇa were the four most renowned teachers of Sāṁkhyam. In tracing back the development of the Sāṁkhya doctrines from the Sāṁkhya-Kārikā to the Vedas, we shall take these four names however mythical they may be, to denote the four traditional landmarks or stages. The first stage of Sāṁkhyam will then be represented by the Puruṣa-sūkta in the Ṛig-veda, the second stage by the Puruṣa-vidha-Brāhmaṇa in the Bṛihad Āraṇyaka Upaniṣad, the third stage by Pañcaśikha's views in the Śāntiparva, and the fourth stage by Īśvara-Kṛiṣṇa's views in the Bhagavad-gītā. The traditional author of the Puruṣa-sūkta is "Nārāyaṇa" or "Kapila."[1] The author of the Puruṣa-vidha-Brāhmaṇa is unknown, but we may suppose that it was Āsuri.

Four prehistoric stages of the development of the Purāṇic Sāṁkhya.

[1] Note that in the Śvetāśvatara Upaniṣad, Kapila (The Fiery) is regarded as the wise son of Brahmā. This is in agreement with the legends in the Śāntiparva, where Kapila is described as the Mind-begotten son (mānasa-putra) of Brahmā. The Mudgala Up. attests that Puruṣa Sūkta was the starling point of Sāṁkhyam.

In the Sāṁkhya tradition Āsuri is hardly more than a name or passing shadow. But his name occurs in all the three genealogies of teachers and pupils given in the Bṛihad Āranyaka Upaniṣad.[1] The first two of these lists mention Āsuri as a pupil of Bhāradvāja, while from the third list it appears that he was the immediate successor of Yājñavalkya, though not necessarily his pupil. This is one of our reasons for ascribing the Puruṣa-vidha-Brāhmaṇa to Āsuri. The other reason is this. The views which this Brāhmaṇa embodies can be traced to "Nārāyaṇa's" hymn in the Ṛig-veda, and Yājñavalkya's philosophy. Admitting this, the next step towards the solution of the question will be to observe how from the time of Āsuri to that of Pāncaśikha in the Śāntiparva the Sāṁkhya nomenclature was gradually coined. In the meantime we must inquire whether or no, such a nomenclature was in use in the time of the Buddha.

Āsuri in the Sāṁkhya tradition.

There are two fragments of Buddha's teaching which throw light on the views of Āsuri. The two fragments are taken from the Brahma-jāla and the Aggañña sutta. In accounting for theistic notion in general Buddha says:[2] There comes a time, now and again, when, after the lapse of a long long period, the world-system (loka, cosmos, the fleeting visible universe) passes away (saṁvaṭṭati). When this happens, living beings (including the gods,—the sun, moon, etc.,) are 'mostly reborn in the World of Radiance' (ābhassara-kāyā), that is to say, assume luminous forms or nebular bodies. In this state they persist for a long long period of time, made of consciousness (manomaya) feeding on joy, self-luminous, traversing the sky (whizzing in the air as dynamic forces),[3] and full of splendour.

Buddha's speculations on the origin of theistic notions.

[1] II. 6. 3; IV. 6. 3; VI. 5. 2.

[2] Dīgha Nikāya, I. 18-20. cp. The story of Baka-Brahmā, Majjhima-Nikāya, I. 326-331; Saṁyutta-nikāya, I. 142-144; Jātaka No. 405. But see Dial. B., II, pp. 30-31.

[3] *Cf.* The Upaniṣad-expressions "Prabhu-vimita," and "vibuuvimita" in the Chāndogya, VIII. 5. 3. and Kauṣītaki, 1. 3.

Thereafter comes also a time, when, sooner or later, the world system begins to develop or re-evolve (vivaṭṭati). When this happens the Brahma-mansion (Brahma-vimāna, the Formed Universe) makes its appearance. But it is at first empty (suñña)—of inhabitants. In course of time, some one of those beings, either at the end of its existence, or because of the exhaustion of its merit (by accident, as we now say), falls from the nebular state, and comes to life in the Brahma-mansion, within the visible universe (say, as the sun).

In this latter state the conscious being spends a long long period of time, feeding on joy, self-illuminated, traversing the sky, and shining in glory. But from the circumstance of 'dwelling there so long alone,' the being begins to feel "a dissatisfaction and a longing: O! would that other beings might come to join me in this place!"[1] Just then, as chance would have it, other beings, descending from the nebular state, come, by a similar process, to life within the formed universe (say, as the moon, the visible stars, and the planetary bodies), which are of a shorter duration, less glorious, and less powerful than the sun.

As time goes on, some of those conscious beings, descending from their solar or lunar or planetary ancestors (phenomenal antecedents) are reborn at last as men on this earth. And among men again, there may be some one who begins to reflect upon the problem of existence,—the speculation about the origin and development of the life-process.

In tracing his existence backward from his present birth to that which he imagines to be his very first, he perceives that his knowledge does not go beyond the sun, the first-born individual in this formed universe,—the first dweller in the solar home. From this thought he is led naturally to the conclusion:—

"He is Brahmā, the Great God, the Supreme Being, the Almighty (or, the Omnipresent), the Omniscient, the Ruler,

[1] Rhys Davids' translation of "Aho vata aññepi sattā itthattam āgaccheyyanti?"

the Lord, the Creator, the Maker, the Best ('Chief of all'), the Ordainer, the Ancient of days, the Father of all that are and are to be. He, the maker of all these beings, is stedfast, immutable, eternal, unchangeable, and the same for ever and ever.[1]

Whereas we, who are made by him, are come here, to this world, being impermanent, mutable, and limited in our term of existence. But on what grounds are we to call him the Creator and us the created ones? We must call him the Creator because when he thought of us,—on his mental resolve (*i. e.*, by the power of his will, mano-paṇidhi),[2] we all came here into existence. We must have been created by him 'because, as we see, it was He who was here first, and we came after him.'"

Buddha's criticism of the doctrine.

The passage of which a summary is given above, seems to have reference to the Puruṣa-vidha-Brāhmaṇa. In the guise of an historian Buddha posed himself as a critic of the notion of a personal author of our mortal being or an individual unmoved mover of the Brahma-wheel (the universe),—a notion which was shaping itself in his time permanently into a legal and moral creed. Proceeding as he did from change or causal genesis as the fundamental fact, Buddha could not conceive any such unchangeable and omnipotent individual as being fully real by himself. For him the world of generation was a constant cycle of change (rather than existence),—a continuous process of evolution and revolution,—of envelopment and development.

Buddha is speaking to two young Brāhmans, Bhāradvāja and Vasiṣṭha, who having disregarded caste-prejudices, are come to join his order: There comes a time when the visible

[1] "Brahmā, Mahabrahmā, abhibhū, anabhibhūto, aññad atthu-daso, vasavatti, issaro, kattā, nimmātā, seṭṭho, sañjitā, vasi, pitā bhūta-bhavyānaṁ. . . . (so) nicco, dhuvo, sassato, avipariṇāma-dhammo, sassati-samo."

[2] *Cf.* The Buddhist Sanskrit expression "praṇidhāna."

universe passes away, and consequently beings are reborn elsewhere in the nebular sphere. This is duly succeeded by a time when the world begins to develop anew. All is then water, and enveloped in darkness, a darkness that blinds. Those beings, falling from radiant worlds, are reborn within the formed universe, made of consciousness, sustained by joy, floating in space, and shining in glory. The formed universe, the juicy earth (rasā paṭhavī 'emerges from the waters like a scum of milk or ghee, odorous and sweet.' Having come in contact with it, feasting thereon, those beings become solidified, and lose thereby part of their own luminance. Thus the sun, the moon, and the stars and planets appear once more, and the natural seasons come into existence. Meanwhile the cooling process goes on. As the juicy earth gradually becomes hardened, it loses its flavour and sweet taste, 'but vegetation, first of low, then higher grade evolves.' Man descends at length from his heavenly ancestors—from the vital sun, or the reflective moon. The human race vary in degrees of comeliness. The fair despise the ugly, the white the black men. Thus a colour distinction arises. Men at first feed on rice grown in abundance without cultivation. But with the gradual loss of fertility of the soil, tilth becomes necessary. In the beginning sex-differences are unknown among the human race. As time passes on, sex-differences evolve, resulting in great social and moral upheavals. From sex-connexion households originate. 'Rice is stored, land is enclosed, and with the rights of property arise dishonesty, strife and injustice.' This leads men at last to think of establishing a ruler,[1] chosen from the best among them, to administer justice. The ruler is supported by the ruled, and he is, to begin with, but a patriarchal or feudal chief, recognised as the lord of the fields (Khetta-pati). From these emerge a class of men, who become known as princes or nobles, upholding a certain standard of morality and social virtue. On the other

[1] Manu, VII. 3; Śānti Parva, Rājadharma, Section 59; Arthaśāstra, I 13.

hand, certain human beings, distressed at the sins of society, leave home-life, retire into woods to meditate, or dwell outside the towns, compiling śāstras - literary treatises. Putting away evil, these come to be distinguished as Brāhmans, who uphold a certain standard of humanity in thought, word and deed. Among others, those who lead household life, develop certain industries, and thereby set up a different standard of morality, come to be called Vessas (Tradesmen). There are others again who take to minor or low crafts, and become known as Suddas, differing from other classes by a certain standard of law.[1]

In this second fragment—taken from the Aggañña sutta—Buddha cites an ancient cosmology (Porāṇa) in support of his opinion that social distinctions among the Aryans were originally based upon moral rather than upon any racial grounds.

The historical importance of the second fragment.

This cosmology, which Buddha indirectly made his own or utilised for his own purpose, presupposes the passage of the Bṛihad Āraṇyaka Upaniṣad referred to above. The main point in which the two accounts differ is that in the Aggañña Sutta Buddha does not attack the theory of creation, as he does in the Brahmajāla and other Suttas. Although, as Prof. Rhys Davids observes, "a continual note of good-humoured irony runs through the whole story"[2] in the Aggañña Sutta, we must not forget the reason of it. Prof. Rhys Davids also rightly points out that this dialogue froms 'a kind of Buddhist Book of Genesis,' and that, in it Buddha replaces an older, but current 'Brāhman legend.' This explains clearly enough why Buddha does not mention the name of God at all when he restates or remodels the Brāhmanic cosmology on his own account.

The historical importance of the Dialogue is indeed very great. It stands mid-way, in point of date, between the Bṛihad Āraṇyaka Upanisad, on one side, and the 'Laws of Manu' and the Mahābhārata on the other. Mrs. Rhys Davids

[1] Mrs. Rhys Davids' Buddhism, pp. 236-238.

[2] Dial. B. II, p. 107.

judges it to be "a striking specimen of archaic science attempting a rational theory of the origin of human institutions."[1] Moreover, it will be noted that both the Upaniṣad-passage and the Aggañña sutta, with all their differences in other respects, agree in exhibiting the doctrine of genesis in its intimate relation to Vedic and post-Vedic thinking, whereas we find in the 'Laws of Manu,' as well as in the Mahābhārata that the doctrine has become altogether what is generally described as the Purānic Sāmkhyam.

As to the teaching of the Puruṣa-vidha Brāhmaṇa, in the first three sections we find a most interesting exposition of "Brahmaṇaspati's" doctrine, combined with the views of Aghamarṣaṇa, "Parameṣṭhin," and "Nārāyaṇa." In the second Brāhmaṇa we read that in the beginning there was nothing else than Death (Mṛityu). Everything was in the womb of chaos concealed by Death, by hunger; for Death is hunger (food-principle). Death is called Aditi because whatever it brings forth, that it tends to devour again. Now Death thought of having an organised body, and so it began to move about, being stirred up with energy. Thereupon water was produced. All was water for the time being. From water was formed gradually froth (śara,[2] protoplasmic matter ?), which being hardened, appeared as the earth. Thereon rested Death (fiery ether) and from it proceeded Fire (Agni), full of splendour. This luminous mass of fire divided itself into three portions; one portion became Āditya (the sun), one portion became Vāyu (the air), and the third portion became this earth, the home of animated beings (Prāṇā). Death wished to have a second body, and it produced the seed which became the Year. Before that time there was no Year,—there were no natural seasons. By natural seasons, all existent

The philosophical views of Āsuri.

[1] Buddhism, p. 285. See also the Mahāvastu, ed, Senart, I, pp. 338-348; and Rockhill's "Life of The Buddha," chap. I.

[2] *Cf.* Pali rasā paṭhavī.

things—men, animals, scriptures and religious ceremonies—were brought forth. As organic beings evolved, the senses developed, and the thinking principle (mind) was already in the living body. In man the mind runs free as a horse fit for sacrifice, while other animals are enslaved by the senses.

The real philosophical views of Āsuri are embodied in the fourth and fifth sections of the Upaniṣad. In view of the imperfection of his terminology it is difficult to judge whether his expressions are those of Pantheism or Dualism. Perhaps they imply both, or neither. Supposing they imply both, this would mean that Dualism furnishes the best ground for explanation of experience, while Pantheism expresses his real philosophical standpoint.

In the beginning Soul (Ātmā) alone was the existent, and Soul was in the form of a self-conscious, self-centred, undivided, individualised, and absolutely pure mass of solar essence (Puruṣa). There being nothing but itself, Soul had no cause to fear a rival. But being alone, Soul felt no delight. It wished for a second. With this thought Soul divided its own body in two, thereby creating a male and a female. The male is called the heaven and the female the earth. It is from the union of these two—heaven and earth—that all beings are born. In this connexion a view of Yājñavalkya is quoted to establish the universal truth that a third something is always the sequence of two opposed facts. Yājñavalkya said: "We two—man and wife—are to each other 'like the half of a split pea' (vṛijala)."[1] Woman (earth) is produced originally from man (heaven). Sex-differences exist among all beings from men down to the ants. Cattle, horses, goats, sheep,—all these were created in pairs, as male and female. Soul knew that it was the creator of all that exists, nay, that it was the creation (sṛiṣṭi). Indeed, soul itself became the creation. Therefore whatever thing is found here, or whatever god is worshipped by men is but a particular manifestation of

[1] Bṛihad Āraṇyaka Upaniṣad, I. 4. 3. *cf.* IV. 3. 21.

the universal spirit. The gods or heavenly bodies are the best creations of this spirit.

Now every particular thing was at first in an indeterminate condition (avyākṛita). The concrete existent became determinate by 'name and form' (nāma-rūpa), by individuality.

The world is pervaded by Soul,—every limb of a living body is animated by the same spirit. Soul is in everything, in every living substance as a razor put into a razor case, or as fire in araṇi wood.

Soul is beyond the apprehension of the senses. The senses can represent Soul only in parts or fragments. For instance, when Soul breathes, we assign to it the name of breath (prāṇa); when it speaks, we assign to it the name of speech (vāk); when it sees, we assign to it the name of sight (cakṣu); when it hears, we assign to it the name of hearing (śrotra); and when it thinks, we assign to it the name of thought (manas). But he who conceives one or other of these, taken alone (ekaikam), to be the Soul, does not know what Soul is. For, as Āsuri maintains in agreement with Mahidāsa, all these represent only the names of one or other function of the soul (asya etāni karmāṇāṁ anyêva); that is to say, breathing, speaking, seeing, hearing and thinking, all bear in varying degrees the name of one and the same act of reasoning (prajñānasya nāmadheyāni). Again, like pratardana, Āsuri holds that the soul acts always as a whole soul. As a whole it breathes, as a whole it speaks, and so forth; and in this sense breathing, speaking, seeing, and other special functions of the soul find unity in it. In fact, the soul, as conceived by Āsuri, is the footstep or foundation (padanīya) of all the functions which we discharge as living thinking beings. It is, by the power of soul, that we know everything. Apart from such a unity, identity and continuity in the soul or mental life, all mental acts would appear to be but so many disconnected events.[1] In his further investigation into the unity of mental life Āsuri

[1] Bṛihad Āraṇyaka Upaniṣad, I. 4, 7.

made an important discovery, namely that the elements of cognition are not confined to understanding, but are involved also in the act of perceiving in general. Even when a man is touched on the back, he becomes aware of this through his mind. Desire, will, doubt, faith, want of faith, retentiveness, forgetfulness, shame (prudence), reflection, fear—all these are constituents of mind.[1] Speech or language is to thought what a wife is to her husband.

The main problem with which the fifth section of the Brāhmaṇa is concerned is how comes it that the world never perishes, in spite of the reckoned cycles of change which it undergoes. In this connection we may recall that Jaivali's question was: How comes it that the world is never full? Strange, to say, the answers given by both Jaivali and Āsuri reach ultimately the same truth. The puruṣa, or the Universe is imperishable. The universal spirit generates the world again and again.

We shall finally consider the social and ethical views of Āsuri. It is important to bear in mind that his views are derived partly from the philosophy of Yājñavalkya, but mostly from that of "Nārāyaṇa." His original contribution is the theory of the origin of society.

God or Soul is nearer to us than anything else: dearer than a son, dearer than wealth, dearer than all the rest. One must, therefore, regard Soul alone as dear. Soul being the true Self, if a man loves soul, he is never disappointed. The highest duty of man is to seek the knowledge of God. But for this reason, Āsuri warns us, we are not to neglect other duties of life and society. According to his view the whole duty of a man may be summed up under these three heads, the Brahman, the sacrifice and the world. A man should carry on the works—social, intellectual and spiritual, of his ancestors. And

[1] Bṛihad Āraṇyaka Upaniṣad, I. 5. 3: Kāma, saṁkalpa, vicikitsā, śraddhā, aśraddhā, dhṛiti, adhṛiti, hrī, dhī, bhī. The Buddhists came to treat these as mental properties (cetasikā dhammā).

there are the three worlds of duty to fulfil—the world of the Gods, the world of the Fathers, and the world of Men. The world of Men is to be gained by a son only, and not by any other work. The world of the Fathers and that of the Gods are to be gained by sacrifice and knowledge respectively.

Āsuri's social and moral views.

As regards his social views, Āsuri maintains that originally there were no class distinctions among men. But society being one or homogeneous did not flourish. With a view to the welfare of society class distinctions were introduced gradually among them, as similar distinctions obtained also among the gods. As society became organised, such distinctions were established permanently. Like "Nārāyaṇa" Āsuri is of opinion that class distinctions and division of labour are necessary for a healthy organisation of society, and are a clear sign of social strength. The moral justification of such distinctions is that some sort of distinction can be found equally among the gods. Briefly, then, homogeneity is as bad for a society as an ill-defined heterogeneity. This is of course a common sentiment in all juristic and theological circles.[1]

The establishment of class-distinctions, or the thorough organisation of the division of labour was not enough for the strength of the community. Brahman, therefore, created at last the most excellent Dharma—Law, Righteousness, Justice. Dharma is protected and administered by the ruling class, and Dharma is the Kṣatra of Kṣatras,—the king of kings, there being nothing higher than the Law. Since the establishment of law or moral justice, a weak man can control one who is physically stronger, by the aid of the Law, as with the help of a king. But Dharma is again Truth, and that which is true is just. The Law and Truth thus being identical, to declare the one is just to proclaim the other.

Later developments on Kauṭilian, Buddhistic and Vedāntic lines of this conception of Dharma as [kṣatrasya kṣatraḥ, or

[1] See Manu-Smṛiti, I 31; Bhagavad Gitā, IV. 13; XVIII. 41-44.

raññо rājā as Buddha puts it, are to be met with in the Kautilīya Arthaśāstra, the Rājavagga of the Aṅguttara, Part III, and the Rājadharma and Gītā sections of the Great Epic. This idea of Dharma, together with the programme of duties of the kings, as set forth in the texts mentioned above, appears to have been realised through the administrations of Candragupta Maurya, King Aśoka, and the Gupta Kings respectively.

Āsuri's religious views.

Āsuri holds that belief in future life is essential to man's moral and spiritual existence. For it alone furnishes a stimulus to all his endeavours. To believe in future life is for him to recognise the law of action, that is to say, to recognise the truth of the maxim that a man reaps as he sows, here as well as hereafter. A man is what he thinks himself to be. He who knows that he is Brahman actually becomes Brahman.[1] If a man worships any other deity, thinking that he is different from Brahman, the highest Deity, is ignorant. In fact, he who worships a god other than God is no more than a beast fit for sacrifice to the gods.

---

[1] Brihad Āraṇyaka Upaniṣad, I. 4. 10: "Ya evaṁ vedâhaṁ Brahmâsmiti sa idaṁ sarvaṁ bhavati."

CHAPTER XV.

PIPPALĀDA.

The philosophical views of the venerable seer Pippalāda are preserved in the Praśnopaniṣad consisting of six dialogues. Each one of these dialogues contains but an answer of Pippalāda to the questions put to him, one by one, by his six contemporaries, who are all said to have been devoted to philosophy (Brahmapara), fulfillers of ideal life (Brahmaniṣṭhā-para), and seekers of divine knowledge (Brahmânveṣamāna). The six contemporaries are—Sukeśas Bhāradvāja, Śaivya Satyakāma, Sauryāyanin Gārgya, Kausalya Āśvalāyana, Bhārgava Vaidarbhi, and Kabandhin Kātyāyana.[1]

The name of Pippalāda does not occur in the three separate lists of teachers given in the Bṛihad Āraṇyaka Upaniṣad. In one of them we have mention of two Gārgyas and of one Gārgyāyaṇa. Gārgyāyaṇa is evidently Gārgyāyaṇi, a contemporary of Uddālaka.[2] We know of one Gārgya, *i.e.*, Gārgya Bālāki, who was a contemporary of Yājñavalkya. The second Gārgya is perhaps the Sauryāyanin (Astronomer) Gārgya, who was a contemporary of Pippalāda. If this be true, we might surmise that Pippalāda belongs to a period later than that of Yājñavalkya.

Probably Pippalāda's date was not far from the Buddha. Among the six contemporaries of Pippalāda, one is Kabandhin Kātyāyana. The early Buddhist records frequently allude to a philosopher named Kakuda Kātyāyana (Pakudha Kaccāyana), who is said to have been one of the elder contemporaries of the Buddha. The two names, Kabandin Kātyāyana and Kakuda Kātyāyana, are practically one and the same. When Buddha was a young man, Kakuda Kātyāyana was getting

[1] Praśnopaniṣad, I. 1.

[2] Bṛihad Ār. Up., IV. 6. 2.

on in years, just as when the latter was a young man, Pippalāda had already reached a venerable age. We suppose that the two names are identical because the real name of the philosopher was merely Kātyāyana. The epithet Kabandhin or Kakuda was attached to his name for no other reason than to distinguish the philosopher Kātyāyana from others of his name. Besides, it is obvious that both Kabandhin[1] and Kakuda have reference to the same physical deformity of the man. This identity, though at first sight hypothetical, is supported by philosophical grounds, as we shall see later.

One thing is certain amid all uncertainty, namely, that we do not know much about Pippalāda's life. In the commentary on Umāsvati's Tattvārtha-sūtra (VIII. 1.) Pippalāda is classed among the ignorant heretics (ajñāni-kudṛiṣṭi's), and in the Praśnopaniṣad he is referred to as a venerable sage, and as a contemporary of Sukeśas Bhāradvāja and others. He was an Ātharvaṇika, the compiler of a recension of the Atharva Veda, recognised as canonical perhaps within a century before the rise of Buddhism.[2] The Garbhôpaniṣad and the Śārīraka, the Parabrahma and the Śarabha also embody his views, and time may come when it will be admitted that he was the historical founder of the Sāṁkhya philosophy of which natural causation and *yoga* were the two cardinal features. This is all that we can say regarding Pippalāda. Only one more trifling point which we might add (from an etymological speculation on his name) to our knowledge of Pippalāda, would be this. He was extremely fond of eating pippala (fruit), in the same way that Kaṇāda, the reputed founder of the Vaiśeṣika school of philosophy, was an eater of kaṇa ('the particles of rice).

[1] A friend suggests that the name implies a headless trunk, *i.e.*, a person having little brain-power or intellect.

[2] In the phraseology of Yājñavalkya the Atharva is not a Veda but Āṅgirasa, Bṛihad Ār. Up. VI. 5 11. Cf. Chāndogya VII. 1, where the Atharva is referred to as the fourth Veda. The Buddhist expression *Itihāsa pañcamaṁ* (Dīgha, I. p. 88) points to the same conclusion (see Sumaṅgala-Vilāsinī, I. p. 247: Athabbaṇa-Vedaṁ catutthaṁ).

His Philosophy.

So far as Pippalāda's philosophy is concerned, we shall vainly go to him for any new ideas. Among the thinkers of the period in question he is perhaps one of the least original. But the precision with which he restated the views of his predecessors was not without its marvellous effect upon the development of the method of systematic thinking and the separation of the Sāṁkhya-Yoga ideas from the older Vedānta. We propose to review, in this light, the following five points, connected with five out of his six answers.

(1) The first dialogue is the answer of Pippalāda to Kabandhin Kātyāyana's question : How and from what are creatures born ?[1] In giving his answer, Pippalāda calls the attention of Kātyāyana to the distinction to be drawn between two Brahma-worlds (Brahma-lokaḥ),—This (eṣa) and That (asau),[2]—Lower and Higher, Material and Spiritual. This Brahma-world is the world of generation (prajā-loka), and that Brahma-world is the ideal world. Pippalāda adopts besides a new term Rayi for Matter, replacing the older term Water.

Pippalāda's answer in brief is this : Creatures are generated from Prajāpati, the lord of creatures,—the creative principle of the universe. Prajāpati is the universal Person (Vaiśvānara Puruṣa),—the sun whose essence is Fire. Desirous of creating, Prajāpati meditated on his own essence, thereby producing out of his own body a pair (mithuna)—Matter (Rayi) and Spirit (Prāṇa)—the notions similar to and anticipating the Sāṁkhya Puruṣa and Prakṛiti.

Pippalāda's views of generation.

The world of concrete existence results, indeed, from the union of these two elements called Matter and Spirit. By

[1] Praśnopaniṣad, I. 3 : " Bhagavān kuto ha vai imāḥ prajāḥ prajāyanta iti."

[2] *Ibid*, I. 15, 16.

Matter Pippalāda understands that element which is dark and passive and feminine, and by Spirit that element which is bright and active and masculine. All that has form and is formless, all that is organised and disorganised—falls under the category of Matter. The formed body is therefore to be called Matter.[1] Matter is that upon which form is imposed by Spirit,—the psychical element. When Spirit is not in close embrace with Matter, the form at once breaks down, that is to say, Matter becomes disorganised. Pippalāda here calls upon us to witness with him the constant play of two opposed phenomena throughout this formed universe,—the sun and the moon, the bright-half and the dark-half of the month, day and night, and the sex-differences, for instance.

Now according as men live in This or That Brahma-world, they are said to travel on the two separate paths of life's journey,—the paths which lead either to repeated death, or to the everlasting home of immortality. Pippalāda is thinking, of course, of the two paths—the southern, ancestral or material path, and the northern, divine or spiritual path—so well marked out for the first time by Jaivali. But his language is more concise than that of Jaivali and of Gārgyāyaṇa, the immediate successor of Jaivali. Besides, it is worthy of note that the earlier expressions for the two paths were Pitṛiyāna and Devayāna, while Pippalāda invented two other expressions —the southern (dakṣiṇa) and the northern (uttara)—for them.[2] And it is not unlikely, as the late Mr. Tilak has sought to maintain, that in the contrast so sharply drawn between the two roads there is a reminiscence of the original home of the Aryans in some northern region especially when the Vedas and later Indian literature abound in Trans-Himalayan reminiscences. As Pippalāda says, to travel on the southern, ancestral or material path is to marry a beautiful

[1] Praśnopaniṣad, I. 5 : " etat sarvaṁ yan mūrtañca amūrtañca tasmān mūrtireva Rayiḥ."

[2] *Ibid*, I. 9. 10.

girl, to generate the race, or, at best, to believe, as some good householders do, in sacrifice and charity,—the two words which sum up the whole duty of a worldly man. Those who do so follow but the rule of Prajāpati,[1] the mundane or prolific god. To them belongs only This Brahma-world here.

Those again, who travel on the northern, divine or spiritual path by means of penance or meditation, abstinence or pure life, faith and knowledge,[2] reach at length that spotless (viraja) Brahma-world which is the dwelling place of the spirits, immortality, fearlessness, the end of the transcendental road,—the world of absolute existence from which there is no return to Rayi—the world of matter. This is the cessation (nirodha)[3] of all materiality, that is to say, of all impurity, and mortality. Such a Brahma-world exists only for those divine sages 'in whom dwell penance, abstinence, and truth,' and in whom there is nothing crooked, nothing false, and no guile.'[4] Here the expression *nirodha* deserves special notice.

(2) The first answer of Pippalāda has shown how a living body is generated from the parents, from the union of Matter and Spirit, and originally from God. In the second dialogue the question is changed, and that partly because the interlocutor is a different man—Bhārgava of Vidarbha. His question is a physio-psychological one: What are the gods (principal things) of which an organised body is constituted, and by which it is preserved and manifested (prakāśita) and, which is the best (variṣṭha) of them? To this Pippalāda gives the following reply:—

A living body is constituted chiefly of ether (ākāśa), air, fire, water, earth, speech, mind, breath, eye, and ear. By

[1] Praśnopaniṣad, I. 15: "Tad yo ha vai tat Prajāpati-vrataṁ caranti te mithunaṁ utpādayante."

[2] Tapasā, brahmacaryyena, śraddhayā, vidyayā.

[3] Praśnopaniṣad, I. 10 "etad vai prāṇānām āyatanam etad amṛita abhayam etat parāyaṇam etasmān na puhar āvartanta ityēṣa nirodhaḥ."

[4] *Ibid*, I. 15. 16; "yeṣāṁ tapo brahmacaryyaṁ yeṣu satyaṁ pratiṣṭhitaṁ; "na yeṣu jihmaṁ amṛitam na māyā cêti."

these the organism is preserved and manifested (developed). The best of them is to be known as Prāṇa, the vital principle. For, when life departs, all other gods are bound to leave the body. Thus Pippalāda holds with Mahidāsa and others that the essential fact is this life, and, therefore, the highest principle is the vital. It is besides the one principle which pervades the universe, and through which we may see the unity of man with the rest of created things. The essence of life itself is Fire or Heat. One of the images by which he illustrates his point indicates his study of nature. The simile is: 'As bees go out of the hive when their king[1] leaves it, so when life, etc.'

His physiological views.

(3) In the third dialogue Āśvalāyana of Kosala asks an even more important question, on a problem having a bearing upon both metaphysics and physiology. As Pippalāda understands Āśvalāyana, his problem is at once the origin, the entry, the place, the supremacy, the five-fold distribution, and the intrinsic fate (subjective condition) of Prāṇa,[2] a term meaning life, a living body, its functions, as well as the soul. Āśvalāyana asks: From what is Prāṇa (the principle of life) itself born (jāyeta)? How does it come into body? Where does it dwell in a fully-developed and fully-active body? Into how many systems are functions of life to be divided? How does the soul leave the body (utkramate)? How again does it bind itself to external objects (bāhyam abhidhatte)? And how does it maintain its inner essence or subjective elements (adhyātmaṁ abhidhatte)?

[1] Should be queen, not madhukara rāja.

[2] Praśnopaniṣad, III.12: "Utpattim āyatim sthānam vibhūtvañcaiva pañcadhā. Adhyātmañcaiva prāṇasya..." Max Müller translates 'adhyātma' by "internal state." But neither "internal state" nor 'intrinsic fate' convey the exact connotation of the term. In philosophical parlance 'subjective' is the word which comes nearest to 'adhyātma,' and 'objective' to 'bāhya.' Unfortunately these words, too, are used not in the same sense by all the philosophers. See for Dr. Stirling's historical note upon this subject, Spinoza's Ethic, translated by W. Hale White, 1910, Preface, pp. VII-VIII.

His Metaphysical views.

Pippalāda cannot help remarking that these questions are all more difficult than one can possibly answer (atipraśna). However, he attempts to answer them all, seeing that Āśvalāyana is very earnest.

The spirit, solar self, or principle of life is generated from the psyche, soul, or ego, that is to say, from itself, from its inner essence. The soul is in life, just as the reflection imaged in the sun.[1] It is by the work of the mind, that is to say, from its inherent desire to be, that the soul comes into body.[2]

As regards the sovereignty (vibhutva) of the vital soul, it is in an organised body, as though a supreme monarch (samrāṭ) who 'commands official, saying to them: Rule these villages or those.' In other words, all separate or special (prithak prithak) functions of the organism are subservient to the central function of life. The above simile is evidently taken from Yājñavalkya.[3]

The soul dwells in the heart from which extend 101 arteries and nerves (nāḍī) towards different parts of the body. In each of these there are a hundred branches, and for each of these branches there are 72,000 (capillaries and nerve-fibres?). It is through all these channels that the supreme ruler sends forth command to his officials who are stationed in various centres of activity, and who are doing special works for the healthy upkeep of his kingdom. Such an enormous number as Pippalāda gives of arteries, veins, capillaries, and nerves was not conceived before the time of Yājñavalkya.[4]

In agreement with Mahidāsa, Pippalāda divides the physiological functions of the body into five systems (pañcadhā),

[1] Praśnopaniṣad, III. 3: "ātmanā eṣa prāṇo jāyate. Yathaiṣa puruṣe chāyā etasminn-etad ātatam."

[2] *Ibid*, III. 3: "manokṛitena āyatyasmiñ charīre."

[3] Bṛihad Āraṇyaka Upaniṣad, IV, 422; IV, 338.

[4] See Chāndogya Upaniṣad, VI.5.3; Kauṣītaki Upaniṣad, IV.20; Kaṭha Upaniṣad VI.16; and Bṛihad Āraṇyaka Upaniṣad, II.1.19; IV.3.20.

to wit, (1) Prāṇa—the respiratory system, (2) Apāna—the alimentary system, (3) Samāna—Metabolism, (4) Vyāna—the circulatory system, and (5) Udāna—the special senses.

The Soul leaves the body by death. Pippalāda maintains that at the time of death, as perhaps at the time of rebirth, the sense-faculties become or remain absorbed in mind.[1] The soul departs free from sense-apprehension and representative cognition, and proceeds towards a world—good, bad, or mixed,—heavenly, infernal, or human—as willed before death (yathā saṅkalpitam lokam). The path of the soul is lighted by its own light, and it is borne by the vital energy inherent in its life. To our utter disappointment, Pippalāda's expressions are too enigmatic and terse to be intelligible without having a constant reference to Yājñavalkya's views.[2]

His psychological views.

(4) The fourth problem is entirely psychological. It was formulated by the celebrated astronomer Gārgya, who was perhaps an elder contemporary of Agniveśya.[3] And so far as Pippalāda's answer goes, there is little in it that is either very new or very peculiar to him. His views remind us at every turn of Yājñavalkya. And yet Pippalāda must be credited with having employed almost all the principal categories of the later Sāṁkhya system. It is indeed in his phrasæology that we come across for the first time such terms as Prāṇa for Puruṣa, Rayi for Prakṛti, Mūrta for Vyakta, Amūrta for Avyakta, and Mātrā for Tanmātrā, the terms Bhūta, Manas, Buddhi, Ahaṅkāra, Sense-faculties (Indriyas) and Sense-objects being all common.[4] We must note that the original problems

[1] Praśnopaniṣad, III. 9; "Punarbhavam indriyair manasi abhisampadyamānaiḥ."

[2] Bṛihad Āraṇyaka Upaniṣad, IV. 4. 1-4.

[3] *Ibid*, IV. 6. 2. Was Agniveśya the traditional writer on medical subjects? See Caraka-Saṁhitā. In any case, we have mention of Aggivessa in the early Buddhist records as a family name or designation of a school, perhaps of thinkers who were interested in the study of medicine.

[4] Praśnopaniṣad, IV. 8.

of the Sāṁkhya type of thinking were two: (1) the genesis of life and the development or manifestation of its potentialities, and (2) the attainment of the highest condition of soul through *yoga*. The solution of the first problem is offered in the light of natural causation, the terms Amūrta, Mūrta, Buddhi, Ahaṅkāra, etc., constituting a series of cause and effect, best understood when studied in reference to the formation of 'sperm' and 'blood,' the development of the foetus in the womb, and the subsequent growth of the organism and the thinking powers, the subject is well dealt with in the Garbha and Śārīraka Upaniṣads and latterly in the Śārīra and Indriya Sthānas of the Caraka-Saṁhitā which is said to have been a later recast of Agniveśya's medical treatise.[1]

Gārgya inquires: What are they that periodically cease during sleep, and are awakened when a man is awake? What is the deity (deva) that sees dream? Who experiences the highest happiness (sukha) during dreamless sleep? And on what first cause are all these dependant ultimately?

The theory of sleep.

Pippalāda's reply is that sensations cease. Sleep in general may be defined psychologically as the cessation of sensations, or rather the absorption of sensations in the mind. When a man sleeps, as they say, he does not hear, see, smell, taste, touch, speak, take (act), enjoy by way of pleasure, excrete, and move about (walk). It is most interesting to notice that Pippalāda is well aware of the fact of his interlocutor being an astronomer,—a student of the solar system, that is to say, a Sauryāyanin Gārgya. Thus he gives for an illustration of his point this simile. "O, Gārgya, as all the rays of the sun, when it sets, are gathered up in that disc of light, and as they, when the sun rises again and again, come forth, so is all this (all the senses) gathered up in the highest faculty (deva), the mind."[2]

[1] Mrs. Rhys Davids has ably sought in her Buddhism to establish a similar interpretation of the 12 *nidānas* conceived by the Buddhists on the Sāṁkhya lines.

[2] Praśnopaniṣad, IV. 2.

Theory of dream.

Pippalāda next takes up the problem of dream, and by dream he understands the state of sleep which is to be carefully distinguished from the dreamless state called Suṣupti. The above definition of sleep applies strictly to the dreaming condition of the mind. Mind is the deity that sees the dream. Pippalāda upholds here the theory of Yājñavalkya, when he maintains that in the state of dreaming, the mind not merely recalls the accumulated impressions of the past, or previous sense-images, but also sees, imagines, or envisages something quite novel or prophetic. In other words, the mind at the stage of dreaming is both a representative and a purely imaginative faculty.[1]

When the mind is overpowered by light (tejasā abhibhūto), then it no longer dreams. And it is then, and then only, that true happiness (sukha) arises in its body.[2]

Soul is defined as a pure cognitive consciousness.

Pippalāda, then, goes on to say that the state of dream, is followed by that of sleep. Between these two he seems to have contemplated an intermediate or transitional state, when the dream is just over and the mind is conscious of nothing but itself. Such a thought-free but self-conscious and blissful state of the mind is the condition of soul (Puruṣa), whose essence is pure consciousness or pure cognition (vijñānātmā). Soul as such underlies all sense-perceptions and sense-actions, and all lower and higher functions of the mind. In this sense Pippalāda regards Soul as that which sees, touches, hears, thinks, understands, and acts.[3]

As sleep deepens, the mind transcends even the state of pure cognitive consciousness (citta=vijñānātmā),[4] and thereby

[1] Praśna, IV. 5: "Dṛiṣṭañca adṛiṣṭañca, śrutañca, aśrutañca, anubhūtañca, ananubhūtañca, sat ca asat ca—sarvam paśyati."

[2] *Ibid*, IV. 6.

[3] *Ibid*, IV. 9: "Eṣa hi draṣṭā praṣṭā ghrātā, rasayitā, mantā boddhā kartā vijñānātmā puruṣaḥ."

[4] *Cf.* Buddha's three terms in "cittaṁ iti pi mano iti pi viññāṇaṁ," Saṁyutta-nikāya, II. p. 94; "That which is called consciousness, that is, mind, that is, intelligence." Mrs. Rhys Davids, "Buddhist Psychology," p. 14.

reaches its highest condition—a condition in which the mind reaches the Divine state, the imperishable essence of our being (para akṣara ātmā).

God denotes the state of mind lying beyond pure cognition.

During sound sleep, when all sensations cease, all imaginations end, and when the mind loses even the consciousness of its own existence, what else can we conceive as existing but the highest indestructible being in which the cognitive soul, together with all the higher faculties of the mind, and all the senses, and the elements, rests? It is therefore on God, who is shadowless, incorporeal, colourless and bright, that all these ultimately depend for their existence. He who knows it, becomes omniscient (sarvajña), comprehends all.

The point on which Pippalāda leaves us in doubt is that he does not say, as Yājñavalkya does, whether the mind is active or passive during sound sleep.

The last point to mention is Pippalāda's enumeration of the 'sixteen phases'[1] (ṣoḍaśa kalā) denoting the sixteen successive changes, *i.e.*, *Ṣoḍaśa Vikārā* in later Sāṁkhya nomenclature. He compares, in agreement with his predecessors, the phenomena of nature to passing phases of the moon, and the abiding element to the sixteenth digit. The world of generation, with all individual beings and particular things, may appear and disappear, while Puruṣa (universal soul) abides for ever. The world develop by 'name and form' (nāma-rūpa). But as soon as the world is absorbed into the imperishable essence, which is one, all names applied to forms or qualitatively distinct things, such as ether, air, fire, water, etc., pass out of use.

Pippalāda's view of the phenomenal world.

CHAPTER XVI.

BHĀRADVĀJA.

(*Muṇḍaka Philosophy.*)

The Muṇḍakôpaniṣad is our sole authority for Satyavāha Bhāradvāja's philosophy, which is honoured in the text itself with the name of the Divine Science (Brahma-vidyā), also described as, the foundation of all knowledge (sarva-vidyā-pratiṣṭhā).[1] The said Divine Science is fancifully traced from Brahmā, the Divine Being himself, down to the great teacher (mahāśāla)[2] named Śaunaka. According to this genealogical tradition, the doctrine was handed down in an unchanged condition from Brahmā to his eldest son Atharvan, from Atharvan to Satyavāha Bhāradvāja, from him to the sage Aṅgiras, and from Aṅgiras at last to Śaunaka.[3]

The teachers of the Muṇḍaka school.

The form in which the Upaniṣad now reaches us shows that it is no more than a spectrum of all contradictory views. In truth, no one can tell in how many ways the text together with the doctrine which it zealously preserves had undergone changes till it was finally recast.

As to the origin or precise historical bearing of the title of the Muṇḍakôpaniṣad, we may quote the following observations of Prof. Max Müller. "The Upanishad is called Muṇḍaka-Upanishad, and its three chapters are each called Muṇḍakam. Native

Origin and historical significance of the name Muṇḍaka.

[1] Muṇḍakôpaniṣad, I. 1.1.

[2] Max Müller translates Mahāśāla "the great householder." It is evident from the Mahāgovinda Suttanta of the Dīgha-nikāya (Vol. II) that Mahāśālā (or rather Brāhmana-mahāśālā) was a technical name for the Snātaka-institution (Post-graduate College, to use a modern phrase). Hence the epithet Mahāśāla would show that Śaunaka was the head (principal) of such an institution.

[3] Muṇḍakôpaniṣad, I. 1.2.

commentators explain it as the Shaving Upanishad, *i.e.*, the Upanishad which cuts off the errors of the mind, like a razor. Another Upanishad also is called Kshurika, the Razor, a name which is explained in the text itself as meaning an instrument for removing illusion and error. The title is all the more strange because Muṇḍaka, in its commonest acceptation, is used as a term of reproach for Buddhist mendicants, who are called 'Shavelings,' in opposition to the Brāhmans, who dress their hair carefully, and often display by its peculiar arrangement either their family or their rank. Many doctrines of the Upanishads are, no doubt, pure Buddhism, or rather Buddhism is on many points the consistent carrying out of the principles laid down in the Upanishads. Yet, for that very reason, it seems impossible that this should be the origin of the name, unless we suppose that it was the work of a man who was, in one sense, a Muṇḍaka (*i.e.*, a Buddhist monk), and yet faithful to the Brahmanic law."[1]

We can not fully agree with Prof. Max Müller because there are no Brāhman works known to us in which the epithet 'Shaveling' is used as a term of reproach for the Buddhist monks only. In these works the Buddhists are commonly represented by such names as 'Saugatas,' 'Śākyas,' 'Bauddhas,' and sometimes reproachfully, in common with the Jainas and Lokāyatas, mentioned as Demons and Atheists (Daityas, Asuras, Nāstikas), but certainly not as Muṇḍakas. The early Buddhist records themselves reveal that Buddha was addressed by his contemporaries as 'Samaṇa Gotama' except in one instance[2] where a sacrificing priest Aggika Bhāradvāja describes him as a *muṇḍaka*, *samaṇa* and *vasala*, and that as the result of his orthodox prejudice not only against the Buddhist Bhikkhus but against the Śramans in general. And 'Samaṇa' (Recluse) was a designation applied

[1] S. B. E. II, Introd., pp. XXVI-XXVII.

[2] Sutta-nipāta, p. 21; Aggika-Bhāradvāja says: "Tatrēvamuṇḍaka tatrēvasamaṇaka."

to all those who distinguished themselves from the Keśins or Jaṭilakas,[1] who wore either long loose locks or hair in braids, and from the Śikhis, who wore a forelock,[2] by seeking to live a pure life as Brahmacārins, by begging food as bhikṣus (mendicants), and by shaving their head clean as muṇḍakas (shavelings). When Buddha said, 'Not by reason of shaving alone a man becomes a recluse' (na muṇḍakena samaṇo),[3] he had, in all probability, kept in his mind the 'Shavelings' other than his own followers. In the list of *religieux*, given in an important passage of the Aṅguttara-nikāya,[4] Buddha unmistakably refers to the Muṇḍa-Sāvakas ("disciples of the Shaveling") as a school distinct from the Magaṇḍikas, Tedaṇḍikas, Ājīvikas, Aviruddhakas, Nigaṇṭhas (Jainas), and such other recluses, mendicants or shavelings. Following Buddhaghosa, Prof. Rhys Davids conjectures that the Muṇḍa-Sāvakas were "perhaps some special sub-division of Jains."[5] But as their name implies, the Muṇḍa-Sāvakas were the disciples or followers of Muṇḍa,—the school after whom perhaps the Upaniṣad in question was entitled Muṇḍaka. Dr. Schrader tells us that in the Jaina Rājavārttika, a commentary on Umāsvati's Tattvārtha Sūtra (VIII. 1.), a Muṇḍa is classed among the Kriyāvādins.[6]

Śramans.

Neither the Ṛṣis or Munis, nor the Keśins or Jaṭilakas, strictly so called, were medicants or shavelings. They were hermits (tāpasas) or ascetics (sannyāsins), without question. In course of time, in the days of Yājñavalkya who alludes to both Śramans and Tāpasas, and also perhaps not long before the rise of Buddhism, a new order of *religieux* was formed, who called themselves

[1] Bühler's Gautama, III. 34. On this authority Rhys Davids, in his Dialogues of the Buddha, Vol. II, p. 221, identifies the Jaṭilakas with those Vaikhānasas ("orthodox hermits") who used to wear, as a rule, their hair in braids.

[2] Gautama, III. 22.

[3] Dhammapada, XIX, 6.

[4] Dialogues of the Buddha, Vol. II, p. 220.

[5] *Ibid*, p. 221.

[6] Indisch. Philoso h

Śramans (to distinguish themselves both from the hermits who practised penance and sacrifice in the wood and the Brāhmans who were householders). They shaved their head clean, and begged their food, instead of feeding like the Munis or Keśins on pot-herbs, wild rice, *nivara*-seeds, water-plants, the powdered grains of rice (kaṇa),[1] the discarded scum of boiling rice, the flour of oil-seeds, grasses, cow-dung, fruits, roots, water, air, or ether.[2] They became known perhaps from the practice of begging, as Bhikṣus (mendicants). The origin of this order of *religieux* is now obscure or uncertain. But we might safely hold with Prof. Rhys Davids that the Bhikṣu order of homeless persons evolved originally from the Brahmacārīns[3] who did not enter upon the stage of the householder,[4] and who customarily begged their food.[5]

According to the *Āśrama*-theory of the leading Brāhman jurists, the life of a member of the twice-born ranks or the three upper classes of the Indo-Aryan people ought to be divided into four periods, representing the four stages of effort or training—intellectual, moral, legal and spiritual, in short, both mundane and transcendental. The names and enumerations of these stages vary with the authorities.[6] But a passage in Baudhāyana's legal manual gives just three stages, omitting

[1] It would seem that Kaṇāda, the founder of the Vaiśeṣika system, received his name from the circumstance of eating Kaṇa.

[2] Dial. B. II. p. 230; Gautama, III. 26, 29; Baudhāyana, III. 3. 1-14.

[3] The word Brahmacārī occurs once in the Ṛig-veda, hymn X. 109: "The Brahmachārī goes engaged in duty: he is a member of the gods' own body." *Cp.* Atharva-veda, XI. 5.

[4] Āpastamba, II. 9. 21. 8; Gautama, III. 2; Manu, VI. 86; Yājñavalkya, III. 56-57.

[5] Āpastamba, I. 1. 3. 28; Manu, II. 49; Yājñavalkya, I. 27; Aśvalāyana Gṛihya-sūtra, I. 22. 10; Mānava-Gṛihya Sūtra, I. 1. 2.

[6] For example, (1) Yājñavalkya gives them as Pāṇḍitya, Bālya, the Muni and the Brāhmaṇa (Bṛihad Āraṇyaka Upaniṣad, III.5.1.); (2) Āpastamba, as Gārhasthyam, Ācārya-kulam, Maunam and Vānaprasthyam (II.9.21.1); (3) Gautama, as the Brahmacārī, the Gṛihastha, the Bhikṣu and the Vaikhānasa (III.2; *cp.* Baudhāyana, II.6.11.12); (4) Manu, as the Brahmacārī, the Gṛihastha, the Vānaprastha and the Yati (V.137; VI.87); and (5) Vasiṣṭha, as the Brahmacārī, the Gṛihastha, the Vānaprastha and the Parivrājaka (VII.2).

the Bhikṣu.[1] The same we find also in a passage of the Manusmṛti.[2] The omission of the Bhikṣu-stage is interpreted differently by Prof. Rhys Davids.[3] While fully cognisant of the weight of his opinion, we think the absence of the name from those passages might well be due to the fact that the stages or periods of training were recognised originally not as four, but as three.[4] It also should be borne in mind that the enumeration of three stages belongs neither to Baudhāyana nor to Manu, but to some older authority, named Asura Kapila (*i.e.*, Āsuri), son of Prahlāda.[5] There are, moreover, the later recasts of a few older Sūtras where the *Āśrama*-theory plays no part, and which might be judged as an evidence of the fact that it was engrafted at some late date on the *Cāturvaṇya* system, though before the rise of a Buddhism.[6]

Prof. Rhys Davids also says: "..... the rules (regarding the Four Efforts) are admitted to be obsolete now. Śaṅkara says these were not observed in his time.[7] And the theory seems to be little more than a priestly protest against the doctrine, acted upon by Buddhists, Jains, and others, and laid down in the Madhura-sutta, that even youths might go forth without any previous Vedic study."[8] But we must understand that the rule enjoined in the Madhura-sutta[9] is in fact far earlier, earlier even than Gautama's work,[10] and most probably laid down in the Vaikhānasa-Dharma-sūtra, also known as the Śrāmaṇaka

1 Baudhāyana, II.6.11.28.

2 Manu, II.230.

3 Dial. B.II., pp. 215-217.

4 Chāndogya Upaniṣad, III.16.1-7.

5 Baudhāyana, II.6. 11.28; Bṛihad Āraṇyaka Upaniṣad, I.5.16.

6 E. G. Saṁkha and Likhita Saṁhitās. The names of these two ancient jurists became proverbial in the time of the Buddha, as may be judged from the latter's expression, *Saṁkha-Likhita Brahmacariya* (Dīgha, I, p. 63). Buddhaghosa has entirely lost sight of the historical significance of the expression.

7 Deussen's 'Vedanta,' p. 40.

8 Dial. B. II., p. 217.

9 See Chalmer's translation in J.R.A.S., 1894.

10 III. 1.

Sūtra.[1] And there is no evidence of the rules of Aśramas being binding or valid, at any time, for all individuals. Thus we can see how the youths had left home-life, and passed straight from schools into the life of homeless recluses, how, in other words, the order of Śramans or Bhikṣus originated from the Brahmacārins.

Opposition between Śramans on one hand, and Brāhmans and Ascetics on the other.

Now among the Śramans, all of whom, in one way or another, broke away from past traditions, revolted against the older Vedic system of sacrifice and self-mortification, or dissented from the later form of Brāhmanic religion, superstition and mysticism, there were various sects or groups or schools. The revolt showed itself in every possible manner. For example, the Śramans as a body shaved their hair and beard, ceased to appeal to the authority of scripture, listened to nothing but their own conscience, sought for inner purity and enlightenment rather than external religiosity, and embraced the wider cause of humanity instead of observing the caste-distinctions which obtained in society.[2] But presumably this battle was a mere question of personal temperament before it became a world-wide phenomenon. And perhaps Bhāradvāja was the first to organise a regular war (the process of which is as old as the Kāvaṣeyas, if not older), to make a firm stand against the champions of ancient rites and usages. He distinguished himself even outwardly from them by shaving his hair and beard. From this latter circumstance we may suppose, his personal name was gradually forgotten, and his nickname, Muṇḍa or Shaveling,

[1] See allusions to the Śrāmaṇaka Sūtra in Gautama, III.27; Vasiṣṭha, IX.10; Baudhāyana, II.6.11.14-15; III.3.15-18: Haradatta's commentary on Āpastamba, II.9.21.21; Bühler's 'Manu,' p. XXVII. Pandit S. Sankar has recently translated the Vaikhānasa Dharma-praśna. Pāṇini refers to the Parāśara Bhikṣu-Sūtra.

[2] The Suttanipāta-comy (Paramatthajotikā, II, 1, p. 175) explains the cause of Brāhmanic apathy for the Śramans. It is said that they did not worship the deities and Brāhmans (deva-brāhmaṇapūjako na hoti); that they did not foster self-mortification (kāya-kilesaṁ na vaṇṇeti); that they received recruits from all grades of society and permitted commensality with all.

took its place. Although following his example, now established as a custom of the land, the Śramans of other schools shaved their hair and beard, yet the designation 'Shavelings' (Muṇḍakas) remained a birth-right for his school only.

His Philosophy.

Two points of investigation in Bhāradvāja.

Bhāradvāja's fundamental views are two. One of these is closely linked with a question, having considerable bearing on moral philosophy in general, and on juristic and social theory in particular. The question is whether, to what extent, and in what manner the transcendental order can be conceived to accord with the concrete activities of life and society. The second view falls within the department of knowledge, and is but a corollary from the first. Here we find an attempted solution of one of the ultimate problems of knowledge, whether the infinite being is within the apprehension of a finite mind, whether the ultimate reality is accessible to ordinary cognition.

I. Transcendentalism[1] *versus asceticism and worldly life.*

In the systems of the leading Brāhman jurists we find certain judgments on the two contrasted types: the life of the householder and the life of the anchorite. Again, in the Sāmaññaphala-sutta the question arises as to the reward (in this present conscious existence) of the life of the recluse; and an answer is given by the Buddha. It is apparent from the

[1] The term is not used here in the Kantian sense of the investigation of that which is *a priori* in human cognition, but approximately in the sense best associated with Emersion. It implies a sort of reaction against the barbarity of ascetic practices and against all so-called self-centred social morality, polity, prejudices and superstitions. Bhāradvāja's predilection for the hermit-life being stronger than his aversion for asceticism, we prefer to call him a transcendentalist rather than a rationalist. 1-2. Dial. B. II, pp. 68-69; *cp.* the Uttarādhya ana Sūtra in Jacobi's Jaina-sūtras, part 2, pp. 61-69.

manner in which king Ajātasattu of Magadha put the question to Buddha that the efficacy of the hermit-life was doubted in the country, especially by those who were immersed in worldliness. But neither was Buddha the first nor Śaṅkara the last to favour the life of renunciation, and at the same time to denounce asceticism. If we be not mistaken, Satyavāha Bhāradvāja was one of the pioneers among those thinkers who bravely faced the problem, upheld transcendentalism against both asceticism as largely practised by the Vedic ascetics and worldly life as regulated with Puritanic strictness by the Brāhman priests and jurists. He thus prepared the way for the rationalism of Buddha who enunciated the Middle-path, and sought for a *via media* of thought, conduct and intellectual training.

Bhāradvāja and Buddha.

Prof. Rhys Davids has justly said, "The intellectual movement before the rise of Buddhism was in large measure a lay movement." For one reason or another, some of the great thinkers of India had found in the order of householders, or life as actually lived in society, nothing in common with the transcendental sphere of existence, the Brahma-world, that is to say, the higher plane of human activities. At the very dawn of intellectual life in India a problem appeared on its horizon, namely, what is essentially and absolutely necessary for a way to the immortal state (amṛitatva). The Taittirīyas tell us that a Truth-speaker or Realist (Satya-vacas) named Rāthītara termed it Truth. An intellectualist (Taponitya) named Pauraśiṣṭi thought that the only thing necessary to the higher life was meditation or constant cultural practice. In the view of Maudgalya, the seeker of rewards in heaven, the essential duty of a man is the study and interpretation of the Vedas (svādhyāya-pravacanam).[1]

Rāthītara, Pauraśiṣṭi, and Maudgalya's views.

[1] *Taittirīya Upaniṣad*, I. 9.

The Taittirīyas themselves, on the other hand, could be content with nothing less than a faithful observance of all these and other duties of man's life. To them, therefore, good principle, truth, the inner culture of faith and intellect, the study and interpretation of the Vedas, self-control or subjugation of the senses, tranquillity or imperturbability, the fires (deities and ancestors), inner offering or prayer, guests (hospitality), fellow men (charity), fellow beings (humanity), marriage and offspring only fall under the various heads[1] of man's duty in the world, home, school, society and solitude. The command, the instruction, or the rule of conduct is presented by them in another form, and accepted and elaborated by all Brāhman legal and moral philosophers. The teacher would say to the pupil who is brought up strictly in Brāhmanic traditions:—"Speak the truth. Walk in righteousness (dharma). Study the Vedas and Vedic sciences. Render pecuniary help to thy teacher. Do not cut off the lineage, spiritual or mundane (prajātantu). Be not thoughtless (na pramaditavyam) as to Truth. Do not swerve from good principles. Do not depart from what is morally good and helpful (kuśala). Do not neglect living beings[2] (cattle, etc.). Be not inattentive to the study and interpretation of the Vedas. Do not deprive the gods and ancestors of offerings and oblations due to them. Honour father, mother, teacher and guests like a god. Esteem only those actions which are blameless (anavadya), and not others. Perform only those good works which have been performed by us (predecessors), and not others. Receive the Brāhmans (wise men) with respect, faith or eagerness, grace, gentleness,

The ethical views of the Taittirīyas.

[1] *Taittirīya* Up. I. 9: ṛitam (dharma), satyam, tapas, svādhyāya-pravacanam, damaḥ, śamaḥ, agnayaḥ, agnihotraḥ, atithayaḥ, mānusam, prajāḥ, prajanaḥ, prajātiḥ. *cp.* Baudhāyana, II. 6. 11. 3-4; Āpastamba, II. 9. 24. 7-8.

[2] Max Müller translates *bhūtāni* greatness.

fear and close attention.[1] Act and behave in doubtful cases[2] as the Brāhmans of ripe judgment (sammarśinaḥ) are wont to act, avoiding meanness and aiming only at righteousness (alūkṣa dharmakāmaḥ), and so, too, in matters exciting the public feeling (abhyākhyāteṣu).

The points about which the Taittirīyas, and with them all Brāhman legal and moral philosophers seem extremely keen are these: (1) the learning and teaching of Vedic literature; (2) an implicit obedience to custom and convention, or so-called revealed laws in the scripture; (3) a gradual advance from professed to realised faith; (4) the worship of deities and ancestors; and (5) marriage.

The first two points mean that we should not care so much to originate new ideas or formulate new rules of conduct as to make explicit what is implicit in the revealed texts,—to go on, in other words, putting new wine continually into old bottles. The third point implies that we should first readily accept what is given in the scripture, and then, if we have time and ability and inclination enough, humbly ask whether it is true or false, in order finally to confirm our faith. The last point relates to marriage or union of the sexes. The Brāhman thinkers in general, and the legal and moral philosophers in particular, viewed, contrary to the warrior thinkers, the idea of celibacy and childlessness with a peculiar dread. Underlying their view of marriage, there is the notion of a kind of heredity, immortality, identity, continuity and progress. Thus nothing is of greater importance for them than this last point relating to marriage.

Referring to the four Āśramas or orders of men, Gautama who is one of the oldest and least philosophical among the writers on legal subjects, declared that the married householder was the source of all other orders of men, obviously for the

[1] Śraddhayā, śriyā, hriyā, bhiyā, saṁvidā. *Cp.* Āsuri's expressions in the Bṛihad Āraṇyaka Upaniṣad, I. 5. 3.

[2] Karma-vicikitsā vā vṛitta-vicikitsā vā syāt.

reason that men of other orders did not generate children.[1]

The legal writers' view of marriage. The antinomian doctrine of Vaśiṣṭha.

Following Gautama, Baudhāyana maintains that there is, forsooth, one order only, the order of the householder. Other orders cannot be conceived as existent because they do not beget offspring.[2] Renouncing good works recommended in the Vedas, severed from the worlds both celestial and mundane, and devoted exclusively to the transcendental sphere of Brahman, these orders of men become at length dust and perish (rajo bhūtvā dhvaṁsate). The other three orders had not existed in the country before a demon named Kapila, son of Prahlāda, disagreeing with the gods, *i.e.*, Brāhmans, introduced them. No wise men, therefore, should take any notice of them. For in accordance with the rule and purpose of Prajāpati, the lord of the world of generation, it is our duty to study the three Vedas, to undergo moral discipline, to marry, to profess and realise faith, to offer sacrifices, and to show liberality to those who deserve it. Quoting an ancient authority,[3] Baudhāyana and Vaśiṣṭha sought to establish their views, that by a son a man conquers the worlds, by a grandson he obtains immortality, and by a great-grandson he rises up to the highest heaven. But we must not put out of sight Vaśiṣṭha's judgment of the moral value of conduct (ācāra) as far outvaluing the mere formal study of the Vedas together with the six Aṅgas and other supplementary works.[4] Baudhāyana's arguments were further worked out later by Āpastamba,[5] as originally derived from the Taittirīyas in the main. Thus Vaśiṣṭha leads us

[1] Gautama, III. 3; III. 36.

[2] Baudhāyana, II. 6. 11. 27; II. 6. 11. 26, 34.

[3] Taittirīya Saṁhitā, VI. 3. 10. 5; Śatapatha Brāhmaṇa, I. 7. 2. 11; Brihad Āraṇyaka Upaniṣad, I. 5. 4. 16. "A Brāhmana is born loaded with three debts: he owes studentship to the sages; sacrifices to the gods, and a son to the manes" (Bühler). Baudhāyaṇa, II. 9. 16. 6; Vaśiṣṭha, XVII. 5.

[4] Vaśiṣṭha, VI. 1-8; *cp.* Manu, IV. 155-158; Viṣṇu, LXXI. 92.

[5] Baudhāyaṇa, II. 6. 11. 34.

back to those who avowedly underrated the moral value of Vedic learning, that is, to the Muṇḍakas, and Baudhāyana leads us to Āpastamba and Āpastamba back to the Taittirīyas.

"Abandoning truth and falsehood, pleasure and pain, the Vedas, this world and the next, one should seek the universal Soul. For an insight into that alone is the attainment of security (kṣemaprāpanam)."[1] Āpastamba considered this Gārgyāyaṇa or Platonic view to be quite the contrary of his own. Strange to say, in one section of his work,[2] if it be not a later interpolation, the same Āpastamba speaks in the Gārgyāyaṇa vein, when like a good philosopher he recognises nothing higher than the realisation of Ātman (ātma-lābhān na param). However, the whole contention of Āpastamba centres round the word "alone." Were security attainable by knowledge alone, then the seeker of it ought not to feel any pain in this life.[3] But the very fact that he feels some sort of pain is enough to prove that insight into truth alone is not enough for security.

Āpastamba and Gārgyāyaṇa.

Āpastamba upholds this view elsewhere,[4] and this time with far greater force. But his reasoning is dialectical, very similar to that of a Pūrva-mīmāṁsin. And the doctrine is at best that of a popular materialist and theologian. He introduces the point of controversy thus: Those who vehemently disparage the order of house-holders assert: Desiring children, a man travels on the southern path of the Āryaman (sun); and desiring no children, he proceeds along the northern path. The southern path leads to the crematorium and 'charnel-fields' (śmaśānam), while the northern path leads to immortality. Moreover, he who travels on the latter path, can accomplish

[1] Āpastamba, II. 9. 21. 13-14. Cp. Kauṣitaki Upaniṣad, I. 4.

[2] *Ibid*, I. 8. 22 ; I. 8. 23 : The section comes in abruptly. It shows no organic connection with what immediately precedes and with what follows. In any case, the author admits that the views are taken over from some older authorities. The commentator Haradatta thinks it is extracted from an Upaniṣad ; we suppose, from the Kaṭha.

[3] *Ibid*, II. 9. 21. 16.

[4] *Ibid*, II. 9. 23. 3-9 ; II. 9. 24. 1-15.

his wishes merely by his will. But their statement is absurd from beginning to end. With us who are well-versed in the three-fold knowledge (traividya-vṛiddhaḥ) the Vedas are the supreme authority (pramāṇam). We maintain accordingly that the works enjoined in the Vedas ought to be performed, and a rule of conduct (ācāra) which is opposed to those works is of no authority.

Now it is declared in the Vedas: offspring is man's immortality (prajātiḥ amṛitam). In other words, the father is reborn in the son, and this is the true immortality of the mortal (martyām amṛitam). That the father is just repro-duced separately (virudhaḥ pṛithak) in the son is perceivable even by the senses (pratyakṣena upalabhyate). For the likeness (sārūpyam) of both is so very apparent that it requires no other evidence to prove it; their bodies are two separate entities, that is all. The son naturally outlives the father, and fulfilling the duties taught in the Vedas, increases the fame and heavenly bliss (kīrtim svargam) of his predecessors. In this way each succeeding generation contributes to the glory and happiness of the preceding ones. It follows that the immortality which the unmarried hermits, ascetics or recluses strive to achieve is but a pure metaphysical fiction. That is to say, those deluded wise men who seek for immortality by means other than marriage 'become dust and perish.' There may be among them some who are good men. But for this reason we are not justified in saying that every one of them is either an intellectual or an ethical superior to every one of the householders. And why should we neglect what is so visible, excellent and concrete for something which is incapable of proof, imaginary or abstract?

The three points of argument of the Taittirīyas.

The arguments which the Taittirīyas brought forward in favour of their opinion were all drawn, as we saw, from the armoury of Mahidāsa, that is, from the philosophy of the Aitareyas. Their arguments are three in all: (1) That the eternal greatness of the Divine being (Brahman) is neither increased by works, nor diminished, and the soul that knows or realises in and through itself the nature of that greatness is not stained by evil deeds. (2) That the development of soul or the manifestation of the Divine essence in and through the world of generation is gradual. And (3) that there is no difference of kind but of degree between varied functions the soul has to discharge in its gradual advance from imperfection to completed actuality.

Thus we see that the opposition is ultimately between two great combatants in history, Mahidāsa and Gārgyāyaṇa[1], and that the real point at issue is whether or no there is any correlation between the Brahma-world and the concrete activities of life. In accordance with his view of development, Mahidāsa found perfect harmony between the two, whereas proceeding from his view of Idea, Gārgyāyaṇa found no other co-ordinating link than the generic character of soul—the soul which alone has the power to contemplate and realise in and through itself the eternal reason of the Divine, or through which the Divine Idea (mānasa) becomes actualised (cākṣuṣa).

The real opposition between Mahidāsa and Gārgyāyaṇa.

In Yājñavalkya we saw something of an attempt at a reconciliation between the views of Mahidāsa and Gārgyāyaṇa. And in making such an attempt he involved himself apparently in self-contradiction. While speaking for himself, he was on the side of Gārgyāyaṇa, as he found, like his predecessor, no harmony between his idea of the Brahma-world, on one hand, and the actual customs and usages of social life, on the other. Society allows, and is perhaps bound to allow, all sorts of distinction between this and that—a thief and not-a-thief, gods and not-gods, and so forth—while the greatest truth is, according to Yājñavalkya,

Ambiguity in Yājñavalkya and its bearing on the antagonism between the Muṇḍakas and the Vājasaneyas.

[1] The dialogue in the Uttarādhyayana, XIII, between Citra and Sambhūta reminds us of Citra Gārgyāyaṇa.

that there is no ultimate ground to justity any such distinctions. Thus he was forced at last to leave home to become a homeless recluse or hermit. For, as is clearly implied by him, we cannot serve both God and Mammon at the same time. Being a god, in other words, we can be among the gods, just as, on the other hand, being a Brahman, we can approach Brahman. Therefore, wishing for the Brahma-world only, the Bhikṣus leave their homes. That is to say, a divine philosopher, rising in thought and conduct above all material conditions of existence, rending asunder all worldly fetters and even putting aside all hankering after heavenly joys, attainable through works, Vedic or sacrificial, adopts the life of a mendicant (bhikṣācaryam carati).[1]

When he spoke for others, Yājñavalkya was on the side of Mahidāsa. As a Brāhman theologian himself, he could hardly get away from his inherited belief in the scripture. It need not surprise us, therefore, when we find that in his estimation the study of the Vedas and Vedic literature was not only useful but essential. The same applies equally to his views on sacrifice, penance and other hum-drums of Brāhmanic religion—the beliefs and practices which the Śramans in general, and the warrior philosophers in particular, either openly condemned, or at least viewed with great suspicion. As a Brāhman, too, he endeavoured to justify on a ground more or less psychological the Divine revelation in the Vedas. It was on a similar ground that he attempted also to defend all existing practices of Brāhmanic religion. As a law-giver, he taught that a Brāhman ought to pass through these four stages of life's training—Erudition (pāṇḍitya), Folly (bālya), Silence (maunam) and the Divine knowledge (brāhmaṇatvam). As a philosopher again, he maintained that the eternal greatness of the Divine being neither increases nor decreases by any kind of work.[2] The view was borrowed

[1] Bṛihad Āraṇyaka Upaniṣad, IV. 4. 22.

[2] Ibid, IV. 4. 22-23.

either from the Taittirīyas or from Pratardana. Supposing that, the view was obtained from the Taittirīyas, we can show that the psychological explanation which Yājñavalkya offered was far more definite and clear than that of his predecessors. Given an eternally active soul, it was very easy for Yājñavalkya to eliminate from the thinking subject an object by substituting for it another, and finally to eliminate from it every object which is foreign, *i.e.*, not-self. When applied to his āśrama-theory, Yājñavalkya's psychological explanation would appear as follows: At the first period of his life, a Brāhman desires Vedic scholarship. Then comes a period when, after accomplishing this object, he desires a wife, by her offspring, and through them immortality, preservation of the race, maintenance of social and religious institutions, and furtherance of knowledge. At the third period again, he, giving up even this object, desires to contemplate in silence the nature of the ultimate reality of things, while at the fourth his mind is intent on nothing but itself. But if, keeping his mind always intent on itself, a man does any work, no evil thereof can attach to his soul. And if it be possible for a man to enjoy all things and perform all life's functions without degrading his nature thereby, then it would certainly be unwise, according to him, to renounce the world and man's various duties in it at an early age.

As for the question, to study or not to study the Vedas, to marry or not to marry, or to be or not to be a monk, his answer was this:—"After erudition, a Brāhman persists in folly (bālyena tiṣṭhati). After that, he contemplates in silence. And finally he becomes a perfect philosopher." Here his expression "persists in folly" refers to marriage, which is the foundation of all social life, and admits of a two-fold interpretation. It may be interpreted either (1) as implying a bitter irony against those recluses or ascetics who looked upon marriage as a mere act of folly or childishness, or (2) as meaning that it is really foolish, even according to Yājñavalkya, to enter upon the life of a house-holder. The same ambiguity of meaning attaches to his sentence—"Everything else is of evil." It may mean either (1) everything except philosophic contemplation, or (2) everything except living in accordance with the āśrama-theory. This ambiguity of Yājñavalkya's expressions is most important historically, since we may suppose that out of it emerged later two distinct and mutually opposed schools of opinion, namely, that of the Muṇḍakas, and that of the Vājasaneyas. By the term folly (bālya) the former understood foolishness, childishness or ignorance, while the latter understood just the opposite of ignorance, that is, wisdom.

A. *The Muṇḍakan view.*

Bhāradvāja is distinguished in history from Rāthītara as a Truth-bearer (satya-vāha) from a Truth-speaker (satya-vacas) or pure Transcendentalist. The real difference between the two thinkers lies in the fact that the former explicitly blends, like Yājñavalkya, moral considerations with his conceptions of the transcendental. Two among the predicates assigned by Bhāradvāja to God (Brahman) are without family and without caste (agotraḥ, avarṇaḥ).[1] By these he clearly implies his detestation of the existing caste-system. But Bhāradvāja has no views to offer other than those of Yājñavalkya save that by which he discountenances the usual ascetic practices of the time. As among the predecessors of the Buddha who is best known as the propounder of the middle-path, it cannot but be of greatest interest to note in Bhāradvāja that as, on the one hand, he was anti-Brāhmanic in his social and religious views, so, on the other, he discouraged unnecessary physical torture, annihilation of the senses, and other ascetic monstrosities. "This self (the ideal self-existence) is not attainable

Bhāradvāja differs from Rāthītara in that he blends moral considerations with his conceptions of the transcendental.

[1] Muṇḍakōpaniṣad, I. 1. 6.

by the Veda, nor by mere intellect, nor by much learning. He whom the self chooses, by him it can be obtained......nor can it be obtained by one who is devoid of strength, thoughtfulness, and right meditation. It is only when a wise man strives after it by means of strength, thoughtfulness or earnestness, and right meditation, that he finds himself at home with Brahman."[1] And we must bear in mind that Bhāradvāja was neither an ascetic or hermit, nor a Brāhman house-holder, priest or jurist. He was a recluse (śramaṇa), mendicant (bhikṣu), or shaveling (muṇḍa).

Bhāradvāja's hostile attitude towards Brāhmanic religion and laws (with which we are mainly concerned) can well be brought out in his own words summarised as follows:—

Bhāradvāja's attitude towards Brāhmanic religion.

There are two kinds of Knowledge (vidyā): the higher or transcendental (parā) and the lower or mundane (a-parā). The knowledge mundane comprises the four Vedas and six Vedic sciences, while the knowledge transcendental is that by which the Undecaying (Akṣara) is rendered accessible—realised or apprehended.[2] "Come hither, come hither!" call the priests, the worshippers of the gods, the preachers of heavenly joys. "This is indeed thy holy well-merited Brahma-world."[3] But fluid and unsteady are those eighteen sacrifices in the form of which the lower ceremonial has been told. Fools who hail these with joy as the highest good (śreyaḥ) are sure to undergo decay and death again and again. Fools who are lodged in ignorance,[4] but consider themselves profoundly wise, and look down upon others, stagger to and fro, like the blind led by the blind. Children (bālāḥ) who are lodged in manifold ways in ignorance, consider themselves

[1] Muṇḍakôpaniṣad, III. 2. 3-4: "Nāyam ātmā pravacanena labhyo, na medhayā,......... Nāyam ātmā balahīnena labhyo, na ca pramādāt tapaso vāpyaliṅgāt,......eṣa ātmā viśate Brahma-dhāma."

[2] *Ibid*, I. 1. 5: "parā yayā tad Akṣaram adhigamyate."

[3] *Ibid*, I. 2. 6: "eṣa vaḥ puṇya sukṛito Brahma-lokaḥ."

[4] Muṇḍaka Upaniṣad, I. 2. 8: "avidyayām antare vartamānāḥ."

happy. Vedic sacrificers who are like children know not owing to their passions (rāgāt) that they will fall and feel miserable, when their life's light is extinguished. Estimating sacrifices and ceremonials as the best (variṣṭha), these blind fools know no better. They having fully enjoyed happiness on the height of their well-merited heaven (nāka-priṣṭhe sukṛite), re-enter this world (of men), or a lower one (of animals and insects). But those venerable sages who meditate in the wood, cultivate faith, and live on alms (bhikṣācaryam carantaḥ), proceed, unperturbed, wise and stainless as they are through the solar gate to the region where dwells the immortal, inexhaustible (avyaya) Person, the supreme Brahman.[1]

He who conceives desires in his mind (kāmān yaḥ kāmayate manyamānaḥ), is reborn here and there, according to his desires. But from him whose desires are fulfilled in that his true self is realised (kṛitātmanaḥ), all desires fall away even here, in this very life or present consciousness. "Two birds, inseparable comrades, are attached to the same tree. Of them, one eats sweet fruit, while the other does not eat but watches. Sunk in the same tree by his own impotence (anīśayā), a man dwells, overwhelmed with grief. But when he sees the other lord (īśa)—the contented and omnipotent Soul, then he overcomes grief. When a seer sees the lordly creative Reason (kartāram īśam), the resplendant soul, having the same origin or close kinship with the Divine (Brahmayonim) then he is truly wise. Shaking off both good and evil, and devoid of all material colouring of the soul (nirañjanaḥ) he reaches the highest unity with himself (paramaṁ sāmyam upeti)."[2]

Like Gārgyāyaṇa and Pippalāda, Bhāradvāja was a Brahmavādin. By the simile of two birds, borrowed from Dīrghatamas,[3] Bhāradvāja controverted the position of the Prāṇa-vādin. "The vital spirit (prāṇa) shines forth in

[1] Muṇḍaka Upaniṣad, I. 2. 9-11.

[2] *Ibid*, III. 1.1-3.

[3] Ṛig-veda, I.164.20; Yāska's Nirukta, XIV. 30.

all beings. Recognising this truth, one may be wise enough, but not a first-rate philosopher (nātivādin).[1]

Bhāradvāja's case against Vitalists or Mechanists.

He who revels in soul, delights in soul, and having performed the higher functions of the soul remains firmly established in his knowledge of Brahman, is indeed the best of philosophers (Brahmavidām variṣṭha)."[2]

In the same tree or world of generation there are two birds or principles. These are Prāṇa and Brahman, spirit and intelligence, life and soul. The functions and tendencies of these two principles are diametrically opposed, and yet they cannot be conceived to exist independently of each other. They are inseparable companions. Apart from Brahman, the intelligent principle of things, Prāṇa or vital spirit is altogether a blind power, just as apart from soul, the element of rationality, the living principle is but an animal soul, guided (as we now say) by mere instincts and impulses. Of life and soul, the former is an active principle, in so far as it tends to increase animality by seeking constantly after the objects of sense, and the latter is a passive factor, in so far as it tends to arrest the growth of animality by refraining from the enjoyment of sensual pleasures. But soul, too, must be said to be active in its own sphere, in so far as it perseveres in developing its rationality or freewill by reflecting upon its own nature, viewing its own purity, *i.e.*, by realising itself. This self-realisation enables soul to rise above all material conditions of its existence, or to reach in this present consciousness the immortal, immaterial Brahma-world, where 'the sun does not shine, nor the moon and the stars, nor lightnings, and much less fire."[3]

Bhāradvāja's conception of the Brahma-world is not that of a material heaven. It is a subjective state of the mind

[1] *Cf.* Chāndogya Upaniṣad, VII. 15-16.

[2] Muṇḍaka Upaniṣad, III. 1.4.

[3] *Ibid,* II. 2. 10; *cf.* Kaṭha, V.15; Śvetāśvatara, V. 14; Bhagavad Gītā, IX. 15. 6.

lying far above sense-perception and imagination. This highest condition of soul is indeed the true self of man, and it can be gained by truth, meditation, right knowledge and pure life, that is to say, by purging the mind of all its distracting and contaminating factors. For such a self-realisation as this neither Vedic learning, nor marriage and offspring, nor sacrifices and penances are at all necessary. It would be a great mistake to suppose that the path to self-realisation involves for Bhāradvāja only a negative process of the mind. He teaches rather that the path-process as a whole is constituted by the mutual counteraction of numerous opposite factors.

B. *The Vājasaneyan view.*

Śramans *versus* Brāhmans.

Bhāradvāja represents the common case of all who called themselves Śramans against all who were known as Brāhman theologians and law-givers. During the long-drawn battle between the philosophers and the theologians, lasting for centuries, the orthodox defenders of Brahmanic religion were always on the defensive. But the new movement evoked such a cry for reformation on all sides that it was impossible for them to remain passive. And whether or not the movement was successful in the long run, its influence penetrated even into ancient orthodoxy. There can, perhaps, be no better evidence of this than the antinomian doctrine of Vasiṣṭha. Perhaps from the beginning the recluse philosophers made a mistake in that they placed themselves out of touch with the people, first, by renouncing the world, and, secondly, by discouraging marriage, which was reasonably viewed as the real foundation of social life. It is doubtful if they really meant to discourage marriage in the case of all. And whether they actually meant it or not, the clever Brāhmans attacked the weak point in their opponents. Chiefly by this one point they were in a position to keep the majority of the people on their side, till they succeeded in slowly and steadily remodelling their own systems with materials obtained from their opponents and other philosophic sources. As the recluse philosophers attempted to interpret the Brahmanic notion of immortality in the light of rebirth and re-decease, so, on the other hand, the Brāhmans interpreted their opponents' conception of immortality or immateriality as virtually amounting to a total extinction of the human race. Nothing could be more an object of dread to the popular mind than this notion of utter annihilation. All this we have noticed in connexion with Āpastamba, Baudhāyana and other legal writers. The Vājasaneyas were, perhaps, the first to answer the charge of the Muṇḍakas.

The Īśopaniṣad; its commentators and exponents.

Their reply is contained in a Upaniṣad, generally known as the Vājasaneya or Īśopaniṣad. It forms the concluding chapter of the White Yajur-Veda. But for this reason we are not prepared to allow with Prof. Max Müller its claim to a 'very early age,' particularly an age prior to that of Yājñavalkya. For, as seems to us, the author of this Upaniṣad was a Vājasaneya or a later exponent of Yājñavalkya's philosophy.[1] Strictly speaking, the Upaniṣad in question represents no philosophical view which is peculiar to itself. Its historical importance is that it contains, in common with the Kenôpaniṣad, an answer or opposition to the Muṇḍakan criticism of Vedic sacrifices, Brāhmanic religion and āśrama-theory. A bitter tone of irony prevails throughout this Upaniṣad, and this cannot be satisfactorily accounted for otherwise than by supposing that it was evoked by the grave charge which the Muṇḍakas, and with them many other schools of recluse philosophers framed against the upholders of the āśrama-theory and of the system of sacrifices.

[1] *Cf.* Īśopaniṣad, 1-2 : "na karma lipyate nare" with Bṛihad Āraṇyaka Upaniṣad, IV. 4-23 : "na lipyate karmaṇā pāpakena."

The Muṇḍakas said: The sun does not shine there (na tatra sūryo bhāti), that is to say, the Brahma-world is not the Vedic material heaven, where the sun shines forth. To this the Vājasaneyas replied: If that world be sunless (asūryaḥ), then it must be covered with blinding darkness.[1]

The Muṇḍakas thought that the highest duty of a man is to gain the Brahma-world by truth, meditation, right knowledge and pure life or celibacy. The Vājasaneyas, on the other hand, considered the action of those who sought for the Brahma-world only by such means as suicidal.[2]

The Muṇḍakas considered generation of offspring as ignorance (avidyā), and self-realisation as knowledge (vidyā). The Vājasaneyas, on the contrary, thought: Death is overcome through such ignorance, while immortality is obtained through such knowledge. This clearly explains why the Vājasaneyas considered the conduct of unmarried recluses as suicidal. As they seem to have understood in agreement with Yājñavalkya, immortality is of two kinds: physical and psychological. Immortality in the physical sense is possible only through the perpetuation of the race. And immortality in the psychological sense is not more than a state of self-realisation—a state of the mind when it thinks of itself.[3] In the latter sense, then, the term immortality implies but the immortality of soul. Whilst thus controverting the Muṇḍakan view, the Vājasaneyas did not intend to undervalue in any way knowledge by way of self-realisation. The real point of their controversy was that in seeking philosophic knowledge one ought not to neglect the duties of life. So they taught: Those who persist in ignorance enter into blinding darkness, but those who delight only in

[1] Īśopaniṣad, 3.

[2] *Ibid*, 9. This seems to be the historical interpretation of the expression *ātmahano janāḥ*.

[3] Note that by the term Immortality Buddha understood the extinction of passion, the extinction of hatred, and the extinction of dullness. "Yo kho .. vuccati rāgakkhayo dosakkhayo mohakkhayo idaṁ vuccati amataṁ." Saṁyutta, V. 8.

knowledge enter, as it were, into greater darkness.[1] He who experiences, therefore, both knowledge and not-knowledge, overcomes death through not-knowledge, and obtains immortality through knowledge.[2]

II. The nature and knowledge of God.

Far more significant than the first is the second point in Bhāradvāja's Divine Science (Brahma-vidyā, metaphysics), as it brings out his definite philosophical view rather than a hostile criticism of polytheistic and juristic errors, committed generally by the professed custodians of Vedic religion and Indian society. It is besides the one point in which he seems to stand nearest to Xenophanes, the reputed teacher of Parmenides.

Bhāradvāja's criticism of the Brahmanic view of life was refuted, as we saw, by the Vājasaneyas. Concerning both the points, and particularly with regard to the second point, his opponents were the Keniya Jatilas whose views are preserved, we think, in the Kenopaniṣad.[3] The contention was not as to the nature of Brahman, but as to the possibility of a knowledge of God.

The Muṇḍakas *versus* the Keniyas.

Following a train of thought of the earlier thinkers, which is very pronounced in Mahidāsa, Gārgyāyaṇa, Uddālaka

[1] Īśopaniṣad, 9.

[2] Īśopaniṣad, 11. "Vidyāṁ ca avidyāṁ ca yas tad vedôbhayam saha. Avidyayā mṛityum tīrtvā, vidyayā amṛitam aśnute."

[3] In the Buddhist Selasutta (Suttanipāta, No. 33) Keṇiya or Keniya is a Jaṭila who lived with his family and kinsmen in a hermitage, built up on the banks of the Mahāmahīgaṅgā (Paramatthajotikā, II. 2. p. 437). In the text itself the locality is referred to as Aṅguttarāpa. Keniya is introduced as a contemporary of the Buddha, and a friend of the Brāhman teacher Sela. On an occasion he entertained in his hermitage the Buddha with his 1250 followers. The commentator points out that Buddha's words *Aggihuttamukhā yaññā, Sāvittī chandaso mukhaṁ* were much appealing to Keniya, a hermit as he was. After reading the Kena Upaniṣad we cannot but feel that a case has been made out in favour of the Tāpasa religion. The very first question—"*Keneṣitaṁ patati preṣitaṁ manaḥ kena prāṇaḥ prathamaḥ praiti yuktaḥ?*" is full of reminiscence of an *āśrama* where a resident pupil would discuss the deep questions in this sweet and genial manner with the Ṛiṣi. Thus elsewhere (Suttanipāta, Sutta No. 56) we meet with a pupil of the hermit Bāvarī who asks the Buddha in a similar way: "*Kena-ssu nivuto loko, Kena-ssu na-ppakāsati?*"

and Yājñavalkya, Bhāradvāja maintained that the one which is the source of many is knowable by the cognitive mind. According to the Keniyas, on the contrary, "The know-all does not know at all."[1] "Brahman is the ear of the ear, the mind of the mind, the speech of the speech, the breath of the breath, and the eye of the eye...... The eye does not reach it, nor speech, nor mind. Without knowing or cognising it, how can anyone instruct others about it?" Referring evidently to "Viśvakarman,"[2] they add: "We have heard from the teachers of old that Brahman is different from that which is known (to our sense-experience), and even beyond that which is known (thought by the mind)."[3] "That which is by its nature inexpressible but by which speech itself is expressed, that which is by its nature unthinkable but by which thought is rendered thinkable, ... or that which is by its nature inaudible but by which the hearing itself is made audible is the real Brahman, not that which people here worship."

The scepticism of the Keniyas.

One of the favourite maxims of Mahidāsa was: "As far as Brahman reaches, so far reaches speech."[4] Discarding this maxim, the Keniyas affirmed: Should anyone ask us, what form of Brahman (Brahmaṇo rūpam) is in itself, and what form of Brahman in the gods do you judge to be known, as it were, to you? our reply would be this: "I do not think I know it well, nor do I know that I do not know it. He among us who knows this, he knows it, nor does he know that he does not know it. He by whom it is not thought, by him it is thought; he by whom it is thought, knows it not. It is not understood by those who understand it, it is understood by those who do not understand it."[5]

[1] Kenôpaniṣad, II. 1: "Yadi manyase suvedeti dabhram evāpi nunam tvam vettha" = Lit. "If thou thinkest thou knowest it well, then thou knowest surely but little."

[2] Ṛig-Veda, X. 82.7.

[3] Kenôpaniṣad, I.4: "anyad eva tad viditādatho aviditād adhi."

[4] Aitareya Āraṇyaka, I. 3. 8. 9.

[5] Kenôpaniṣad, II. 2-3: "nāham manye suvedeti no na vedeti veda ca. Yo nas tad veda tad veda no na vediti Veda ca......" (Max Müller's Translation).

This sarcasm has been variously explained by the commentators and modern scholars. But the general trend of thought or argument seems to be this. Brahman is in essence unknowable. Hence those who boast that they have power to apprehend it are ignorant. But those who are fully aware of their incapacity to apprehend it, and do not endeavour to apprehend it by neglecting the duties of life are wise indeed. "(The Muṇḍakas, for instance are) of opinion that Brahman is known by an inner awakening or a kind of intuition (pratibodha-viditam matam), and that by such knowledge we obtain immortality. (If it be true that) by knowledge we obtain immortality, (even then it must not be forgotten that) by the self (physical being, living body) we acquire strength (vīrya, to overcome real death)."[1] The gods are powerless without Brahman. True. But it must be remembered that the gods, such as Fire, Air, Lightning and others, are nearest unto Brahman.[2] (The worship of these is, therefore, not altogether worthless.)

According to the Muṇḍakas God can be known by pure cognition.

There is every reason to believe that here the Keniyan Sarcasm applies to the Muṇḍaka opinion according to which Brahman is knowable only by inner understanding or intuition (pratibodha-viditam). For it is explicit in Bhāradvāja, although not so explicit as in Naciketas, that "a man, whose nature is purified by the grace of knowledge, alone can see God, meditating on him as without parts—as a whole. The infinitesimal self is to be known by cetas (pure reason) or vijñāna (pure cognition)."[3] God is invisible, incomprehensible, without family, without caste, without eyes, ears, hands and feet, the eternal, the really existent, the omnipresent, the infinitesimal, the inexhaustible, and the origin of all beings.[4] Just as the

[1] Kenôpaniṣad, II. 4.

[2] *Ibid*, III. 1-12; IV. 2-3.

[3] Muṇḍakôpaniṣad, III. 1. 8-9: "Jñāna-prasādena viśuddha-sattvas tas tu tam paśyate niṣkalam dhyāyamānaḥ."

[4] *Ibid*, I. 6.

spider spreads and winds up its thread, or as plants grow on the earth, or as hairs spring forth on the head and body so does everything originate from the inexhaustible. The Divine Person is devoid of form, unborn, without breath, without mind, pure (śubhra), undecaying, higher than the high (parāt paraḥ). From him is generated breath, mind, all organs of sense, ether, air, fire, water, and earth.[1] The earth is the support of all, while the Divine Person is the inner self of all that is (sarvabhūta-antarātmā). In the physical world there is no god—the sun, the moon, lightning, or the like—who can be conceived as God. In man God is the soul that assumes the nature of mind and acts as a guide to the senses.[2] That which is the purest in external nature and that which is the purest in our inner life are one. That is to say, God and Soul are indentical in nature. That which is uncreated (akṛita) cannot be gained by that which is created (kṛita). And that which is pure cannot be obtained by that which is impure. Neither God in nature nor God in man can be apprehended by the study of the Vedas and Vedic sciences or by the senses. The sacrifices to the gods and ancestors and penances and fasting cannot purify our nature. The rivers cannot wash off our sins. The best means of apprehending God or purifying our nature is Yoga—meditation or inner culture of faith and intellect When the wise apprehend God, and realise the immortal in them, which is full of bliss, then the fetter of their heart is broken, all doubts are solved, all their works perish.[3] And when they die, the elements are dissolved, and the sense-faculties vanish in a similar way, but soul, the imperishable element, becomes united with God.[4] In this connexion Bhāradvāja quotes a Pippalāda view, *viz.*—"Just as the flowing rivers disappear in the sea, so a wise man, freed from individuality, goes to the Divine Person."

[1] Muṇḍakôpaniṣad, II. 1. 3.
[2] *Ibid*, II. 2. 7.
[3] *Ibid*, II. 2. 8.
[4] *Ibid*, III. 2. 7-8.

CHAPTER XVII.

Naciketas.

(Gotamaka Philosophy.)

The place of Naciketas in Indian philosophy is very similar to that of Parmenides in the history of Greek thought. The precise position assumed by both is that of an Absolutist[1] as opposed to that of a Mechanist.[2] The analogy between the views of the two thinkers is in certain points very close.[3] But we shall not for this reason be justified in supposing one of them to have been a borrower from the other.[4]

Position of Naciketas and Parmenides in the history of philosophy.

Even as to the point of close resemblance between them, Mrs. Rhys Davids seems more doubtful than we are, when she says, "Nor, in the absence of any fuller statement of the former extreme (That everything is) alluded to by the Buddha, can we say whether that view coincided with the position taken by Parmenides." She readily grants, however, the probability of some coincidence. Prof. Max Müller, on the other hand, discovers some points of similarity between Naciketas and Plato, especially in regard to the simile of the chariot in the Kaṭhopaniṣad, although he, too, is not ready to presume that the latter borrowed the simile from the former. Instead, then, of raising any question of borrowing, we might observe with profit that in India Naciketas' thought on the lines of Gārgyāyaṇa; in Greece Plato thought on the lines of Parmenides. In India Uddālaka, who resembles Anaxagoras, was a predecessor of Naciketas. Furthermore, the immediate

[1] Brahma-vādin. Ātma-vādin.

[2] Prāṇa-vādin. Bhūta-vādin.

[3] All. Gesch. der Philos., p. 121.

[4] Mrs. Rhys Davids, Buddhism, p. 83.

predecessor of Naciketas was Bhāradvāja as that of Parmenides was Xenophanes.

Historical interpretation of the descent of Naciketas from Uddālaka Āruṇi. The Gotamaka views in the Kaṭha Upaniṣad. The Gotamaka philosophy in relation to the Muṇḍaka and the Nyāya philosophy.

It is a received opinion that the historical reality of Naciketas is extremely doubtful.[1] In the Taittirīya story he is introduced as a Gautama, the son of Vājaśravasa,[2] while in the Kaṭha version of the same story he appears as a Gautama, the son of Auddālaka Āruṇi, *i.e.*, of Vājaśravasa the son of Uddālaka and the grandson of Aruṇa.[3] But however fictitious the ascribed descent of Naciketas from Uddālaka of the Gotama clan may have been, it is of the greatest historical importance as affording a legendary basis for the chronology of the philosophy of Uddālaka and the teaching of the Kaṭhôpaniṣad, centred round Naciketas. The name of Naciketas is no more than a suitable designation for referring to the particular individual behind that teaching, and we are inclined to think that this particular individual was but an influencial leader of a school of wanderers whose origin can be traced back to Uddālaka Āruṇi. We might, indeed, go so far as to identify this band of Bhikṣus with the Gotamakas[4] appearing in the Aṅguttara list of *religieux*, along with the Muṇḍa-sāvakas whose views have been discussed in the previous chapter. The positive advantage of this identification is that we are enabled thereby to account for the close resemblance between the teachings of the two Upaniṣads, the Muṇḍaka and the Kaṭha, in both of which we cannot help being struck by a spirit of reaction against Vedic ritualism. The truth of a common legendary descent of Uddālaka Āruṇi

[1] Vedic Index, I, p. 432.

[2] Taittiriya Brāhmaṇa, III. 1. 8.

[3] Kaṭhopaniṣad, I. 1. 11.

[4] Prof. Rhys Davids thinks that the Gotamakas were either the followers of Devadatta or the followers of a Brāhman of the Gotama clan (Buddhist India, pp. 145-146; Dial. B. II. pp. 220-22). Budhoghosa says that the Gotamakas were a school of non-Buddhistic teachers or a class of heretics, which is really saying nothing about them.

and Naciketas is clearly brought home to us as we realise how closely is bound up the Nāciketa doctrine of Being with the logical postulate of Uddālaka's philosophy. And the same is still more clearly brought home to us when we see how the Kaṭha dialogue between Naciketas and his father was constructed on the model of the Chāndogya dialogue between Śvetaketu and Uddālaka. The difference between Bhāradvājā and Naciketas, considered as representatives of the Muṇḍaka and the Kaṭha or Gotamaka philosophy, is of such a nature as is inevitable when one teacher thinks on the lines of the other. Speaking generally, it is such a difference as exists between Xenophanes and Parmenides in Greek thought. On the other hand, in the light of the legendary descent of Naciketas from Uddālaka it is easy to understand the process of the growth of a Gotamaka philosophy which in its Chāndogya, Kaṭha or Gītā stage is but the same theistic doctrine (Īśvara-vāda) in a special form. The time may come, and we firmly believe that the time will come when the historian will be able to prove beyond dispute that the Nyāya system of Gautama Akṣapāda which is in its ultimate analysis a theistic doctrine was the consummation of the Gotamaka attempts to establish a valid theory of the singleness of cause (eka-vāda) by the method of induction by way of inference.

His Philosophy.

The most authentic document now available for the philosophy of Nacikeast is the poem of the Kaṭhopaniṣad. It has been translated into Persian, French, Latin, German, Italian and English by many distinguished scholars. The first translation is that in Persian, and associated with the name of the enlightened Mogul Prince, Dara Shukoh, the eldest son of Shah Jehan. And the view has been generally maintained since Prof. Weber that the said poem consists of portions

The source of information.

or fragments some of which are older than others. Even actual attempts have been made to separate the more modern from the more ancient portions. But Prof. Max Müller finds no justification for an attempt on the part of modern scholars to ransack the Upaniṣad in its present form. "In its original form," he says, "it may have constituted one Adhyāya only, and the very fact of its division into two Adhyāyas may show that the compilers of the Upaniṣad were still aware of its gradual origin. We have no means, however, of determining its original form, nor should we even be justified in maintaining that the first Adhyāya ever existed by itself, and that the second was added at a much later time. Whatever its component elements may have been before it was an Upaniṣad, when it was an Upaniṣad, it consisted of six Vallis, neither more nor less."[1]

But one important point seems to have escaped the great scholar's notice, namely, that the poem of Naciketas, precisely as that of Parmenides, consists not of two parts but of three. The first part serves as an introduction, the second part treats of 'the way of truth,' and the third part of 'the way of opinion.' We propose to examine these parts separately, one after another.

I. Introduction.

There are two versions of the first part now extant, and it furnishes 'a peg on which' hangs the whole philosophy of Naciketas. The prose version of which the date is unknown is given in the Taittirīya Brāhmaṇa (III. 1. 8); the poetic version forms the first chapter of the Kaṭhopaniṣad. This part introduces Naciketas as the son of Vājaśravasa, descendant of Uddālaka. Vājaśravasa wishing for heavenly rewards, spent all his wealth on performing a cow-sacrifice to the gods, and on giving presents to the priests. When the sacrifice

[1] S.B.E., XV. p. xxiii.

was being performed and the presents were being given, a conviction arose in the heart of Naciketas, and he began to think "Unblessed (anandā), indeed, are those heavenly worlds to which a man goes by sacrificing cows, old and sterile,—too old to be able to drink, eat, give milk, or to calve."[1]

The boy Naciketas questioned thrice his father saying, "Father, unto whom wilt thou give me?" The father replied rather angrily, "Unto Death (Yama)." Here the two versions differ in some respects. The Taittirīya version introduces a third interlocutor, Voice or Wisdom, saying to Naciketas, as he was waiting for further reply from his father: "Thy father asked thee to go to the house of Death—Death to whom he has offered thee. Go, therefore, to Death while he is away from his house, and stay there three nights without eating. When Death inquires of thee, 'How long hast thou been here?' then say, 'For three nights.' If he asks thee, What didst thou eat all the while? say, "I ate the first night thy offspring, the second night thy cattle (animals for sacrifice), and the third night thy good works (sacrifices)."

According to the Kaṭha version after listening to his father's words, Naciketas said, "Father, I go as the first, at the head of many who are still to die, and I go as one of many who are now dying. But how will Yama, the king of the dead, dispose of me?" The father replied, 'consider what has happened to those who have gone before thee, or what will befall those who are still to come. Verily a mortal ripens like corn, like corn he springs forth anew.[2] Metempsychosis is, in other words, the lot of a mortal on this earth."[3]

The prose version of the introduction further relates that Naciketas, following the voice of Wisdom, came to the house

[1] Kaṭhopaniṣad, I. 1. 3.

[2] Kaṭha, I. 1. 6: "Śasyam iva martyaḥ pacyate śasyam ivājāyate punaḥ."

[3] The last sentence is our own addition and it is meant to sum up Vājaśravasa's views about metempsychosis on the analogy of the animation of corns.

of Death when the latter was not at home, and did all the rest exactly as he was instructed to do. Seeing that Naciketas consumed his offspring, cattle, sacrifice, in short, all that tie a man down to mortal existence, Death showed respect to him instead of subjecting him to his rule, and granted him three boons. The first boon chosen by Naciketas was the knowledge of the way of returning alive to his father; the second was the knowledge of the way of rendering one's good works imperishable; and the third was the knowledge of the way of conquering death itself for ever. Death's reply to Naciketas was, by means of the three-fold Nāciketa-fire or zeal for truth as distinguished from the three-fold fire, kindled generally by Vedic sacrificers or Brāhman priests, by way of marriage, penance and sacrifice.

The poetic version only sets forth in detail what is given in the earlier prose version in a concise form. The interest of the introduction is two-fold: (1) That it sets forth the attitude of Naciketas towards Brāhmanic religion and laws. (2) That it gradually leads up to the real philosophical stand-point of Naciketas. And upon the whole, it shows that the subject of his investigation is neither the world of generation or realm of repeated birth and death, nor the heavenly world or the realm of relatively unchangeable being. The latter point is very clearly brought out in a verse of the Kaṭhopaniṣad (I. 1. 12-13), where Naciketas, referring to the ordinary popular belief in the happiness of celestial beings, says: "In the heavenly world (svarge loke) there is no fear (they say). Thou art not there, O Death, and no one need be afraid owing to decay. Leaving aside hunger and thirst, and out of the reach of sorrow, all rejoice in heaven. Vedic fire-sacrifice leads us to heaven. But tell me, if thou knowest, whether the lovers of the heavenly world obtain true immortality or not." Thus Naciketas in his introductory statement implies a sharp distinction of the realm of one absolute being, which is his immediate task to investigate, from the world of constant changes, as also from heaven, the realm of relatively unchangeable being. As the absolute being is in his view far beyond the sensuous, no idea of change or relativity can attach to it.

II. The way of Truth.

The second part of the Kaṭhopaniṣad really begins (I.1.20) where the Taittirīya version of the introduction ends (I.1.19). It is entirely a dialogue between Naciketas and Death. Scanning this part closely, we can perceive that it was added at a later period to the first part. A similar relation may be said to exist between the second and the third part. Whatever that may have been, dealing as it does with the way of truth, none can dispute that the second part alone gives us the real view-point of Naciketas, the doctrine of Being, presupposed or implied in what is known in the Buddhist literature as Sakkāya-diṭṭhi or Ātmanistic philosophy,[1] and in the Sāṁkhya literature as Sat-kārya-vāda. Mahāvīra and Buddha seem to have described it as a type of Eternalism,[2] or rather of the doctrine of oneness[3] or Semi-eternalism.[4] It is somewhat difficult to distinguish between what Buddha calls Eternalism and what he calls Semi-eternalism. So far as we can judge from his language, Eternalism has direct reference to the philosophy of Kakuda-Kātyāyana, and Semi-eternalism to the philosophy of Naciketas.[5] The doctrine of Being constitutes the logical standpoint of the philosophies of Naciketas and Kakuda Kātyāyana. Not less important is the distinction drawn by Buddha between the two types of Eternalism: Intuitional and Sophistic, Physical and Logical.[6] In reference to the first type of Eternalism, Buddha thought that the absolutist

1 Atta-vāda; Attānudiṭṭhi.
2 Niya-vāda; Sassata-diṭṭhi.
3 Ekkā-vāda.
4 Ekacca-sassata-ekacca-asassata-vāda.
5 Dial, B. II. 26-35.
6 Dial, B. II. 27-29.

position, that everything is (sabbam atthi), was reached from the notion of the world of generation. "For one who views in the light of right insight the coming-to-be of the world, as it really is, there is no such thing in the world as non-Being (natthitā). (Thus his mind fastens upon this one extreme: Everything is.)"[1]

Buddha's opinion is expressed elsewhere, in a passage of the Brahmajāla Sutta. There by the term everything Buddha understands the soul and the world, the self and the not-self (attā ca loko ca). In this passage Buddha clearly states that a full recollection of former existences leads a man to the following conclusion: "Eternal are the soul and the world. These are barren, stedfast as a mountain peak, as a pillar firmly fixed. And though living beings continually run in transmigration, decease from one state of existence to be reborn into another, yet they exist eternally and are for ever the same."[2]

The position taken by Naciketas was different from that of an Eternalist. In truth his was the point of view of a Semi-Eternalist or Monist. Accordingly, his fundamental thesis was not that 'Everything is,' but only that 'He is' (astîti). As we have seen, the introduction ascribes the former view to Vājaśravasa, father of Naciketas. The point gains in importance as it clearly shows how Naciketas made a wide departure from his predecessors—"Parameṣṭhin", Uddālaka, Varuṇa, and others. "Parameṣṭhin" approached the notion of Being entirely from the physical world: whatever is, springs from that which neither is nor is not. Although Uddālaka's doctrine of Being was in the same stage, it was in his hands that the doctrine came to be distinctly formulated as a logical postulate: How can there be transition into Being but from Being? The way in which Uddālaka asked himself this question shows that he made a great advance upon "Parameṣṭhin" as to the actual formulating

[1] Saṁyutta-nikāya, II.17; III.135. *Cf.* Mrs. Rhys Davids, Buddhism, p. 83.

[2] Dīgha-nikāya, II, pp. 14 foll.: "sassato attā ca loko ca vañjho kuṭaṭṭho......atthitveva sassati samanti."

of the doctrine. Gārgyāyaṇa, too, paved the way for Naciketas by defining Being (Sat) as that which is different from the gods and the sentient beings.

Now Naciketas said to Death, "There is the doubt (vicikitsā) as to man's existence after death. Some say, he is; others, he is not. This would I like to know, taught by thee. This is the third boon which I ask of thee. Naciketas does not choose any other boon but this."[1]

Death said, "The good is one thing, the pleasant another; these two, having different objects, chain a man. It is well within him who clings to the good; he who chooses the pleasant, misses his end. The good and the pleasant approach man: the wise goes round about them and distinguishes them. Yea, the wise prefers the good to the pleasant, but the fool chooses the pleasant through greed and avarice."[2]

"Wide apart and divergent are these two: ignorance and what is known as knowledge. Fools who are lodged in ignorance, consider themselves profoundly wise and look down upon others. They stagger to and fro, like the blind led by the blind. The existence after death never appears in the vision of the careless child (ignorant fool), deluded by the possession of wealth. This is the world, he thinks, there is no other. Thus he subjects himself repeatedly to my rule."

(There can be no doubt that the verse relating to the doctrine of Being is missing from the Kaṭhopaniṣad as we now have it. We supply it from the Bhagavad Gītā (II. 16) seeing that the Gītā-slokas relating to the doctrine of Being are all quoted from an Upaniṣad which is no other than the Kaṭha.)

"Being is, non-Being is not. Being cannot come out of non-Being nor can there be non-Being, when there is Being."[3]

"Being is not born, it does not die. As it sprang from

[1] Kaṭhopaniṣad, I 1. 20-29.

[2] *Ibid*, I.2. 1-2 (Max Müller's translation).

[3] Bhagavad Gītā, II.16: "nâsato vidyate bhāvo nâbhāvo vidyate sataḥ."

nothing, so nothing sprang from it. Being is unborn, eternal, immutable, ancient. Being does not perish when the body perishes. If the killer thinks that he kills, if the killed thinks himself killed, both of them are ignorant; the one does not kill, nor is the other killed......He who has not ceased from his wickedness, who is not tranquil, and subdued, or whose mind is not composed, cannot obtain the Being (even) by knowledge."[1]

Being is, non-Being is not. Nothing comes out of nothing, there is no becoming. Birthless it is and deathless. Being is the self, the immaterial in the material, the changeless among the changing. Such is the doctrine of Being as propounded by Naciketas, an Eleatic postulate of Being which Bergson aptly describes as a paradox. The important point to observe is that all the predicates assigned by Naciketas to Being are negative in character.

III. The way of Opinion.

The second part of the Kaṭhopaniṣad comprises the second section of its first chapter, and the third part covers the third section of the same chapter. Such being the case, the whole second chapter would seem redundant and unnecessary. Indeed, its usefulness is that it furnishes a detailed exposition of all that is expressed by way of opinion in the third section of the first chapter.

The question has been raised with respect to the Parmenidean conception of Being, whether it has in its background anything material or that which occupies space or not. Prof. Zeller, who is supported by many modern scholars, maintains that Parmenides, like all previous Greek speculators, kept in his mind the general structure of nature. Prof. Adamson and Prof. Dawes Hicks[2] contend that Parmenides approached the

[1] Kaṭhopaniṣad, I. 2. 18. ff.

[2] Senior Professor of Philosophy, University College, London. Here the reference is to his lecture notes.

notion of Being entirely from an abstract point of view. In other words, the postulate of Being was for Parmenides altogether a logical doctrine. In such case Parmenides could not append to his truth any opinion—application of truth to experience—without doing violence to his own position. A similar question is apt to arise in the case of Naciketas or Gotamaka philosophy, especially when the connexion between the second and the third part of the Kaṭhopaniṣad is so mechanically maintained. The philosophy of Naciketas, no less than that of Parmenides, begins and ends with the definition of Truth. As regards the Naciketa or Gotamaka philosophy, the truth of the logical postulate of Being can be realised psychologically through Yoga, and not by reasoning (tarka).

And as to opinion, Naciketas had nothing to say which is new, that is, nothing that neither Pippalāda nor Bhāradvāja had said. However, the precise way in which he stated his opinion is interesting enough. Another point of interest in his opinion is the definition of the term Yoga. We sum up below his opinion:

Unity of God and Soul.

There are two principles, dwelling in the same cavity of the heart. One is life; the other is soul. The knower of Brahman distinguishes between them as shade and light (chāyā-tapau). The true self of man is soul which sits in the chariot called the body. Intellect or the faculty of understanding (buddhi) is the charioteer, the mind (manas) is the reins, the senses (indriyāni) are the horses, and the sense-objects are the roads. When Soul is united with the body, the senses and the mind, then it is called by the wise the Enjoyer (bhoktā).[1] He who has no understanding (vijñāna), and he who is weak-minded, his senses run riot like vicious horses of a charioteer. But he who has understanding and is strong-minded, his senses are well

[1] Kaṭhopaniṣad, I. 3. 3-4: "Ātmānaṁ rathinaṁ viddhi, śarīraṁ ratham eva tu. Buddhiṁ tu sārathiṁ viddhi, manaḥ pragraham eva ca. Indriyāni hayān āhur viṣayaṁ steṣu gocarān. Ātmendriya-mano-yuktaṁ bhoktetyāhur maniṣinaḥ."

controlled like good horses of a charioteer. He who is without understanding, and he who is thoughtless and impure (aśuci), never reaches the immortal immaterial state, but enters into the round of births. But he who has understanding, and he who is thoughtful and pure, reaches indeed (in thought) that state (tat padam) from which there is no return to the realm of change. It is he who reaches the destination of his (mind's onward) journey, the highest state of Viṣṇu.

Yoga is the subjective or meditative mode of attaining to God or reaching unity of self.

Beyond the senses there are the impressions or the contents of perception (arthā), beyond them there is the mind (the inner sense), beyond it there is the intellect or the faculty of understanding (buddhi), beyond it there is the great soul (mahat, pure cognitive consciousness), beyond it there is avyakta—the indeterminate and beyond it there is the Divine Person (Puruṣa). Beyond Puruṣa there is nothing or no other state of consciousness. Thus Godhood is the goal, the highest condition. This ideal self-existence cannot be gained by the Veda, nor by more intellect, nor by much learning. God is hidden in all beings, the inner self of man (antarātmā). Subtle seers can see God by their sharp and subtle intuition. In fact, knowledge is to be obtained by the mind (manasā vedaṁ āptavyaṁ)—a mind that is purified and elevated through Yoga.

By the term Yoga we are to understand, with Naciketas, 'the firm holding back of the senses' (sthirām indriya-dhāraṇām) a mode, in other words, of reaching unity with ourselves. As in the process of meditation the mind rises higher and higher from one state to another, the realm of absolute existence appears at length in the mental vision of the Yogin, like an image reflected in a mirror. Such a knowledge of God as this cannot be reached by speech, mind or sight. God can be apprehended by none but he who recognises the truth of the dictum "He is" (astīti). There is no better expression according to Naciketas, for God than that "He is."

One can hardly fail to notice in these views the Yoga or psyco-religious aspect of the Sāṁkhya philosophy in the making. The cosmological or biological aspect of the same philosophy is altogether absent from the Kaṭha Upaniṣad and in this respect the teaching of the Kaṭha differs from that of the Praśna.

Before we take leave of Naciketas, it is necessary to mention that the whole of his philosophy is beautifully reproduced in a section of Āpastamba's legal manual (I. 8. 22-23). This fragment of Āpastamba has besides some points in common with the Mahāgovinda Suttanta of the Dīgha-nikāya. The dialogue between Kesi and Gotama in the Jaina Uttarādhyayana Sūtra (XXIII), too, reminds us, here and there, of the older dialogue between Yama and Gautama in the Kaṭhopaniṣad. In the Brahmajāla sutta again Buddha gives an analysis of a view, similar to that of Naciketas. It is presented partly in a mythical garb. Nevertheless, it is obvious that the terms—the gods 'spoilt by play' (khiḍḍā-padosikā) and the gods 'debauched in mind' (mano-padosikā)—as Buddha employs them, have reference to such passages in the Kaṭhopaniṣad as: "the careless child" (I. 2. 6.); "Children follow after outward pleasures"; and the like. The fourth passage in Buddha's analysis is: "The sentient soul comprising eye, ear, nose, tongue and body, is impermanent, mutable, limited and changeable, while the self called thought, mind or cognitive consciousness (citta, saññā, viññāṇa) is permanent, stedfast, eternal and immutable."

CHAPTER XVIII.

Pūrṇa Kāśyapa.

(Pūraṇa Kassapa.)

The Buddhist records[1] speak of Pūraṇa Kassapa as an old, experienced and venerable teacher, the head of a religious order, the founder of a school (tittha-karo), one who was followed by a large body of disciples and honoured throughout the country. According to a fabulous legend of Buddhist origin, Pūraṇa Kassapa drowned himself near Śrāvastī, the capital of Kosala, in the sixteenth year of Buddha's career. We may infer from this that Kassapa died in 572 B.C. if the traditional date 543 B.C. of Buddha's demise be accepted as true. On the other hand, in the Sāmaññaphala sutta, Kassapa is referred to as a contemporary of King Ajātasattu of Magadha. But he is similarly alluded to in the 'Questions of King Milinda' as a contemporary of Milinda. Buddhaghosa tells us that Pūraṇa Kassapa was a naked ascetic (acelaka). He apparently confounds Acelaka Kassapa[2] with Pūraṇa. Buddhaghosa further tells us that Kassapa was formerly a slave, that he completed the number of one hundred slaves of a family, and that from this circumstance he came to be known as Pūraṇa.[3] Apparently this is not true, for, as his name shows, Kassapa was born in a Brāhman family.

The true significance of the Pāli epithet Pūraṇa seems to be that Kassapa claimed to have attained perfect wisdom (pūrṇa jñāna), or that his disciples believed that he was replete with perfect wisdom. This is borne out by the passage

[1] Sāmañña-phala-sutta, Dīgha-Nikāya, I. 47 (Dial. B. II. 66); Milinda-pañho, p. 4; Rockhill's 'Life of the Buddha,' pp. 80, 96 foll.

[2] Dīgha-Nikāya, I, p. 161.

[3] Sumaṅgala Vilāsinī, I, p. 102.

of the Aṅguttara Nikāya (IV, p. 428) where two Lokāyatika Brāhmans are said to have stated that according to Pūraṇa Kassapa's theory only an infinite mind can comprehend the finite world, whereas according to Nigaṇṭha Nātaputta's theory, the finite world can only be a content of finite knowledge.

Curiously enough, in a passage of the Aṅguttara-nikāya[1] Ānanda ascribes part of Gośāla's doctrine to Pūraṇa Kassapa.

Kāśyapa and Gośāla.

In this passage Kassapa comments upon Gośāla's term Chalābhijātiyo[2] (six classes of beings). Buddhaghosa's explanation[3] of this term was evidently based on the Nikāya passage above referred to. The primary object of Ānanda was to label Kassapa's philosophy as the doctrine of non-causation (ahetu-vāda), and so far he was perfectly right. This leads us further to think that the first portion of the doctrine ascribed to Gosāla in the Sāmañña-phala-sutta ought to be separated from the rest on the ground that the doctrine of non-causation or the hypothesis of chance does not fit well into the deterministic theory of Gosāla. We think there is no other conclusion to be drawn from the significant passage in the Saṁyutta-nikāya (V, p. 126). Ārya-Śūra also identifies the doctrine of non-causation with that of nature (svabhāva-vāda).[4]

A later text, the Milinda, ascribes to Pūraṇa Kassapa a puerile doctrine, that the earth rules or sustains the world. Whereas an older authority, the Sāmañña-phala-sutta, applies the name Akiriya-vāda, the doctrine of non-action, to the philosophy of Kassapa. Buddhaghosa also admits that Kassapa discarded the theory of action.[5] The Jaina Sūtrakṛitāṅga[6] furnishes a parallel passage, where the doctrine

[1] III, p. 383 foll.

[2] Dīgha-Nikāya, I, p. 54.

[3] Sumaṅgala-Vilāsinī, I, p. 162.

[4] Jātaka-mālā, pp. 148-149.

[5] Kammaṁ paṭibāhati.—Sumaṅgala-Vilāsinī, I, p. 166.

[6] I. 1. 1. 13 (Śilāṅka's commentary).

under discussion is expressly called Akiriyavāda. Śīlāṅka calls it Akāraka-vāda.[1]

Thus our authorities for the philosophy of Pūraṇa Kassapa are two,—the Sūtra-kṛitāṅga and the Sāmañña-phala-sutta. And we must give preference to the evidence of the former, as the Buddhist document does not make perfectly clear the real position taken by Kassapa,—a position which can truly be indicated by the term Akiriya-vāda.

The doctrine of passivity of soul.

From these authorities we learn that according to Kassapa's view, when we act or cause others to act, it is not the Soul that acts or causes others to act. The Soul is, in other words, passive (niṣkriya).[2] This being the case, whether we do good or bad, the result thereof does not affect the soul in the least. Kassapa's view is rather exaggerated by King Ajātasattu.[3] That ultimate reality is beyond both good and evil is a view which has been upheld, more or less, by all the previous thinkers. The immediate background of Kassapa's theory of the passivity of soul must be sought in the philosophy of Bhāradvāja and Naciketas, who maintain that contrasted with the functions and tendencies of the living principle, the soul is passive. It is interesting to see that Śīlāṅka identifies Kassapa's doctrine with the Sāṁkhya view.

Kāśyapa's logical standpoint.

It seems that the Buddha, in the Brahmajāla-sutta, distinguished the logical standpoint of Pūraṇa Kassapa from his own, as a hypothesis of fortuitous origin (adhicca-samuppāda) from what he called the theory of causal-genesis (paṭicca-samuppāda).[4] Elsewhere he describes the former as a theory of non-causation (ahetu-appaccaya-vāda).[5] According to the

[1] I. 1. 1. 13 (Śīlāṅka's commentary).

[2] Sūtra-Kṛitāṅga, I. 1. 1. 13; "Kuvvaṁ ca kārayaṁ cêva, savvaṁ kuvvaṁ na vijjai; evaṁ akārau appā." *Ibid*, II. 2.

[3] Dial., B. II. 69-70.

[4] *Ibid*, II. 41-42.

[5] Saṁyutta Nikaya, III, p. 69.

hypothesis of fortuitous origin, something comes out of nothing, whereas according to the theory of causal-genesis, nothing comes out of nothing.[1] From this it is clear that the logical standpoint of Kassapa's philosophy was diametrically opposed to that of Naciketas. A similar doctrine was propounded long ago by "Brahmaṇaspati" and re-appears in the teaching of Varuṇa. But the Buddha draws distinction between the two types of the postulate of non-Being: the Vedic and the Sophistic, the physical and the metaphysical. In the case of Pūraṇa Kassapa, we can interpret the doctrine as meaning that the caused comes out of the uncaused.

[1] Dīgha, I, pp. 28-29.

CHAPTER XIX.

KAKUDA KĀTYĀYANA.

(*Pakudha Kaccāyana.*)[1]

Kakuda Kātyāyana was an elder contemporary of the Buddha,—a Sophist (titthiya) of whom the Buddhist annals[2] speak in the same terms as of Pūraṇa Kassapa and others. A Wanderer named Sakula Udāyi informs the Buddha that in days gone by Aṅga and Magadha seethed with sophistic discussions.[3] That these two countries were among the centres of intellectual activities in northern India is evident also from the Sāmañña-phala account of King Ajātasattu's interview with six sophistic teachers. The interview of King Milinda alluded to in the Milinda-pañho is evidently the outcome of a naïve plagiarism on the part of a later Buddhist writer. We have reason even to doubt if King Ajātasattu could have had the opportunity to meet those teachers, considering that he usurped the throne of Magadha only eight years before Buddha's death. On the other hand, it is manifest from Udāyi's statement, that the memory of those teachers became a thing of the past even in the life-time of the Buddha. This is confirmed by the mention of Kakuda Kātyāyana in the Praśnopaniṣad as a younger contemporary of Pippalāda. The author of the Upaniṣad applies to the name of Kātyāyana, the epithet Kabandhin which like Kakuda points to a physical deformity of the philosopher. Their significance is that Kātyāyana had a hump on his neck or shoulder. Thus the

[1] *Cf.* Saṁyutta-nikāya, I, p. 66: "Pakudhako Kātiyāno."

[2] Sāmañña-phala-sutta, Dīgha-nikāya, I, p. 48; Majjhima-nikāya, I, p. 198; I, p. 250; etc. The Tibetan version of the Sāmañña-phala-sutta confounds Kātyāyana with Ajita Gosāla and Sañjaya. See Rockhill's 'Life of the Buddha,' pp. 102-104, 257.

[3] Majjhima-nikāya, II, p. 2.

philosopher was distinguished by his contemporaries from all his namesakes.

Kātyāyana, like Pūraṇa Kassapa, came of a Brāhman family. Buddhaghosa tells us that Kātyāyana avoided cold water,[1] and used hot water, whenever possible. All that he says respecting Kātyāyana amounts to this—that the religious order founded by Kātyāyana betrayed its ascetic tendency in matters of external conduct.

His Philosophy.

In order to get an insight into Kātyāyana's philosophical views we must leave aside the trivialities of later traditions. It is quite sufficient for our present purpose to know that he was a younger contemporary of Pippalāda and an elder contemporary of the Buddha. As he has left us no records of his own, we have to depend for a knowledge of his doctrine entirely on the mercy of those, the Jains and the Buddhists, who were not his friends but opponents. The author of the Praśnopaniṣad tries to maintain an air of neutral dignity, but that, too, is a mere false pretence, his real hero being Pippalāda. However, it is important to note Kātyāyana's question to Pippalāda as to the roots of things? He was told that the roots were Matter (Rayi) and Spirit (Prāṇa). Besides the Praśnopaniṣad, there are two other authorities for his philosophy, *viz.*, the Buddhist Sāmañña-phala-sutta[2] and the Jaina Sūtra-Kṛitāṅga.[3] In the former his philosophy is described as the doctrine of seven categories (satta-kāya-vāda), and in the latter, as the doctrine of soul as a sixth (ātma-ṣaṣṭha-vāda). The fragment of the Sūtra-Kṛitāṅga would seem in a sense more important and interesting than the passage of the Sāmañña-phala-sutta,

Sources of information.

[1] Sumaṅgala-Vilāsinī, I, p. 144. "Sit-udaka-paṭikkhitto esa .... nissirika-laddhiko esa."

[2] Dīgha-Nikāya, I, p. 57.

[3] Sūtra-Kṛitāṅga, I. 1. 1. 15-16. (See Śīlāṅka's Commentary.)

as it clearly shows that Kātyāyana adopted the Gotamaka or Eleatic postulate of Being that nothing comes out of nothing (nôye uppajja-e asaṁ).[1] It appears from both the fragments that the term Eternalism[2] was strictly applied by Mahāvīra and Buddha to the doctrine of Kātyāyana. It also comes under the definition of what Mahāvīra calls Pluralism (Aṇikka-vāda).[3]

The relation between Kātyāyana's philosophy and the system of the Bhagavad Gītā and the Sāṁkhya.

Śīlāṅka identifies the doctrine of soul as a sixth with the doctrine of the Bhagavad Gītā, as well as with the Sāṁkhya and some of the Śaiva systems.[4] He is so much struck by the close resemblance between the expressions of Kātyāyana and the second chapter of the Bhagavad Gītā that he actually quotes passages from the latter in support of his opinion. Although Śīlāṅka is not justified in identifying Kātyāyana's doctrine either with the system of the Bhagavad Gītā or with the Sāṁkhya system, we cannot deny that there is some sort of historical relationship between them. In this connexion the testimony of an earlier authority like Aśvaghoṣa is of some interest. The latter in his Buddhacarita[5] attributes to Kapila a view which he seems to have described by the name of the doctrine of soul as a sixth. In Kātyāyana's six or seven categories, considered as the permanent elements of thought and existence, one may trace a background of the Vaiśeṣika categories, six or seven, which were in their main conceptions but so many logical predicaments and existences.

As regards the broad outlines of his philosophy, Kātyāyana cannot be denied his rightful claim to be singled out as the Empedocles of India. Following Uddālaka, Kātyāyana

[1] *Cf.* Sūtra Kṛitāṅga, II. 2 : Sato n'atthi viṇāso, asato n'atthi saṁbhavo.

[2] Sthānāṅga, IV ; Dīgha-Nikāya, I. 13-17.

[3] *Ibid,* IV. 4.

[4] Ihasmin Saṁsare ekeṣāṃ veda-vādināṁ sāṁkhyānāṁ śaivādhikārināṁ ca.

[5] Buddhacarita, XII. 17. ff.

maintained that the elements of being are so distinct qualitatively from one another that there is no transition from the one into the other. Empedocles upheld the same view in agreement with Anaxagoras. Again, just as Empedocles is called, justly or unjustly, an Eleatic,[1] so is Kātyāyana called an Eternalist, and an Eternalist is but an Indian Eleatic. Both agree with the Eleatics or Gotamakas, when they maintain unchangeable Being as opposed to the coming into existence. In the view of both becoming is impossible. Both conceive Being as a plurality of unchangeable elements, while with the Eleatics or Gotamakas Being is one, one only, without a second. According to both, the four roots of all things are the four elements, earth, water, fire and air. These are in their nature permanent, that is to say, they know no qualitative change. In addition to these unchangeable substrata, Empedocles conceives some ground or cause of change. This ground of change or this formative principle is two-fold: "Love"—the force which combines; "Hatred"—the force which separates. Over and above the four elements, Kātyāyana regards in like manner Pleasure and Pain (sukha, dukkha) as two principles of change. Finally, they resemble each other in admitting that there are pores (vivara)[2] in organic bodies, and they also deny the void. They found the conception of void space incompatible with the postulate of Being upon which their doctrines were based. We see, moreover, in Kātyāyana, no less than in Empedocles, that metempsychosis takes the place of immortality. According to the interpretation of both Mahāvīra and Buddha of the eternalistic thesis, the elements of being are eternal, imperishable and immutable by their very nature. They are neither created, nor can be caused to be created. But they produce again nothing new but are

Kakuda and Empedocles compared.

[1] Erdmann, History of Philosophy, I, under Empedocles. Prof. L. T. Hobhouse says, "The philosophy of Empedocles is in the main one of change and evolution."

[2] Buddhaghosa paraphrases *vivara* by "chiddo," Sumaṅgala-Vilāsinī, I, p. 167.

barren, steadfast as a mountain peak, as a pillar firmly fixed.[1] Hence concrete individual beings may come and go without affecting in the least either the nature or the existence of the substrata of change. The only point of difference between the two thinkers of two distant countries is that in the case of Empedocles it is unknown whether he left any room for the conception of soul in his scheme of existence, whereas in the case of Kātyāyana it is positive that he did. It is important to bear in mind that the passage of the Sūtra-Kṛitāṅga is silent about the grounds or principles of change. It also differs from the fragment of the Sāmañña-phala-sutta as to the number and enumeration of the substances. The former gives them as earth, water, fire, air, ether or space, and soul; the latter gives them as earth, water, fire, air, pleasure, pain, and soul or the living principle.[2]

Significance of the terms employed by Kātyāyana.

The terms kāya, sukha, dukkha, and jīva which Kātyāyana is said to have employed in the Sāmañña-phala-sutta require some explanation. As for the word kāya,[3] it does not mean for Kātyāyana what Gosāla and Mahāvīra called body or group or species, but corresponds to Uddālaka's term dhātu (a thing with its distinctive properties or characteristics), or what Aśvaghoṣa terms Sthirasattvaḥ (permanent elements of being). In the phraseology of Kātyāyana the terms sukha and dukkha (pleasure and pain) are far more general in meaning than with us. They imply, so far as their specific sense goes, exactly what Mahidāsa and Varuṇa conveyed by Hunger and Thirst. We may infer from this that Kātyāyana agreed with his predecessors in conceiving a relation of food and feeder between the five elements of being. The elements combine, in other words, into unity by their inherent tendency to eat one another, and separate by a contrary tendency that

[1] Dīgha, I, p. 56: Satta ime...kāyā akaṭā akaṭavidhā animmitā animmātā, etc.

[2] "Paṭhavi-kāyo āpo kāyo tejo kāyo vāyo kāyo sukhe dukkhe jīve sattame."

[3] Buddhaghosa understands by *Kāya* 'samūha,' or 'group.'

perpetually disunites them. Lastly the term soul or living principle (appā, jīva) bears almost the same sense as Mahidāsa's term Prāṇa or Uddālaka's term jīvātmā.

The question may perhaps be asked, why is it that Mahāvīra and Buddha considered Kātyāyana's doctrine to be a doctrine of non-action (akiriya-vāda)? With regard to this question, we cannot do better than examine the ethical bearing of his metaphysical speculation.

The theory of non-action involved in Kātyāyana's philosophy.

If the elements of being be eternally existent and unchangeable by their very nature, if they mechanically unite or separate by Pleasure and Pain, inherent in each of them, if there be, in other words, no volitional activity of consciousness, then where is the ground for the conception of or distinction between good and bad, between knowledge and ignorance, and so forth? From a literal interpretation of his expressions it at once follows that in reality there is no act of killing or hearing or knowing or instructing. The act of killing, if it is possible at all in the world, means nothing but the act of separating from one another the elements of being in their organic unity. "When a man with a sharp sword cleaves a head in twain, he does not thereby deprive anyone of life, a sword has only penetrated into the interval between seven elementary substances."[1] These expressions occur, more or less, in the language of three previous thinkers—Pratardana,[2] Naciketas[3] and Pūraṇa Kassapa,[4] and are repeated in the Bhagavad Gītā.[5] It would seem that they were suggested by a long state of war, which existed in the country at the time.

[1] Dial. B., II, p. 74. The Cartesians in Europe declare that there is no sin in taking the life of lower animals, because they do not possess a soul; whereas Kātyāyana and others in India inspired men to dismember their fellow beings, because they could not destroy either soul or any component element of being. And Pascal says, "I cannot forgive Descartes."

[2] Kauṣītaki Upaniṣad, III. 8.

[3] Kaṭhopaniṣad, I. 2. 18-25.

[4] Dial. B., II, p. 70.

[5] II, vs. 16-24.

CHAPTER XX.

Ajita Keśa-Kambalin.

(*Ajita Kesa-Kambala.*)

Since the illustrious Colebrooke many Indian and European scholars have dealt with the subject of Indian Atheism or Materialism. As far back as A.D. 1862, Prof. Muir in an instructive article[1] was concerned to show that there was freedom of thought in ancient India, giving as proof extracts from a few later texts illustrating materialistic tenets.

Introductory. Ajita's relation with Cārvāka and Bṛihaspati.

But we are far from having anything in the shape of a complete treatise on the subject. In 1907 Dr. Pizzagalli has published an excellent work, the "Nāstika Cārvāka e Lokāyatika." The way for this work was prepared by Prof. Rhys Davids in his valuable introduction to the Kuṭadanta Sutta.[2] Regarding the sources we must use discrimination as to the actual position of Indian materialistic thinkers. The later works ascribe materialistic utterances to a mythical figure to whom they give the name Cārvāka (Demon). In the Sarva-darśana-saṅgraha, Cārvāka is represented as a disciple of Bṛihaspati, another mythical figure. The Mahābhārata alludes to a Cārvāka rākṣasa, disguised as a Brāhman who had the courage in the midst of the flattering Brāhmans, to condemn civil strife.[3]

Sāyaṇa-Mādhava in his Sarvadarśana-saṁgraha actually quotes a few sayings of Bṛihaspati which are ascribed in the Viṣṇupurāṇa to Delusion the Great (Mahā-moha, *i.e.*, the

[1] J. R. A. S., Vol. XIX, 1862, art. xi.

[2] Dial. B., II. 160-172.

[3] Śāntiparva, Chaps. XXXVIII and XXXIX. Note that Cārvākarākṣasa is said to be a *bhikṣu* or a parivrājaka, nay, a Brāhman Tridaṇḍin.

Buddha), and in the Rāmāyaṇa to Jābāla.[1] Similar but earlier utterances can be traced in the Bhagavad Gītā, where they are characterised as the Demoniac-Estate (Āsura-sampatti). The Sarvadarśana account of Cārvāka philosophy is a curious combination of the materialistic views of Ajita and Pāyāsi, the biological theories of Makkhali Gosāla and others, the political tenets of Bṛihaspati and the naïve hedonism of the common folk. There is no other good grounds for ascribing the so-called Cārvāka or Demoniac philosophy to Bṛihaspati than the fact that in his political views as cited in the Kauṭilīya Arthaśāstra and embodied in the Bṛihaspati Sūtra, recently edited and translated by Dr. F. W. Thomas, we find the application of the principles of Ajita's metaphysic to politics and morals. We must draw the same conclusion from Bṛihaspati's morals cited by Draupadī, in a dialogue of the Mahābhārata[2] in favour of the Pāṇḍavas going to war with those members of the Kuru clan who had humiliated her in public. The Cārvāka of the Great Epic has nothing to do with Bṛihaspati or his school. On the other hand, as a Brāhman wanderer and mendicant and an advocate of the doctrine of non-killing, he seems to have a close historical connexion with Ajita. In point of fact, the name Cārvāka doctrine denotes no more than a type of the materialistic view of soul which has been condemned throughout the Sanskrit literature as *āsura* or demoniac but very popular (lokāyata). Passing over these works and mythical figures, we shall confine our attention to Ajita, the historical founder of Indian Materialism.

The oldest known Jaina and Buddhist works furnish us with some stereotyped extracts relating to two materialistic thinkers, Ajita of the Hair-garment and Pāyāsi. The latter was a royal chieftain, while the former was the head of a religious order and was the founder of a system of philosophy. Ajita was an elder contemporary of the Buddha, while Pāyāsi

[1] Rāmāyaṇa, II, Canto 108.

[2] Mahābhārata, III, Chap. XXXII.

belongs to the first century of Buddha's demise. Ajita is classed by the Buddhists with such Sophists as Pūraṇa Kassapa, Kāccāyana and others. In a passage of the Aṅguttara-nikāya the Buddha seems to have confounded Ajita, as Mrs. Rhys Davids points out, with Makkhali Gosāla. The passage is: "Just as......of all kinds of woven robes, a hair-garment is known to be the least desirable—cold in cold weather, hot in hot, unpleasant to the touch, so of all the many assertions by recluses, the Makkhali theory is the most undesirable."[1] It is evident from this that Ajita was distinguished in his life-time from his namesakes by the hair-garment which he wore. It is also probable that his disciples followed his example by wearing similar garments, and that from this circumstance they came to be known as Keśa-kambalins.[2]

The Keśa-kambalins and the Epicureans compared.

After the manner of the Muṇḍakas and the Gotamakas, the Keśa Kambalins were opposed as Śramans to the Brāhman priests and jurists. Perhaps among the successors of the Muṇḍakas no other school was so contemptuous of Brahmanic religion as that of the Keśa-Kambalins. All older and later accounts of the Lokāyata doctrine agree on this point. Nevertheless, it would be a mistake to suppose that their mission was only to oppose the dogmas of the Brahmanic faith. They were equally opposed to all those idealistic thinkers who, feeling extreme distrust for the senses and sense-objects, revelled in the knowledge of the universal; giving up the simple joys of life, sought to obtain the joy born of contemplation; and neglecting this present existence, strove continually to fix their attention upon the unknown future. In this respect they may be best compared with the Epicureans. Indeed, like the Epicureans, the Keśa-Kambalins with their

[1] Aṅguttara-nikāya, I. 286; Buddhism, p. 86; Oldenberg's "Buddha," p. 70.

[2] Dīgha-nikāya, I. 167, Majjhima-nikāya, I. 77, 238; II. 161, Aṅguttara-nikāya, I. 240, etc., Dial. B., II. 281. Note that in these passages there are references to a class of ascetics who used to wear hair-garments.

later designation, the Lokāyatas or Cārvākas, have generally been misunderstood by their contemporaries and posterity. As a matter of fact, both Ajita Keśa-Kambalin of India and Epicurus of Greece were good men at heart, lovers of simple living and high thinking. Thanks to modern research, we are now in a position to be able to fully appreciate the teachings of Epicurus. And it was Bacon who was the first to define an Atheist as one who thinks. In India it was Rāj Kṛiṣṇa Mukhopādhyāya who in his 'Miscellaneous Essays' (Bibidha-prabandha), attempted to appreciate the value of what he calls the philosophy of Cārvāka. Not less remarkable it is that even in olden times the Buddha did not fail to accord due attention to the view of one whom he always regarded as his opponent. Now the result of modern research is that we are all prepared to investigate the causes which compelled a Cārvāka to teach us to eat ghee even though we run into debts, or a Preacher to eat and drink and be merry, or an Omar Khayyam to fill the cup.

His Philosophy.

The sources of information.

As to Ajita's philosophy, we have evidences, supplied by the Buddhists, the Jains and the Brāhmans. The best known Buddhist passage on Ajita's doctrine is that which is incorporated in the Sāmañña-phala Sutta.[1] In the Patisambhidā-magga and Dhamma-saṅgaṇi[2] the passage has been broken up in two portions. The same breaking up reappears in the Tibetan and Chinese versions of the Sāmañña-phala Sutta.[3] However, these earlier fragments are the same to all intents and purposes. Thus the passage of the Sāmañña-phala Sutta may be taken as the most typical of the oldest Buddhist records, and compared

[1] Dīgha-nikāya, I, p. 55; *cf.* Majjhima, I, p. 515; Saṁyutta, III, p. 307.

[2] Dhamma-saṅgaṇi, 1215, 1362, 1364.

[3] Rockhill's Life of the Buddha, pp. 100-101; 255-257.

with a parallel passage in Candrakīrti's commentary on the Mādhyamika Sūtra.[1] As a departure from the older authority, the fragment of Candrakīrti is attributed to the Lokāyatas and it is said that the Lokāyatas compared the origin of intelligence from the chemical mixture of four elements to that of generation of the inebriating power of liquor from a kindred mixture of its ingredients. The simile which Candrakīrti adds as a new element to our knowledge occurs in all later Buddhist, Jaina and Brāhman works,[2] and not in the texts which are older.[3]

The philosophical views of Pāyāsi are to be found in a Buddhist Suttanta named after him,[4] and in the Rāya Paseṇi, the second Jaina Upāṅga. Besides numerous scattered fragments, the Jaina Sūtra-Kṛitāṅga[5] contains a parallel passage, where the expressions and arguments of Ajita and Pāyāsi seem to have been mixed up. The Bhagavad Gītā,[6] in common with the older Buddhist and Jaina authorities, differs from the Rāmāyaṇa,[7] the Viṣṇu-purāṇa and the Sarvadarśana-saṅgraha in that it does not allude to the analogy employed by the materialists as an argument against the practice and utility of offering food to the dead. Their argument is : If it be possible that food set for the dead can feed them, then why not prepare food for those who are away on a journey in the belief that it can appease their hunger ? The later texts[8] differ again from the Rāmāyaṇa and the Viṣṇupurāṇa in referring to the dialectical and epistemological aspect of the Materialist doctrine. The Viṣṇupurāṇa[9]

[1] Ed. Bibl. Buddhica, IV, p. 336.

[2] *E.g.* The Tamil Mani-Mekhalai, XXVII ; Śīlāṅka's Sūtrakṛitāṅgaṭīkā : Saptabhaṅgataraṅginī ; Yoga-Vāsiṣṭha Rāmāyaṇa ; Sarva-darśana-saṅgraha.

[3] *E.g.* Bhagavad Gītā, XVI ; Rāmāyaṇa ; etc.

[4] Pāyāsi Suttanta, Dīgha-nikāya, II.

[5] II. 1. 16.

[6] XVI.

[7] Ayodhyā-kāṇḍa, Canto 103.

[8] *E.g.* Vaiśeṣika Sūtra, III. 2. 17 ; Sāṁkhya Sūtra ; Vedānta-sāra ; Śiva-jñāna-siddhiyar ; Alberuni's India ; etc.

[9] Wilson's translation, III, Chap. XVIII.

in particular lays stress on the rejection of the doctrine of revelation of the Vedas by the Materialists in common with the Jainas and Buddhists. "The received or authoritative word (āpta-vākya) does not fall from the sky." The discussion of the same problem finds its place in all the philosophical Sūtras, notably Jaimini's Pūrvamīmāṁsā. Three other characteristics of the later Brāhman works are: first, that in them the Materialist doctrine is interpreted as implying pleasure (kāma) to be the sole end of life's activities[1]; secondly, that the Materialists are said to worship in common with the political writers the king as the supreme lord, present in his corporeal form[2]; and thirdly, that Materialism, better known in former ages as Annihilationism (Ucchedavāda), is harmoniously combined with Naturalism. The first of these three characteristics cannot be directly inferred from the extracts on Ajita and Pāyāsi, as supplied by the Buddhist and Jaina canonical texts. As to the second characteristic the process which resulted in intermingling the Materialist doctrine with the rules of polity (nīti) can be seen in its initial stage in a passage of the Maitri Upaniṣad (VII. 8-10) where Bṛihaspati transformed as Śūkra misleads the demons. But in the Kauṭilīya Artha-śāstra[3] Materialism (Lokāyata) together with the Sāṁkhya and Yoga systems is scrupulously distinguished from the doctrine of polity as something speculative (ānvīkṣaki) from a practical way of life (loka-yātrā). In the Mahābodhi Jātaka,[4] too, the doctrine of annihilation is kept separate from Khatta-vijjā, which means literally the Militarist doctrine according to which a man ought to seek his own advantage even by killing his parents. The term Kṣatravidyā occurs in a list of sciences given in

[1] *E.g.*, Bhagavad Gītā, XVI. 8. 11-12. *cf.* Śivajñānasiddhiyar (Nallasami's translation), pp. 13-14.

[2] Pratyakṣa-siddhaḥ-rājā Parameśvaraḥ.

[3] I. 1.

[4] Fausböll's Jātaka, V. 489-490.

the Chāndogya Upaniṣad,[1] and is explained by Śaṅkara as the science of archery (Dhanurveda). Buddhaghosa and Āryaśūra understand by it the science of government (nīti-sattha, nīti-kauṭilya).[2]

The examination of the sources of information leads us to the conclusion that the rather long and eventful history of Indian Materialists, like perhaps the history of the Stoics, may be divided into many periods, but our concern being here the doctrine of Ajita, we shall regard the passage of the Sāmañña-phala Sutta as our principal authority.

Two aspects of Ajita's philosophy—negative and positive.

Our next task is to determine the positive thesis or constructive aspect of Ajita's doctrine. It is remarkable that his categorical assertions (abhinivesā)[3] are all negative in form: There is no such thing as liberality shown to the priests; no such thing as sacrifice; as offering food to the dead; as reward or retribution; as future life, as father or mother after death; as 'chance-born beings' (opapātika sattā), no perfect saint who can instruct us about future life or existence of individuality after death. All this may be summed up in the expression: There is no individuality after death. "A living body is constituted of the four elements of existence. When a man dies, earth returns to the earth, water to the water, heat to the fire, air to the air, and the sense faculties pass into space. It is a doctrine of fools, the talk of existence after death (atthika-vāda), for all alike, fools and the wise, on the dissolution of the body, are cut off, annihilated, ceasing to be after death."[4] Ajita in the negative aspect of his doctrine shows a resemblance to Epicurus, while on the positive side of his speculations, he seems to be more a Stoic than an Epicurean, his fundamental point being that nothing is real but that which is corporeal.

[1] VII. 1. 2.

[2] Dial. B. II. 18. cp. Śikṣā-samuccaya, p. 192.

[3] Patisambhidā-magga, I.

[4] Dial, B, II. 73-74.

Again, referring to the passage of the Sāmañña-phala-sutta, we can see that Ajita was neither a political writer like a Bṛibaspati or a Śūkra, nor a sensualist like a Vātsyāyana or a Ghoṭakamukha, nor a naturalist like a Gośāla. As contrasted with the point of view of Gośāla, the stand-point of Ajita seems purely subjective. As the passage of the Bhagavad-Gītā[1] seems to imply, the term Naturalism or Atheism is applicable to the demoniac doctrine only because it teaches that a living being comes into existence by a natural process of reproduction. Ajita only reproduced what other previous thinkers had said in so many words. Even then we should bear in mind that Naturalism, so far as it is implied in Ajita's doctrine, was not the subject of his main investigation. The problem with which Ajita and Pāyāsi, his immediate successor, were confronted was rather epistemological. That is to say, their main contention was not so much against the dogmas of the Brahmanic faith (which may appear at first sight) as against the doctrine of Kakuda Kātyāyana and others who made a hard and fast distinction between the body and the soul, matter and spirit, in short, who conceived soul as an entity existing independently of anything corporeal or material. From this point of view his doctrine was described by Mahāvīra and Buddha as Taṁ-jīva-taṁ-sarīra-vāda, in contradistinction to the doctrine of soul being distinct from the body (Aññaṁ-jīva-aññaṁ-sarīra-vāda). Thus in one sense like a Stoic he identified the corporeal with the mental, and in another sense he did not. His intention was not to identify body with soul, judged as concepts, for what he sought to establish was that the real fact of experience is always a living whole, a whole which the apprehending mind can conceive in its various aspects.[2] Hence the distinction which Kakuda Kātyāyana made between the elements of being is in the view of Ajita untenable, the

Ajita the critic of Kātyāyana and other dualistic thinkers.

[1] I.XVI, 8: "jagad āhur anīśvaraṁ."

[2] *Cf.* Vedānta-sāra (ed. Cowell), p. 32.

distinction being only an act of our mind. No such distinction exists in the living concrete individual, taken as a whole. This view of Ajita was, made more intelligible by Pāyāsi. The soul is not an entity distinct from the body. As a man drawing a sword from the scabbard can say "This is the sword and that is the scabbard," so we are not able to separate the soul from the body, pointing out, this is the soul and that's the body.[1] Without multiplying the references, we may add that Pāyāsi's argument implies a serious protest against the proposition of all earlier dualistic thinkers, who held that "Soul is in body, as fire in the araṇi-wood," a proposition corresponding to Aristotle's formula, Universalia in Re—the Universal in things. Ajita and Pāyāsi viewed the corporeal from the point of view of self,[2] on the ground that form cannot exist apart from matter.

According to Mahāvīra's opinion, Ajita denying the future life, taught men to kill, burn, destroy,[3] and enjoy all the pleasures of life. The truth seems quite the contrary. He taught us, as we may infer from a Upaniṣad passage forming the background of his views, to believe rather in life than in death, to show proper regard to persons when they are alive rather than showing honour to them after death.[4] It was the Eternalists, as we saw, who, maintaining a theory of the unchangeable being, appeared to inspire man to take life. In another Jaina passage we are told that Ajita was an Akriyā-vādin, as he upheld the doctrine of non-Being. On the other hand, Buddha distinguished the Annihilationists from the Eternalists, that is, he distinguished those who by right insight saw the

The moral deductions of Ajita's theory of self.

[1] Jacobi's Jaina Sūtras, part 2, pp. 340-341 ; Dial. B, III, 358-361.

[2] "Rūpaṁ attato samanupassati."

[3] Jacobi's Jaina Sūtras, part 2, p. 341.

[4] *Cf.* Chāndogya Upaniṣad, VII, 15, 2-3 : prāṇo hi pitā prāṇo mātā......sa yadi pitaraṁ vā mātaraṁ vā......kiṁcid bhṛiśam iva pratyâha dhiktvâstvityevainam āhuḥ "pitṛihā vai tvam asi mātṛihā vai tvam asi......Atha Yadyapi enān utkrāntaprāṇān śūlena samāsaṁ vyatiṣaṁ dahen naivainaṁ brūyaḥ : "pitṛihâsîti na mātṛihâsîti...... "

ceasing-to-be of the world, as it really is, from those who saw how the world comes to pass. Thus in the estimation of the Buddha, the Annihilationists were as much wise, or as much in error, as the Eternalists themselves. The fault which he found with both was that both were extremists and dogmatists.

The basis of Ajita's doctrine, as of Kātyāyana's, is in the philosophy of Mahidāsa, who formulated the proposition: "I am the five-fold hymn." The study of the views of Śīlāṅka and Sāyaṇa Mādhava leads us to think that the foundation of Ajita's doctrine was laid in a statement of Yājñavalkya which is—that the intelligible essence emerging from the five elements vanishes into them at death.

CHAPTER XXI.

Maskarin Gośāla.

(*Makkhali Gosāla.*)[1]

Maskarin Gośāla is best known as the third or last Tīrthaṅkara of the Ājīvika School. The school is thrice mentioned in the edicts of King Aśoka whose grandson Daśaratha gave them some cave-dwellings.[2] Among modern scholars who have dealt with the philosophy of the Ājīvikas, the chief is Dr. Hoërnle. But his account paints them in rather shocking colours, as he is influenced by the Buddhists and the Jainas, who were bitter opponents of the Ājīvikas. The Ājīvikas cannot be identified entirely with the Acelakas (naked ascetics) alluded to in numerous Buddhist texts. For the Acelakas as described in the Buddhist literature do not certainly represent one single corporate body but several religious orders. Part of the description of the naked ascetics in the Buddhist texts applies to them. This part emphasizes only the Ājīvika sense of self-respect, conscientiousness, continence, and very tender regard for animal and all forms of life.[3] We learn from the Majjhima-nikāya[4] that an Ājīvika never incurred the guilt of obeying another man's command. He refused to accept food which was especially prepared for him. He did not accept food from people when they were eating, lest they

Gośāla and the Ājīvikas.

[1] A separate monogram on Makkhali's philosophy has been written by the author. Those who are interested to know the results of his later investigations into the subject must read this monogram, "The Ajivikas" (Calcutta University publication).

[2] See Senart, 'Inscriptions de Piyadasi,' II. 82, 209.

[3] Dīgha-nikāya, I. 166. This is a stock passage; see Dial. B. 2, 227. Aṅguttara-nikāya, III. 383, foll.; *cf.* Sumaṅgala-Vilāsinī, I, p. 162. Jaina Sūtras, Part 2, XXXI. Majjhima I, pp. 238, 524.

[4] Majjhima-nikāya, I, p. 238.

should go short or be disturbed. He did not accept food collected in time of drought. He did not accept food where a dog was standing by, or flies were swarming round, lest they should lose a meal. He did not eat fish, or meat, nor use intoxicants.[1] Even from this meagre account we may infer that the Ājīvikas were men of right living and that in this mode of right living they were followed by both the Jainas and the Buddhists.

A certain amount of mystery hangs round the name and life of Maskarin Gosāla. In the Jaina records the name is given as Gosāla Maṅkhaliputta,—Gosāla the son of Maṅkhali.

His name and life.

He was born at Saravaṇa near Sāvatthi. His father was Maṅkhali and his mother's name was Bhaddā. His father was a Maṅkha, that is, a dealer in pictures. Gosāla himself followed his father's profession before he became a monk.[2] In the Buddhist records the name is spelt differently as Makkhali Gosāla. According to Buddhaghosa's comment on the name, Gosāla means one who was born in a cow-shed, and Makkhali means one who stumbled in the mud. Buddhaghosa hands on the tradition that during the early years of Gosāla he was employed as a servant, who, while carrying an oil-pot stumbled from carelessness, and from the fear of his employer fled away naked, leaving his garment behind (acelako hutvā).[3]

Neither of these accounts is historical. The true name of the philosopher seems to be Maskarin, the Jaina-prakrit form of which is Maṅkhali, and the Pali form Makkhali. The term Maskarin is explained by Pāṇini[4] as meaning one who carries a bamboo-staff (maskara). A Maskarin is also known as Ekadaṇḍin. According to Patañjali's comments[5] the name

[1] Dial. B., II, pp. 227-229.

[2] Hoërnle's extract from the Bhagavatī, XV. 1, Uvāsaga-dasāo, p. 1.

[3] Sumaṅgala-Vilāsinī, I, pp. 143-144.

[4] Pāṇini's Grammar, VI. 1. 154.

[5] Patañjali's Mahābhāṣya (ed. Kielhorn) III. 96. See Hoërnle's "Ājīvikas" in the Encyclopedia of Religion and Ethics. Ind. Ant., Vol. XLI, 1912, p. 289.

indicates a school of Wanderers or Sophists who were called Maskarins, not so much because they carried a bamboo staff about them as because they denied the freedom of the will. Thus in the estimation of Patañjali, as also in that of Mahāvīra and Buddha, the Maskarins were fatalists or determinists. We know next to nothing of Gośāla's early years. We do not know exactly when he was born or what led him to renounce the world. In the absence of any record left us either by him or by his disciples we can only say that it was perhaps in the fashion of his day that he left home-life to be a homeless wanderer. Dr. Hoërnle's extract from the Bhagavatī sūtra[1] shows that Mahāvīra had withdrawn himself from the world shortly before Gośāla, and that in his second year he received the latter as a disciple. Nālandā was their meeting place. They lived happily together for six years at Paṇiyabhūmi, and afterwards separated owing to a doctrinal difference. They never met again but once after the lapse of sixteen years in Sāvatthi, where Gośāla had founded a separate school of thought. The doctrinal difference which the Bhagavatī sūtra alludes to was that according to Gośāla there is no matter unformed and nothing without life, while Mahāvīra distinguished between the concrete and the abstract. This account regarding the chronology of Gośāla and Mahāvīra does not agree with the authority of the Kalpa-sūtra,[2] where we are told that Mahāvīra spent the first twelve years of his monkhood not as a teacher (jina) but as a mere learner or pupil. Even in the malicious Bhagavatī account it is stated that Gosāla predeceased Mahāvīra by sixteen years, and was recognised as a teacher sometime before the latter. Gosāla's death was coincident with a great political event, namely the war "which King Kūṇiya (Ajātasattu) of Magadha waged with King Cheḍaga of Vesāli." From this it follows that the statement with regard to Gośāla's position as a disciple of

[1] Appendix to Uvasāga-dasāo, pp. 2-4.

[2] Jacobi's Kalpasūtra, Introd., p. 9.

Mahāvīra is disputable. The Buddhist records,[1] too, invariably distinguish between Gosāla and Mahāvīra, and allude to both as the renowned leaders of two separate religious orders, and of two distinct schools of thought. The order of the Ājīvikas or Maskarins is of older standing than that of the Jainas or the Buddhists. Gosāla was not a disciple of Mahāvīra, but the latter was in all likelihood either a disciple of, or at least in some way connected with, the former. The Kalpa-sūtra which is one of the most authoritative works on Mahāvīra's life informs us that immediately after his renunciation Mahāvīra spent more than a year as a clothed monk, while in the second year he became a naked ascetic. Dr. Hoërnle says that the two teachers separated because of their difference of 'character and temper,' and 'owing to the insincerity and trickery of Gosāla.' Here we cannot agree with Dr. Hoërnle, as we find in his extract from the Bhagavatī Sūtra that the cause of their separation was a difference of opinion between the two thinkers.

In a passage of the Sūtra-kritānga[2] Gosāla is confounded with a Sensualist, as in a passage of the Anguttara-nikāya[3] the Buddha appears to have confounded Makkhali with Ajita Kesa-kambalin. On the authority of the Uvāsaga-dasāo[4] we may add that Śrāvastī was the head-quarters of the Ājīvikas or Maskarins, and that Gosāla was there held in great respect by the people.

To sum up: Maskarin Gosāla predeceased Mahāvīra by sixteen years, and spent his whole life in biological researches. The tender regard which he showed for every form of life was a natural outcome of his philosophical doctrine. It appears from the evidence of Aśokan edicts and Patañjali's commentary on Pāṇini that his school survived after him, and were known as the Maskarins or "Idlers."

[1] Dial. B. II. p. 66.

[2] Sūtra-Kritānga, II. 6.

[3] Anguttara, I. 286.

[4] Uvāsaga Dasāo, VI-VII.

I. Physics.

Gośāla's philosophy may conveniently be divided into two sections: Physics and Ethics. In dealing with the former, we have to determine at the outset the historical relationship of Gośāla to Mahāvīra.

The relationship of Gośāla and Mahāvīra as thinkers.

With regard to this point we ought first of all to examine the fragment of the Bhagavatī Sūtra (XV. 1) which clearly sets forth the relative position of the two thinkers. In it we are told that Gosāla and Mahāvīra were once travelling together from Siddhatthagāma to Kummagāma. On their way they passed a large sesamum shrub which was then in full bloom (tila-thambhae pupphie). Gośāla inquired of Mahāvīra whether the shrub would perish or not, and what would be the fate of its seeds, if they had perished. To this the latter's reply was that the shrub would perish, though the seeds would be formed in seed-vessels. Disbelieving what Mahāvīra had said, Gośāla uprooted the shrub and dislocated it. As chance would have it, just then a shower of rain fell, enabling the shrub again to take root and flower. The result of it was that shortly afterwards the seeds were formed in the seed-vessels, as Mahāvīra had predicted. Thereupon Gośāla concluded that just as the sesame seeds after having completely perished, come to life from their inherent force or will-to-be, so are all living beings capable of reanimation.[1] Mahāvīra was unable to accept Gośāla's general theory of the perpetual reanimation of things,[2] seeing that in the above case the shrub revived not because its soul having left it came back to it again, but only because it had not altogether perished. The difference of opinion which thus ensued led ultimately to their separation.

[1] "Tila-puppha-jīva uddaitā uddaitā ...... ajjhattie jāva samuppajjittha evaṁ khalu sabbajīvāvi pauṭṭa parihāraṁ pariharaṁti." The passage is rather obscure. The term puppha-jīva is literally the flower-souls, the commentators take uddaitta as equivalent to mṛitvā. Pauṭṭa = parivarta. It seems more accurately = pravritta. *Cf.* Kaṭha, I. 1. 6, quoted *ante* p. 268, f. n. 2. 1.

[2] Parivarta-vāda, the doctrine of transformation.

It is somewhat difficult to understand the exact significance of Gośāla's view or of Mahāvira's contention. We cannot believe that in Gośāla's opinion the shrub having been uprooted, either perished altogether, or having perished came to life again. Perhaps the passage means that according to Gośāla's theory, there is nothing without life or nothing that is not capable of transformation, while from the point of view of Mahāvīra there are not only living substances (jīvā), but also things which are non-living (a-jīvā). If so, the importance of the above passage is that for Gośāla the ultimate category is one,—*jīva* or concrete living things, while for Mahāvīra they are two: *jīva* or concrete facts and *a-jīva* or judgments about things.

Proceeding on this assumption, we may also note that historically the two categories of Mahāvīra were derived from the one category of Gośāla, his predecessor. Strictly, we may suppose that all the various classifications of living beings adopted by Mahāvīra belong not to him but to Gośāla. With regard to the relation, personal as well as doctrinal, between Gośāla and Mahāvīra, Prof. Jacobi observes: "The relation between them probably was different from what the Jainas would have us believe.... The fact that these two teachers lived together for a long period, presupposes, it would appear, some similarity between their opinions....the expressions *sabbe sattā sabbe pāṇā sabbe bhūtā sabbe jīvā* is common to both Gośāla and the Jainas, and from the commentary we learn that the division of animals into *ekendriyas, dvīndriyas*, etc., which is so common in Jaina texts, was also used by Gośāla. The curious and almost paradoxical Jaina doctrine of the six Leśyas closely resembles, as Prof. Leumann was the first to perceive, Gośāla's division of mankind into six classes; but in this particular we are inclined to believe that the Jainas borrowed the idea from the Ājīvikas and altered it so as to bring it into harmony with the rest of their own doctrines."[1] Here the last point of Prof. Jacobi's remark

[1] The Jaina-sūtras, Part 2, pp. XXIX-XXX.

requires a little modification. It is the Buddhists who tell us that by the term 'six classes' Gośāla meant the six types or classes of men, whereas in point of fact the division is in accordance with Gośāla's view not only applicable to men, but to all beings. As a matter of fact, the idea of such a division seems to have been inherited by Gośāla from the teaching of Pārśvaṇātha, as may be inferred from the expression *cha jiva-nikāyā* of Mahāvīra's parents who were lay followers of Pārśvanātha.[1]

Gośāla, Mahāvīra, Kaṇāda and the Stoics.

Now as to the historical relation between Gośāla and Mahāvīra on one hand, and Kaṇāda on the other, we shall provisionally take it for granted that the Vaiśeṣika system of Kaṇāda has many points in common with the early Stoic philosophy, as also with the Atomistic theory of Democritus. Uddālaka by his doctrine of the mixture and infinite divisibility of things prepared the way for the Atomistic doctrine of Kaṇāda; and Kātyāyana's doctrine of six substances which are all qualitatively distinct was not without its marvellous effect upon the development of the Vaiśeṣika system. The two points which Kaṇāda seems to have derived from Gośāla relate to his two grounds of explanation: nature peculiar to each type of existence, and fate or necessity.[2] And Mahāvīra, who thought on the lines of Gośāla and partly adopted the hypothesis of nature or necessity, prepared further the way for the development of Kaṇāda's doctrine. As Prof. Jacobi points out, the doctrine of Mahāvīra in common with that of Kaṇāda or Hindu Zeno is to be distinguished from the view of Kātyāyana as the doctrine of action (kriyāvāda) from that of non-action (akriyāvāda). Kriyāvāda is the doctrine according to which the soul acts and is acted upon.[3] Supposing Ajita's doctrine that the real is throughout

[1] Āyāramga Sutta, II. 15. 16.

[2] Gough's Vaiśeṣika Sūtra, VI. 2.12-13: adṛiṣṭāt; jāti-viśeṣāt.

[3] Jacobi's Jaina-sūtras, Part 2, p. 240: "Things depend partly on fate, and partly on human exertion" (niyayâniyaya).

single and corporeal corresponds to the Stoic theory of knowledge, we may perhaps say that Gośāla's doctrines roughly represent the Stoic physics and ethics. Moreover, the substrata of Gośāla's doctrine are in the philosophy of Mahidāsa, just as perhaps the real basis of the Stoic physics is constituted by the philosophy of Aristotle. In other words, just as Gośāla's view is thoroughly post-Vedic, so the Stoic philosophy at its first stage of development is thoroughly Greek.

Gośāla's fundamental thesis and its signification.

The fundamental thesis of Gośāla's physics is Stoic in its nature. It is summed up in the Jaina Bhagavatī Sūtra and its commentary as the doctrine of transformation (Pauṭṭa parihāra-vāda), and in the Buddhist texts as the "theory of purification through transmigration" (saṁsāra-suddhi).[1] The term employed by Gośāla himself is transformation,—pariṇāma implied in pariṇata.[2] In the Buddhist phraseology, purification is the equivalent of 'the end of pain' (dukkhassanta), and the word transmigration by which Prof. Rhys Davids translates saṁsāra, signifies the passing of soul from one state of existence to another. In reference to Gośāla's physics, however, we must interpret the expression "purification through transmigration" as meaning perfection through transformation,—transformation which implies for him not only the process of constant change, but also a fixed orderly mode of progression and retrogression.

According to Gośāla's view, the law of change is a universal fact, because all types of things and all species of beings[3] are individually capable of transformation, that is, of elevation or degradation in type. Judging from this point of view, his fundamental thesis would seem to be rather too narrowly

[1-2] Dīgha-nikāya, I. 54; Jātaka, V. 489; Dial. B, II. 72-73. Buddhaghosa explains pariṇatā as nānāppakārattaṁ pattā, "diversified or made manifold,—attaining different conditions of existence."

[3] Sabbe sattā, sabbe pāṇā, sabbe bhūtā, sabbe jīvā. See Hoërnle's translation of the extract from Buddhaghosa's Sumaṅgala-vilāsinī, I. 161, in Appendix II, Uvāsaga Daśao; Jacobi's Jaina-sūtras, Part 2, p. XXVI.

stated by the Buddhists when they state it thus: Both fools and wise alike shall reach perfection by gradual transformation. In strict accordance with his view the thesis ought to be stated in a more general form: All beings, all lives, all existent things, all living substances attain, and must attain, perfection in course of time.

In Buddhaghosa's explanation the term "all beings" denotes for Gośāla all kinds of animals, camels, cows, asses, etc.; "all lives" comprise all sensitive things and sentient creatures, divided into those with one sense (ekendriyas), those with two senses, and so forth; "all existent things" are living beings divided into generic types, to wit, those which are produced from an egg, or born from the womb, or (sprung from moisture, or propagated from seeds); and the term "all living substances" is used with reference to rice, barley, wheat, and the like.

The reliability of Buddhaghosa's expositions.

In the absence of the recorded words of Gośāla or of his disciples, one may reasonably ask, are we justified at all in relying upon Buddhaghosa's exposition, and using it as an argument in favour of the opinion that the division of living beings into those with one sense, those with two senses, and so forth, is common to both Gośāla and Mahāvīra? With Prof. Jacobi we are convinced that there is after all no reason for disputing Buddhaghosa's comments. In this particular case, we can safely regard him as our best authority. Buddhaghosa drew on some older authorities. There can be no better evidence of this than that his comments upon Gośāla's expression 'six classes' are traceable in an identical form in the Aṅguttaranikāya (III. 383-384). Nevertheless his explanation of the terms all beings, all lives, etc., seems ingenious enough, but not quite in accord with Gośāla's own enumerations and classifications of living things and beings. But the passage of the Sāmaññaphala Sutta itself is corrupt and disjointed; it has, moreover, the critical purpose of making Gośāla's doctrine collapse.

"There are fourteen hundred thousands of principal genera and species (pamukha-yoniyo), again six thousand others, and again six hundred. (Thus the sum total is 14,06,600.)" "There are ; forty-nine hundred Ājīvakas,[1] hundreds of Wanderers or Sophists (Parivrājakas), hundreds of Nāga-abodes-or-species, two thousand sentient creatures (vise indriya-sate), three thousand infernal states, thirty-six celestial, mundane or passionate grades (rajo-dhātuyo),[2] seven classes of animate beings (saññigabbhā) or beings having the capacity to generate by means of separate sexes, seven of inanimate production (a-saññigabbhā), seven of production by grafting (niganṭhi-gabbhā), seven grades of gods, and of men, and of devils, etc."

Buddhaghosa found it a hopeless task to explain this passage. However, what he says with respect to Gośāla's three expressions *saññi-gabbhā*, *a-saññi-gabbhā* and *niganṭhi-gabbhā* is very instructive: "Camels, cows, asses, goats, sheep, deer and buffaloes are generated by means of separate sexes. Rice, barley, and five other cereals are of inanimate production. Sugar-cane, bamboo, reeds, etc., propagate from joints.'

The above passage indicates that for Gośāla there are infinite gradations of existence. In his view each individual thing has eternal existence, if not individually, at least in type. He has definite conceptions of numerous grades of beings, celestial, infernal and mundane, as also of the infinity of time and the recurrent cycles of existence. In particular the expression twenty thousand sentient creatures (vise indriya-sate) shows that Gośāla had in mind something of a division of animate things according to the number of senses each type possesses. In order to render his views and classifications of beings intelligible, it is necessary to take into consideration the classifications that we find in previous thinkers, and in his successors.

[1] *Cf.* The Tibetan version of the Sāmaññaphala Sutta in Rockhill's Life of the Buddha, p. 103.

[2] Following Buddhaghosa, Hoërnle translates it "dust-depositories."

Buddhaghosa's explanation of the term "all existent things" (sabbe bhūtā) shows that Gośāla adopted Mahidāsa's division of the animate world. The latter, as we saw, vaguely conceived a two-fold classification : physical and psychological. In his physical division the heavenly beings stand highest in the scale. Below them come the five elemental beings (pañca mahābhūtāni). All these are to be regarded as *sui generis*. The sentient beings are divided into the movable and the immovable (jaṅgama, sthāvara), the viviparous, the oviparous, the moisture-sprung, and plants. According to his psychological division, all forms of life up to plants possess life but hardly any sensation. Among higher forms of life, some possess intelligence (citta), while others do not. The highest among the animals is man who alone possesses intellect, prudence and moral sense. Among men again the most perfect is the philosopher who can seek immortality by means of the mortal.

The two-fold classification of the animate world.

In turning to Gośāla's classifications we shall assume that they are essentially the same as those of Mahāvīra. The two-fold classification of living things is found in many Jaina texts, earlier as well as later.[1] Here we shall consider only one text, the Uttarâdhayayana Sūtra, in which the classifications are given in an elaborate manner. The noticeable point in the biological classifications of Gośāla and Mahāvīra is that the living things are divided according to the number of senses each type possesses.

Those with one sense comprise the four elemental groups and the vegetable kingdom.[2] This one sense is the fundamental sense of touch. The four elemental groups are the Earth-group (Pṛithivīkāya), the Water-group (Āpa-kāya), the Fire-group (Teja-kāya) and the Wind-group (Vāyu-kāya). Of these, the first two groups are distinguished from the other two as the

[1] Sūtrakṛitāṅga, II. 2-5 ; Bhagavatī-sūtra, I. 1 ; Uttarâdhyayana Sūtra, X ; XXXVI. 74-77.

[2] *Cf.* Paramatthajotikā, II, Vol. I. p. 3 ; rukkhaṁ...ekindriyaṁ...jīvaṁ.

immovable or passive from the movable or active, or to use Mahidāsa's phraseology, food from the feeder. Each of these groups is further divided into the developed and the undeveloped. In the Earth-group are placed clay and dust of different colours, rocks, minerals, metals, and other inorganic things. The Water-group comprises rain, dew, fog, etc. The Fire-group includes flame, lightnings, sparks, etc. Gentle breezes, hurricanes, cyclones, monsoons, etc., form the Wind-group. All these differ in size, shape, colour, motion, force and so forth.

The plant-life or vegetable kingdom, like the elemental life, is possessed of only one sense, the sense of touch. Gośāla admits, however, that plants in general stand higher in the scale than elemental lives. All plants are organic beings, capable of reanimation. We should note that in the Mahābhārata one can meet with a criticism of this view. It is maintained that the plants possess the same number of senses as we possess. "The trees bear flowers and fruits, drop their leaves, wither and die. Therefore they are sensible to touch . . . . A creeper, for instance, winds round a tree on all sides. Had it been blind how could it find its way? etc., etc."[1]

Next in the scale are the creatures with two senses—touch and taste—animalculæ, worms, etc. Above these are placed those with three senses—touch, taste and smell—such as ants, bugs, moths, etc. Still higher are those with four senses—touch, taste, smell, and sight, *e.g.*, mosquitos, gnats, scorpions, locusts, butterflies, etc. Highest in the scale are beings with five organs of sense. They are sub-divided into infernal beings, animals, men, and the gods.

In all these divisions we have to suppose a graduated scale of existence. Living things and beings differ in their physical formation, strength, and duration of life.[2]

[1] Mahābhārata, Śāntiparva, Mokṣadharma, Canto 184, IV. 6 foll.

[2] Carefully compare Manu's classifications, 'Laws of Manu,' I. 37-39; I. 49-50; XII. 4 foll.

In dealing with Gośāla's psychological classification we need only to explain the significance of his term Kāya or Mahāvīra's term Leśya. In commenting upon Gośāla's expression six-classes (chalābhijātiyo), the Buddhist authorities tell us that it has reference to his division of mankind into six colours: the black, the blue, the red, the yellow, the white, and the supremely white. In the black class are placed all the workers of iniquity such as sheep-butchers, boar-hunters, thieves, murderers, and so forth, while in the supremely white class are the three Ājīvika Tīrthaṅkaras.

This is what the Buddhists say of Gośāla's doctrine. Without denying that this division is, in accordance with Gośāla's view, applicable to human beings, we have reason to think that the division is in fact of a far wider application. Colour here is a metaphorical expression corresponding to Manu's term Quality (guṇa).[1] In a passage of the Majjhima-nikāya we have from the Buddha a short note on the term Colour (kāya or leśya) as employed by Gośāla and Mahāvīra: Just as a piece of cloth absorbs the colours or impurities from different dyes, so does the mind become tinged or tainted by its different tendencies and associations.[2] The term Leśya is explained in the Uttarâdhyayana-sūtra[3] in a similar way, *i.e.*, in the sense of "Seelen-typus" or "Soul-type," as Prof. Weber explains it.[4] Both these explanations indicate that in the conception of Gośāla and Mahāvīra soul is in its nature absolutely pure. The colouring is the effect of actions on its life. Putting it otherwise we can say that soul has a colour of its own which is supremely white, and it is discoloured when it is affected by things which are foreign to its nature.[5]

[1] Majjhima-nikāya, I, p. 36. "Vatthaṁ saṅkiliṭṭhaṁ malaggahitaṁ . . . . parisuddhaṁ pariyodātaṁ . . . . . yadi nīlakāya yadi pītakāya . . . "

[2] Manu, XII. 12-14; also I. Uttaradhyayana, 49-50; XII. 4.

[3] XXXIV.

[4] Leumann's Aupapātika Sūtra, Glossary.

[5] The Stoic and Lockean notions of soul or mind as *tabula rasa* were very common among Indian thinkers, earlier and later. For example, Yājñavalkya predicated "self-luminous" (svayaṁ jyotis) of soul; Bhāradvāja predicated "white" (śubhra). Buddha assigned the

Particularly we can observe in Gośāla's theory how soul is acted upon by things external.

Gośāla's classifications of living things are essential to the discussion of the theoretical aspect of his physics. So far as this aspect goes, he offers for his theory of perfection through transformation three grounds of explanation : Fate or Necessity, Class or Species, and Nature (niyati-saṅgati-bhāva-pariṇatā).[1]

I. Fate (Niyati).—Like the Stoics, Gośāla maintains that in the world as a whole all comes about by necessity ; fate regulates all. As Mahāvīra, Buddha and others[2] interpret his doctrine, there is no such thing as power, energy, strength or vigour. All beings, all lives, all existent things, all living substances are without force and power of their own. They are bent this way and that by their fate. That which is to be, must be; that which is not to be, cannot be. All things are unalterably fixed. Fixed are the periods of existence, the properties of things, and the functions of the senses. The nature of action, fortune, wisdom and death is fixed in the case of a being even while he is in the womb, so to speak. Just as when a ball of string is cast forth it spreads out just as far as, and no farther than, it can unwind, so every being lives, acts, enjoys, learns and dies in the manner in which it is destined to do so.[3]

Following Mahidāsa, Gośāla conceived the world as a rational purposive order, a system in which everything has that place and function assigned to it which contribute to the well-being of the whole. It is to one and the same order that we may give the name fate, necessity, nature, destiny, providence, reason. It is the system in which chance has no

predicate "radiant" (pabhassara) to mind (citta), or rather to the life-continuum (bhaṅga-citta). Aṅguttara-nikāya, I, p. 10.

[1] Dīgha-nikāya, I. 53.

[2] Uvāsaga Dasāo (with Abhayadeva's commentary), VI-VII; Sāmaññaphala-sutta (with Buddhaghosa's commentary); Hitopadeśa, Introd., 17-19.

[3] Dial. B. II, 72-73.

place, and which admits of no other cause whatever for the depravity or purity of beings than all that is implied in the word Fate or Destiny.[1]

II. Class or Species (*Saṅgati*).—The attainment of a certain peculiar condition, and of a certain peculiar character on the part of all things, all lives, all beings, depends in part on the class or type or species to which they belong. It is partly according to their position in this class or that that they possess certain special properties, that they have certain physical characteristics, that they inherit certain peculiar habits, develop certain faculties, and so on. Thus for example fire is hot, ice is cold, water is liquid, stone is hard, a thorn is sharp, a peacock is painted, the sandal tree possesses fragrance, the elephant's cub, if it does not find leafless and thorny creepers in the green wood, becomes thin; the crow avoids the ripe mango, etc.[2]

III. Nature (*Bhāva*).—Buddhaghosa explains Gośāla's term nature as 'the peculiar nature of each being.'[3] With reference to Naturalism Aśvaghoṣa speaks of Nature (prakṛiti)[4] as being a property or tendency (pravṛitti), such as heat is of fire, and fluidity of water. We have the same explanation from Śaṅkarācārya, Śīlāṅka and others.[5] Āryaśūra, following some older Buddhist authority, speaks of a Non-Causalist (Ahetu-vādin) as professing the view that "the universe is self-caused, self-generated" (svābhāvikaṁ jagad idaṁ).[6]

[1] Niyati, dṛiṣṭa, daiva, Pubbekata-hetu. *cf.* Gough's Vaiśeṣika-sūtra, pp. 189-190: A certain desire or aversion arises through destiny. In illustrating this the commentator refers to these two facts: the need of youth for love, without previous experience, and natural aversion towards snakes.

[2] Buddhacarita, IX. 47, 48, 52; Śīlāṅka's Sūtrakṛitāṅga Ṭīkā, p. 30; Sarvadarśana-saṅgraha, p. 7. The same is the view of Kaṇāda (*vide* Vaiśeṣika sūtra, VI. 2. 13: A certain desire or aversion arises through particularity of race or species (jātiviśeṣāt), and also of the Buddhist Naturalists of Nepal (*vide* Illustrations of the Literature and Religion of the Buddhists, by Hodgson, pp. 105-110.

[3] Sumaṅgala Vilāsinī, I. 161: "bhāvo ti sabhāvo."

[4] Buddhacarita, IX. 47.

[5] Comy. on the Śvetāśvatara Upaniṣad, I. 1: svabhāvo-padārthānāṁ pratiniyatā śaktiḥ; Sūtra Kṛitāṅga-ṭīkā, 8.

[6] Jātaka-mālā, p. 148.

Thus according to Gośāla's view the world originates and develops from its inherent force or immanent energy. It is also probable that he sought for the explanation of the diversity of appearance, characteristics, habits and behaviour of things in nature. He conceived Nature as a self-evolving activity. Nature has two modes of operation: by one mode things come to pass and by the other they cease to be (pravṛitti and nivṛitti). More accurately, he seems to have understood by Nature the specific faculties or characteristics of a living substance other than those which it possesses in common with the race or species.

Ethics.

The details of Gośāla's ethics are unknown. But the little that we know enables us to say that there are many points of similarity between him and the Stoics. We may preface our discussion of Gośāla's ethics with the following remarks of Prof. Adamson on the Stoic Physics. "The Stoics will not admit in the universe any element of chance, nor any element of freedom of will. It is true......that the wise man...is at the same time called free; but what the Stoics meant by 'free' in this connexion is best explained by the one illustration which they employ—a dog tied under a chariot." "Their emphasis on the mechanical side tends to give great prominence to the Stoic notion of the fate under which all things operate. The difficulties for their moral system involved in that conception they endeavoured to evade by giving equal emphasis to the teleological interpretation. The world is not only a mechanical system but a system of reason."[1]

Among the views of the Sophists, Buddha regarded the fatalistic doctrine of Gośāla as the least desirable. In his opinion the doctrine of fate, like the doctrines of chance, Providence, and so forth, does not afford a rational ground

[1] Development of Greek Philosophy, pp. 273-274.

upon which to base a moral philosophy.[1] Buddhaghosa in particular draws a distinction between the moral effect of Gośāla's doctrine on one hand, and that of the doctrines of Pūraṇa Kassapa and Ajita on the other. Pūraṇa by propounding a theory of the passivity of soul denied action. Ajita by his annihilationistic theory denied retribution. Whereas Gośāla by his doctrine of fate or non-causation denied both action and its result.[2]

Mahāvīra's criticism is in effect the same. For he too thinks that if all things be unalterably fixed and there be no such thing as strength or power or exertion, then where is the ground for moral distinctions between good and evil, or where is the ground for our moral responsibility or freedom.[3] (This criticism will be modified later.)

Gośāla had to say something regarding the many paths of virtue (paṭipadā). He spoke of eight kinds of action, five of which are sensuous and the rest are mental, vocal and bodily. He perhaps distinguished mental acts from word and deed as half-action (upaḍḍha-kamma).

The *āśrama*-theory of the Brāhman jurists was based on a notion of the gradual development of self. As a Brāhman mathematician (Gaṇaka) told Buddha, the Brāhmans laid down their moral injunctions in an ascending order (anupubba-sikkhā), as a mathematician counts the numbers, one, two, three, and so on. But it was at Gośāla's hands that the Brahmanic *āśrama*-theory came to be distinctly formulated as a biological principle of evolution in its application to education.[4]

The gradual development of self.

Babyhood begins with the day of birth, and lasts for a period of seven days. It is the dull or semi-conscious stage of

[1] Aṅguttara-nikāya, I. 286 ; III. 61.

[2] Sumaṅgala-Vilāsinī, I. 166.

[3] Uvāsaga Dasāo, VI-VII.

[4] Majjhima-nikāya, III. 1. See Deussen's note on Kramamukti in his All. Gesch. der Philosophie.

a man's life. Babyhood is followed by the play-time, and that again by the trial-time, when the child attempts to walk. The trial-time is duly succeeded by the erect-time, when the child is able to walk. When he becomes older he is sent to learn under a teacher. In course of time he renounces the world and masters, sooner or later, all that his teacher knows. Subsequently comes a time when he realises that what his teacher taught was not all, that in fact it was nothing (na kiñci āha). These are the eight developmental stages (aṭṭha purisa-bhūmiyo) through which every man must pass in order to reach perfection, to become a Jina.[1] It is not difficult to understand that Gosāla's doctrine of the eight developmental stages of man was a physical antecedent of Buddha's doctrine of eight higher spiritual ranks (aṭṭha purisapuggalā). In Gosāla's division an infant is placed in the lowest stage of development, while in Buddha's division the lowest rank is filled by a *Sotāpanna*, *i.e.*, a recluse who has advanced in his religious efforts far enough to be sure of his final success. The contrast between the two doctrines is important historically as indicating a transition from a biological division to a moral or spiritual one.

3. *Post-script.*

The results of our latest investigations into Makkhali's views are thus summed up in our paper on "The Ājīvikas," Pt. I, pp. 23-27, together with a short account of the sources of information :—

1. *Jaina Sources*—(*a*) Sūyagaḍaṁga (I. 1. 2. 1-14; I. 1. 4. 7-9; II. 1. 29; II. 6) with Sīlāṅka's Ṭīkā.
   (*b*) Bhagavatī Sūtra (Saya XV, Uddesa I) with Abhayadeva's Commentary.

[1] Dial. B. II, p. 72; Appendix to Hoernle's Uvāsaga-Dasāo, II, p. 24. The eight stages are : manda bhūmi, khiḍḍā bhūmi, vīmaṁsā bhūmi, ujngata bhūmi, sekha bhūmi, samaṇa bhūmi, jina bhūmi, paṇṇaka bhūmi. *Cf.* Fausböll's Jātaka, IV, pp. 496-97 : manda-dasaka-bhāvaṁ, khiḍḍādasakabhāvaṁ, vaṇṇadasakabhāvaṁ, etc.

(*c*) Bhagavatī Sūtra (Saya XV, Uddesa I) with Abhayadeva's Commentary.

(*d*) Leumann's Das Aupapātika Sūtra (Secs. 118 and 120).

2. *Buddhist Sources*—(*a*) Sāmaññaphala Sutta (Dīgha, I, pp. 53-54) with Buddhaghosa's Commentary.

(*b*) Saṁyutta Nikāya, III, p. 69, ascribes the first portion of the Sāmaññaphala account of Gosāla's views, N'atthi hetu, n'atthi paccayo, etc., to Pūrana Kassapa.

(*c*) Aṅguttara Nikāya (Pt. I, p. 286) with the Manorathapūraṇi confounds Makkhali Gosāla apparently with Ajita Kesa-kambala.

(*d*) Aṅguttara Nikāya (Pt. III, pp. 383-84) with the Manoratha-Pūraṇi represents Kassapa as if he were a disciple of Makkhali Gosāla.

(*e*) Mahasaccaka Sutta (Majjhima I, p. 231); *cf.* also I, p. 36.

(*f*) The Chinese and Tibetan versions of the Sāmaññaphala Sutta, translated in Rockhill's Life of the Buddha, where the doctrines of the six Heretics are hopelessly mixed up.

(*g*) Trenckner's Milinda Pañho, p. 5.

(*h*) Mahābodhi-Jātaka (No. 528), *cf.* Āryaśūra's Jātaka-Mālā, XXIII.

1. Gosāla was, to start with, the propounder of a 'doctrine of the change through re-animation' (*pauṭṭapariahārvāda*),[1] or, better, of a theory of natural transformation (pariṇāmavāda),[2] which he came to formulate from the generalisation of the periodical re-animations of plant life. This is the central idea of his system according to the Bhagavatī account.

[1] The term is so rendered by Prof. Leumann. See his translation of the extracts from the Bhagavatī, XV, in Rockhill's Life of the Buddha, Appendix II, p. 251.

[2] The term implied in the adjective pariṇata, *cf.* the Dīgha, I, p. 53.

2. The basic idea of this theory as explained and illustrated in the Bhagavatī and in the Sāmaññaphala Sutta implies a process of natural and spiritual evolution through ceaseless rounds of births and deaths,[1] *i. e.*, *saṁsāra-suddhi*, as the doctrine is aptly summarised in the Majjhima[2] and in the Mahābodhi Jātaka.[3]

3. The *Pariṇāmavāda* seeks to explain the diversity of the organic world by these three principles—

(*a*) Fate (niyati=niyai)[4]

(*b*) Species (saṅgati=saṅgai[5]=pariyāya)[6]

(*c*) Nature (bhāva=sabhāva)[7]

"Niyati-saṅgati-bhāva-pariṇatā."[8]

4. The organic world is characterised by six constant and opposed phenomena, *viz.*, gain and loss, pleasure and pain, life and death.

"Savvesiṁ pāṇāṇaiṁ savvesiṁ bhūyāṇaiṁ
Savvesiṁ jīvāṇaiṁ savvesiṁ sattāṇaiṁ
imāiṁ saṇaikkamaṇiāiṁ vāgaraṇāiṁ
vāgarai—taṁ lābhaṁ, alābhaṁ, suhaṁ
dukhaṁ jiveyaṁ, maraṇaṁ."[9]

5. The *Pariṇāmavāda* involves a conception of the infinity of time with the recurrent cycles of existence, and the same theory conveys a great message of hope by inculcating that even a dew-drop is so destined as to attain in course of natural evolution to the highest state of perfection in humanity.

[1] Dīgha, I, p. 54: sandhāvitvā saṁsaritvā dukhass' antaṁ karissanti, *cf.* the Bhagavatī text quoted by Prof. Leumann (Rockhill's Life of the Buddha, App. II, p. 253, f. n. 3):—anupuvveṇaṁ khavaitta pacchā sijjhanti bujjhanti jāva aṁtaṁ kareṁti.

[2] Majjhima, I, p. 31.

[3] Fausböll's Jātaka, V, p. 228.

[4] The Prākrit form of *niyati* occurs in the Sūyagaḍaṅga, I. 1. 2. 4.

[5, 6] The forms saṅgai and pariyāya are to be found in the Sūyagaḍaṅga, I. 1. 2. 3; I. 1. 4. 8.

[7] According to Buddhaghosa's comment, bhāvo=sabhāvo, Sumaṅgalavilāsinī, I, p. 161.

[8] Dīgha, I, p. 53. Buddhaghosa explains *pariṇatā* as meaning diversified (nānāppakāraṁ pattā).

[9] The passage is an extract from the Bhagavatī, Saya, XV, Uddesa. I.

6 The longest period or duration fixed for the evolution of life from the meanest thing on earth to the greatest in man covers 84 hundred thousand *mahākalpas.*[1]

7. This necessitates a division of time into *mahākalpas, kalpas, antarakalpas* and so forth, during which the universe of life progresses onward along the fixed path of evolution.[2]

8. The theory of progression itself necessitates the classification of the living substances on different methods, and groups them on a graduated scale in different types of existence which are considered as unalterably fixed.

9. The *Pariṇāmavāda* seeks to establish, even by its fatalistic creed, a moral government of law in the universe where nothing is dead, where nothing happens by chance, and where all that is and all that happens and is experienced are unalterably fixed as it were by a pre-determined law of nature.

10. It teaches that as man is pre-destined in certain ways and as he stands highest in the gradations of existence, his freedom, to be worth the name, must be one within the operation of law, and that the duty of man as the highest of beings is to conduct himself according to law, and so to act and behave himself as not to trespass on the rights of others, to make the fullest use of one's liberties, to be considerate and discreet, to be pure in life, to abstain from killing living beings, to be free from earthly possessions, to reduce the necessaries of life to a minimum, and to strive for the best and highest, *i.e.*, Jinahood, which is within human powers.[3]

11. The fatalistic creed which is a logical outcome of *Pariṇāmavāda* confirms the popular Indian belief that action

[1] Bhagavatī text quoted by Prof. Leumann. See Rockhill's Life of the Buddha, App. II, p. 253, f. n. 3, Dīgha, I, p. 54.

[2] Rockhill's *Life of the Buddha*, App. II, 253-54; *Dīgha*, *I*, p. 54.

[3] Dīgha, I, p. 54; *Aṅguttara*, III, pp. 383-84; *Majjhima*, *I*, p. 238; *Aupapātika Sūtra*, Sec. 120.

has its reward and retribution and that heaven and hell are the inevitable consequences hereafter of merits and demerits of this life.

12. In accordance with the deterministic theory of Gośāla, man's life has to pass through eight developmental stages or periods (aṭṭhapurisabhūmiyo),[1] at each of which the physical growth proceeds side by side with the development of the senses and of mind with its moral and spiritual faculties[2]; and from this underlying theory of interaction of body and mind it follows that bodily discipline (kāya-bhāvanā)[3] is no less needed for purification of soul than mental (citta-bhāvanā).

13. The division of mankind, or, better, of living beings, into six main types (abhijātis) involves a conception of mind which is colourless by nature and falls into different types—*nīlakāya*, *pītakāya*, etc.—by the colouring of the different habits and actions, and hence the supreme spiritual effort of man consists in restoring mind to its original purity, *i.e.*, rendering it colourless or supremely white by purging it of all impurities that have stained it."[4]

II. The Sceptics.

(*Ajñāna-vādins.*)

Mahāvīra's expression Aṇṇāniya or Ajñānika has reference to Sañjaya and his school[5]; Buddha's expression is Amarā-vikkhepika, or 'Eel-wriggler,' its alternative form being Vāca-vikkhepika, Equivocator or Prevaricator.[6] The former

[1] Dīgha, I, p. 54.

[2] Sumaṅgala-Vilāsinī, I, pp. 162-163.

[3] Majjhima, I, p. 238.

[4] Dīgha, I, 53; Aṅguttara, III, pp. 383-84; Sumaṅgala-Vilāsinī, I, p. 162; Majjhima, I, p. 36.

[5] Uttarādhyayana Sūtra, XVIII. 22-23, *cf.* Sūtra-kritāṅga, I. 6, 27; I. 12, 1-2; II. 2, 79.

[6] Dīgha-nikāya, I. 24-28; I. 58 (Dial. B. III, 37-41; 75): Sumaṅgala-vilāsinī, I, p. 168; "Sañjaya-vādo Amarā-vikkhepe vutta-nayo eva."

expression has been freely translated by Prof. Jacobi as Agnostic,[1] a term coined by Huxley in 1869.

The correspondence between the two terms Ajñānikas and Agnostics.

In spite of the fact that the two terms Ajñānikas and Agnostics are the same both etymologically and morphologically, we must be cautious in using a modern English term as a synonym for an ancient Indian expression. In India it was "Viśvakarman" who was the first to define an Agnostic or a Sceptic,[2] as one who is "enwrapt in misty cloud" (nīhārena prāvṛita), and "with lips that stammer" (jalpya).[3] "Viśvakarman" had evidently in mind one or all of these hymn-chanters or Vedic thinkers: (1) Those who doubted the existence of Indra[4]; (2) "Parameṣṭhin" who saw no possibility of knowing any cause or reality beyond the original matter: "who verily knows and who can here declare it, whence it was born and whence comes this creation? The gods are later than the world's production. Who knows then whence it first came into being?......(the Sun) verily knows it, or perhaps he knows not"[5]; (3) Dīrghatamas who was ignorant for the sake of knowledge of the nature of a first cause.[6] In the language of subsequent thinkers we come across these two expressions: Avidyā or ignorance and Vicikitsā or perplexity. The connotation of the term Avidyā, as employed by the Muṇḍakas and Vājasaneyas, is anything but transcendental knowledge (parāvidyā), the knowledge of Brahman (Brahma-vidyā), and anything but that which is conducive to an ideal self-realisation. The Muṇḍakas employed another term saṁśaya or doubt, probably in reference to the Keniyas who were of opinion that the know-all does not know at all, while the know-nothing knows everything. In Āsuri's opinion Perplexity (vicikitsā) Faith

[1] The Sanskrit word for Agnostic or Sceptic is not to be found in Viśvakarman hymn.

[2] Jacobi's Jaina-sūtras, Part 2, p. XXVI.

[3] Griffith's Ṛig-veda, X. 82, 7.

[4-6] Griffith's Ṛig-veda, VIII. 89, 3; X. 129, 6-7; I. 164, 6.

(Śraddhā), want of Faith (aśraddhā), and the rest, are all mind or mental states[1]; and in the teaching of Naciketas Vicikitsā is a philosophic doubt as to man's existence after death: Some say, he is; others, he is not.[2]

In Mahāvīra's definition the Agnostics (aṇṇāniyā) are those who pretend to be intelligent, but are in fact unfamiliar with truth and have not got rid of perplexity or puzzlement (*vitigicchatiṇṇā*). They are ignorant teachers who teach ignorant pupils, and without proper investigation or examination of knowledge speak untruth.[3] Mahāvīra employs two terms Ignorance (aṇṇāna) and Perplexity (vitigicchā) to convey almost the same sense, and Śīlāṅka speaks of various types of ignorance or doubt.[4]

Buddha's expression 'Eel-wriggling' (amarā-vikkhepa) corresponds to King Ajāta-sattu's term 'manner of prevarication' (vācavikkhepa). Both are connected with the name of the Sceptic Sañjaya, and signify a sort of indifferent or neutral attitude of some thinkers toward certain problems of metaphysical speculation,—such problems as those which are concerned with *pre-ens, post-ens,* the first cause, the final cause, future life, retribution, and so forth. However, both of these terms are rather vague in their connotation, and we need not feel wonder if they are replaced elsewhere by such terms as Perplexity (vicikitsā), Doubt (saṁsaya), and the like.[5]

In the Buddhist literature we have mention of three types of Perplexity: the hindrance-type (nīvaraṇa), the fetter-type (saṁyojana), and the Orambhāgiya fetter-type. The first type can be put away by an ordinary reflective mind by means

[1] Bṛihad Āraṇyaka Upaniṣad, I 5, 3

[2] Kaṭhopaniṣad, I. 20: "yêyam prete vicikitsā manuṣye: astîtyeke nâyam astîti caike."

[3] Sūtra-kritāṅga, I. 12. 2.: "Aṇṇāniyā te kusalāvi saṁtā, asaṁthuyā no vitigicchatiṇṇā. Akoviyā āhu akoviyehiṁ, ananuvi-ittu musaṁ vayaṁti" *Cf.* Jacobi's translation. ananuvritta = Pali ananuvicca.

[4] Śīlāṅka's commentary on *ibid*

[5] Dhammasaṅgaṇi, 425; Vibhaṅga, pp. 255-258; Mrs. Rhys Davids' Buddhist Psychological Ethics, pp. 115-116.

of faith (saddhā) and discursive judgment (vicāra); the second can be got rid of only by an unwavering faith and a deep insight into truth; and the third by the power of faith and introspection.

Nīvaraṇa is generally defined as that state of mind which acts as a hindrance to higher life and insight.[1] It is otherwise called *ceto-khila* or something that locks the door of the heart, *manovilekha* or something that scarifies the heart,—in other words something that steels the heart against all tender and higher feelings and aspirations.

The number of Hindrances is generally calculated to be five, the fifth being 'Perplexity.' The Abhidhamma texts on the other hand, give them as six, the fifth and sixth being 'Perplexity' (vicikicchā), and 'Ignorance' (avijjā) respectively.[2] "In the Sutta Piṭaka," says Mrs. Rhys Davids, "the Hindrances form a category of five, ignorance being excluded......This discrepancy is not noticed by Buddhaghosa."[3]

The category of six hindrances was only an extension of the category of five,—the outcome of a further analytical distinction of the fifth—Perplexity—into Doubt proper and Ignorance. Patañjali's Yogasūtra and Vācaspati's gloss throw further light on the point, for obviously Buddha's term 'hindrance' (nīvarana) is the same as Patañjali's term 'obstacle' (antarāya). Patañjali, in agreement with Buddha, defines an obstacle as that which causes distractions to the mind (citta-vikṣepa).[4] Patañjali's category of obstacles includes two terms—Doubt (saṁśaya) and Erroneous view (bhrāntidarśana),[5] corresponding to Buddha's category of

[1] Buddhist Psychological Ethics, IX. 310: "The Hindrances are to be understood as states which muffle, enwrap or trammel thought." *Cf.* Compendium of Philosophy, p. 172.

[2] The Dhammasaṅgaṇi, 1152; The Compendium of Philosophy, p. 172.

[3] The Buddhist Psychological Ethics, p. 310.

[4] Yoga-sūtra, I. 30.

[5] *Cf.* Vātsyāyana bhāṣya on the Nyāya-sūtra, IV. 3.

six hindrances which includes the two terms Doubt and Ignorance.

Vyāsa's Comments on the Yogasūtra (I. 30) is practically the same as Buddhaghosa's on Buddha's expressions. Neither Vyāsa nor Buddhaghosa determines the nature of the psychological relation between Doubt and Ignorance, Scepticism and Agnosticism. In the commentary of Vācaspati on the Yogasūtra the point has been properly threshed out. According to Vācaspati, Doubt and False-knowledge do not differ much from each other, and yet the former is separately mentioned with a view to specifying its precise signification. The special characteristic of doubt is the touching and evading of both sides of a question,[1] indeed in this respect doubt may be regarded as a sub-head of false-knowledge.

Now in accordance with the general Buddhist view the difference between the Hindrance and the Fetter type of doubt, as that between the Fetter and the *Orambhāgiya* type, is one of degree rather than that of kind. In the Abhidhamma Books the two pairs of words are set forth in definition in identical terms, although it is not to be supposed that their underlying conceptions are identical. An 'average man' can put away the Hindrance by a professed faith in the Teacher, the Doctrine and the Order; a young inquirer by an implicit faith in the system which he aspires to be acquainted with; a reflective student by his discursive judgment (vicāra). A 'stream-attainer' can, on the other hand, put away the Fetter by his faith unwavering (aveccappasāda) and insight philosophic (dassana), while an Āryan in a higher stage of spirituality can put away the Fetter inherent in the lower nature (orambhāgiya) by the power of faith (saddhā-bala) and introspection (bhāvanā). Thus each type has two sides—religious comprising the emotional and volitional, and intellectual comprising the metaphysical and psycho-ethical. The religious

[1] *Cf.* Nyāya Sūtras, I. 1. 23; IV. 2. 4.

doubt can be got rid of by the faith professed, articulated or confirmed, and the intellectual by discursive judgment, philosophic insight or introspection. The religious aspect of the Hindrance is technically called *cetokhila* or 'bolt of the heart,'[1] a term similar in meaning to the Jaina *duhasejjā* or 'bed of suffering'[2]; the intellectual aspect is known as *tamas* or 'darkness.'[3]

Cetokhila is not far removed from, and touches indeed in many essential points *assaddhā*, "the absence of faith" or "irreverence" as defined in the Vibhaṅga (p. 371). Similarly *tamas* can be shown not to differ much from *avijjā* or *aññāna* (ignorance) as defined in the Dhammasaṅgaṇi (1152, 1162), both being at bottom grounded in the lack of understanding, the lack of knowledge. The same remark holds true of other higher types of doubt, the Fetter and the *Orambhāgiya* fetter. Thus in this analysis the sceptic appears as an enemy 'of the divines and the gravest philosophers.' But the Fetter type might be broadly distinguished from the Hindrance as doubt 'consequent to science and inquiry' from scepticism 'antecedent to all study and philosophy.'[4] It needs no mention that *tamas* as defined in the Vibhaṅga (p. 371) denotes a philosophic doubt or Scepticism proper, or that *avijjā* or *aññāna* as defined in the Dhammasaṅgaṇi (1152, 1162) denotes Agnosticism even as we now understand it. Moreover it may be seen from the views of Sañjaya that the same philosopher tends to be an Agnostic when he freely confesses his inability to know

[1] Majjhima, I, p. 101; Dīgha, III, Saṅgīti Suttanta, *sub voce cetokhila*; etc.

[2] Sthānāṅga (ed. Dhanapati), p. 289.

[3] Vibhaṅga, p. 367.

[4] *Cf.* Hume's distinction between two types of scepticism. "There is a species of scepticism [such as the Cartesian doubt], antecedant to all study and philosophy." "There is another species of scepticism, consequent to science and inquiry when men are supposed to have discovered either the absolute fallaciousness of their mental faculties or their unfitness to reach any fixed determination in all those curious subjects of speculation about which they are commonly employed." An Inquiry concerning Human understanding, section XII.

the ultimate beginning and end of things which is virtually the same as admitting that these are unknown and unknowable; and a sceptic when he doubts or hesitates to admit the correctness of all bold assertions about matters beyond human cognition.

CHAPTER XXII.

SAÑJAYA.

In the Buddhist annals Sañjaya is best known as a Sceptic. It is not clear from the existing accounts if he is the same personage as Sañjaya the wanderer, the previous teacher of Sāriputta, the chief disciple of Buddha. The Buddhist records on the latter's life are all based upon the account in the Mahāvagga.[1] There we are told that Sāriputta was before joining the Buddhist school an adherent of Sañjaya. One may reasonably object to the identification of Sañjaya the sceptic who is designated in the Sāmaññaphala Sutta as Sañjaya Belaṭṭha-putta (ŏr Belaṭṭhi-putta) with Sañjaya described in the Vinaya Mahāvagga and the Dhammapada commentary as a Paribbājaka. The historical justification of such an identification is that scepticism is associated in the Buddhist records with the name Sañjaya. We must also remember that the Mahāvagga is at least a century later than the portions of the Buddhist canon where the name of the Belaṭṭha-putta occurs in several connexions and where one can expect to find not a single reference to Sañjaya Paribbājaka. We have also to consider that the Belaṭṭha-putta, too, was a wanderer and the founder of a religious order and of a school of thought in Rājagaha. The story of Sāriputta's conversion to the Buddhist faith is of considerable importance as it shows how ripe was the intellect of the disciple of a sceptic to welcome the Buddhist theory of causation which lay at the root of a critical method of inquiry.

An account of his life.

[1] Mahāvagga, I. 23-24. *Cf.* The Aggasāvakavatthu in the Dhammapada-Commentary, I.

The Buddhists tell us that when Sāriputta, accompanied by Moggallāna and two hundred and fifty other disciples, left the school of Sañjaya, the latter fainted, bled and died. Sāriputta joined the Buddhist school in the second year of Buddha's career. Neither the Jaina nor the Buddhist account seems wholly true. In the Sāmaññaphala and other Suttas, Sañjaya of the Belaṭṭha clan is spoken of in the same terms as Pūraṇa and other Sophistic teachers. Buddhaghosa, although a later authority, furnishes some useful information. He informs us that a certain Wanderer named Suppiya was a disciple of Sañjaya Paribbājaka.[1] In the Brahmajāla Sutta Suppiya is referred to as a teacher who was opposed to the Buddhist school and who disparaged the Buddha and his doctrine and disciples.[2] King Aśoka dedicated a cave-dwelling to a school of Wanderers, namely the Suppiyas.[3] In the list of the Aṅguttaranikāya (III. 276) Buddha expressly mentions the name of the Aviruddhakas (Un-inimicals or Friends) as a school of thought distinct from the Muṇḍa-sāvakas and others. The two names—Friends or Good-natured ones seem to have been applied by Buddha and the Buddhist emperor Aśoka to one and the same school, namely, that of Sañjaya of the Belaṭṭha clan. The disciples of Sañjaya were from the point of view of their philosophical doctrine known as Agnostics, Sceptics or Eel-wrigglers, and from the point of view of their moral conduct as Friends or Good-natured ones. If so, we may conclude that the school of Sañjaya survived long after his death, at least, till the reign of King Aśoka, *i.e.*, 3rd century B. C. Sañjaya was an elder contemporary of the Buddha. He was the Pyrrho of India,—a famous wanderer and founder of school, highly honoured in the country. No further details of his life are known.

1, 2 Sumaṅgala Vilāsinī, I. 35; Dial. B. II, p. 1.

3 The Cave Inscription, No. 3.

His Philosophy.

The Dogmatists and the Sceptics contrasted.

In the estimation of Mahāvīra and Buddha, particularly of the latter, the Eternalists and the Annihilationists, the Extensionists and the non-Extensionists,—all are Dogmatists (Diṭṭhi-vādins, Diṭṭhigatas), their cant being: 'Nothing save the doctrine we uphold, nothing save the dogma we preach, is true.'[1] These Dogmatist philosophers were divided in opinion on such knotty questions of metaphysics as these: Is the world eternal or is it non-eternal? Is the world finite or is it infinite? Is there another world or is there not? Is soul after death subject to decay or not, corporeal or incorporeal, conscious or unconscious? Is there or is there not any reward or retribution? Are there any 'chance-born' beings or are there not? Does a perfect man continue to exist after death or not? Whilst thus a fierce battle was raging in the country there arose a school of thinkers, who kept themselves aloof from all those conflicts of speculation, and cultivated an attitude of indifference or suspended judgments as the best way of securing the imperturbability of mind. They were the Friends or Good-natured ones, the disciples of Sañjaya, who agreed with the Eternalists and the Annihilationists in regarding happiness as the end of life's activities. But they differed from the latter as to ways and means. Whereas for the Dogmatist philosophers the path to happiness lay through the heroic grappling with problems and ascertainment of truth, for the Sceptics the path was just the reverse, being the evasion of problems and suspension of judgment.

Sañjaya and Pyrrho.

In all these points the disciples of Sañjaya are at one with the disciples of Pyrrho, notably Timon. Sañjaya, like Pyrrho, raised scepticism to a scientific doctrine, and thus prepared the way for a critical

[1] Sthānāṅga, IV. 4; Sūtra-Kritāṅga, I. 1. 2. 21; Dīgha-nikāya, I. 13-39; Majjhima-nikāya, I. 483-489; Kosala-Saṁyutta; etc. "Idam eva saccaṁ, moghaṁ aññanti evaṁ diṭṭhi."

method of investigation in philosophy. Sañjaya differed from Dīrghatamas, who was ignorant for the sake of knowledge, (and from the Keniyas who made this definite statement that the know-all does not know at all, while the know-nothing knows everything), just as Pyrrho differed from some of the Academic Sceptics who doubted in order to know. As the former with the Eternalists and Annihilationists, so the latter together with the Stoics and Epicureans, marks a distinct period of thought and furnishes a connecting link in the movement of philosophy. Again the former was an Indian, and the latter is said to have accompanied Alexander in his Indian campaign. Pyrrho of Elis "studied philosophy under Indian Gymnosophists and Chaldean Magi."[1]

Colebrooke identifies the Gymnosophists in Greek accounts with the Jains, but they should be identified rather with the Suppiyas, the disciples of Sañjaya. Lastly, the little that is known of Pyrrho's teaching is summed up by Prof. Zeller in the three following statements: "We can know nothing about the nature of things: Hence the right attitude towards them is to withhold judgment: The necessary result of suspending judgment is imperturbability."[2] Now let us sum up Sañjaya's doctrine in the words of two critics—Buddha and Śīlāṅka.

First, Buddha says: "There is a school of thinkers, who are Eel-wrigglers (Amarā-vikkhepikas). When they are asked a question on this or that, they equivocate and wriggle like an eel (or slip through like quick-silver), and their reason is one or another or all of the following four:—

Buddha's account of Sañjaya's doctrine.

(1-2) We neither know the good (kusala) nor the evil (akusala), as it really is. In such case, if we make a positive declaration either with regard to good or to evil, we may be

[1] Rolleston's "Teaching of Epictetus," p XXI.

[2] The Stoics, Epicureans and Sceptics. Reichel's translation, p. 492.

led away by conceit or pride,[1] or influenced by ill-will and resentment.[2] Under these conditions we may be proved wrong (musā), and that may cause us the pain of remorse and ultimately a hindrance to the tranquillity we aim at. Or, in the second place, we may fall into a grasping condition of heart (upādāna), which will culminate in a similar disturbance of peace.

(3-4) We neither know the good nor the evil as it really is. There are persons who are clever, subtle, expert, controversialists, hair-splitters (vāla-vedhi-rūpā), who go about, as it were, shattering the dogmas (diṭṭhigatas) of others. But we, on the other hand, are dull and stupid. Hence if we make a definite statement with regard to good or evil, they may join issue with us, ask us for reasons, and point out our errors. This may cause us, as before, the pain of remorse and disturb our imperturbability.

Thus fearing and abhorring the being wrong in an expressed opinion, the falling into a grasping condition of heart, or the joinder of issue, we declare nothing to be either good or bad; but on a question being put to us on this or that, we answer thus: Is A B? No. Is A not-B? No. Is A both B and not-B? No. Is A neither B nor not-B? No.

(1) "I don't take it thus—evam pi me no.

(2) But I don't take it the other way—tathā ti pi me no.

(3) But I advance no different opinion—aññathā ti pi me no.

(4) And I don't deny your position—iti ti pi me no.

(5) And I don't say it is neither the one nor the other—no ti ti pi me no."[3]

[1] Chando vā rago vā. Rhys Davids translates this "feelings or desires." We have followed here Buddhaghosa.

[2] Doso vā paṭigho vā. According to Buddhaghosa's comments, the two terms mean wounded vanity or revengeful feeling.

[3] Buddhaghosa says that by (2) the Eel-wrigglers rejected the doctrine of Eternalism (sassata-vāda); by (3) that of modified Eternalism (Ekacca-sassata-vāda); by (4) that of Annihilation (Ucchedaṁ); and by (5) the view of the Dialecticians (Takkivāda Sumaṅgala-Vilāsinī, I, p. 116. Dial. B, II. 37-41.

Secondly, Śīlāṅka says: Literally, the 'Agnostics' are those in whom there is 'ignorance,' or 'who walk about in ignorance.' They think: "Even if we avowedly maintain a view—'That this is good' (kuśala), we are conscious that we are not acquainted with truth, the matter is not familiar to our knowledge. Indeed we have not as yet got beyond 'perplexity'—perplexity which is blindness and delusion of the mind (cittâśuddhi, cittabhrānti)

Śīlāṅka's account.

"Some conceive the existence of an all-seeing soul, while others controvert it. Some speak of an all-pervading self (sarvagatâtmā); others contend that the body being such an entity, it cannot be all-pervading. Some estimate that soul is equal to a digit in size, while others say that it is equal to a grain of rice. Some posit a soul that has a material form (mūrtam), while others maintain that it is formless (amūrtam). Some point out that the heart is the seat of soul, while others oppose them by saying that the forehead would be the right place......"

How can there be an agreement of views among these philosophers?......Many moral injuries (bahudoṣāḥ) may result from the issues of such antagonistic blunders. (Hence let us keep far from the madding crowd and ignoble strife). For us ignorance is far better than these follies."[1]

The underlying motive of the above accounts is to make Sañjaya appear as an intellectual coward. These are correct only in so far as we are told that his studious evasion of certain great questions of human mind and equivocal statements of his own position were apt to produce an intellectual torpor. But his views were probably not so confounding as they appear in the Buddhist or the Jaina representation thereof. If the matters were so simple as his opponents would have us believe, they might

Criticism of the Buddhist and Jaina accounts of Sañjaya's position. His place in the history of Indian philosophy and of philosophy generally.

[1] Sūtra-Kṛitāṅga-ṭīkā, pp. 451-452.

have been completely ignored. The very fact that his opponents were compelled to put his views to the hardest test argues that these could not be so easily shelved. Sañjaya had a large following in Northern India, a fact which goes at once to prove that there was some truth in his teaching that could appeal to so many thoughtful men. It is clear that he had studiously suspended his judgments only with regard to those great questions of which a decisive answer will ever remain a matter of speculation. Indeed the effect of his teaching on the course of Indian philosophy seems to have been twofold: first, that he by suspending his judgments on certain great questions of human mind came to indicate that their final answer lay beyond the domain of speculation; and secondly, that he called away the attention of the philosophers from fruitless inquiries and directed it towards the *Summum bonum* which is the attainment and preservation of mental equanimity.

Thus he came to be a true precursor of Mahāvīra who propounded a doctrine of antinomies (syādvāda) and of the Buddha who advocated a critical method of investigation (vibhājyavāda). Both Mahāvīra and Buddha were unanimous in declaring that there are certain mooted questions of cosmology, ontology, theology and eschatology on which a man is unable, constituted as he is, to pronounce a bold, authoritative or dogmatic opinion. And the questions which they put aside as inscrutable dilemmas are precisely those with regard to which Sañjaya had deliberately suspended his judgments. The main point in which his successors differed from him is that like him they did not consider those questions as fruitless inquiries. The inculcation of a Buddhist theory of causal genesis (paṭiccasamuppāda) afforded a new scientific way of approaching those questions. This fact is nowhere so clearly indicated as in the story of the conversion of Sāriputta, formerly a disciple of the veritable sceptic, to a system of philosophy which judges things critically in the light of a partly *a priori* principle, namely, the principle of causation. If it be admitted that Pyrrho of Elis had imbibed his sceptical bias from an Indian school of sceptics, one can at once see that the sceptical propaganda such as those of Sañjaya were the antecedents of critical philosophies alike in India and in Europe.

3. The Moralists.

(Vinaya-vādins)

According to Mahāvīra's definition, the Vinaya-vādins are those who consider truth to be untruth and call a bad man good. They are those various upholders of the doctrine of discipline who, without comprehending the truth (anovasaṁkhā), expound their tenets briefly as follows: "The objects of desire (atthā) are realised by us by means of *vinaya* alone."[1] The doctrine of discipline, no less than the doctrines of non-action and ignorance, is opposed to the Jaina doctrine of free-will activity (kiriya-vāda).[2] In commenting upon Mahāvīra's definition Śīlāṅka says: The Moralists (Vainayikas) act according to the principles of morality or moral discipline. They seek to gain a better future existence by set moral precepts alone.[3]

The definition of Vinaya-vāda.

Corresponding to Mahāvīra's Vinaya-vāda we have from the Buddha the expression *Sīlabbata-parāmāsa*, which is generally translated the affectation of moral vows, but really signifies the doctrine of moral discipline. In the Dhamma-saṅgaṇi[4] the above term is defined as that doctrine of teachers other than the Buddhists according to which the purity of character

Sīlabbata-parāmāsa.

[1] Sūtra-kṛitāṅga, I. 12, 3-4.

[2] *Ibid*, II. 2. 79; Uttarādhyayana Sūtra, XVIII. 23. Note that Jacobi translates Vinaya-vāda as "idolatry."

[3] Sūtra-kṛitāṅga-ṭīkā, p. 447: "Vainayikānāṁ vinayād eva kevalāt paralokam apicchataṁ." Śīlāṅka quotes from some older authority: "Vinaittā Vinayavādi."

[4] *Dhamma-saṅgaṇi*, 1005, 1119, 1138, etc:

"Ito bahiddā samaṇa-brāhmaṇānaṁ sīlena suddhivatena suddhi-sīlabbatena suddhīti—evarūpā diṭṭhi—ayaṁ vuccati sīlabbata-parāmāso."

is attainable only by morality, the observance of moral precepts, the fulfilment of the vows of chastity. Buddhaghosa says that by 'purity' we are to understand purity both moral and mental, ordinary and philosophic,[1] and that the term 'moral vow' includes the bovine vow, the canine vow, and such other vows, resorted to by some of the ascetics and penitent Brāhmans.[2] In the Vinaya texts Buddha is asked by a Brāhman if he was a Vinayavādi or mere Moralist. Apparently according to the Brāhman, a Moralist was one who cared only for a blind adherence to an accepted code of moral discipline. Although Buddha's answer was in the affirmative, his meaning was different from that of his interlocutor. He was ready to be called a Moralist only in the sense that he taught the subjugation of all immoral tendencies, that is to say, of all that is rooted in greed, hatred and delusion. Buddhaghosa wrongly takes the term *vinayavādi* to mean the destroyer of all moral laws of society.

The doctrine of outward morality or Formalism, along with Ātmanistic philosophy (also called Sakkāya-diṭṭhi) and Perplexity, yields under the critical analysis employed by the Buddha three pairs of opposite errors. The Ātmanistic philosophy, for instance, involves such a pair of opposed blunders as Eternalism and Annihilationism, the speculations about the finiteness and infinity of the world and the like. The pair of blunders involved in Perplexity comprises 'Agnosticism' and 'Scepticism.' Now the two extremes (dve antā) to be avoided or reconciled in regard to the Buddhist system of morals are briefly described by Buddha as 'the frivolity of worldly life' (kāmasukhallikānuyoga) on the one hand, and 'the barbarity of asceticism' (attakilamathānuyoga) on the other.[3]

[1], [2] Atthasālinī, pp. 348, 355, 377, etc. : "suddhiti kilesa-suddhi paramatthasuddhi bhūtaṁ vā nibbāṇam eva." See for Govata, Kukkura-vata, etc., Majjhima-nikāya, I. 397.

[3] Dhamma-cakka-pavattana Sutta: *cf.* Majjhima-nikāya, I. 166 foll.

All these dogmatic errors can be overcome by a true insight into truth.[1] The doctrine of outward morality was regarded by Buddha both as an erroneous dogma and a false path. The real meaning of the term Sīlabbata or Vinaya-vāda, as contrasted with the doctrines of Mahāvīra and Buddha, can be gleaned from the fragment on Morality (Sīla-kkhandha) incorporated in the first thirteen suttas of the Dīgha-nikāya.[2] Throughout this fragment Buddha's object is to make it quite clear that he was not a Moralist in the accepted sense of the term. Buddha says that the uninstructed might praise him only with regard to things trivial, matters of little value, and mere morality (sīla-mattaṁ). They might say, for example: "Abandoning slaughter and destruction of life, he is compassionate and kind to all living creatures: Abandoning theft, he takes only what is given and lives in honesty and purity of heart, and so forth." "It is not with regard to these things, but mainly with regard to matters more profound, subtle, comprehensible only by the wise, that he could be rightly praised (or blamed)." This fragment containing a statement of the moral precepts of the Buddhists occurs in a scattered form in the four corners of the Jaina and Buddhist literatures, and enables us to determine the moral teachings of other schools as contrasted with the ethical views of both Mahāvīra and Buddha. The fragment is divided into three sections: the short, the medium-length and long paragraphs on conduct. The rules of conduct contained in the first section were those observed by the Buddhists, Jains and other recluses. Each of these rules implies an antithesis which relates to the moral conduct of others. The following two sections are only an elaboration of the first. The details have reference to manifold practices and activities of the time. These may

The fundamental rules of conduct common to both the Jains and Buddhists: contrast with the codes of other schools.

[1] Dhamma-saṅgaṇi, 1009.

[2] Dial. B., pp. 3-26.

be broadly arranged under the following heads : (1) Religious, comprising rites and ceremonies—performance of various sacrifices ; polytheistic worship (deva-dhamma), such as the worship of the sun, moon and earth, the invocation of Siri, the goddess of luck ; making vows to the gods and paying them when the wishes are fulfilled ; pilgrimage to holy places ; bathing in the rivers in order to purify one's soul ; oracular answers from the gods ; etc. (2) Scientific, comprising the mathematical, the astrological, and the medical : foretelling the eclipses and aberrations of the heavenly bodies, the occurrences of earthquakes, the rainfall, the food-supply, the general conditions of existence and health, fixing lucky days for marriage, hostilities and other purposes ; counting numbers, summing up large totals ; practising as an oculist or as a surgeon, or as a doctor for children, etc. (3) Artistic, comprising architecture (vatthu-vijjā), painting, music, poetry, etc. (4) Popular practices—games, sports, amusements, festivities, and so forth. (5) Social, moral and political.

For our present purpose the fragment with its counterpart in the Jaina Aupapātika Sūtra[1] has value only in so far as it illustrates the moral teachings and practices prevalent in the country before and during the time of Mahāvīra and Buddha. These teachings may be taken to represent three systems of moral discipline : *first*, the system as expounded in the Dharma-sūtras and Gṛihya-sūtras ; *secondly*, that elaborated in the existing Nīti-literature ; and *thirdly*, that embodied in the Kāma-sūtras. The first system is concerned with the discussion of general principles of social morality, justice, and the duties of individuals in various capacities. The subject matter of this system is Dharma or juristic morals providing a standard mainly for the Brāhman. The second system is concerned with questions of polity and government, and the object which it seeks to secure is Artha—material advantage or prosperity. It provides a

[1] Secs. 62-130.

standard mainly for the King. The third system aims at teaching us how to regulate our individual and natural desires for pleasure (Kāma); it provides a standard mainly for the lover.

Thus all these systems are distinguished from a system of speculation (ānvikṣaki) of which the subject of investigation is Mokṣa or final release. Ānvikṣaki provides a standard mainly for the dispassionate recluse. Accordingly, we propose to make a brief survey of the moral standards of the time under Kāma (Erotic morals or Hedonism), Artha (Political morals or Utility), and Dharma (Juristic morals or Equity). These three systems were, according to tradition,[1] later developments out of a common mass of Vedic lore and their inter-dependence in secular Brahmanism is amply borne out by the fact that the general principles of morality which they inculcate are embedded in the treatises of veritably the same Brahmanical writers or schools. These systems can claim a place in the history of Indian philosophy on the ground that their teachings rest upon two accepted ideas of Brahmanical philosophy: (1) that all human arts inclusive of all human institutions such as those of marriage and the rest must be an imitation of or a conformation to divine arts as manifested through the purposive order of nature[2]: and (2) that all human systems must be conceived on a graduated scale in accordance with the fundamental truth of the gradual development of self-consciousness.[3]

[1] *Cf.* Kāmasūtra by Vātsyāyana, Chap. I, and Mahābhārata, Śāntiparva, Canto 9, V, 28. See Mr. H. C. Chakladar's paper on Vātsyāyana (Calcutta University Journal of the Dept. of Letters, Vol. IV).

[2] See *Ethics* of Mahidāsa Aitareya.

[3] See the Taittirīya philosophy under Varuṇa.

CHAPTER XXIII.

Teachers of Erotic Morals.

A gross hedonistic end implied in Erotic Morals.

Since Mahidāsa it has been recognised by many thinkers that happiness is the one end of all things. What we call bliss (ānanda) or contemplative joy is nothing but a culmination of the happiness resulting from satisfaction of various desires (kāmā). Hence as of existence, so of happiness there are infinite gradations. The lowest form of desire or feeling is appetitive. The next higher form is sensual in its varying degrees. It seems that Mahāvīra's expression Sensualism (sāya-vāda)[1] has direct reference to the sensualistic principles such as those expounded in Vātsāyana's Kāma-sūtra. (Abhaya-deva identifies *sāya-vāda* with the Buddhist system.) Buddha has a similar expression, Pañca-kāma-guṇa-diṭṭha-dhamma-nibbāṇa-vāda.[2] It is defined as an opinion of some teachers according to which the soul attains Nirvāṇa, *i.e.*, the fulfilment of all desires, through full indulgence of the five pleasures of sense. The term 'sensual desires' (kāmacchanda)[3] which is explained in numerous Buddhist texts, and considered as a hindrance to higher life (nīvaraṇa), has bearing upon the system of Kāma-sūtra.

The Buddhist Kāma-sutta[4] presupposes treatises on Erotic or Eugenic Morals, latterly systematised in the Kāma-sūtra ascribed to Vātsyāyana. The date of this work in its present form is unknown.[5] In its general structure it seems to resemble the Kauṭiliya Arthaśāstra.[6] It is particularly remarkable that

[1] Sthānāñga, IV. 4.

[2] Mahāniddesa, p. 2.

[3] Dial. B., II. 49-50.

[4] Suttanipāta; Mahāniddesa, 1-22.

[5,6] Mr. Chakladar has placed the date of the Kāmasūtra in the 3rd century A.D., and sought to prove that there is a wonderful agreement between the Kāmasūtra and the Kalpasūtra of Āpastamba.

the two works have each a chapter called 'Aupaniṣadikam' dealing with medicine and charms. The following fragment of Buddha seems to have reference to such Ātharvaṇa doctrine: "Some recluses and Brāhmaṇas make use of charms to make people lucky or unlucky, to procure abortion, to bring on dumbness . . . . . . cause virility, deprive a man of potency . . . . . ."[1]

Vātsyāyana and his predecessors.

In the concluding verses of the existing Kāmasūtra we are told that Vātsyāyana wrote a systematic treatise on the subject of Erotic Morals after the due consultation of older treatises of Bābhravya and others. And in the introductory chapter we have mention of Śvetaketu, the son of Uddālaka, Bābhravya of Pañcāla,[2] Dattaka, Cārāyaṇa, Suvarṇanābha, Ghoṭaka-mukha, and others as teachers who left only fragmentary works. Of these Śvetaketu is referred to as the earliest of them. In the body of the text their opinions are quoted and discussed. Ghoṭaka-mukha is mentioned in the ancient Buddhist records as a Brāhman teacher who had some conversation with the venerable Udena while the latter was staying at Benares. He plainly told Udena that he could not believe that there could be a virtuous hermit (*n'atthi dhammiko paribbājo*).

In the Majjhima-nikāya we have mention of four Vacchas or Vātsyas, all of whom were Wanderers and one was named Tevijja-Vacchagotta. Tevijja-Vacchagotta had a philosophical discussion with Buddha as to whether it is possible for a worldly man with worldly ties to make an end of suffering after death, *i.e.*, to attain immortality. Buddha answered in the negative, but he added that he knew of one within his experience who, even being a worldly man, succeeded in obtaining eternal life. Buddha did not give the name of the person,

[1] *Dial. B.*, II. 23-25.

[2] See Mr. Chakladar's remarks about Vābhravya (C. U. J. D. L., IV, pp. 87-89). His surmise about the association of the early history of *Erotic Science with Pañcāla seems quite sound.*

but merely mentioned him as an upholder of the doctrine of action, a believer in free-will activity (kamma-vādi kiriya-vādi).[1] But there is also mention of a Wanderer, Pilotika Vacchāyana. It would show that there was at the time a distinct school of Wanderers, known as the Vacchāyanas.[2] His question clearly shows that he was interested in mundane matters.

According to Hemacandra, Vātsyāyana was one of the names of Cāṇakya, the traditional author of the Kauṭiliya Artha-śāstra. This is at variance with the account of the Pañcatantra, which tells us that the Dharma-śāstras belong to Manu and others, the Artha-śāstras to Cāṇakya and others, and the Kāma-śāstras to Vātsyāyana and others.[3] Nevertheless Vātsyāyana's Kāma-sūtra shows, in its general structure and style, a resemblance to the Kauṭiliya Artha-śāstra.

Inter-connexion of Kāma-sūtra and Artha-śāstra.

It is expressly mentioned in the two works that the systems which they embody are, as contrasted with a philosophical system, altogether a practical way of life (lokayātrā). The point in which they differ is that the former lays the whole stress on Kāma or Pleasure, and the latter on Artha, Material advantage.[4] But we must remember that Kauṭilya assigns due place to pleasure in his system, when he says: One ought to enjoy pleasure or happiness, in so far as it does not conflict with the principles of law and polity; none should be deprived of happiness. Pleasure, advantage and righteousness form a category of three (trivarga). They are of equal (practical) value, and inter-dependent. When one of them is not cultivated the other two are impaired thereby.[5]

1, 2 Majjhima-nikāya, II. 158. Majjhima-nikāya, II. 183; I. 175.

3 "Tato Dharma-śāstrāni Manvādīni, Artha-śāstrāni Cāṇakyādīni, Kāma-śāstrāni Vātsyāyanādīni." Quoted by Shama Shastry, Indroduction to Kauṭiliya Arthaśāstra, p. VIII. The personal name of Vātsyâyana probably was Mallanāga.

4 Arthaśāstra, I. 7; XV. 1: "Artha eva pradhāna"; "Artha-mūlaṁ hi dharma-kāma iti."

5 Ibid, I. 7; XV. 1: "Dharmārthavirodhena kāmaṁ seveta, na nissukha syāt."

And we must note in justice to Vātsyāyana that in his introductory statement and concluding words he points out that the ultimate aim of his work is to teach the subjugation of the senses or self-conquest (indriya-jaya). With regard to this point his position is similar to all the Nīti-kāras, the writers on Polity. Particularly in his introductory chapter, he teaches us not to indulge in sensuality. He admits that of the three—good principle, advantage and sensuality, the first two are far superior to the last-mentioned object. He warns us of the dangers we have to meet on the way of pleasure: the loss of friendship with the good, association with obnoxious people, waste of fortune, impurity, fear, nervous weakness, distrust, and fall in public estimation. We may hear of many persons who brought ruin upon themselves and their families by their subjection to sensual desires. Yet sense-indulgences, like daily food, are required for the preservation of the body. Good principle and advantage are at the root of desired result which is happiness.[1] Another point in which Vātsyāyana agrees with the Nīti-kāras is that he is not a believer in a Deity or in over ruling Fate, but only in manly strength (puruṣa-kāra).

Vātsyāyan's doctrine summing up Hedonistic morals.

The ethical value of Vātsyāyana's doctrine, judged as a summary of Hedonistic morals, is slight. However, it contains matters which may interest the students of modern science of Eugenics, the division of men and women into four sexual types, for example. Following his predecessors, Vātsyāyana divides man's life into three periods: boyhood, youth and old-age. According to his view, boyhood should be spent in learning, youth in enjoyment of pleasures and riches, and old-age in good principle and detachment from all material concerns. He defines pleasure (kāma) as the activity of the special senses—hearing, touch, sight, taste and

[1] Kāma-sūtra, II.

smell—which is brought into exercise by their natural affinity for the specific objects, and the pleasurable feeling which results therefrom.[1] The senses are inseparable from the self and are all based upon the mind. From this is apparent the appropriateness of the name—the doctrine of pleasures of the five senses—given by the Buddha to such a view as this. The name is a descriptive one—*pañca-kāmaguṇa-diṭṭha-dhamma-nibbāṇa-vāda*, and the implied sense is that we can realise Nirvāṇa, the *summum bonum*, the fulfilment of all desires, in this present consciousness, by indulgence of the senses. No doubt Vātsyāyana speaks of self-conquest or subjugation of the senses, but his real view is that we should proceed through indulgence to achieve this end of desires. Thus we see that his teaching was in a sense a mockery of selfconquest. If the Kāmasūtra be studied in relation to the voluptious life of Indian princes and rich bankers and to the general immorality of human society, one cannot but agree with Dr. F. W. Thomas that it does not represent after all any vicious system. Its primary object, as set forth in the closing chapter of the Bṛihad Āraṇyaka Upaniṣad, is to teach a way of life which is essential to the preservation and betterment of the race, and as such the system forms an integral part of Brahmanic ethics. The system as a whole emanated undoubtedly out of the Brahmanic theory of art (see Aitareya ethics, p. 83 f.) None should fight shy of claiming ancient Indian treatises of erotic science as a rich heritage.

CHAPTER XXIV.

Teachers of Political Morals.

By the term Artha,—Wealth or Material Advantage, Vātsyāyana understands the acquisition and increase of good in general, land, gold, cattle, furniture, etc. The science which treats of the subject of wealth is called Vārtā. Commerce and agriculture fall within the province of Vārtā, the science of Wealth or Economics. Bṛihaspati is traditionally known as the first author of the science of wealth (artha-śāstra).[1]

Definition of Artha

The above definition of wealth is implied also in Buddha's Kāma-sutta: "If the desire cherished by a man be fulfilled, the mortal becomes glad-hearted indeed, obtaining what he desired. On the other hand, his desires being unfulfilled, he feels himself distressed, like one pierced with an arrow. The thoughtful man who renounces all ambitious desires, as one runs away from a snake, overcomes the torments of desire. The man who hankers after land, houses, gold, cattle, horses, slaves, women, friends and various other possessions, allows these minor things to overpower him and enemies—internal and external—to trample him down........"[2]

According to Kauṭilya the Sciences (vidyās) are four: Philosophy, the three Vedas, Economics, and the Science of

[1] Kāma-sūtra, I, 7; II, 8-9.

[2] Commentary on Kāma-sutta in the Mahāniddesa, 1-22.

Administration.[1] Philosophy, he says, is the light or guide to all other branches of knowledge, to all particular sciences, it opens the way for all our activities, and it is the foundation of all principles, the giver of eternal life.[2] The three Vedas, together with all supplementary works and sciences, lay down the general rules relating to men of four castes and of four 'estates' or orders of training. So by the three Vedas Kauṭilya really means the Dharma-śāstras. The subjects of enquiry of Vārtā, the science of wealth, are agriculture, cattle-rearing, trade and commerce. The science of Administration (Daṇḍanīti) enables a man to gain what is not gained, to protect what is gained, to increase what is protected, and to benefit public institutions therewith.

Place of Daṇḍanīti among the Sciences.

Although from one point of view Kauṭilya accords the highest place to Metaphysics and from the other point of view he gives the same place to Daṇḍa—the science of Administration. In fact, he considers Daṇḍa to be at the root of other three sciences. Vinaya or Discipline is at the root of Daṇḍa. His definition of Vinaya is that which provides a safe-guard for all living beings. Discipline may be either cultivated or natural. For instance, Nature governs substances—living individuals—not non-substances (kriyāhi dravyam vinayati

[1] Kauṭilya tells us that the Mānavas regarded philosophy as a particular phase of the three Vedas. Those of the Bṛihaspati school recognised only two Sciences, Economics and the science of Government. They considered the three Vedas to be a mere system of moral conduct, that is to say, a mere way of life. Auśanasas, on the other hand, recognised only one science, namely the science of Government. The three philosophical systems recognised by Kauṭilya are Sāṁkhyam, Yoga and Lokāyata. The three Vedas investigate the good and bad principles; Economics prosperity and adversity; and the science of Government the good and the bad policy. From his further discussion it appears that he accords the highest place to Philosophy. Bṛihaspati-sūtra, I.3: "Dandānītir eva vidyā." The Bārhaspatyas recognised only the science of Government as the science. However, the statement is modified elsewhere, in the later portions of the sūtra, III, 9 following.

[2] "Pradīpaḥ sarva-vidyānām upāya-sarva-karmaṇām. Āśrayaḥ sārvadharmāṇām śāśvadānvīkṣaki mata." Arha-śāstra, I.1.

nâdravyaṁ). Discipline which is cultivated includes reverence for the teacher, attention, reception, retention, understanding, and so forth.[1]

Kāma-śāstra and Nīti-śāstra.—Sensualism and utilitarian morality compared.

The same broad division of the science of utility (Artha-śāstra), also known as the science of polity (Nīti-śāstra, Rāja-śāstra), into Economics (Vārtā) and Politics (Daṇḍa-nīti) is adopted by all the leading political writers.[2] It is clear from Kauṭilya's division and definition that the principles of utility, no less than the principles of self-perfection, rest ultimately upon Vinaya,—order, discipline, restraint, social organisation or moral culture in the widest possible sense But we must not lose sight of the difference between a Kama-śāstra and a Nīti-śāstra, or between Sensualism and Utility. With regard to the first difference, we are told in the Śūkra-nīti that whereas an Arthaśāstra enumerates the public and private functions of kings in accordance with the dictates of Śruti and Smṛiti, a Kāma śāstra describes the characteristic marks—physical and mental—of living beings, both male and female.[3] In addition to this scientific difference we have to consider the difference in the moral means by which the sensualist and political teachers seek to realise their objects, pleasure and material advantage. As we have seen, with the former the royal road to happiness is the full indulgence of the five senses. According to the latter, sense-indulgence cannot be conducive to material advantage. Hence all political teachers insist on self-conquest (indriya-jaya) as the essential duty of the king and his servants. But they concede this much to the sensualist view that a man should enjoy the pleasures of life in so far as they do not conflict with the principles of good conduct, justice and economy, and that none

[1] Artha-śāstra, I. 1.2.

[2] Bṛihaspati-sūtra, I-3; II.1-4; Śūkra-nīti, I.303-316.

[3] Śūkra-nīti, IV.3.110-114. cf. Dial. B. II.19.

should be deprived of happiness. Thus we see that Sensualism and Utility agree in considering happiness to be the highest good.

These early developments of political theory have a real and close connexion with the progress of philosophy and ethics.

Development of political speculations previous to Kauṭilya's Arthaśāstra.

Divergent as the traditions are, they seem to agree on this point, namely that they all mention Cāṇakya, Kauṭilya, or Viṣṇugupta as the greatest landmark in the development of Indian political science and literature. A fairly large number of works[1] are associated with the name of Cāṇakya, the prime minister of king Candragupta Maurya of Magadha. The best known of these works is the Artha-śāstra, discovered a few years ago in South India by Pandit Shama Shastri of Mysore. Prof. Jolly considers the Kauṭiliya Artha-śāstra to be "one of the most important discoveries ever made in the whole range of Sanskrit literature," as it has thrown a flood of light "on the political condition of India in the very times when Megasthenes visited it."

While scholars are unanimous in their verdict on the great historical value of the work, they are divided in opinion on the question as to its real author. There are three schools of

Three schools of opinion as to the authorship of the Kauṭiliya Arthaśāstra.

opinion. Prof. Hillebrandt,[2] who is supported by Prof. Jolly, maintains that it was the work of Kauṭilya Cāṇakya's school, rather than of himself. Pandit Shama Shastri and Prof. Jacobi[3] maintain an individual authorship of the work.

[1] Nīti-śataka; Nīti-sāra; Laghu-cāṇakya-rājanīti-śāstra; Vṛiddha-cāṇakya-rājanīti-śāstra; Cāṇakya-śloka; Cāṇakya-sūtra; Hitopadeśa.

[2] Ubèr das Kauṭilya-śāstra und Verwandtes, Breslau, 1908.

As to the progress made by scholars in the study of the Indian science of polity previous to the discovery of the Kauṭiliya Artha-śāstra, Dr. Thomas points out that "The propagation of the policy in fable (the Fables of Pilpay) was first adumbrated by Sir William Jones—. In its technical form the Indian science first became known by the publication of the Kāmandaki-Nītisāra—. The next stage is represented by two valuable publications of Prof. Formichi—." Bṛihaspati-sūtra, p. 131.

[3] Uber die Echtheit des Kauṭiliya in Berlin Academy Sitzungberichts, 1911 and 1912.

Prof. Keith, on the other hand, holds "that the Artha-śāstra is based on his (Kauṭilya's) teaching, though not by his own hand."[1]

Prof. Rhys Davids agrees with Prof. Keith in saying that "the maxims [of state-craft in the Artha-śāstra] constantly refer to Chāṇakya under the suggestive name of Kauṭilya ("cunning," "deceptive"), as if one were to speak of Machiavelli as "the trickster." They refer also to China, and they refer to royal mints in constant work. Neither of these was possible till long after Chāṇakya's time (4th century B.C.). They breathe, too, the spirit of a later time, the time in literature of the writing of manuals, and, in politics, not of a great empire like Chandragupta's, but of contending states."[2]

It would be idle on our part to speculate here whether the Artha-śāstra in question was composed by Kauṭilya himself, or by his school, or by someone else. The work in its present form embodies the views of Kauṭilya along with those of others, and thus enables us to discriminate the opinions which are strictly Kauṭilya's own from those which are not his, *i.e.*, which are older. And so long as we can do that it is immaterial to enquire when the work was written or by whom.

Kauṭilya's predecessors.

As Pandit Shama Shastri and Prof. Jacobi point out, in the body of the work the opinions of Kauṭilya's predecessors are frequently quoted and discussed. They include both schools and individuals. The schools are the Mānavas, Bārhaspatyas, Auśanasas, Āmbhiyas (of Taxila ?), and the Pārāśaras ; and the individuals are Bhāradvāja, Kaṇiṅka Bhāradvāja, Viśālākṣa, Piśuna, Piśunaputra, Kātyāyana, Kaunapa-danta, Vāta-vyādhi, Bāhudanti-putra, Kiñjalka, Dīrgha Cārāyaṇa, and Ghoṭaka-mukha. Some of these names occur in the Mahābhārata : Vaiśālākṣa, Manu, Indra, Bahudantaka, Bārhaspatya, Kavi (Uśanasa),

[1] J. R. A. S., January, 1916.

[2] The Economic Journal of the Royal Economic Society, Dec., 1916, p. 519.

Gauraśiras, etc. ; two in Vātsyāyana's Kāma-sūtra : Cārāyaṇa and Ghoṭaka-mukha;[1] one in the Mānasāra-Vāstuśastra: Viśālākṣa.

With regard to the predecessors of Kauṭilya, our conclusions are : (1) That the schools referred to were not strictly and exclusively political schools, but legal and ethical schools who had certain opinions on political and artistic matters. Law in ancient times was mingled with religion, morality and politics. The existing legal manuals, both ancient and modern, " devote some of their chapters to discussions of political subjects like the duties of kings, public finance, civil and criminal laws, and judicial procedure."[2]

(2) That the allusion to Dīrgha Cārāyaṇa and Ghoṭaka-mukha in Vātsyāyana's Kāma-sūtra and the Kauṭiliya Artha-śāstra throws light on the close relations between Sensualism and Utilitarian morality. Dīrgha Cārāyaṇa (Dīgha Kārāyaṇa) and Ghoṭaka-mukha were both younger contemporaries of Buddha. Of them, the former was a near attendant of king Pasenādi of Kosala.[3]

(3) That the individuals who placed the science of royal polity on an independent footing by gradually separating its province from that of the older legal systems were mostly known as Parivrājakas,—the wanderers as distinguished, on one hand, from the Hermits, Ascetics and Recluse philosophers, and on the other hand, from the Brāhmans with kingly powers, the ministers and officers of state, the Mahāśālas or teachers of various sciences and arts, and the priests. In the early Buddhist records[4] we have frequent mention of a number of such Wanderers, all of whom were the contemporaries of Buddha, e.g., Poṭṭha-pāda, Dīgha-nakha, Sakula Udāyi;

[1] Cf. Thomas' Brihaspati-sūtra, p. 132.

[2] Public Administration in Ancient India, p. 5.

[3] Majjhima-nikāya, II.118.

[4] Dīgha-nikāya, I. 178 ; Majjhima-nikāya, I. 359, 481, 483, 489, 491, 501, 513 ; II. 1, 22, 29, 40 ; III ; 207. Aṅguttara-nikāya, II. 30. 1 ; II. 185. 1 ; etc.

Aṇṇa-bhara, Varadhara, Poṭāliya or Potali-putta, Uggahamāna, Vekhanassa Kaccāna, Māgaṇḍiya, Sandaka, Uttiya, three Vaccha-gottas, Sabhiya, and Pilotika Vacchāyana. Besides these Wanderers we have to take into account many celebrated Brāhman teachers of Buddha's time, such as Pokkharasāti (Puṣkarasādi), Sonadaṇḍa, (Śaunadanta or Śaunaka), Kuṭadanta, Lohicca, Kaṅki (Caṅki), Tarukkha (Tārukṣya), Jānussoṇi (Jātaśruti), Todeyya, Todeyya-putta or Subha, Kāpaṭhika Bhāradvāja, Aggika Bhāradvāja, Piṇḍola Bhāradvāja, Kāsi Bharadvāja, Vāseṭṭha, Assalāyana, Moggallāna, Pārāsariya, Vassakāra and others.[1]

Distinction between the Wanderers and the Recluse philosophers.

The best way of distinguishing between the Wanderers, strictly so called, and the Recluse philosophers—who were in a sense a class of Wanderers is probably this. We may here suppose that in speaking of "harsh language" (parusavācā) or "wrangling phrases," Buddha had in mind the disciples of such Recluse philosophers as Pūraṇa Kassapa, Kakuda Kātyāyana, and others, while in speaking of "vain conversation" (samphappalāpa) or "manifold beastly talk" (aneka-vihita tiracchāna-kathā), he had in mind chiefly the disciples of the Wanderers. The disciples of the six famous Recluse philosophers would say to one another: "You don't understand this doctrine and discipline, I do. How should you know about this doctrine and discipline? You have fallen into wrong views. It is I who am in the right........"[2] The disciples of the Wanderers, rather of Brāhmaṇa-paribbājakā as distinguished from aññatitthiya-paribbājakā, were addicted to such vain and low conversation as talk about kings, robbers and rebels, ministers of state, war and warfare; talk about foods and drinks, clothes, beds, garlands, perfumes; talk about relations, equipages, villages, towns, cities, and countries; tales about women, heroes, streets, departed spirits;

[1] Dīgha-nikāya, I. 87, 111, 127, 224, 234; Majjhima-nikāya, I. 16, 164, 175, etc.

[2] Dial. B. II. 14-15. Majjhima-nikāya, II. 3.

miscellaneous talk; speculations about the origin of the world including human institutions, the apparition and distribution of land and water, or briefly, about the successive phases of existence and non-existence."[1]

The historical importance of the list of low talks.

The above list given by Buddha of low topics is of great importance from the historical standpoint. First, it sums up the manifold topics which fall within the province of the science of utility or royal polity. Secondly, it sets forth the view of Buddha and other Recluse philosophers on politics. Politics was to them mere gossip or foolish talk. And thirdly, it shows that although with the Wanderers in general the subjects of constant and habitual discussion comprised all social and political questions and though the discussion of philosophical problems was but a hobby, so to speak, they were not altogether indifferent to the great spiritual striving which was going on in the country all round, side by side with its intellectual and material progress.

The Buddhist accounts of the Wanderers are extremely meagre, and appear in places too symmetrical to be susceptible of historical proof. For instance, almost all the Wanderer teachers are represented as having three hundred followers each. Nevertheless they place before us a few broad facts relating to the Wanderers.

The Brāhman Wanderers furnished a connecting link between the Recluses and the Brāhmans.

In the first place, the Buddhist records agree with the Brāhman law-books in representing the Wanderers as those Brāhmans who cut off connection with the world, and passed into a new mode of life which admitted of no caste-system or class-distinctions.[2] In this they were in no way different from the Recluse proper. Another point of resemblance between them and the Recluses is that they sought to

[1] Dial B. pp. 13-14. This is one of the stock-passages in the Jaina Aṅgas.

[2] Śaṅkara in his comments on the Vedānta-sūtra, II. 3. 15, sarcastically remarks: "As sometimes the Parivrājakas are distinguished from the Brāhmans,"

build up a system of moral philosophy entirely upon a human or rational ground rather than on a theocratic basis. They differed, however, from the latter by the strong moral justification which they offered for the current Āśrama-theory of life, and other social laws and usages. Thus we can easily see that the Wanderers proper by their views and ways of life furnished a connecting link between the Recluses, on one hand, and the Brāhmans on the other, the Recluses who were inspired with ideas of sweeping reform in religion and philosophy, and the Brāhmans who, in their various capacities, governed society, and were naturally anxious to safeguard their interests and influence against every dangerous change. Hence is the justification of the significant name Brāhmaṇa-paribbājakā. Further, understanding this connecting link we can see near relation in which ethics and politics, or a Dharma-śāstra and an Artha-śāstra stand to each other. In the second place, it is manifest from these records that travellers as the Brāhman Wanderers were, they were in a position to learn the languages, customs and usages of the people living in different parts of the world in which they themselves lived. And we must remember that in those early ages of civilisation when there was neither any printing press nor any easy means of communication between one country and another, elements of knowledge could be gathered, disseminated or utilised for scientific purpose by no better means than such travelling. The Brihaspati-sūtra, therefore, rightly insists: "Manliness consists in rising superior to one's weaknesses. A man learns endurance by residence in other countries. A prince should acquire knowledge of all powers, times, countries, conciliations, natures (views, ways and temperament), strengths, exercises and ages."[1] It is hardly necessary to mention that even in the time of Buddha the knowledge of different languages (deśa-

[1] Cf. Thomas' Bṛihaspati-sūtra, III. 1-3.

bhāṣā-vijñāna) and usages (deśādi-dharma) was recognised sciences or branches of learning. And in the third place, we may learn from these records that the Brāhman Wanderers were known to their contemporaries generally by some nick-names. Let us consider, for instance, the names Poṭṭha-pāda, Uggahamāna, and Dīgha-nakha. The name Poṭṭha-pāda literally means one who was a prosṭha or pusṭa-pāda,—sufferer from elephantiasis. The name Vāta-vyādhi (The rheumatic) given in the Kauṭilīya Arthaśāstra is a similar example. Another name is Uggahamāna, which literally means one who gazes upward, one with rolling eyes, that is to say, one who is goggle-eyed (Viśālākṣa). Similiarly the name Dīgha-nakha signifies one with long nails. By the nick-names we trace some of the teachers whose views are quoted and discussed in the Kauṭilīya Arthaśāstra as Wanderers mentioned in the oldest Buddhist records.

Furthermore, from the discussions reported by the Buddhists we find traces of the personal views upheld by the Wanderers. These views may be arranged under three heads: philosophical, ethical, and political. Of these we need only consider the philosophical and the ethical.

The philosophical views of the Wanderers.

As regards their philosophical views, the Brāhman Wanderers seem to have drawn inspiration from post-Vedic philosophies rather than neo-Vedic or pre-Buddhistic. The problems with which Poṭṭha-pāda, Aggi-Vacchagotta and Uttiya (Ātreya) were confronted were these: Is the world as a whole enternal or not? Is the psychical identical with the corporeal, or are the soul and the body two separate entities? Does a human being who has by his enlightenment and character reached the highest conceivable standard of perfection continue to exist after death or not? All these problems may be reduced to one: Is there an incorporeal and extra-mental soul or not? Aggivessana Dīgha-nakha is said to have maintained this view: Nothing of me abides (sabbaṁ me na khamati). Buddha said in reply: If it be, as you say, that nothing of yours abides, then it follows that the dogmatic assertion which is yours also does not abide.[1] Sakula Udāyi who declared himself to be a disciple of Mahāvīra (Nigaṇṭha Nātaputta) was of opinion that soul is the highest self or entity which remains untouched after death, and that our real self-existence is one of unmixed happiness (ekanta-sukha),—the absolute bliss which can be realised by means of moral restraint and religious penance (tapoguṇa).[2] A fuller discussion of the philosophical views of the Brāhman Wanderers appears in the Poṭṭha-pāda Sutta. It is a dialogue between Poṭṭha-pāda and Buddha, which adopts, as Prof. Rhys Davids points out, the Socratic method of securing a dialectical advantage over opponents' views. This dialogue reminds us of the episode of Indra and Prajāpati in the Chāndogya Upaniṣad. In it we are told that the Wanderer Poṭṭha-pāda or Vāta-vyādhi was a believer in three grades of soul: the gross or corporeal (Oḷārika, *i.e.*, sthūla or bhūtāmā); the mental (manomaya), and the incorporeal, immaterial or purely cognitive (arūpa or saññāmaya, *i. e.*, vijñānātmā).[3]

The ethical views of the Wanderers and other Moralists.

Turning to the ethical views of the Wanderers and other ancient Moralists (Vinaya-vādins), we observe that they all conceived unmixed happiness (ekanta-sukha) as the highest good. Accordingly, all efforts of life should be directed to this one end. But their method of self-training was imperfect or defective. Indeed, the fault which Buddha, in agreement with his predecessor Mahāvīra, found with their method of self-training was that it emphasised only the negative or privative side of virtue. In other words, the Moralists attempted to regulate outward conduct or behaviour of man rather than build up his character by developing all active moral

[1] Majjhima-nikāya, I. 497.
[2] *ibid*, II. 35-37.
[3] Dial. B. II. 241-264.

faculties. "A Bhikṣu shall not possess any store. He must be chaste. He must not change his residence during the rainy season....He shall abandon all desire for sweet food. He shall restrain his speech, sight and actions. . He shall not take parts of plants and trees....Out of season he shall not dwell a second night in the same village....He shall avoid the destruction of seeds. He shall be indifferent towards all creatures, whether they do him an injury or a kindness. He shall not undertake any work for his livelihood."[1] Such are the rules which are laid down in the Brāhman law-books, and which apply to the Wanderers and Recluses. The Wanderer Sakula Udāyi, as we saw, maintained that the formulated path (ākāravati paṭipadā) to the realisation of unmixed happiness is twofold: abstention from killing, robbing, adultery and lying, and various penances.[2] The Wanderer Uggahamāna or Viśālākṣa, son of Samaṇa-maṇḍikā, was of opinion that a person may be said to have performed all his moral duties (sampanna-kusala), if he does not commit any sin or crime by way of deed, does not utter any harmful speech, does not entertain any sinful thought, and does not follow a wrong mode of living.[3] When this view of Uggahamāna was brought to the notice of Buddha by the Architect named Pañcakaṅga, Buddha said, "Well, if that be so, then a baby must be regarded as one who has performed all his moral duties, who is extremely clever, who has attained the best of attainments or who is a Recluse without a rival. For such a baby has even no body, and what to say of his committing any sin by way of deed; he has even no language, and what to say of his uttering any sinful word; he has even no mind, strictly speaking, and what to say of his cherishing any sinful

[1] Bühler's Gautama, III. 11-25.

[2] *Cf.* Baudhāyana, II. 10. 18. 1-3: The precepts to be observed by a Saṁnyāsin are—Abstention from injury to living beings, from falsehood and theft or dishonesty, continence, liberality, freedom from anger, obedience to the Guru, avoidance of rashness, cleanliness and purity in eating.

[3] Majjhima-nikāya, II. 24.

thought; he has even no profession, and what to say of his wrong mode of living!"

From Buddha's further criticism it appears that mere avoidance of sinful acts cannot exhaust man's moral functions, and cannot lead to unmixed happiness. The result of abstinence or self-restraint is not unmixed happiness, but something which is mixed (sukha-dukkha).[1] In his opinion, therefore, the path to unmixed happiness is threefold; avoidance of all that is evil, rooted in greed, hatred and ignorance, performance of all that is good, rooted in disinterestedness, love and knowledge, and inner enlightenment. Buddha declared action to be volition (cetanā vadāmi kammaṁ). His definition was anticipated by Yājñavalkya who said, "As a man's will is, so is his act". According to this definition, an act whether good or bad is an act only when it has reference to man's will, is prompted by a certain motive, and carries out a certain definite purpose or intention. This definition of an act was open to misunderstanding. A Wanderer named Potali-putta took it to mean that in Buddha's view a true act is that which is mental (manokammaṁ), and neither that which is vocal nor that which is bodily.[2] Another view of Buddha, which was misunderstood by some of the Wanderer teachers is this: "Painful is the life of a house-holder, and free is the life of renunciation (sambādho gharāvāsā,—abbhokāso pabbajjā)." The Brāhman law-givers, on the contrary, extolled the life of a house-holder and denounced the life of renunciation. In this respect, neither Buddha nor the Brāhman law-givers were extremists. When Subha, the son of Todeyya, consulted Buddha on the Brāhman view, Buddha frankly confessed that he had no reason to judge every householder an ethical or intellectual superior to every hermit, and every hermit an ethical or intellectual superior to

Buddha's criticism of the views of the Wanderers.

[1, 2] Majjhima-nikāya, II. 36; III. 207.

every house-holder. In such case the best thing would be to judge every person, whether he be a house-holder or a hermit, individually, on his own merits.[1] Similarly, although it might appear that they with one voice extolled the order of house-holders, and with one voice denounced the order of hermits, a careful examination of their systems as a whole would reveal that this was really not the case. By extolling the order of house-holders they did not mean in their heart of hearts to disparage the spiritual life which the hermits sought to live. The point which they insisted on was that in seeking the higher life, we should not neglect the humbler, preliminary but useful functions of man's life. However, taking literally Buddha's general opinion, that painful is the life of a house-holder, and free is the life of a recluse, the Wanderer Māgaṇḍiya[2] judged Buddha to be an exterminator of the human race (bhunahu, bhruṇahan), in the same way that the Vājasaneyas judged the Muṇḍakas to be self-murderers (ātmahano janāḥ).

Now to return to Uggahamāna. Although his was a negative definition of goodness, it is most remarkable historically, as it exhibits a rational attempt on his part to form a distinct and clear notion of what goodness is. That his conception of good implies a lofty morality is unquestionable. We shall perhaps be not far wrong in holding that the Brāhman Wanderers, in conjunction with the Recluse philosophers, effected a transition from the older conventional standards of judgment of conduct to later rational or scientific standards. The determining fact with the Wanderers, as with all later political writers, is psychogenetically will or volition (saṅkalpa, cetanā), and ethically the end to which activities are directed. In their teachings God, Time, Fate, Chance, or the like has no place. Manliness or self-reliance

[1] Majjhima-nikāya, II. 198.

[2] *Ibid*, I. 502. As the name implies, Māgaṇḍiya was either an adherent of the Māṇḍukeya, or the founder of the Mārkaṇḍeya (Māgaṇḍika) school.

(puruṣakāra) is the *raison dêtre* of their ethics.[1] Thus they thought it necessary first to investigate which of the current theories of life was adequate to furnish a high and at the same time attainable standard of ethical or moral judgment.

CHAPTER XXV.

TEACHERS OF JURISTIC MORALS.

As employed in the Vedic literature, the three terms Truth (satya), Good Principle (ṛita), and Righteousness (dharma) appear to be almost synonymous. Of these, the term Ṛita is of more frequent occurrence than the other two. A Vedic sage conceived Truth as that on which the universe rests. Truth was, in other words, for this sage Ṛita, the law, principle or order of things.[1] In the view of Aghamarṣaṇa Ṛita is the eternal law and order of the universe.[2] Following these earlier thinkers, Āsuri assigned a Divine origin to Dharma. In his phraseology, the term Dharma implies the most excellent law, right or justice which is protected, exercised or administered by the ruling class,—by the State—of which the origin is equally divine. He declared Dharma to be the Kṣatra of Kṣatras,—the king of kings, there being nothing higher than it. Since the establishment of Government, of which the main weapon is law or justice, one who is physically weaker is able to control another who is physically stronger, who follows the simple rule of might. For Āsuri again justice is truth, just as conversely that which is true is just.

Satya, Ṛita, Dharma.

Thus we see that the term Dharma in its narrowest sense signifies just what we now call justice. But we are here concerned with Dharma, as understood in the Dharmasūtras and Dharmaśāstras. As Cāṇakya points out, the term Dharma is employed by writers on equity in the sense of Varṇāśrama-dharma,—the discipline which considers man's actions or duties

[1] Ṛig-Veda, X. 85. 1. [2] *Ibid*, X. 190. 1.

from the point of view of social grades and periods of life. The literature which embodies such a discipline is briefly known as *Trayī*, the three Vedas, whereas, strictly speaking, it includes the four Vedas, Itihāsas, Purāṇas, and the six Vedāṅgas.[1] The author of the Śukranīti, in agreement with Cāṇakya, defines a Dharmaśāstra or Smriti as that system of discipline which investigates the nature of castes and the duties enjoined by the revealed texts, and which sets forth the social and economic principles.[2] The Buddhist expression for the system is even more interesting : *Anussava or Itiha-itiha-paramparā-piṭaka-sampadā Dhamma*,[3]—a system of moral discipline which is based upon customs, usages, or traditions handed down from time immemorial.

The Dharma Sūtrakāras and the Mīmāṁsakas.

The dialectical defenders of these partly-religious, partly-social, partly-moral, partly-legal systems were known as Mīmāṁsins whose views were later systematised in the Pūrva-mimāṁsā of Jaimini. In the Buddhist literature they are referred to as Takkis and Vimaṁsins. With regard to this close alliance or kinship between the Dharmasūtrakāras and the Mīmāṁsakas, the following observations of Dr. Bühler are instructive. Referring to Āpastamba, one of the oldest known writers on Indian law, Dr. Bühler says,[4] "In two passages he settled contested questions on the authority of those who know the Nyāya, *i.e.*, the Pūrva-Mīmāṁsā, and in several other cases he adopts a line of reasoning which fully agrees with that followed in Jaimini's Mīmāṁsā-sūtras......... The wording of the passage in the two works does not agree so closely that the one could be called a quotation of the other. But it is evident, that if Āpastamba did not know the

[1] Kauṭiliya Arthaśāstra, I. 3.

[2] Śukra nīti, IV. 3. 106-107.

[3] Majjhima-nikāya, I. 520.

[4] Bühler's Āpa stamba, XXVII ; II. 4. 8. 13 ; II. 6. 14. 13. *cf.* Mimāṁsāsūtras, I. 3. 3-4.

Mīmāṁsāsūtras of Jaimini, he must have possessed some other very similar work."

In dealing with the subject of Dharma, we have first to consider that branch of Vedic literature which is called the Kalpa. The Kalpa in its purely literary sense is but a common designation applied to a number of Sūtras or codes, such as Śrauta-sūtras, Dharma-sūtras, Gṛihya--sūtras and Sulva-sūtras Of these, the Dharma-sūtras may be regarded as the essence of each Kalpa. How many Kalpas there were in all we do not know, but presumably their number was large. Probably each Kalpa represented the manual of a separate school of Brāhmans, who were the legislators of life and society, the teachers of morals.

The Kalpa-sūtras; their relation to the Dharma-sūtras.

The Kauṭilīya Arthaśāstra quotes and discusses the opinions of five schools: the Mānavas, the Bārhaspatyas, the Auśanasas, the Āmbhiyas and the Pārāśaras. Pāṇini in his grammar alludes to two schools: the Pārāśariyakas and the Karmandinas. The Mānavas and Pārāśariyakas are mentioned in the Mānasara Vāstuśāstra as being recognised authorities on architecture and kindred arts; the names of Vasiṣṭha, Nārada and other Dharmasūtrakāras, too appear in the list of such authorities. Baudhāyana and Vasiṣṭha quote in their legal manuals the opinions of Gautama, Manu, Kātyāyana, Hārita, Aupagandhini and other ancient teachers of Dharma; Āpastamba cites the opinions of Eka, Kāṇva, Kuṇika, Kutsa, Kautsa, Puṣkarasādi, Varṣyāyani, Śvetaketu and Hārita. Dr. Bühler tells us that Kāṇva, Kautsa, Puṣkarasādi and Vārṣyāyani are quoted by the expositors of Pāṇini as authorities on phonetics, etymology and grammar. A string of names also appears in the existing Gṛihya-sūtras. And we must not be surprised when those who are quoted in one group of texts as authorities on law and morals should be quoted in other groups as authorities on other subjects—medicine, astronomy, and astrology, for instance.

The philosophers and the councillors.

The Dharmasūtrakāras were Brāhmans by birth. But for historical purposes we should remember that there were two distinct types of Brāhman teachers, namely, the Dharmasūtrakāras and the Wanderers. Megasthenes was inclined to represent the philosophers as a class of Indian population quite distinct from those to whom he applied the name of the councillors.

But although the philosophers were not necessarily either householders or hermits and recluses, the one characteristic fact about them was that none of them cared for material gains. The point may be illustrated by reference to Uddālaka and his son Śvetaketu. The former was a philosopher or original thinker; the latter was a famous Vedic scholar, a writer on the subject of Kāma and Dharma. Śvetaketu was proud and conceited, as Vedic scholars generally were and are, and he lacked originality of thought.[1] The Dharmasūtrakāras as distinguished from the philosophers were those Brāhmans who held high social positions. They were either ministers of state, councillors, or served the state in other capacities. Besides these Brāhmans, there were others who were established in different parts of the country as land-holders by Royal Grant. Some idea of their position may be formed from the modern Mohāntas, from whom they differed, however, in that they were married householders[2] and their position and rights were hereditary. They are known in the Upaniṣad literature as Mahāśālas or heads of Vedic institutions. Also they were diplomats of ancient times, and knew exactly where to draw the line between theory and practice.

It is a remarkable fact that several discussions which Buddha had with these Brāhmans all turned upon the subject of caste system. The only question they discussed was: " who

[1] Chāndogya Upaniṣad, VI. 1.

[2] Dial. B. II, 150.

is a Brahmin and who is not"? This is the main point in their ethical teachings to be specially noted. For other points we refer the reader to the chapters on the Taittirīya system and Muṇḍaka philosophy.

PART IV.

PHILOSOPHY OF MAHĀVĪRA.

Introductory.

The aim and scope of Part IV.

It is not part of our plan to undertake in these pages so large and important a task as an enquiry into the philosophy of the Buddha. We content ourselves with a general survey from within of the development of what is known as the Dynamistic philosophy of Mahāvira. And our object will be attained if we succeed to any appreciable extent in indicating the nature of the precise historical relation in which Mahāvīra stands to his predecessors as well as to the Buddha, his younger contemporary and far-famed successor.

Review of modern studies in Jainism: Lack of historical method.

A distorted picture of history has been the inevitable result of attempts to represent Jainism, Buddhism, or Hinduism as a system, complete once for all and in all its aspects. The reason is obvious. No one of these three names denotes any one system of thought, but several. For example, Jainism, taken as a whole, presents to us a long and eventful history not of one individual thinker but of many. And if we may rightly suppose that no two individuals are exactly alike in their views, character, outlook and environment, then it follows that the development of Jainism is unintelligible when considered apart from those individual thinkers to whom it is mainly or largely due. In such case the subject of our investigation should be not what Jainism as a whole is, but who Mahāvīra was, what his teachings were, how his doctrines were expounded after his death by Sudharman, and others.

There remains much to be done because scholars have hitherto sought to measure the philosophical views of India not by the standpoint of the philosophers themselves, but in part by those of later commentators and in part by what they call modern, European or Christian standpoints. Referring to this latter mode of judgment Mrs. Rhys Davids acutely observes, "A specific tradition in knowledge, and a vehicle of expression that has not coincided in its growth of that knowledge should make us wary in estimating another tradition, another standpoint, other modes of expression. We may fancy that we are measuring other views by standpoints that are not only absolutely true, but the only standpoints possible or conceivable. But in fact we are measuring, by what is relatively true.........a different range of standpoints, which have come to hold good, analogously and equally, for other sections of humanity."[1]

Again the point where modern exponents of Indian philosophy show want of historical insight is that they have hitherto directed all their energetic efforts towards ascertaining what a particular system of thought is, instead of answering at the same time the question why the system should be what it is, and not otherwise. That is to say, they have failed to display the necessity lying behind the evolution of a system of philosophy. According to the modern scientific theory of history, it is not the primary concern of the historian to furnish expositions of any system, but to bring out, so far as is practicable, the parts played by three factors in the appearance of a system and its supersession by another which went ahead. The factors, as enumerated by Prof. Windelband, are the pragmatic or logical, the cultural, and the individual, while in the view of Hegel, who was the first to make the history of philosophy a genuine science, the factor was just one, namely, the pragmatic or logical. Corresponding to these three factors, in dealing with a system it is the task of the historian to render

[1] Buddhism, p. 16.

an account of the threefold necessity arising, *first*, from the existing types of speculation; *secondly*, from the prevailing education of the time; and *thirdly*, from the personality of the individual thinker.

Nevertheless, the fact remains that "we are now beginning to reap the harvest sown by certain pioneers." With regard to Mahāvīra's philosophy in particular, it may be observed that the first gatherings of a harvest rich in promise are to be found in Prof. Jacobi's introduction to the Jaina Sūtras, Part II. It is most remarkable that Prof. Jacobi, relying largely as he did upon guesswork, could raise in his introduction all the fundamental problems with which we are confronted in the following pages, and also vaguely point out the nature of their solutions. Among earlier treatises Prof. Bhandarkar's 'Report on the Search for Sanskrit Manuscripts,' Prof. Weber's Indischen Studien, and Prof. Leumann's paper in the Actes du VI Congres des Orientalistes are particularly worthy of note. Colebrooke's Essays do not contain much information about the early history of the Jains. The principal authority with which the illustrious scholar was acquainted is a work by Hemachandra. However, the references to Gymnosophists in Greek accounts, collected by Colebrooke, are interesting enough. Prof. Hopkins' chapter on Jainism in his Religions of India is contaminated by prejudice, and utterly destitute of broad intellectual sympathy. M. Barth's review of our knowledge of Jainism in the Bulletin des Religions de l'Inde does not enlighten us in any way either. Mr. Barodia's History and Literature of Jainism, Dr. Bühler's Indian Sect of the Jains, M. le Milloue's Essai sur la Religion des Jains, Dr. Hoernle's Annual Address to the Asiatic Society of Bengal and his article on the Ājīvikas,[2] and other good works by previous

Acknowledgment of debts to the Jaina scholars.

[1] Indian Antiquary, IX, 158 foll.

[2] Encyclopædia of Religion and Ethics.

scholars may be read with interest and profit, though not for definite historical knowledge of Mahāvīra's philosophy.

The chief among later writers who have considerably widened our knowledge of the early history of Jainism is Prof. Rhys Davids. He has, more than any one else, tried to hold before our eyes a picture of Indian society at the time of Mahāvīra and Buddha, which is as vivid as perhaps true to fact. Mrs. Stevenson in her *Heart of Jainism*, seems to think that if Jainism possesses a heart at all, it is empty—an Indian faith "in which death, not life, is the prize, cessation, not development the ideal."[1] Although she is not without reverence and sympathy for an Indian faith, her observations only prove how difficult it is for a Western mind to comprehend the inner meaning of the spiritual life of India.

But when we speak of Mahāvīra and Buddha, we have to think with Dr. F. Otto Schrader of an age "seething with speculative ferment," or with Mrs. Stevenson of the times "ripe for revolt." We have to imagine a time when there was no organised religion or established church in the country to interfere with the freedom of speculation by imposing upon its adherents its professed dogmas, and when conversion implied in the case of a learner or truth-seeker no more than a transition from one mode of self-training to another which he deemed more suitable to his temperament. Nor even in the case of a layman did it ever demand that unflinching devotion or that profession of blind faith which leads men by imperceptible steps to harbour bigotry, to become religious fanatics, and to shut the gate of benevolence upon every fellow being who is a stranger.[2]

A general reflection on Indian life in the time of Mahāvīra and Buddha.

A religion there was,—a natural religion, later known as Brahmanism or Hinduism, bound up with polytheism, animistic

[1] The Heart of Jainism, p. 1.

[2] Majjhima-nikāya, 1. 380.

beliefs, popular superstitions, ancestral worship, rituals, ceremonies, law, morality and mythology. It was at once a form of nature-worship, a way of life, a rule of conduct, a principle of righteousness, a civil and criminal procedure, and a conventional standard of ethical judgment. So long as people who lived within its jurisdiction conformed to the established rules of society and did not infringe the laws of the state, it did not matter much what were their personal beliefs. And that religion, if religion we may call it, with all its defects, cherished within itself polite literature, poetry, music, and various other useful sciences and arts. The philosophers were left entirely free to indulge in any amount of speculation and argumentation. In the tradition of the time there was known only one sage, Māṇḍavya, a contemporary of Kriṣṇa Dvaipāyana or Vyāsa, who was impaled[1] for reasons other than his bold theories. In fact, this part of our reflection upon ancient Indian society may be made clearer in the light of Hume's reflection upon the history of ancient Greece and Rome. "The singular good fortune of philosophy," says Hume, "which, as it requires entire liberty above all other privileges, and chiefly flourishes from the free opposition of sentiments and argumentation, received its first birth in an age and country of freedom and toleration, and was never cramped, even in its most extravagant principles, by any creeds, concessions, or penal statutes. For, except the banishment of Protagoras and the death of Socrates, which last event proceeded partly from other motives, there are scarcely any instances to be met with in ancient history of this bigoted jealousy with which the present age is so much infested. Epicurus lived at Athens to an advanced age in peace and tranquillity; Epicureans were even admitted to receive the sacerdotal character, and to officiate at the altar in the most sacred rites of the established religion. And the public encouragement of pensions and salaries was afforded

[1] Fausböll's Jātaka, IV, pp. 28-29.

equally, by the wisest of all the Roman emperors, to the professors of every sect of philosophy."[1]

To return to India: Mahāvira's life-time, which coincides with the greater part of Buddha's career, marks a short period when peace began to smile over the whole land after centuries of war, resulting in the final overthrow of the power of Kāśi by the Kosalans, and in the ascendency of Magadha. Or rather it was a period when civil war ceased for a while, yielding place to fights for civic rights and higher ethical ideals. The appearance of this new factor, the kingdom of Magadha, was full of presage, as it was destined to determine to a large extent the future of India.

According to a Jaina tradition, recorded by Prof. Jacobi, the Licchavi and Mallakis were once the chiefs of Kāśi and Kosala.[2] But during the period under discussion the descendants of the Licchavi were just one of the eight small clans or powers, constituting together the strong Vajjian confederacy of Vaiśāli.[3] The influence of the Mallas, on the other hand, was confined to Kusinārā and Pāvā.[4]

As the researches of Prof. Rhys Davids have shown, in the time of Mahāvīra and Buddha there were in Northern India four powerful monarchies, while the remaining powers were represented by a number of small states and oligarchies of various description. The ruling chiefs of the time were often united by matrimonial alliances. The inhabitants of South India were till that time looked down upon by the Aryans or Northerners as the unclean or barbarians. The inference from this fact is that till the time of Mahāvīra and Buddha the Dravidian countries, situate for the most part below the Godāvari, did not come within the pale of Aryan civilisation.

We need hardly emphasize the importance of the existence of these independent powers or states to the historian of

[1] An Enquiry concerning Human Understanding, section XI.

[2] Jaina-sūtras, Part 2, p. 321. [3, 4] Mahāparinibbāna-suttanta, chaps. I and VI.

Indian religion, philosophy, politics, language, literature, sciences and arts. For it was under the auspices of one or other of these states that various sects of religion and contending schools of philosophy flourished side by side in the country. Each power left the indelible marks of its specific traditions, language, laws and principles. While each city wall enclosed within itself a royal capital with all its grandeur, outside it might be seen the headquarters of this or that school. In the language of the Mahāparinibbāna-suttanta, a King of kings within, a King of kings without, both were heroes, although in different senses, and both equally worthy of a memorial mound, Dagaba or national shrine (thūpa, cetiya).[1]

The bearing of political history upon the progress of thought and the development of language.

In the absence of any fixed residence, royal parks, public halls and potters' premises generally afforded shelter to the recluses, all of whom were, in one sense at all events, travellers in the boundless realm of knowledge, the seekers of truth divine, and above all, the teachers of humanity. Other places accessible to these homeless Wanderers were an open meadow, a distant wood-land, a solitary forest, a deserted house, a cave, and a crematorium or a charnel-field. The continual coming and going of the Wanderer teachers had something of a spectacular effect upon the mind of an observer.

The founders and leaders of Wanderer schools are best known to posterity—to modern historians, as religious reformers, whose vehicle of expression was the language of the people, instead of Sanskrit, the language of the learned. Their intellectual activities thus soon led to the development of vernacular literatures. As Professor Rhys Davids has pointed out, the Recluse teachers of the time carried on their religious and philosophical discussions [*] in a language intelligible

[1] Buddhist suttas, S. B. E, XI, pp. XVIII-XIX, pp. 93-94.

to the people to whom they partly addressed their views, and thus gradually raised the conversational dialects to a literary status. This is proved by the existence and survival of two special languages, Ardha-Māgadhi or Jaina Prākrit and Suddha Māgadhi or Pāli, in which the teachings of Mahāvīra and Buddha respectively are embodied. Even the short extract of Gośāla's doctrine, preserved by the Buddhists, conclusively proves that his vehicle of expression was neither Ardha-Māgadhi nor Pāli but something allied to both.[1]

Uninterrupted growth of Sanskrit.

With the progress of thought, the growth and enrichment of colloquial dialects proceeded side by side with the growth of Sanskrit which was never interrupted. Sanskrit never ceased to be a language of the country, as Brāhmans—the ministers of the state and teachers of many public institutions, never ceased to be a power.

The origins of pessimism.

The direct influence of political history of the time over the course of philosophy was even greater than we usually suppose. Although, as we said, peace followed upon centuries of war, the gloom cast over the mind of ignorant people by terrible experiences and painful recollections of the past was too deep to be so easily removed. As the contemporary literature vividly paints it, within the living memory of the people many places, which were in former days populous, prosperous and closely situated, had so fallen into ruin that now villages appeared to be no villages, countries no countries, and cities no cities. The devastation was partly a periodical work of the hand of nature, being brought about by famine, disease and other natural causes, and partly by war, tyranny, lawlessness, and general immorality.[2]

If we think of the misery of the people, the domination of one caste over another, of men over women, and of masters

[1] Our 'Ājīvikas,' Pt. I, p. 46 f.

[2] Aṅguttara-nikāya, I. 159 f.

The problem of misery and other ethical problems.

over slaves and servants, the ruthlessness of criminal laws, the system of usury, and such other corrupt social practices, we may almost say that the general conditions of society brought the problem of misery to the forefront. The problem really arose long before, and was still awaiting solution. It was bound up with all ethical problems. The most disputed question of the time was: Is there any valid metaphysical ground for moral distinctions? When this last question forced itself upon Pratardana, he naively suggested that we are just so many puppets in the hands of Chance or Providence and that there is no sin whatever in killing a Brāhman or parents and teachers. The Gotamaka paradox of Being left the question entirely in the dark: If the killer thinks he kills or the killed thinks himself killed, both are ignorant. In Pūraṇa Kassapa's view, the soul is absolutely passive, and not affected in the least by our sense-experiences. It is therefore all the same whether a person makes "all the living creatures on the earth one heap, one mass of flesh," or he gives alms, shows liberality, and practises generosity, self-mastery, and so forth. Kakuda Kātyāyana's eternalistic theory was even more surprising: "There is neither slayer nor causer of slaying, hearer or speaker, knower or explainer. When one with a sharp sword cleaves a head in twain, no one thereby deprives anyone of life, a sword has only penetrated into the interval between seven elementary substances." Ajita Keśa-Kambalin opposed to this eternalistic error, an error which is of an annihilationist character. Denying future existence and retribution, he deprived human life of all its zest. Maskarin Gośāla's biological researches supplied the thinkers with a strong argument in favour of the doctrine of non-injury to every form of life, but he sold men altogether to fate, nature and heredity. Another belief which took possession of people's mind is that time is the first and only cause of our happiness and sorrow.

At the time when these philosophers indulged in all sorts of extravagant theories, pernicious in their moral consequences and detrimental to the source of distinctions between 'truth and falsehood, vice and virtue, beauty and deformity,' Sañjaya embarked upon a vigorous sceptical campaign against them all. Seeing that the current views were so widely opposed as to defy every attempt at their reconciliation, and at the same time so remote from the sentiments and comprehension of common men, he considered suspension of judgment the best pathway to peace. Thus Sañjaya's attitude served to throw speculative philosophy into disrepute, and it remained for Mahāvīra and Buddha to rectify by means of sounder methods of examination the current belief that abstraction has no connexion with ethical self-development. Another great service rendered by Sañjaya to philosophy was this. Most of the philosophers of his time adopted a dogmatic method of investigation, whereas the exploitation of the sceptical method loosened the bonds of affirmative philosophies and paved the way for a critical method. With the awakening of new ethical consciousness the hypothesis of time, Providence, Chance, Fate, Nature or Soul as the first cause of our happiness or misery was abandoned and the thinkers concentrated their attention upon manly strength. But we are yet far from having a conception of positive good.

CHAPTER XXVI.

MAHĀVĪRA.

The time is now past when we should give a detailed account of the life of Mahāvīra. But a few salient facts regarding it will be deemed necessary for an introduction to our discussion of his philosophy.

A short account of Mahāvīra's life: his names and birthplace.

To begin with, Mahāvīra—the Great Hero—was not the personal name of the thinker. He was better known to his contemporaries as Nigaṇṭha Nāta-putta—Nigaṇṭha of the Nāta or Nāya clan. He is sometimes alluded to as Vardhamāna and Veśālie (Vaiśālīya),[1] the latter being evidently a local name which signifies that Vaiśāli was his birthplace. As we noticed, the government of Vaiśāli was a confederation of eight small clans, powers or states collectively known by the name of the Vajjis. Dr. Hoernle describes it as "an oligarchic republic," the government of which "was vested in a senate, composed of the heads of the resident Kṣatriya clans, and presided over by an officer who had the title of King and was assisted by a viceroy and a commander-in-chief."[2] Presumably the Nātas, Nāyas or Jñātris were one of these eight clans. It is important to record that Buddha, too, came of a similar republican clan, the Śākyas of Kapilavāstu, as in the light of this fact we can easily trace the source from which both Mahāvīra and Buddha derived their democratic tendencies.

His parentage: the source of his anti-Brahmanical feelings.

The Jaina tradition places the birth of Mahāvīra in the year 599 B. C. His father, Siddhārtha, was an influential member of the well-known Nāta clan, who married the daughter of the then king of Vaiśāli. She was a Kṣatriya lady, Triśalā by name. Obviously then the family in which he was born was

[1] Uttarādhyayana-sūtra, VI. 17. [2] J. R. A. S., 1808, p. 40; Heart of Jainism, p. 22.

anything but "beggarly or Brahmanical."[1] Even the whole of Vaiśāli, his birthplace, was removed from the centres of Brahmanical influence. This latter fact may well explain in the case of Mahāvīra, as also in the case of Buddha, why his attitude towards Brahmanic religion was not quite friendly.

According to a Śvetāmbara tradition, Mahāvīra, no less than Buddha, fully entered into the experience of the world in

Marriage.

that he married Yaśodā, a Kṣatriya lady, and thus experienced what Śtrīveda or 'amorous enjoyment'[2] is. A daughter was born to them, Anojjā or Priyadarśanā by name. She was married to Jamāli, a kṣatriya 'who, after becoming one of Mahāvīra's followers and fellow-workers, ended by opposing him.'

All the Jaina authorities agree in relating that when Mahāvīra was about thirty years old, he withdrew himself from the

Renunciation. Pārśvanātha and Mahāvīra.

world. There are good reasons to believe that he joined at first, and remained for a year with, the religious order founded by Pārśvanātha, who is said to have lived some two hundred and fifty years before Mahāvīra. The members of this ancient order used to cover their nakedness by wearing clothes, and were noted for their fourfold vow (cāujjāma).[3]

We learn from the Kalpa-sūtra that Mahāvīra was a mere learner during the first twelve years of his monkhood, and that

Gośāla and Mahāvīra.

in the second year he became a naked monk. In the fifteenth chapter of the Bhagavatī-sūtra we are told that in the second year Mahāvīra received Gośāla Maṅkhali-putta as a disciple at Nālandā. They lived in concord for six years, after which they separated on account of a doctrinal difference. After this

[1] *Cf.* Bühler's Baudhāyana, II. 2. 4. 26; Mahābhārata, I. 78: A Kṣatriya princess says to the daughter of a Brāhman: "Thou, forsooth, art the daughter of one who praises (others), who begs and accepts (gifts); but I am the child of one who is praised, who gives gift and does not accept them."

[2] Sūtra-kṛitāṅga, I. 4. 1-200; Uttarâdhyayana sūtra, XXIX. 5. itthi-veda.

[3] Uttarâdhyayana sūtra, XXIII. 12.

separation they never met in sixteen years but once in Sāvatthi. Gosāla predeceased Mahāvīra by some sixteen years, and it follows from the account in the Kalpa-sūtra that he was recognised as a teacher at least two years before the latter. Another discrepancy between the accounts of the Bhagavatī and the Kalpa-sūtra is pointed out by Dr. Höernle as follows: "According to the former, Mahāvīra spent six years in Paṇiyabhūmi (in the company of Gosāla), while the latter gives him only one year in that place, but six years in Mithilā."[1] The inference from these two somewhat contradictory accounts seems to be this—that in the second year of his monkhood, Mahāvīra left the religious order of Pārśvanātha, and joined the school of Gosāla. And when six years afterwards the difference of opinion led Mahāvīra to leave that school, he founded a new school of his own and organised a religious order mainly after the model of that of Pārśvanātha. The only innovation which he made was the introduction of the vow of chastity in addition to the fourfold vow of Pārśvanātha, and that was perhaps suggested by the moral corruption of the naked ascetics. However, the fact that he retained all the vows of the latter induced his old friends, the followers of Pārśvanātha, again to meet him, nay, to accept him as their teacher. But although the two orders were thus amalgamated, and Mahāvīra was recognised as the common spiritual father and leader, the followers of Pārśvanātha could not but be shocked at the sight of nudity. This furnished a psychological cause of difference, which led at last immediately after the teachar's death to a dissention among his disciples.[2] The after effect of it was of course the appearance of two rival sects, the Digambara or sky-clad and the Śvetāmbara or white-clad. This schism may accordingly be viewed in a sense

[1] Uvāsaga Dasāo, p. 111.

[2] Dīgha-nikāya, III. 137; Majjhima-nikāya, II. 243.

as a 'reversion' to the original separation between the two orders, referred to above.

Mahāvīra died in 527 B.C. at Pāvā, after a successful career of thirty-five years as a teacher. Among his disciples, Gautama Indrabhūti was the 'earliest and greatest.' He survived his master for twelve years. Sudharman is another great disciple who survived Mahāvīra.

Among other notable facts we have to record, first, that the main centres of Mahāvīra's activity were Rājagṛiha, Campā, Vaiśāli and Pāvā; secondly, that Prince Abhaya, the son of Bimbisāra, was the chief patron of his order[1]; and thirdly, that from the beginning the lay supporters of his order were merchants and rich bankers.

His Philosophy.

I. In dealing with Mahāvīra's philosophy it is necessary first to discriminate the sources of information which broadly fall under two heads; the direct and the collateral. The former comprise documents preserved to us by the Jains themselves; the latter represent fragments procurable from the Buddhist records.[2] Of the Jaina authorities, some are older or more authentic than others. By older authorities we mean of course the twelve Aṅgas, and by later authorities the twelve Upāṅgas and other works. In pursuing our present investigation, nothing perhaps would be wiser and safer than to draw our information chiefly from the twelve Aṅgas, the last of which, the Dṛiṣṭivāda, containing fourteen discourses or sections (pūrvas), has been lost. The loss is great, because, as its name implies, this particular text, perhaps more

Sources of information.

[1] Nāyādhammakahā, 81 f. *Cf.* Majjhima-nikāya, I. 392.

[2] *E.g.* Sāmaññaphala and Pāsādika suttas in the Dīgha-nikāya; Saccaka, Upāli, Sakula-Udāyī, Abhaya-Rājakumāra, Devadaha and Sāmagāma suttas in the Majjhima-nikāya; Aṅguttara, III. 70. I. 3; etc.

than any other, contained a systematic criticism of pre-Jaina philosophies. And yet we have reason to believe that the remaining eleven Aṅgas, which still survive together with the Upāṅgas and other extra-canonical works, cannot fail to give us a fairly definite idea of the content of the Aṅga now lost.

The existing Aṅgas do not seem to have been put together at one time. Their growth was gradual. None the less, the date of composition of the main bulk of Jaina canonical literature must be placed between the life-time of Mahāvīra on one side, and the reign of Chandragupta Maurya (4th century, B.C.) on the other. For, according to a well-founded tradition, the Jaina canon was fixed for the first time at the council held at Patna under the auspices of Sthūlabhadra, who was prime minister to the ninth or last Nanda king. On the other hand, it will be wrong to suppose that Jaina literature sprang up suddenly, without a causal connexion with earlier processes, dating from the life-time of Mahāvīra onward.

We also have reason to suspect that the Aṅgas, as we now have them, underwent considerable changes, here and there, at later redactions, or in the course of being handed down orally. The second Aṅga—the Sūtra-Kṛitāṅga for instance, which is supposed to have been composed originally in Ardha-Māgadhi, has in its present form a section[1] containing many Sanskrit words. Similarly, although the Samavāyāṅga is generally enumerated as the fourth in the list of Aṅgas, even a superficial acquaintance with the text will reveal that, a synthesis or summary as it is of all the Aṅgas, it is really not the fourth but the very last Aṅga.

In view of such uncertainty of chronology, it would certainly be a mistake to accept the evidence of any particular text. The best we can do under the circumstances is first to conceive the historical data upon the collective evidence of the Aṅgas now available, and then to test them further by the

[1] II. 4. 3 f.

collateral evidence of the Buddhist literature, as well as to verify them in the light of later development of the Jaina doctrine. The task is not so difficult as may appear at first sight, considering that the existing Jaina texts, in common with those of the Buddhists, abound in stock or parallel passages. Even then in order to achieve this critico-philological task, the historian will have to discriminate the passages ascribed to his disciples from those ascribed to Mahāvīra himself. Let this suffice for an introduction.

Kiriyam or Kriyāvāda was the original name of what is now known as Jainism.

II. The doctrine to which modern usage freely applies the name Jainism was designated by its author as Kiriyam or Kriyāvāda. Its upholders, the Kriyāvādins, who are now called Jains, were then generally known as Nigaṇṭhas. The designation Ārhatas for the Jains is of frequent occurrence in the medieval literature of the Brāhmans.

Significance of the name Nigaṇṭha. In which sense Pārśva may be called a precursor of Mahāvīra.

Mahāvīra himself was best known to his contemporaries as a Nigaṇṭha or Nirgrantha,—the unfettered one,—he who is free from all worldly bonds or mundane desires. The name has been applied to the religious order of Pārśva whom the Jains idolise as the last Tīrthaṅkara (school-maker) but one. Here a question is apt to arise if we are really justified in regarding Pārśva as a precursor or philosophic predecessor of Mahāvīra. Evidently we are not. There is not, as yet, a single proof that he was in any sense a philosopher. A predecessor Pārśva nevertheless was, but that in quite another sense. He was an ascetic of the ancient hermit type, who, like the king Nimi of Mithilā, Ariṣṭanemi, and other common predecessors (Jinas, Bodhisattvas) of Mahāvīra and Buddha, strongly favoured the life of renunciation. It appears that Mahāvīra, on leaving home-life, joined a religious body who followed the rule of Pārśva.

The whole clan of Nātas,[1] or at any rate Mahāvīra's parents,[2] were among the lay supporters of this body of ascetics. If so, we can easily imagine how Mahāvīra's attention was naturally turned to Pārśva's order.[3]

Prof. Jacobi has thrown light on the exact relationship between Pārśva and Mahāvīra as teachers.[4] He is the first to discover that there were at first two separate Nigaṇṭha orders, having nothing in common save the 'four vows' or 'four restraints,' and to assume that this original diversity between the two orders 'ripened into division, and in the end brought about the great schism.'

The original Nigaṇṭha order.

He has again clearly perceived that a doctrine attributed to Mahāvīra in the Buddhist Sāmaññaphala sutta 'properly belonged to his predecessor Pārśva,' of course, in so far as the mere expression *cātuyāma-Saṁvara* is concerned. The doctrine is that, according to Mahāvīra, the way to self-possession, self-command, and imperturbability consists of 'a four-fold self-restraint' such as restraint in regard to all water, restraint as regards all evil, and restraints by way of the purification of sin and feeling a sense of ease on that account.[5] Buddhaghosa interprets the first restraint as meaning that Nigaṇṭha Nāta-putta did not use cold water, believing it to be possessed of life (satta-sāññi),[6] and remarks that although founded upon an erroneous view of life, the doctrine of four restraints was in some measure favourable to moral discipline.

Pārśva's doctrine.

Prof. Rhys Davids seems to have misunderstood Prof. Jacobi when he says that in the opinion of the latter "the

[1] Uvāsaga Dasāo, p. 6.
[2] Ācārāṅga, II. 15. 16.
[3] Heart of Jainism, p. 31.
[4] Jaina-sūtras, Part 2, pp. xix-xxii.
[5] *Cf.* Dial. B., II, pp. 74-75.
[6] Sumaṅgala-Vilāsinī, I. 166; cp. Rhys Davids' 'Milinda,' II. 85-91.

four restraints are intended to represent the four vows kept by the followers of Pārśva." Prof. Jacobi nowhere maintains that the four restraints, as enumerated in the Sāmaññaphala-sutta and explained by Buddhaghosa, correspond to the four vows as enumerated in the Jaina texts, notably the Sūtra-Kṛitāṅga.[1] On the other hand, he shows that the term *Cātuyāma-saṁvara*, employed in the Buddhist dialogue, is but the Pali equivalent of the Prakrit *Cāujjāma*, a well-known Jaina term denoting the four vows, which, according to the testimony of two followers of Pārśva, Keśi and Udaka, were held binding upon their fraternity.[2] We are thus convinced with Prof. Jacobi that the enumeration of four restraints in the Sāmaññaphala-sutta is wrong, and that the doctrine attributed to Mahāvīra in the same sutta is neither an accurate representation of his opinion, nor that of the view of his predecessor, though at the same time it contains nothing alien from either. For even apart from the convincing proofs adduced from the Jaina authorities, we learn from a sutta in the Majjhima-Nikāya[3] that in Mahāvīra's view the established path to the realm of highest bliss lies through abstinence from killing, abstinence from theft, from adultery, from lying, and such austere practices (tapoguṇa) as nudity, penance, confession, and the rest.[4] That these five modes of self-restraint correspond to the five great vows[5] (pañca mahāvvaya) of Mahāvīra is beyond question. And if so, we may conclude on the authority of both Jaina and Buddhist texts that the first four of these precepts were

Modern interpretation of the term *cātu-yāma saṁvara*.

[1] Sūtra-Kṛitāṅga, II. 7. 17.

[2] *Ibid*, II, 7. 39; Uttarādhyayana-sūtra, XXIII. 12.

[3] II. 35-36. *Cf.* Digha-nikāya, III, pp. 48-51, where Buddha interprets the term *cātu-yāma-saṁvara* as meaning four moral precepts, considered each under three serial heads. This is the meaning the Buddha wishes to pnt on the phrase.

[4] *Cf* Saṁyutta-nikāya, I. 66.

[5] Ācārāṅga, II. 15 (1-5).

originally laid down by Pārśva, while the fifth was added later by Mahāvīra himself.

Contrast between Pārśva and Mahāvīra: the former was a mere religious teacher, the latter a religious-philosopher.

We can now see the contrast between the two time-honoured Jaina teachers, Pārśva and Mahāvīra, or where we can attempt to give a definite answer to the question whether the former might be regarded as a philosophic predecessor of the latter. The scanty account we now have of Pārśva clearly shows that he was a man of practical nature, remarkable for his organising genius. The religious order founded by him enjoyed the reputation of a high and rigid standard of conduct, verging upon the Stoic or ascetic. He made four moral precepts binding upon his followers, precepts which were later enforced by Mahāvīra and Buddha among their followers. We shall, however, not judge Pārśva aright if we suppose that his rules were confined to these four precepts. Conceivably, they embraced many other practical rules laid down for guidance of the fraternity and laity. We might even go further and maintain that all the fundamental rules of the Nigaṇṭha community were due to Pārśva and his followers. But this set of rules, taken by themselves, constituted just another system of austere moral discipline (vinaya-vāda or sīlabbata) which Mahāvīra and Buddha deprecated with one voice. That is to say, Pārśva's rules of conduct, however good they were, needed a philosophic justification in order that they might not appear in any sense arbitrary, or be confounded with the conventions of society.

The Uttarādhayana sūtra furnishes a dialogue shedding abundant light on this obscure point. The interlocutors are the two leading representatives of the Nigaṇṭha orders of the time. Keśi, who was a follower of Pārśva's rule, asks Gautama, who was one of the chief disciples of Mahāvīra: "When the four precepts promulgated by the great sage Pārśva are held equally binding upon our two orders, what is the cause of difference between us?" The latter replies, "Wisdom recognises the truth of the law and the ascertainment of true things. The first saints were simple but slow of understanding, the last saints prevaricating and slow of understanding, those between the two simple and wise; hence there are two forms of the Law. The first could only with difficulty understand the precepts of the Law, and the last could only with difficulty observe them, but those between them easily understood and observed them."[1] Here the purport of Gautama's reply is that Pārśva's was a mere religious order, while Mahāvīra's was not only a religious order, but also a distinct school of thought.

Mahāvīra's philosophic predecessor was Gośāla.

III. If neither Pārśva nor any one among his followers were the philosophic predecessor of Mahāvīra, who then was there in India who might be honoured with that name? The reply must go against the Jaina tradition which represents Gośāla as a disciple of Mahāvīra. We have sought to show that Gośāla was the one among his many predecessors or elder contemporaries with whom he was most intimately associated for a number of years.

Three questions relating to the ecclesiastical history of the Jainas, and their answers.

In connection with the ecclesiastical history of the Jainas these are the three important questions: How was it that there were originally two Nigaṇṭha orders instead of one? When were the two amalgamated into one, to be separated again after Mahāvīra's death? What benefit did the followers of Pārśva derive from such an amalgamation?

We may attempt to answer these questions by assuming that Mahāvīra, after undergoing Pārśva's discipline for a year joined the Ājīvikas, who, as we saw, cultivated a high sense of dignity and independence. This naturally brought him

[1] Jaina-sūtras, Part 2, pp. 122-123.

into close contact with Gośāla whose biological speculations created a sensation in the country. There is evidence enough that his naturalistic researches were soon followed by others upon social and moral problems of varied description. In religious circles the burning questions of the day were: Is there any moral justification for killing living beings? Can we, on the other hand, literally avoid, while we live, the act of killing? And what is the proper way of dealing with those fellow beings who sin against society and morals?

Although the religious bodies did not all actually keep to a vegetarian diet, it was recognised universally that every object of nature should be handled gently and treated with the utmost tenderness. As Buddha expressed it, "Living beings are all desirous of happiness," "all are afraid of the rod, all fear death. Thus, comparing oneself with others, one should cease from the act of hurting or killing."

In order to avoid killing, some of the hermits used to subsist upon the flesh of animals which had died. There were a few others, the Hatthi Tāpasas,[1] for instance, who with a view to lessening the slaughter of living beings, killed for food each year one elephant instead of destroying many lives daily and hourly.

It is from Gośāla that Mahāvīra first learnt to think philosophically as it was afterwards mainly in opposing this teacher's deterministic theory that he was led gradually to the discovery of nine categories (nava tattva). The opposition led to the severance of the tie that bound them for a period of six years. We do not know by what name Mahāvīra was known during the time when he associated himself with the Ājīvikas or Maskarins. Subsequently he assumed his old epithet Nigaṇṭha, though he did not actually go back to Pārśva's order. The epithet proved very useful to him owing to the popularity which the Nigaṇṭhas of the old order had so long enjoyed.

[1]. Sūtra-Kṛitāṅga, II. 6. 52.

When in course of time Mahāvīra succeeded in founding a new Nigaṇṭha order and in organising it partly after the model of the Ājīvikas and partly after that of Pārśva's followers, some sort of distinction between the two orders became inevitable. It is implied in the dialogue between Udaka and Gautama[1] that the followers of Pārśva were known as Nigaṇṭha Kumāra-puttas, while Mahāvīra's disciples were known as Nigaṇṭha Nāta-puttas.[2] Thus we can see how two rival orders arose.

Whilst the intellectual superiority of the new order was throwing the old order into the shade, the adherents of the latter were compelled to think of some way of maintaining their existence and prestige. Obviously the best means was not rivalry, but reconciliation. The dialogue between Keśi and Gautama in the Uttarādhyayana sūtra shows that there was a time when Pārśva's followers were contemplating an amalgamation of the two orders. Keśi was perhaps the Nigaṇṭha of the old order who is designated by Buddha as Dīgha-tapassi. If so, the Dīgha-tapassi-sutta belongs to a time when the two orders were actually amalgamated into one school of philosophy. The Pāsādika and Sāmagāma suttas again take us to a time when, soon after Mahāvīra's death, his disciples were divided into two contending parties. However, the benefit which Pārśva's followers derived from the amalgamation was the philosophy of the new school.

Definition of Kiriyam.

IV. The Kiriyam of Mahāvīra, in common with the vibhajja-vāda of the Buddha, denotes a doctrine which is diametrically opposed to Akiriyam, and also sharply distinguishable from Aṇṇānam or Vicikicchā and Vinayam or

[1] Sūtra-Kritāṅga, II. 7.

[2] In the Buddhist records (Aṅguttara-nikāya, III. 383 ; Sumaṅgala-Vilāsinī, I. 160-165) the Nigaṇṭhas are alluded to as recluses of " the red class " (lohitābhijāti), also as " those with one garment " (ekasāṭakā). The term Wearers of white clothes (odātavasanā or śvetāmbaras) is applied to the lay adherents of the Ājīvikas.

Sīlabbatam. In a passage the Sūtra-Kṛitāṅga[1] we read that the upholders of this doctrine gaining a true view of the world, maintain that misery is caused by oneself, and not by others—time, providence, fate, chance or soul (sayaṁkaḍaṁ ṇannakaḍaṁ ca dukkhaṁ). Liberation is obtainable by knowledge and good conduct (vijjā-caraṇaṁ pāmokkhaṁ). Thus they teach a path which is conducive to man's moral and intellectual progress. They declare the world of generation to be eternal (sāsaya), because beings live in it for ever and ever, and because sinners are subject to repeated births and deaths.

Again, while recognising the inflexibility of the law of action, the Kriyāvādins maintain that fools are unable to stop the course of their evil actions by actions which are equally evil. The wise saints can arrest the course of evil only by abstaining from all wrong-doing.[2] For they believe that those who have overcome greed (lobha) and are contented, cannot commit sin; they are indeed wise and happy.

Averse to slaughter of life, they neither kill nor incite others to kill. Keeping always the senses under control, these pious men become heroes, armed with the weapon of knowledge. A Kriyāvādin regards all beings, large and small, and the whole world as like to himself. He comprehends the immensity of the universe, and thus awakened he guards himself among the careless or unguarded.

He who knows himself and the world, who knows the nature of man's future existences and immortality, who knows what is eternal and what is not, and so forth, alone is entitled to expound the Kriyāvāda, since he is unattached to the pleasures of the senses, free from desires as to life and death, and self-controlled.

It is not easy to elicit from this verbose and obscure passage any clear-cut definition of Kiriyam. However, in attempting

[1] Sūtra-Kritāṅga, I. 12. 11-22.

[2] Ṇa kammaṇā kamma khaveṁti bālā, akammaṇā kamma khaveṁti dhīro.

a definition of this significant term we shall do well first to consider the light in which Buddha viewed the doctrine of his predecessor:

V. The Psycho-ethical aspect of Kiriyam.

Buddha, in agreement with Mahāvīra and contrary to the deterministic theory of Gośāla, expounded the doctrine of Karma, dynamism, or the moral effect of manly strength. It was again following his predecessor that Buddha judged Gośāla's to be the worst of all doctrines, subversive of the ground for all moral distinctions, responsibilities and freedom.[1]

Gośāla, Mahāvīra and Buddha.

Besides this hostile attitude towards Gośāla's fatalistic doctrine, Mahāvīra and Buddha had many points in common. They were, for instance, both nobles by birth, and came of two republican clans. They classified the philosophers of their time as unmoral metaphysicians, ignorant eel-wriggling sceptics and selfish pleasure-seeking moralists. They pursued neither a dogmatic nor a sceptical method of investigation. And yet Buddha often appears to think that his doctrine of causal genesis (paticca-samuppāda) was in some way antagonistic to Mahāvīra's dynamistic philosophy or doctrine of free-will activity.

Buddha understood that Mahāvīra, in opposition to current beliefs that our happiness and misery are caused by others—determined wholly and solely by external factors and conditions—formulated a new theory, namely, that they are caused by the individual agent of our free-will. That our weal and ill are conditioned solely by or dependent upon external causes is one extreme, and by opposing to this a new individualistic theory,

Buddha's interpretation and criticism of Mahāvīra's doctrine.

[1] Aṅguttara-nikāya, I. 173-174, 286-287; Uvāsaga Dasāo, VI. 166; VII. 196-209: "Mahāvīrassa dhamma-paṇṇatti: atthi uṭṭhāne iva...jāva parakkame iva, aniyayā sabba-bhāvā."

Mahāvīra ran to the other extreme, neither of which can a man of true insight reasonably accept.[1]

Buddha is right in ascribing to Mahāvīra the individualist position above-mentioned. His expression in the original is practically identical with the Jaina affirmation in the Sūtra-Kṛitānga.[2] It must be noted here that this particular Jaina text contains several disconnected passages where, according to the testimony of Sudharman, Mahāvīra, like his successor Buddha, throws into clear relief the contrast between existing philosophical notions and his own theory. And important as they are, these passages can be rendered intelligible only when we consider them in reference to those individual theorisers to whom they actually apply.

Mahāvīra's criticism of pre-Jaina and contemporary philosophers from the standpoint of his ethics.

First, with regard to ancient Vedic thinkers, Mahāvīra said: "Some of the seers thought that the world has been created and is governed by the gods; others by Brahmā. Some of them have ascribed to the hand of Iśvara, the mundane Lord, the creation of this universe of beings and things, with its manifold vicissitudes; in the opinion of others, this phenomenal world is but the outcome or gradual manifestation of primitive undifferentiated matter (pahāna = pradhāna). Some maintain that the world emanates from a self-existent being; its origin is spontaneous and it appears to be non-eternal and unreal because of the illusion (māyā) thrown over man's mind by Death (Māra); according to the view of others, the world is produced from a primeval germ,—the original solar body.

[1] Aṅguttara-nikāya, III. 440; "Abhabbo diṭṭhisampanno puggalo sayaṁkataṁ sukha-dukkhaṁ paccāgantuṁ, abhabbo diṭṭhisampanno puggalo paraṁkataṁ sukha-dukkhaṁ paccāgantum." *Cf.* Saṁyutta, II. 22. ff. We are indebted to Dr. M. H. Bode for these valuable references. *Cf.* Peṭakopadesa, opening paragraphs. "Sayaṁ kataṁ paraṁ katanti, etc., dve antā."

[2] Pāli—Sayaṁkataṁ sukha-dukkhaṁ, (na) paraṁkataṁ sukha-dukkhaṁ. Prakrit—sayaṁkaḍaṁ ṇannakaḍaṁ ca dukkhaṁ.

I do not, however, see how these cosmological speculations can afford a rational, clear and distinct theory of misery or its origin and cessation."[1]

Secondly, as to Post-Vedic thinkers (*e.g.*, Yājñavalkya and Uddālaka), we are told: "Some of the philosophers postulate these five gross elements—earth, water, fire, air and ether—as the five roots of things. It is from them that another—the intelligent principle or soul—arises, inasmuch as on the dissolution of the body living beings cease to exist. However, as the earth, though it is but one mass, presents manifold forms so the intelligent principle appears under various forms or manifests itself in varying degrees of development.

Such is the pantheistic view of some teachers, which, verging as it does upon materialism, fails to explain how and why an individual wrong-doer should suffer pain due to his iniquities."[2]

And lastly, among his elder contemporaries, Pūraṇa Kassapa was evidently the first object of Mahāvīra's attack: "There is a class of philosophers who maintain that when a man acts or causes others to act, it is not his soul which acts or causes to act. But how can those who hold such an opinion account for the moral distinctions as known in our daily experience?"[3]

"There is another class of philosophers (say, the Kātyāyanas) who regard five elements as the five permanent substrata of change. To these they also add soul as the sixth substance. What is, is imperishable,—eternally existent; nothing comes out of nothing. On these grounds they who make a hard and fast distinction between mind and body, view life and death as a kind of recurrent mechanical combination (samavāya) and separation of the elements of existence. The moral inference

[1] Sūtra-Kritāṅga, I. 1. 3. 5-9. See for literal translation, Jacobi's Jaina-sūtras, Part 2, pp. 244-245.

[2] *Ibid*, I. 1. 1. 7-10.

[3] *Ibid*, I. 1. 1. 13.

drawn from these delusive metaphysical arguments is that whether a man buys or causes to buy, kills or causes to kill, he does not thereby commit any sin."[1]

"There is a third class of philosophers (say, the Keśakambalins) who oppose to the dualist or pluralist doctrine above mentioned a theory which goes to identify the mental with the corporeal. They maintain that the real is always a living whole,—an individual who comes into existence from the union of four or five elements and passes out of existence after death. Life ends here, there is no world beyond, say they. Thus these murderers teach men to kill, slay, burn, cook, cut and destroy. Denying the hereafter and the efficacy of all social institutions founded upon beliefs in the future existence of man, the annihilationists cannot inform us whether an action is good or bad, virtuous or vicious, well-done or otherwise, whether it is in man's power to reach perfection or not, or whether there is a heaven or a hell."[2]

"The Maskarins or Fatalists are the next to be considered. They represent a class of philosophers who admit that there are infinite numbers and grades of concrete existents,—of living beings who, as individuals, experience pleasure and pain and pass by death from one state of existence to another which is better, equal or worse, but they deny that our happiness and misery, weal and ill, are caused by us individually or determined by any other cause except what they term fate or necessity (niyai). All things are pre-arranged by nature and unalterably fixed. Some beings are capable of bodily movement, others not; it depends upon certain conditions whether they are in the one state or in the other (sangai). Proceeding from these erroneous notions, they deny all exertion, struggle, power, vigour or manly strength. Those who boldly

[1] Sūtra-Kṛitāṅga, I. 1. 1. 15; II. 1. 22-24.

[2] *Ibid*, I. 1. 11-12; II, 1. 16-17.

proclaim these opinions are really deluded. They, too, cannot account for moral distinctions."[1]

"There are yet again a class of philosophers[2] who maintain that the soul has power to attain the highest state of purity or sinlessness, but just as distilled water may again be defiled on coming into contact with impurities, so may be the soul defiled by pleasant excitement or hate. In upholding such a view these philosophers really deny the possibility of the soul attaining an undecaying or immaterial condition (nijjarā) within its living experience, and final release (mokṣa) after death. They betray, in other words, just their faulty notion of immortality here and hereafter."[3]

"The philosophers hitherto considered differ from one another in intellect, will, character, opinion, taste, undertakings and plans, but their views in their moral effect are the same, being actuated by the same motive, prompted by the same unmoral sentiments. We may take for instance the views of Pūraṇa Kassapa and Gosāla Mankhaliputta. The former denies causation in that he denies activity on the part of soul; the latter, on the other hand, assigns fate as the cause of everything. What is the difference between the two, in so far as the moral bearings of their doctrines are concerned? When these philosophers are judged from the ethical standpoint of a Kriyāvādin, all appear in one sense or another as so many unmoral metaphysicians—(akriyāvādins)."[4]

"Those who, besides unmoral metaphysicians, are in some way opposed to a Kriyāvādin are the sceptics and moralists. The former, ignorant as they are, do not themselves apprehend truth, how then can they teach it to others? To follow their lead is to be as a man who has lost his way in a strange

[1] Sūtra-Kritāṅga, I. 1. 2. 1-5; I. 1. 4. 8-9; II. 1. 32; Uvāsaga Dasāo, VI. 166.

[2] According to Śīlāṅka, they are the followers of Gośāla and later Jaina Trairāśikas.

[3] Sūtra-Kritāṅga, I. 1. 3. 11.

[4] *Ibid*, II. 1. 30; II. 1. 34; Sthānāṅga, IV. 4.

wood and follows a guide who also does not know it. Their views are, in short, no good."[1]

"The moralists are those teachers who seek to govern society by set rules, compose treatises directing people how they should gratify their amorous passions, encourage acquisition of wealth, tolerate all superstitions and corrupt social practices, judge men by their outward conduct, behaviour and circumstances, do not recognise the rights of individuals as individuals, and so forth."[2]

The fundamental categories and maxim of Mahāvīra's ethics.

"It is chiefly, then, in opposition to the views of unmoral metaphysicians and selfish moralists that a Kriyāvādin recognises that there is virtue (puṇṇa), that there is vice (pāpa), that there are 'channels,' that there is in-flux of sin (assava), that there are restraints (saṁvara), that there is bondage (bandha), that there is the path to freedom (nijjarā), and that there is final liberation (mokkha). These are the five categories of his ethics. The standpoint from which he judges the standard of conduct is that of an individualist, his fundamental maxim is: I am the maker of my own happiness and misery, and not others."

Modification of Buddha's interpretation of his predecessor's fundamental ethical thesis, and of Mahāvīra's interpretation of pre-Jaina philosophies.

Now we must modify Buddha's interpretation of Mahāvīra's ethical position just as we must modify Mahāvīra's interpretation of pre-Jaina philosophies. We have endeavoured to show that Mahāvīra, in direct antagonism to Purāṇa Kassapa's doctrine of non-causation or theory of the inactivity of soul, put forward this proposition: "When I suffer, grieve, repent, grow feeble, am afflicted, or experience plain, I have caused it, and when another man suffers in a similar way, he has caused it.

[1] Sūtra-Kritāṅga, I. 1. 2. 17-19.

[2] *Ibid*, I. 1. 4. 8; I. 4. 1. 20-23; II. 1. 45-46; Sthānāṅga, IV. 4; etc.

Pleasures and amusements are not able to help or save me. They are one thing, and I am another; they are foreign to my real being. Even the friends and relations who are more intimately connected with me cannot experience, still less take upon themselves, the pains I actually undergo. That is to say, as an individual a man is born, as an individual he dies, as an individual again he deceases from one state of existence to be reborn into another. The 'passions, consciousness, intellect, perceptions and impressions' of a man belong to him exclusively."[1]

If we compare these expressions of Mahāvīra word for word with those of Buddha, it is hardly possible for us to detect any difference between their opinions. For Buddha, too, declared that evil is done by oneself, born of oneself, produced from oneself, affects oneself, and that while self is the lord of self, there is no other lord but self.[2] In the same vein he instructed Ānanda to be zealous in his own behalf and to devote himself to his own good.[3] The question then arises, where lies the real point of difference between their views?

Difference between the views of Mahāvīra and Buddha, and the correlation of Niyativāda and Kriyāvāda.

We must first examine the Buddhist fragment—the Devadaha sutta of the Majjhima—where Buddha sharply criticises the ethical position of Mahāvīra, as represented after his death by his disciples, the Niganthas.[4] This dialogue throws some light upon the signification of Mahāvīra's terse expression: "Fools cannot annihilate works by works; the wise can annihilate works by abstaining from works."[5]

Buddha says to the Niganthas, "Are you, friends, of this opinion, is it your view: Whatever a living individual

[1] Sūtra-Kritānga, II. 1. 31; II. 33-41.

[2] Atta-vagga, Dhammapada.

[3] Rhys Davids', Buddhist Suttas, p. 91.

[4] Majjhima-nikāya, II. 218.

[5] Sūtra-Kritānga, I. 12. 15: "Na kammaṇā kamma khevaṁti bālā, akammaṇā kamma khevaṁti dhīro."

experiences in this life, whether it be pleasant or painful or neither pleasant-nor-painful, all that is predestined by fate, due to works of a previous life. Because of the exhaustion of former works through austerities, and because of the abstention from new works, (there is) arrest of the influx of sin in future. Because of that, the extinction of karma. Because of that, the extinction of pain. Because of that, the extinction of misery. Thus the entire body of ill perishes ?"[1]

The latter replying in the affirmative, Buddha goes on,[2] "You admit, then, that our pleasure and pain, happiness and misery, depend in part upon fate or actions of the past existence and in part upon free-will activities of the present life ?"

The reply being in the affirmative, "If so, I must ask you, Do you positively know whether you, as present individuals, had existed in the past or not ? Whether you had committed such and such sins or not ? Have you any definite idea of the *quantum* of pain already exhausted, or of the *quantum* of pain still to be exhausted, or of the *quantum* of pain which being exhausted, the entire body of ill will be exhausted ? Above all, are you acquainted with any right method of avoiding all that is evil in the negative and of performing all that is good ?

The answer being, "No" "If not, then how can you maintain your premises......I also should like to know from you, my good Nigaṇṭhas, if you intend so to change the course of action by means of your initial effort and vigorous exertion that it should produce its result in the future instead of at present, and *vice versâ* ?......"

The answer being still in the negative, "If not, where then is the utility of your energetic moral efforts ?"

[1] "Yaṁ kiñcâyaṁ purisa-puggalo patisaṁvedeti......sabbaṁ taṁ pubbekata-hetu; iti pūrāṇānaṁ kammānaṃ tapasā vyanti-bhāvā, navānaṁ kammānaṁ akaraṇā, āyatiṁ anavassavo; āyatiṁ anavassavā kammakkhayo; kammakkhayā dukkhakkhayo, dukkhakkhayā vedanākkhayo, vedanākkhayā sabbaṁ dukkhaṁ nijjiṇṇaṁ bhavissatîti ?"

[2] The translation of following paragraphs of the discourse is not literal owing to the *great length of the original ; and the substance only has been given.*

The sceptic Buddha at last concludes by saying: "If it be true that living beings experience pleasure and pain as predetermined by actions of their past lives, then the Nigaṇṭhas must have been all great sinners formerly in that they now undergo such painful austerities. Or if it be true that living beings experience pleasure and pain according as they are created by a God, then the Nigaṇṭhas must have been created by a wicked God (pāpakena Issarena). Or if living beings be happy or miserable because of the species (saṅgati) to which they belong, then the Nigaṇṭhas must have been of a very low species; or if because of their mentality (abhijāti) then they must have been persons of the worst possible mental type, etc., etc."[1]

In accordance with Mahāvīra's view I am not, as a thinking subject, wholly and solely the maker of my moral being, but I am partly a creature of circumstances. This important point is well brought out in a passage of the Sūtra-kṛitāṅga where Mahāvīra, in criticising Gosāla's doctrine, declares that "things depend partly on fate, and partly on human exertion."[2] The proposition is significant. It illustrates his antinomian theory (syād vāda) that has its full play throughout Kriyā-vāda. It may be that in one sense, looking from one point of view, A is B. It may be that in another sense, looking from another point of view, A is not-B. It may be that looking from a third point of view, A is both B and not-B, and so forth. In other words, the Dynamism of Mahāvīra leaves room enough for determinism, or the hypothesis of time, providence, nature, chance.

VI. The biological and psychological aspects of Kiriyam.

"There are things which are determined, and there are things which are not-determined (niyayāniyayaṁ saṁtaṁ)."[3]

[1] Majjhima-nikāya, II. 216-222. *abhijāti=jīvavarṇa* (Mbh. XII. 279. 32).

[2] Sūtra-Kritaṅga, I. 1. 2. 4. (Jacobi's translation).

[3] *Ibid*, I. 1. 2. 4.

Following the commentators Prof. Jacobi translates it—"Things depend partly on fate, and partly on human exertion." But keeping to the actual words of the commentators, we must interpret the dictum as meaning that "our happiness and misery are wrought partly by fate, soul, time, God or nature, and can be regulated partly by our personality or manly strength."[1] This shows that in the view of Mahāvīra, as later in the view of Kaṇāda, we are in some respects bound and in some respects free. Here Mahāvīra appears to be in sharp antagonism with Gośāla.

The category of Jīva.

But the supposed antagonism between the two thinkers may easily break down the moment the historian can prove that it rests upon a difference of standpoints. This brings us to Mahāvīra's important category of *Jīva*, a term which we take to denote the biological and psychological aspects of Kiriyam.

Gośāla also taught that all living beings experience pleasure and pain, each individually. But Mahāvīra differed from Gośāla in teaching that the sole determining factor of our entire existence is not fate or anything of the kind but the individual agent of our free will. A dialogue in the Uvāsaga Dasão[2] embodies Mahāvīra's moral contention raised against Gośāla's fatalism or denial of free-will activities.

Mahāvīra asks Saddāluputta, a lay adherent of Gośāla, who was a rich potter, "How is this pot made? Is it made by dint of exertion and manly strength or without them?" The latter replies: "It is made without them, because, according to our master's view, there is no such thing as exertion or manly strength, everything being unalterably fixed." "Supposing, Saddāluputta, some one of your men should behave in an improper manner, how would you deal with him?" "I would punish him as severely as I could or

[1] "Kiṁcid ṇiyati-kṛitaṁ ca puruṣa-kāleśvara-svabhāva-karmādi-kṛitaṁ tatra kathaṁcit sukha-dukkhādeḥ puruṣa-kāra-sādhyatvaṁ apyaśrīyate."

[2] Höernle's Uvāsaga Dasāo, VII. 196-200.

should." Thereupon Mahāvīra retorts: "But what moral reason have you for doing so, when, as you say, there is no such thing as exertion or manly strength, but all things are unalterably fixed? According to your belief, the man behaved in such a manner because he could not help it, ruled as he was by an overpowering fate."

It is difficult even to imagine that Gośāla really intended to bring arts such as pot-making within the operations of the laws of fate. It is likewise difficult to think that he actually meant to deny all moral distinctions, responsibilities and freedom as enunciated by Mahāvīra himself. On a close examination of his doctrine as a whole, we can soon discover that his determinism did not exclude Mahāvīra's notion of freedom of the will, just as, on the other hand, Mahāvīra's Dynamistic philosophy did not altogether set aside Gośāla's rule of fate. They are complementary, one being imperfect and unintelligible without the other. We conceive nevertheless that in attempting to banish the possibilities of chance from the world of fact, and of belief and reason, Gośāla carried his determinism rather too far, and that in consequence he confused or at least did not keep quite distinct the two standpoints—the biological and psychological, or the physical and ethical. Accordingly the task which Gośāla had left for his immediate successor was to draw a sharp distinction between these standpoints by employing the sober method of analysis of the laws of action (Karma) and their effects in the world of experience.

Gośāla's Determinism did not exclude the notion of freedom of the will, nor did Mahāvīra's dynamism altogether set aside the rule of fate.

The problem was discussed by Buddha also. The three teachers handled it differently and found a different solution. Gośāla set himself to show how we, as living individuals and in common with the rest of sentient existence, are acted upon by various natural causes and manifold external conditions. The main object of Mahāvīra was to determine

Gośāla, Mahāvīra and Buddha: transition from a biological to a psychological, or from a physical to an ethical standpoint.

how we, as living individuals and thinking subjects, are both acted upon and capable of acting of our own accord. Buddha sought to show how we, as rational beings, can act according to the laws or principles of reason itself. That is to say, the main standpoint of Gośāla was biological or objective, that of Mahāvīra both objective and subjective, and that of Buddha psychological or subjective.

The following argument will perhaps give some support to these general observations. As we know, Gośāla, Mahāvīra and Buddha, in common with the Moralists, followed a threefold division of actions into Deed, Word and Thought, or into Thought, Word and Deed. The same threefold division is to be found in the existing Zend-Avesta, but there is as yet no proof that anyone of them borrowed it from the ancient Persians. There is, on the other hand, sufficient evidence to prove that Gośāla laid stress mainly upon Deed and Word, Thought being to him a mere half action (upaḍḍhakamma)[1]; that Mahāvīra laid almost equal stress upon the three—Deed, Word and Thought, while the whole emphasis was laid by Buddha upon Thought (manokamma),[2] his very definition of action being volition (cetanā vadāmi kammaṁ).[3]

Threefold division of actions into deed, word, and thought.

Mahāvīra laid almost equal stress upon Deed, Word and Thought. This point is so important that if we loose sight of it we are apt to ignore half the significance of Kiriyam and the whole of the significance of Mahāvīra's psychology and ethics. In order to establish it, we may separately examine two lines of evidence, the Jaina and the Buddhist. In the first place, the Jaina Sūtra-Kṛitāṅga preserves a dialogue where Adda, a disciple of Mahāvīra, discusses a view put into the mouth of the Buddhists: "If a savage thrusts

[1] Dīgha-nikāya, I. 54.

[2] Majjhima-nikāya, III. 2. 7.

[3] Aṅguttara, III, p. 415. Cf. Mrs. Rhys Davids' "Buddhist Psychology," p. 93.

a spit through the side of a granary, mistaking it for a man; or through a gourd, mistaking it for a baby, and roasts it, he will be guilty of murder." "If a savage puts a man on a spit and roasts him, mistaking him for a fragment of the granary; or a baby, mistaking him for a gourd, he will not be guilty of murder." "If anybody thrusts a spit through a man or a baby, mistaking him for a fragment of the granary, puts him on the fire and roasts him, that will be a meal fit for Buddhas to breakfast upon." Adda, then, turns upon the Buddhists with this powerful argument: "Well-controlled men cannot accept your denial of guilt incurred by (unintentional) doing harm to living beings........ It is impossible to mistake a fragment of the granary for a man; only an unworthy man can say it. How can the idea of a man be produced by a fragment of the granary? Even to utter this is an untruth.......They kill a fattened sheep, and prepare food for the sake of a particular person; they season the meat with salt and oil, and dress it with pepper. You are irreligious, unworthy men, devoted to foolish pleasures, who say that partaking heartily of this meat you are not soiled by sin......In compassion to all beings, the seers, the Jñātiputras, avoid what is sinful; afraid of it, they abstain from food specially prepared for them."[1]

The same text contains a few other passages in which the Kriyāvādin view is contrasted apparently with the Buddhist view of delicts and crimes. We learn from one of them that for a Kriyāvādin "He who intends to kill a living being, but does not do it by an act of his body, and who unknowingly kills one, both are affected by that act through a slight contact with it only, but the demerit in their case is not fully developed."[2]

And in the second place; the Buddhist Upāli-sutta records that of the three measures of sin and crime, the bodily (Kāyadaṇḍa) had greater weight with Mahāvīra than either the vocal or the mental, while that which weighed heaviest for Buddha

[1] Jacobi's Jaina-sūtras, Part 2, pp. 414-416; *cf. ibid*, I. 1. 2. 28.

[2] *Ibid*, p. 242.

was the mental. "Even in his coming and going a Nigaṇṭha is apt to cause the slaughter of many animalcules. What does Nigaṇṭha Nātaputta consider to be the moral consequence of such an act?" When this question was pressed home by Buddha to Upāli, then a lay disciple of Mahāvīra, the latter replied: "Our master does not attach the notion of any great sin to an unintentional (unavoidable) act, but only to an act which is intentional." "Then you see, Upāli, the main determining factor of an act is the volition, motive or intention (cetanā)."[1]

The most important of Buddhist documents to consider as to the doctrine of Kiriyaṁ is the Mahā-Saccaka-suttā in which the practice of the Ājīvikas has been contrasted with that of the Buddhists as follows: "Whereas the former devote themselves to culture of the body, neglecting culture of the mind, the latter devote themselves to culture of the mind, neglecting culture of the body." Saccaka clearly implies that the followers of Mahāvīra cultivate equally both the modes of self-training on the ground that which affects the body, affects the mind, and *vice versâ* (kāyanvayaṁ cittaṁ hoti, cittanvayo kāyo hoti).[2]

We can easily understand from this that the theory of interaction of mind and body was the physio-psychological ground by which Mahāvīra sought to justify austerities in religious practice, bodily restraints in daily life, and corporeal punishment in criminal justice.

The main question remains yet to be answered. What are the things which depend on fate, necessity, time, providence, nature and the like? Which are determined by natural causes and general conditions of existence? and what are again the things which are not determined in a similar way? Mahāvīra's answers may be summed up in the modern expression, that there is physical determinism. He agreed with

There is physical determinism: Soul is in its nature absolutely pure.

[1] Majjhima-nikāya, I. 377.

[2] *Ibid*, I. 237-238.

Gosāla in many respects. For instance, he accepted the classifications of living beings and things as given by the latter. He too believed that there is no matter unformed, nothing in nature which is dead. It was readily granted by him that our duration of life, physical formation,[1] number of sense-faculties, certain mental qualities and tendencies and intellectual and spiritual powers depend upon the species or types of existence (saṅgati) to which we belong; that nature (sabhāva) implants in our breast certain passions and emotions which develop as we grow up, or that as we advance in life we pass through many ups and downs, experience many agitations of passion; as in the life of a finite individual, so in the life of the whole, the duration of existence is limited, the duration of the world as a whole is marked by periods which succeed each other alternately and uniformly, showing the predominance of good (*su*, corresponding in some way to love of Empedocles) over evil (*du*, corresponding to Hate), on the predominance of evil over good, on the equipoise of both in an ascending or a descending, a progressive or a retrogressive (utsarpiṇi and avasarpiṇi) order[2]; and so forth.

The one point which Gosāla left in obscurity and which Mahāvīra and Buddha brought into prominence was that soul or mind is in its nature supremely white or absolutely pure. The various pleasures and amusements, passions and emotions, thoughts and impressions which stain it with this or that colour, give to it this or that habit and disposition, are quite foreign (āgantuka) to its nature. The realm of soul is in other words the realm of absolute bliss.[3] The soul is not only open to the influx of sin, but also has that peculiar capacity of its own by which it can regain its native purity by shaking off all alien elements. There, indeed lies the scope for our manly strength, the value of education, nay, the foundation

[1] Sūtra-Kṛitāṅga, II. 3. 37.

[2] Jaina-sūtras, Part 2, p. 227 f.; Heart of Jainism, pp. 272-276.

[3] Majjhima-nikāya. I. 36; II. 31-36; I. 483.

of our whole moral freedom. For it is in resisting and rising superior by the goodness and wisdom of the soul to all natural forces and tendencies, passions and emotions, that we build up our moral self, and attain immortal life. This doctrine of soul belongs historically to Yajñavalkya, whom Buddha seems to have esteemed as the upholder of Kiriyāvāda.[1]

VII. The Epistemological aspect of Kiriyam.

As we have seen, the Bhagabatī Sūtra attributes the separation of Gośāla and Mahāvīra to a doctrinal difference, while the former maintained that there is nothing in nature without life, no matter unformed, the latter contended that there are certain things which do not strictly come under the category of life (jīva). This contention on the part of Mahāvīra may perhaps be interpreted in two ways: either (1) that Mahāvīra tried to modify Gośāla's general hylozoistic theory by pointing out that there is as a matter of fact death for every living individual; or (2) that he implied that there are besides the objects of nature or others which are of a purely subjective origin. Accepting one or other of these two interpretations, we see that whereas for Gośāla the category was just one, that of Jīva, for Mahāvīra the categories were two, that of Jīva and that of Ajīva. This was an advance on the part of the latter. We propose here to take the category of *Ajīva* to denote the epistemological aspect of Kiriyam, as distinguished from the biological and physical aspects.

The category of Ajīva: its signification.

The first thing which Mahāvīra was anxious to do in connexion with his theory of knowledge was to see clearly what the problems of knowledge are. He seems to have felt in common with Buddha that the question could be settled only by first settling what cannot be the problems of knowledge.

The problems of knowledge.

[1] Majjhima-nikāya. I. 36; II. 31-36; I. 483.

So far as this latter question was concerned, the sceptic Sañjaya had already suggested the lines of its answer. The questions with regard to which Sañjaya suspended judgment were in fact the questions to be excluded from the problems of knowledge. Is the world eternal, or is it non-eternal? Is it both eternal and non-eternal, or is it neither eternal nor non-eternal? Is the world finite or infinite? Is there any individual existence of man after death, or is there not? Is the absolute truth seen face to face by a seer, comprehended by a philosopher, part of real tangible existence or not? It was with regard to these and similar questions that Sañjaya refused to put forth any affirmative proposition. To avoid error he contented himself with the four famous negative propositions: A is not B; A is not not-B[1]; A is not both B and not-B, A is not neither B nor not-B. It is with regard to the self-same questions that Mahāvīra declared: "From these alternatives you cannot arrive at truth; from these alternatives you are certainly led to error."[2] "The world exists, the world does not exist. The world is unchangeable, the world is in constant flux. The world has a beginning, the world has no beginning. The world has an end, the world has no end, etc. The persons who are not well-instructed thus differ in their opinions, and profess their dogmas without reason."[3] And these were precisely the questions which Buddha regarded as unthinkable (acinteyyāni) on the ground that those who will think about them are sure to go mad, without ever being able to find a final answer, or to reach apodeictic certainty.[4]

Sañjaya, Mahāvīra and Buddha:

However, even with regard to these problems Mahāvīra differed from Sañjaya, and Buddha from both, if not in any

[1] Dial. B. II, pp. 39-40; 75.

[2] Sūtra-Kṛitāṅga, II. 5. 3: "Eehiṁ dohiṁ ṭhānehiṁ vavahāro na vijjai. Eehiṁ dohiṁ ṭhānehiṁ anāyāraṁ tu jānae." (Jacobi's translation.)

[3] Ācārāṅga, I. 7-3.

[4] Aṅguttara-nikāya, II. p. 80.

other respect, at least in attitude. For the cowardly manner in which Sañjaya tried to evade them shows that he did not himself feel certain whether error lay on his side or on that of others. As a successor and younger contemporary of Sañjaya, Mahāvīra's position was somewhat better, something intermediate between that of an ignorant sceptic and that of an enlightened philosopher of the critical school. His was the standpoint of the antimonian (syādvādin), who is represented by later Jaina writers[1] and Buddhist Sarvāstivādins (Syādvādins) of the 3rd century B.C.[2] in the following manner: If he has to answer any questions touching "matters of fact," he should answer them by saying, contrary to both a dogmatist and a sceptic: "It may be that in one sense, looking from one point of view, A is B. It may be that in another sense, looking from another point of view, A is not-B. It may again be that looking from a third point of view, A is both B and not-B. It may equally be that when viewed from a fourth point of view, A is neither B nor not-B."

Syādvāda.

It is then clear that in the view of Mahāvīra and Buddha metaphysics could not be a science, and also that the sceptic Sañjaya had prepared the way for both of them. Prof. Jacobi thought that "in opposition to the Agnosticism of Sañjaya, Mahāvīra has established the Syādvāda." Besides Gośāla, Sañjaya is a great land-mark in the development of the philosophy of Mahāvīra and Buddha. It is remarkable that Sāriputta, formerly the chief disciple of Sañjaya, the founder of the sceptical school, became later the chief disciple of Buddha, the founder of the analytical school,—a fact which Prof. Jacobi was the first to emphasize, and which has almost the same force as Kant's famous dictum that the

[1] See Syādvāda-mañjarī; Sapta-bhaṅgi-taraṅgini; Bhandarkar's Report for 1883-84, p. 95 f.; Jacobi's Jaina-sūtras, XXVII-XXIX: "Syād asti; syād nāsti; syād asti nāsti; syād avaktavyaḥ; syād asti avaktavyah; syād nāsti avaktavyaḥ; syād asti nāsti avaktavyaḥ."

[2] Kathāvatthu, I. 6. 55 58.

sceptic is the true school master to lead the dogmatic speculator towards a sound criticism of the understanding and of reason.[1]

To return to our main question: if the problems stated above cannot be the proper subjects of investigation of knowledge, then what were for Mahāvīra the real problems? The problems were: what and in what manner can we become aware in and through our mind of ourselves and of others who are finite individuals like us? What are the modes of cognition, or categories of thought? What are, in other words, 'demonstrable facts' relating to a concrete individual as distinguished from the 'probable'?

Pañca asti-Kāya.

According to the view, the demonstrable facts are these five (pañca asti-kāya): Dhamma (sense-data), Adhamma (data other than those furnished by the senses), Āgāsa (space), Jīva (soul or finite consciousness), and Puggala (Matter or the material).[2] Each one of these facts is to be understood according to the following categories[3]: Substance (dabba), Attribute (guṇa), Field of action (khetta), Time (kāla), Sequence or causal relations (pajjava),[4] Division (padesa), and Transformation (pariṇāma).

In view of the fact that there is nowhere to be found in the older texts any systematic exposition of Mahāvīra's theory of knowledge, we shall here content ourselves with urging two points regarding it. First, in a passage of the Samavāyāṅga, the five demonstrable facts (pañca asti-kāya) are spoken of as being immutable, permanent or eternal elements of knowledge to which no notion of temporal relations can attach; they are above time—past, present and future, and yet hold good universally and for all times. The great interest of the

[1] Max Muller's translation of Kant's Critique of Pure Reason, Vol. II, p. 659.

[2], [3] Samavāyāṅga, 15; 193; 199. It also refers to similar passages in the Sthānāṅga and the Bhagavati-sūtra.

[4] According to later Jaina writers, pajjava = Sanskrit paryāyaḥ. But it seems that the word equates with the Pali paccaya or Sanskrit pratyayaḥ.

passage is that it enables us to see the sharp contrast between the views of Mahāvīra and Kakuda Kātyāyana: Whereas the latter identified the concepts of a finite mind with concrete things existing eternally in space and time, the former did not.

Secondly, Mahāvīra so far agreed with Kakuda Kātyāyana that he too conceived a plurality of substances. In dismissing the notion of a single universal soul, Mahāvīra's object was to protest against subjective idealism which was continually tending to make the 'transcendental self' into a sort of entity. In dealing with Mahāvīra's philosophy as a whole it must be borne in mind that there are in its background Gośāla's biological speculations.

CHAPTER XXVII.

CONCLUSION.

Here we have to close the rather incomplete survey from within of the development of Indian philosophy before the advent of the Buddha. Incomplete, because according to our original plan, the history was to have been brought down to the time of Sāyaṇa-Mādhava (14th century A.D.). We could hardly realise, until experience actually revealed, the vastness of the field chosen even for a rapid survey, and the immensity of the task to achieve with materials requiring a careful sifting and necessitating in places a great deal of historical reconstruction. Consideration of practical difficulties happily suggested curtailment of the scope of the work, with the result that we had to be satisfied with a modest plan, bringing the history down to the 6th century B.C., and closing it with Mahāvīra. But the plan, however modest, covers centuries of thought-evolution which in respect of antiquity and importance merits the deepest reflections of the modern student, whether in the East or in the West. We must say with Dr. Oldenberg that "hundreds of years before Buddha's time movements were in progress in Indian thought, which prepared the way for Buddhism, and cannot therefore be separated from a sketch of the latter,"[1] or with Dr. Paul Deussen that "the thoughts of the Upanishads led in the post-Vedic period not only to the two great religions of Buddhism and Jainism, but also to a series of philosophical systems."[2] Buddha's analytic method of enquiry (*vibhajja-vāda*) imparted a great synthetic landmark to the history of Early Indian Philosophy. A perusal of the foregoing pages will have, we hope, made it abundantly clear that the synthetic

[1] *Buddha*, Hoey's translation, p. 6. [2] Outlines of Indian Philosophy, p. 34.

development presupposes a large number of philosophical thoughts that constituted its immediate background—negative as well as positive. It has also been indicated how Buddha grouped the current philosophical notions under four pairs of *extremes* (*antā*) comprising *thesis* and *antithesis* and how he endeavoured by his system of the Middle Path to avoid as well as reconcile them without jeopardising his own position. These four pairs of *extremes*, as presented in Buddhist literature, are :—

1. (*a*) Eternalist thesis—that everything exists (*sabbaṁ atthîti*). This is one extreme.

   (*b*) Annihilationist antithesis—that nothing exists (*sabbaṁ n'atthîti*)—This is another extreme.[1] Between these two *extremes* lay whole centuries of metaphysical evolution.

2. (*a*) Determinist thesis—that everything is pre-determined (*sabbaṁ pubbekatahetu*). This is one extreme, yielding the postulate of Being—what is is ; something comes out of something ; nothing comes out of nothing.

   (*b*) Fortuitist antithesis—that nothing is caused and conditioned (*sabbaṁ ahetu-appaccayā*)—This is another extreme,[2] yielding the postulate of non-Being—What is not comes to be (*ahutvā hoti*) ; something comes out of nothing. Between these two extremes lay whole centuries of logical evolution.

3. (*a*) Individualist thesis—that weal and woe are caused by the moral agent of an act (*sukhadukkhaṁ sayaṁkataṁ*). This is one extreme.

   (*b*) Fatalist antithosis—that weal and woe are caused by agents other than self (*sukhadukkhaṁ paraṁkataṁ*).—This is another extreme.[3]

[1] Saṁyutta, II, pp. 17, 96 ; III, p. 135.
[2] Aṅguttara, I, p. 173 f. ; Digha, I.
[3] *Ante*, p. 386, f. n. 1.

Between these two extremes lay whole centuries of ethical evolution.

4. (*a*) Hedonist and Utilitarian thesis—that adherence to pleasures of the sense constitutes the path to the goal (*kāmesu kamasukhallikânuyoga*). This is one extreme.

(*b*) Ascetic antithesis—that self-mortification constitutes the path to final release (*attakilamathânuyoga*). This is another extreme.[1] Between these two lay whole centuries of socio-religious evolution.

The mental attitude implied in Buddha's analytic method of enquiry differs merely in degree from that implied in Mahāvīra's antinomian[2] mode of reviewing the many dogmatic but conflicting assertions of philosophers about the origin, existence and destiny of the world and of life as a whole. These two methods lead us back to Sañjaya of the Belaṭṭha clan, whose scepticism suggested the suspension of judgment as the best path-way to peace. The questions on which he suspended his judgment, whether for or against, embraced, as we have seen (p. 331), a number of problems of metaphysical and theological character. We have further seen that the sceptical or agnostic attitude can as well be traced in the speculation of earlier thinkers. In the Kaṭhopaniṣad, for instance, there is reference to doubt entertained by some school of thinkers regarding the possibility of future existence of man. The teaching of the Kena Upaniṣad has a ring of agnosticism, and it is clearly brought out in the paradoxical assertions about the incognisability of mental events whereby objects are cognised. If we carry our enquiry back to the philosophical hymns of the Ṛig-Veda we should not be astonished to find a similar sceptical or agnostic attitude in them. As a matter of fact, we read in Hymn X. 129 that the sun shining in the highest heaven being later in origin than the cosmic process

[1] Dhammaçakkapavattana Sutta.

[2] The word has been used here to denote a dialectic method of judging two sides of a question.

as a whole, no one can say whether the sun himself knows the genesis of the cosmos or not (*veda yadi vā na veda*). In another hymn (I. 164) the Ṛiṣi Dīrghatamas proclaims in an agnostic vein : "What thing I truly am I know not clearly: mysterious, fettered in my mind I wander." If we push our enquiry farther back to the mythological poetry which constituted the immediate background of the philosophical hymns, it is curious that there too we would find indication of some school of ṛiṣis doubting the existence of Indra.[1] The pursuit of this one line of enquiry lays bare the fact that there is no abrupt beginning in history. In every age there have been sceptics and agnostics, though not technically so called. Although from the psychological point of view the sceptical or the agnostic attitude has expressed itself in every age, it has differed from time to time in regard to the subject of speculation and the mode of expression. In the mythological poetry the doubt was entertained with regard to the existence of Indra; in the philosophical hymns, with regard to the knowledge of the single, the first cause of the Universe, and the knowledge of the genesis of the cosmos; in a subsequent age represented by the older Upaniṣads, the same doubt arises with regard to the cognisability of mental events and the future existence of man, while we find that scepticism came to be formulated as a definite method of philosophic investigation in the hands of Sañjaya who was an elder contemporary and common predecessor of Mahāvīra and Buddha; it also came to be exercised over a wider range of problems. Thus investigating a known period of history from the Vedas to Mahāvīra, we could discover certain broad divisions, characterised each by the predominance of some special problems, that is to say, that with every change of problem a new epoch had commenced. The divisions thus marked out are three, *viz.*, (1) Vedic, (2) Post-Vedic, (3) Neo-Vedic-and-Sophistic. The main problem of Vedic thought

[1] Ṛig-veda, VIII. 89. 3.

is cosmological, that of the Post-Vedic period is Physico-Psychological and that of the Neo-Vedic-and-Sophistic, logico-ethical. Each of these synthetic divisions follows upon a cruder stage of mythology, casuistry or sophistry. The cruder stage intervening two synthetic landmarks is naturally a transitional period during which the cosmological problem tended towards the physico-psychological or the latter towards the logico-ethical.

The general movement of thought was continuous. This is not to say that newer ideas did completely supplant the older ones and in their turn were replaced by still newer ones. On the other hand, it is clearly manifest from many instances that an idea of a certain period never became extinguished, although it had given rise to and was superseded by a newer one. In fact, every period has contributed to the multiplication of philosophic thought, and the older ones exist side by side with newer offshoots and modifications. The whole process, viewed in one way, would seem to be a gradual unfolding of philosophic consciousness of a certain section of humanity, and viewed in another, it would appear to be a process of supersession and supplementation. This two-fold process of evolution was instrumental to the accumulation of myriads of conflicting views and dogmas, differing from each other in slight shades, blurring the intellectual vision, towards the close of the 7th century B.C. It was at such a stage that Sañjaya entered upon his vigorous sceptical campaign and paved the way for Mahāvīra, who adopted a new antinomian test to judge the current theories and dogmas and religious practices in their ultimate logical, ethical and practical issue. It remains to be seen how these diverse issues came to be handled by the Buddha and what the result was that followed upon the introduction of an analytic method of enquiry and true valuation of concepts and things in the light of the Buddhist theory of causal genesis.

II

Though we have said that there is no abrupt or absolute beginning in history, it is indispensable that for historical purpose we have to define the period chosen for investigation in respect of time and place, in order to conceive a beginning and an end, an upper and a lower limit. To our purpose, the hymn of Aghamarṣaṇa marks the commencement of Indian philosophy, for it is here that we find that not only a problem has been clearly stated but also that it has been definitely attempted. It is this test of clearness and definiteness in statement and handling of problems which we have taken to distinguish philosophy from its background of mythology and popular casuistry. Although the innumerable hymns composing the vast collection of the Ṛig-Veda are full of inquisitive questions as to the *what*, the *whence*, the *how*, the *whither*, of things, none of the earlier hymns are so definitely philosophical as the hymn ascribed to Aghamarṣaṇa It was not to our purpose to set up an enquiry into the time and place of the composition of these earlier hymns, the task being left to those who would study them from the antiquarian point of view. In Part I dealing with Vedic philosophy we have considered only those hymns which have been recognised by Vedic scholars as of philosophic interest, and almost all of which are to be found in the tenth or last Book of the Ṛig-Veda. We hold that the Xth Book and some of the philosophic hymns scattered in the 1st Book were added at a later date to an earlier redaction of the Ṛig-Veda, and it is quite possible that the latest hymn may be separated from the most ancient by a long interval of time. The philosophical hymns with which we are concerned must be relegated to the closing period of the Ṛig-Veda, which judging from the chronology of thought may not be dated before 1500 B.C. In respect of place, they seem to have been composed or uttered in the land of the Seven Rivers or, more precisely, in that tract of land which was bounded on the north-west by the Sindhu and the Sarasvatī, and on the north-east by the Jamunā and the Gaṅgā. Roughly speaking, this tract is taken to comprise the region covered by the Punjab and the North-western Frontier Provinces. So much about the upper limit of our history in regard to time and place.

The internal investigation as to the chronology of the philosophical hymns has been carried on mainly in the light of the chronology of thought, and the general trend of thought has been judged by the test, how far it has represented the development of the idea of God, of course, on the cosmological basis. The chronology of the philosophical hymns thus conceived is merely tentative and provisional. It is left to the future historian to test this chronology by considering the inter-relation of those hymns in the light of some other problem, *viz.*, a problem other than that of the development of the idea of God. Vedic philosophy commenced, as set forth in Part I, with an enquiry into the nature of the first cause or cosmic matter and of the cosmic process and its successive stages, and the unity and order of the visible universe. The attempted solution of the questions which arose on cosmological plane goes to prove that the Vedic seers differed widely from one another, although their speculations all tended to the conception of the singleness of the first cause, whether it be Water, or Air, or Fire, or the Solar Substance, and to the recognition of a wonderful order, a rhythmic progress of things in the physical universe. Thus their speculations supply a number of ancient types of cosmological theory, more varied and numerous than the types supplied by Greek philosophy in its first stage. The instances of close resemblance have been noted in their proper place.

As to the striking points of resemblance, we have noticed that first philosophic reflections originated in India and Greece in religion; that a peaceful time was a necessary condition of pondering over the riddles of existence; and that the first conception of God was within the realm of the physical. But Vedic philosophy went far ahead, culminating in the abstract conception of one God, represented as the Divine Architect. In these cosmological speculations, the importance of which has been indicated in its proper place, lay the germs and possibilities of later Indian thought and the basis upon which the structure of Hindu society was built. For instance, Aghamarṣaṇa's hymn contains the first philosophic conception of the Year, which can be traced in a developed form in the Atharva Veda, the Mahābhārata and the Purāṇas as a Doctrine of Time which influenced the popular mind so largely as to become a by-word of faith. The famous Puruṣa-sūkta yields a conception of the universe as an organic whole, constituted by different groups of beings and things with distinct places and functions, all inter-connected, and it supplied a philosophic exposition of the *Cāturvarṇya* system which, with the progress of civilisation and advancement of thought, had a supergrowth in the *āśrama* theory of individual training and culture. But everything is so vague and indefinite. One may as well go back to the Brahmaṇaspati and Viśvakarman hymns for the origin of the Vedāntic conception of Brahman, as also of the Nyāya conception of God. The Upaniṣadic tradition traces, as we have seen, the origin of the Sāṅkhya conception of Puruṣa to the Puruṣa-sūkta ascribed to Nārāyaṇa, but one may as well derive the whole cosmological aspect of Sāṅkhya philosophy from the Nāsadiya-sūkta (X. 129) where the cosmic changes have been conceived as gradual transformation of the primitive matter (Water), due to the influence of the creative fervour (Warmth), immanent in it, and where the terms *sattva*, *rajas* and *tamas* denoting vaguely the threefold divisions of the physical universe are met with.

III

We have closed the first part—the Vedic philosophy—with the abiding impression that Vedic thought was in its fundamental character geo-centric, and its main interest lay in speculations about the physical world. But taking a retrospective view and scanning the hymns we discovered that the problems of the subsequent period, called post-Vedic, was anticipated in Dīrghatamas' hymn (I. 164) in the expression "What thing I am I know not clearly," and a few other detached hymns embodying the conception of Truth (Satya) and Right (Dharma) as *ṛita* denoting the eternal order of things (X. 85); the conception of Faith (śraddhā) as the yearning of the heart for better condition of existence (X. 85); the vague notion of the four stages of the development of the fœtus in the womb (X. 85); and the equally vague notion of rebirth and the two paths, *devayāna* and *pitṛi-yāna*, along which the soul after death proceeds to its destination. In the conflict between the worshippers of Indra standing for absolute power and Varuṇa standing for order, and in Dīrghatamas' conception of two birds, *i.e.*, of the play of two opposed factors of active vitality and passive mentality in the cosmos, we find anticipated the subsequent antagonism between the Brāhman philosophers upholding social order and the mechanistic conception of life (*prāṇavāda*) and the Kṣatriya philosophers advocating the idea of renunciation and upholding the rationalistic view of soul (*Brahmavāda*). The Brāhmaṇa portion of the older Brāhmaṇas disclosed to us a transitional stage marked by a fusion of racial elements, an intermingling of Vedic speculations, admixture of philosophy, mythology and popular casuistry, elaboration of rituals and interpretation of the Vedic hymns. It is in the Brāhmanic efforts that we find the beginning of various sciences and arts, of the method of classification and systematization, and of the growth of the consciousness that man is the best of creatures. With the dawning of this consciousness we find that the attention of the philosophers came to be concentrated upon the problem of man in his relation to the material world, the organic world, to society, to his senses, mind and soul. The Second Part dealing with post-Vedic philosophy covers the period from Mahidāsa Aitareya to Yājñavalkya. Going by the Paurāṇic tradition about the age of Parīkṣit[1] who lived just a generation before Yājñavalkya, the lower limit of the post-Vedic period can be brought down to 1300 B.C. But judging from the process of thought-evolution the limit may as well be brought down nearer to Buddha, say, to 900 B.C.

Another point to be noted is that the centre of Aryan activity and culture was shifted to the land of Kuru-Pañcāla, which retained its importance down to the time of Pārīkṣita or Janmejaya. No doubt, it was under the patronage of Pārīkṣita and his forefathers that post-Vedic philosophy flourished so much. A prominent landmark in philosophy of this period was reached in Uddālaka Āruṇi. Towards the close of this period, with the death of Janamejaya and Uddālaka, the centre of Aryan influence and culture was shifted further south-east to Videha, where Yājñavalkya, the last landmark of post-Vedic philosophy, successfully pursued his philosophic career under the patronage of King Janaka, challenging in philosophical controversies, great thinkers, especially those hailing from Kuru-Pañcāla; and it was now that the Aryan sovereignty spread over the greater portion of Northern India from Gandhāra to Videha and Kāśi.

The history of the post-Vedic period has been built up with materials drawn mainly from the works of a few ancient Brāhman schools such as the Aitareyas, the Chāndogyas, the Kauṣītakeyas, the Taittirīyas and the Śatapathas. A distinction had to be made between the chronology of literature and

[1] The date of Parīkṣit, in round numbers, is 1400 B.C. Ray Chandhuri's 'Early History of the Vaishnava Sect,' p. 38. *Cf.* Pargiter's 'Dynasties of the Kali Age,' p. 58.

that of thought especially where a particular text like the Chāndogya Brāhmaṇa-Upaniṣad is a compilation, containing the views of several teachers, differing in content from one another. The Aitareya Brāhmaṇa and the Āraṇyaka, omitting the Upaniṣhad portion, represent together a homogeneous body of doctrines which may be judged as the system of a particular individual or of a particular school of thought, say that of Mahidāsa Aitareya or of the Aitareya school. The case of the Upaniṣad is different, as it contains the views of many individuals and schools other than those of the Aitareyas. This holds true of the Kauṣītaki and the Bṛihadāraṇyaka Upaniṣads, while the Taittirīya represents the views of one and the same school, *viz.*, that of the Taittirīyas. In cases where the texts do not represent coherent systems, we have analysed their component elements, and arranged them on internal evidence in a chronological order. We have shown how the post-Vedic period commenced with the Aitareya system, which was the greatest synthetic landmark in pre-Buddhistic Indian thought. In tracing the development and exposition of the doctrine of "*so'haṁ*"—" I am He "—*i.e.*, of the identity of the individual with the universal self in its morphological, physiological and psychological aspects, we have noticed how different lines of investigation issued forth from one common substratum, leading to the scientific conceptions of astronomy, anatomy, physiology, embryology, biology, logic, psychology and ethics. During this period we came across different types of thought, some with old Vedic characteristics, some resembling Pythagorean and Anaxagorean, the predominant types being Aristotelian and Platonic. Indian philosophy took a systematic turn in the teachings of Uddālaka, for it is here that we find that different lines of thought branched off to give rise in later times to the fundamental conceptions of Vedānta, Bauddha, Sāṅkhya, Yoga, Nyāya and Vaiśeṣika systems. In this period Indian philosophy would appear to be on the whole a lay movement, almost all the teachers being married householders. We have noticed that the antagonism prevalent during this period was between Brāh*mans and Kṣatriyas, and that Brāhmanic thought tended to justify the civic duties of man on the ground of the gradual* development of self or gradual manifestation of the potentialities of life, while the Kṣatriya thought tended contrarywise to give preference to the subjective mode of attaining true self-hood and living an ascetic life in the forest, practising penance and cultivating inner culture and faith. The development of Āraṇyaka life which commenced during the closing period of the Ṛig-Veda is one of the prominent features of the post-Vedic period. One of the mooted questions of philosophy was whether the higher plane of man's activity could be co-ordinated or harmonised with the lower functions that a man has to discharge as a living body and social being. In the development of many psychological theories of the senses, the mind, and the soul and their functions and inter-relations we notice the basis of the fundamental conceptions of Buddhist psychology which holds a unique position in ancient human thought, especially in the whole of Indian philosophy. The period closed with the philosophy of Yājñavalkya in whose teachings we discovered a conscious attempt to compromise the claims put forward by the Brāhman and Kṣatriya thinkers. It is again in his teachings that we could discover the logical trend of entire post-Vedic thought tending towards the psycho-ethical. Yājñavalkya's psychological speculations about the waking, the dreaming and the sleeping states of soul, and his theories about birth, death and rebirth laid the foundation of the Jaina, the Buddhist and the Hindu doctrines of Karma.

IV

With the close of post-Vedic thought we entered upon another period which may be designated in history as the neo-Vedic-and-Sophistic. During this period the principal combatants in philosophy were no longer the Kṣatriya and Brāhman householders, but the Śramans and Brāhman wanderers, who were divided into numerous religious orders and schools of thought. In the light of the evidence of Buddhist literature one can see that no less than 50 orders and schools of recluses and wanderers, some anti-Brahmanic in their attitude and the majority in favour of the Brahmanic system of morals yielding the Hedonistic, the Utilitarian, the Juristic and the Ascetic standards of judgment. It seems that these religious orders and schools of philosophy arose as if to bridge over the gulf widely separating the two modes of thought, the two modes of life, the two modes of expression. The centre of activity was shifted farther eastwards towards Gayā, Campā and Vesāli. This period closes with Mahāvīra. The prominent feature of its political history, as may be ascertained from the ancient Jaina and Buddhist texts, is the existence of many independent Aryan or semi-Aryan powers in Northern India divided into 4 monarchies and a number of oligarchies of various descriptions. Since Yājñavalkya there seems to have been a long state of war which resulted in the conquest of Kāsi by the Kośalans, Videha by the Vajjis and the ascendancy of the kingdom of Magadha. As may be inferred from the Epic kernel of the Mahābhārata, the absolute powers had developed from a tribal stage and gradual subjugation of one tribe by another. The powers were generally related to one another by matrimonial alliances, and, according to the Jaina evidence, the alliance of 18 eastern tribal powers existed down to the demise of Makkhali Gosāla and Mahāvīra. The influence of these independent powers and warring factors upon the course of Indian philosophy and on the development of Indian language, literature, sciences and arts cannot be overstated, for it was under the auspices of one or other of these princes that the religious orders and schools of philosophy flourished. The main characteristic of this period, so far as philosophy is concerned, were the freedom of thought and the general spirit of toleration. The philosophical controversies carried on in a spoken language by the recluses and wanderers on matters ethical, social, religious and philosophical, served to enrich Sanskrit language, and give rise to Vernacular literatures. Every shade of opinion was advocated with the utmost subtlety of reasoning and sophistry, with the result that gradually all the pre-historic conditions of the development of logic and dialectic as a science made their appearance. One can easily discover that some of the conflicting opinions emerged out of the ambiguity in the earlier thoughts. Although in most cases we do not find the discovery of a new truth, the interest of the period as a whole lies in the emphasis laid upon certain logical consequences of earlier thoughts discriminated and tested with utmost logical acumen. Through this conflict of opinions two facts come to be emphasized.

(1) That there is a higher self which has got the power to rise above material conditions and can arrive, by its own efforts, to a condition where it is not touched by our sensuous experiences.

(2) That this ideal state of self, reachable by a subjective mode of effort, constitutes the supreme goal of man.

As a result of the antagonism between the Śramans and Brāhman wanderers the *āśrama* theory came to be synthesized with the earlier *cāturvarṇya* system. But the possibility of such a coalition was clearly indicated in the Taittirīya philosophy, just as the beginnings of Sophistic movements can also be traced in the personal example set by Uddālaka Āruṇi and in the many philosophical controversies between Yājñavalkya and his contemporaries. It is not at all surprising that the earlier thoughts of the Upaniṣads were continued in the intellectual activity of the period with many ramifications and newer scientific and artistic developments. It is in the teachings of the Philosophers and Sophists of this period that we begin to see a clearer differentiation of earlier thoughts, some proceeding towards Sāṅkhya-Yoga, *e.g.*, the views of Pippalāda, Pūraṇa

Kassapa and Pakudha Kaccāyana; some towards the Vaiśeṣika philosophy, *e. g.*, the views of Pakudha Kaccāyana, Gosāla and Mahāvīra; some towards Vedānta and Nyāya, *e.g.*, the views of the Muṇḍakas and the Gotamakas; and some towards Buddhist philosophy, *e.g.*, the views of Pakudha Kaccāyana, Ajita, Sañjaya, Gosāla and Mahāvīra. Here again we find a close resemblance between the Ancient Indian and the Greek types of speculation, *e.g.*, between the views of Naciketas and Parmenides; between the views of Pakudha Kaccāyana and Empedocles; between those of Ajita and Epicurus. One very important point has been emphasized in Part III, *viz.*, that the Īśa, the Kaṭha, the Kena, the Muṇḍaka and such other texts which have hitherto been considered as the oldest among the Upaniṣads have been all found to be later in point of date than Yājñavalkya. The records of most of the schools of recluses and Brāhman wanderers have not come down to us, but we have found reason to believe that the views of these schools can still be found in one or other of these later Upaniṣads in the vast accumulation of the Māhābhārata and the Purāṇas, but we leave all these surmises to the future historian of Indian philosophy to test.

V

In dealing with the history of Indian Philosophy before the rise of Buddhism we have to move in a period when it is difficult to speak of a system of philosophy in its later technical sense, but mainly of some daring and far-reaching speculations forming the earlier landmarks or stages of later schools of philosophy, whether Brāhmanic, Jaina or Buddhistic. We trust that we have not failed to indicate, wherever possible, the types of speculation which tended towards one or other of the six schools of Hindu philosophy. The subject, however, requires a closer investigation and independent study, which is quite out of place in our work. Only a word remains to be said regarding the comparison we have instituted, here and there, between Indian philosophy and Greek thought. It was really not our purpose to bring Greek philosophy under our survey and raise any question of borrowing. Wherever we have resorted to a comparison, we have done so with no other end in view than orientation of Indian thoughts themselves. The point of prehistoric contact between the Indian and the Greek thought is generally sought in the Pythagorean doctrine of transmigration of soul, but, having no conclusive evidence to hand, we have refrained from dealing with that disputed point. But it has been pointed out that with Alexander's Indian campaign in the 4th century B. C. an intellectual connection came to be established through Pyrrho of Elis who is said to have studied philosophy under the Indian Gymnosophists and Chaldean Magi, or, as we hold, who imbibed his sceptical bias from the followers of Sañjaya, the Sceptic. The Greek ambassador Megasthenes, as is well-known, was much impressed by the prevalence in northern India of philosophical views similar to those of Plato and Aristotle when he visited the court of Chandragupta shortly after Alexander's departure.

"The East is East and the West is West." This has already passed into a maxim of our time. Although it would not be easy to say how far the dictum is literally true, we concede that one can derive from it, if not a truth, at least a precious warning which is—one must not hold comparison between two countries, nations or races, and much less between their cherished teachers until one has discovered a common trait to judge and appreciate them. A comparative study of Greek and Ancient Indian philosophy, attempted in our work, has yielded cases of resemblance, more or less close. Those who are still in doubt as to the possibility of a history of philosophy as a genuine science can discover in the history of Indian philosophy a great world of ideas furnishing many interesting parallels to western thought. Should such a time ever come for a thorough comparative study, those of wider outlook can find in its light what is commonly given in the human reason, and how that original gift develops as time goes on in manifold forms. It will doubtless set forth the same human spirit manifesting itself among different peoples in different climes and exhibit certain eternal problems preoccupying the thoughtful section of humanity of all ages. However looking back to the past, the historian cannot but be impressed by the fact that however ancient the Semitic and Chinese civilizations may be, the Indo-Aryans and the Greeks with their Roman neighbours stand out in history as the originators of philosophy and scientific thought.

The peculiar interest of the study of Indian philosophy is that from the Vedas onwards we have almost a continuous record, in the light of which a mighty movement and progress of human thought can be visualized. It is certainly not our object to extol the past which is in a sense dead and therefore indifferent to praise and blame. We have taken pains, therefore, to judge history as it is and not as it ought to be, with reservation—so far as practicable. In fact, with Lord Acton we have searched earnestly and sympathetically certain past records of mankind to learn wisdom for the present, to study the lives and teachings of ancient Indian teachers on their purely human and historical side. Much has been said and much remains yet to be said. But the process of evolution of Indian thought, as discovered in our investigation, has served to supply us with the key to the development of other aspects of Indian culture.[1]

[1] Our "Asoka's Dhamma—a Landmark of Indian Literature and Religion"—which is a joint-work, is an instance of what an investigation on the same lines has done. The work will be published soon by the University of Calcutta.

NOTES AND APPENDIX

1. **Complement or Entelechy (p. 66)**—The meaning attached by Aristotle to this expression is that soul is nothing but a complement of the living body, *i.e.*, something added to life. We do not know of any Sanskrit equivalent of the expression, but there is a passage in the Aitareya Āraṇyaka (III. 12), where it is clearly stated that soul enters (or is inserted) into the body, after it has reached an advanced stage of embryonic development, through the suture at the top of the skull. *Cf.* Taittirīya Up. (I. 6.1). Note Rhys Davids' observations in his Buddhist India, p. 253.

2. **Pūrṇa Kāśyapa**—The Pāli epithet Pūraṇa has been Sanskritized on p. 277 as Pūrṇa, which seems incorrect. Nowhere in the Buddhist Sanskrit Texts *Pūrṇa* has been used as the Sanskrit equivalent of it. *Pūraṇaḥ* would have been the right equivalent. In the Mahābhārata *Pūraṇaḥ* occurs as the name of a distinguished teacher. This does not affect our remark that the meaning and derivation of the epithet are very different from those suggested by Buddhaghosa.

3. **Supiya, Suppiya (p. 326)**—This word *supiya*, as we are informed by a friend, occurs in some of the Kharoṣṭhī incriptions, edited by Rapson, (*e.g.*, No. 272) apparently as the designation of an itinerant body of ascetics. It would be worth while to investigate whether any new light could be thrown thereof on the interpretation of the word.

4. **Gymnosophists (p. 328)**—It is not at all clear from either Strabo's description or Plutarch's Life of Alexander that the Gymnonosophistae or Naked sophists formed a compact or

homogeneous body of Indian philosophers. They are represented no doubt as in some way attached to a royal court, though not precisely in service of the state. No definite clue to their identification either with the Ājīvikas, Jains, or with Sañjaya's followers can be elicited from Plutarch's account of the replies of ten Gymnosophists to the ten questions severally put to them.

5. **Paṇṇaka-bhūmi (p. 314 f. n. 1)**—We have sufficient reasons to dispute Buddhaghosa's explanation of this expression and accept Hoernle's interpretation that it denotes the *Prostrate stage* of an Ājīvika saint—(App. to the Uvāsaga-Dasāo, II. p. 24). This was a common practrice of Indian ascetics, particularly that of the Ājīvikas and the Jainas, as has been shown elsewhere (The Ājīvikas Pt. I. p. 53), that they committed religious suicide. It is all the more interesting to note that the word *Parṇaka*, which is a Sanskrit equivalent of the Pāli Paṇṇaka, is used in the Vedic texts in the sense of a human-victim at the *Puruṣa-medha* (Vedic Index, *sub voce* Parṇaka).

6. **Interpretation of the Īśa Upaniṣad (p. 259)**—in the light of the ancient Sanskrit and Pāli texts.

(*a*) ईशावास्यमिदं सर्वं यत् किंच जगत्यां जगत्।
तेन त्यक्तेन भुञ्जीथा मा गृधः कस्य स्विद्धनम् ॥१॥
कुर्वन्नेवेह कर्माणि जिजीविषेच्छतं समाः।
एवं त्वयि नान्यथेतोऽस्ति न कर्म लिप्यते नरे ॥२॥ (Īśa)

Cf. Bṛihad Āraṇyaka Up., III, 7. 23 नान्योऽतोऽस्ति द्रष्टा नान्योऽतोऽस्ति श्रोता...मन्ता...विज्ञाता"; IV. 4.23 : "तस्यैव स्यात्पदवित्तं विदित्वा न लिप्यते कर्मणा पापकेनेति"।

(*b*) असूर्या नाम ते लोका अन्धेन तमसावृताः।
तांस्ते प्रेत्याभिगच्छन्ति ये के चात्महनो जनाः ॥३॥ (Īśa)

Cf. Bṛihad Āraṇyaka Up. IV. 4. 11

अनन्दा नाम ते लोका अन्धेन तमसावृता: ।
तांस्ते प्रेत्याभिगच्छन्त्यविद्वांसोऽबुधो जना: ॥

Being the apt rejoinder of the Muṇḍaka, II. 2. 10; Kaṭha, II. 6. 5; Śvetāśvatara, VI. 14

न तत्र सूर्य्यो भाति, न चन्द्र तारकं,
नेमा विद्युतो भान्ति, कुतोऽयमग्नि: ?
तमेव भान्तमनुभाति सर्वं,
तस्य भासा सर्वमिदं विभाति ।

Udāna, I. p. 9:

न तत्थ सुक्का जोतन्ति, आदिच्चो नप्पकासति,
न तत्थ चन्दिमा भाति, तमो तत्थ न विज्जति ।
यदा च अत्तनावेदि मुनि मोनेन ब्राह्मणो
अथ रूपा अरूपा च सुख-दुक्खा पमुच्चति ॥

Kaṭha, I. 1. 3:

पीतोदका जग्धतृणा दुग्धदोहा निरिन्द्रिया: ।
अनन्दा नाम ते लोकास्तान् स गच्छति ता ददत् ॥

For the significance of the expression *ātmahano janāḥ*, *cf.* Baudhāyana's (or, Bodhāyana's) expression "rajo *bhūtvā dhvaṁsate,*" discussed on pp. 247—49. Also ascertain what led the Brāhman wanderer Māgaṇḍiya (Mārkaṇḍeya ?) to call Buddha a *Bhunahu,* Sk. *Bhruṇahā* (Majjhima, II. p. 198)

(*c*) अविद्यया मृत्युं तीर्त्वा विद्ययामृतमश्नुते ॥११॥

(Īśa, Bṛihad Āraṇyaka)

For the meaning of *avidyā* and *vidyā cf.* the Muṇḍaka I; the Kaṭha I. 2; the Praśna I. 15: तद्ये ह वै तत्प्रजापतिव्रतं चरन्ति ये मिथुनमुत्पादयन्ते तेषामेवैष ब्रह्मलोको; येषां तपो ब्रह्मचर्य्यं, येषु सत्यं प्रतिष्ठितम्, तेषामसौ विरजो ब्रह्मलोको ।

SUBJECT INDEX

INDEX OF SANSKRITIC WORDS

A